TOUR DE FRANCE 100

'It never gets easier, you just go faster.'
GREG LEMOND

Foreword by Bernard Hinault
Preface by Stephen Roche

Peter Cossins, Isabel Best,
Chris Sidwells & Clare Griffith

TOUR DE FRANCE 100

The definitive history of the world's greatest race

First published in Great Britain in 2013 by Cassell Illustrated,
an imprint of Octopus Publishing Group Limited, Endeavour House,
189 Shaftesbury Avenue, London WC2H 8JY
www.octopusbooks.co.uk

An Hachette UK Company | www.hachette.co.uk

Distributed in the US by Hachette Book Group USA,
237 Park Avenue, New York, NY 10017 USA

Distributed in Canada by Canadian Manda Group,
165 Dufferin Street, Toronto, Ontario, Canada M6K 3H6

www.octopusbooksusa.com

ISBN: 978-1-84403-742-1

Set in Berthold Akzidenz Grotesk.

Printed and bound in China.

KEY TO THE TOUR DE FRANCE JERSEYS

Yellow: Worn by the general classification leader – the rider with the lowest overall time at the end of each stage. It was introduced in 1919. The rider who receives the yellow jersey after the last stage in Paris is overall winner of the Tour.

Green: Worn by the leader of the points classification – the rider who has the highest number of points awarded for intermediate sprints and time trials. The points competition began in 1953.

Polka dot: Worn by the King of the Mountains – the rider who is designated as the best climber during the Tour's mountain stages. It was awarded from 1933 and the jersey was introduced in 1975.

White: Worn by the Best Young Rider – the rider aged under 26 who is placed highest in the general classification. It was awarded from 1975-1989 and again from 2000.

KILOMETRES TO MILES CONVERSION

Kilometres	Miles
1 km	0.62 m
5 km	3.11 m
10 km	6.21 m
25 km	15.53 m
50 km	31.07 m
75 km	46.60 m
100 km	62.14 m
125 km	77.67 m
150 km	93.21 m
175 km	108.74 m
200 km	124.27 m
300 km	186.41 m
400 km	248.55 m
500 km	310.69 m

Conversion formula: kilometres x 0.6214 = miles

CONTENTS

Le Tour de France: the people's race

FOREWORD BY BERNARD HINAULT

1978, 1979, 1981, 1982 AND 1985 TOUR DE FRANCE WINNER

The Tour de France existed long before I started cycling – long before I was even born. But I witnessed its evolution. And despite all its ups and downs, it has become one of the world's three major sporting events, alongside the Olympic Games and the FIFA World Cup. And it's the only one to take place every year.

I watched the Tour grow throughout the Eighties, with the growing surge of media interest, the creation of the race's portable Start Village and the swell of marketing around the event. These changes are part of life; you can't stand in the way of progress. But the event flourished, and it always managed to keep the sporting element at the forefront. Its directors – the men who created it, such as Henri Desgrange, then Jacques Goddet and Félix Lévitan after him – and those who have developed it, such as Jean-Marie Leblanc in past years and Christian Prudhomme at present, have ensured that cycling has remained at the heart of the Tour. The race's organizers respect this. What's more, the Tour has a dedicated team that oversees every aspect of its planning and execution; nowadays, its 200 cyclists are supported by a mobile village that relocates every day, following their progress. To me, this in itself is a true feat.

I see no reason why the race shouldn't continue to capture the public's imagination. The Tour is greater than its heroes, because it's the Tour that makes the heroes, not the contrary. But one could not exist without the other.

The Tour endures because of the lasting support of the villages, towns, provinces, regions and countries that host it – and because it is a fantastic event that passes, quite literally, in front of people's doorsteps. And it's free!

This is why the Tour lives on, and why it will endure through time.

Le Tour de France: cycling's biggest race

PREFACE BY STEPHEN ROCHE

1987 TOUR DE FRANCE WINNER

I was first aware of the Tour de France during the mid 1970s. I was a teenager getting into cycling, and my compatriot, Sean Kelly, had just become a professional racer in his first Tour de France. He was part of the Flandria team, so he was in the action leading out their star man, Freddy Maertens, for stage victories.

Then Kelly won a stage as well. It was so exciting. The Tour de France was the only bike race in the Irish papers and on the news back then. We didn't even have a cycling magazine in Ireland – I had to order *Cycling Weekly* from London and I'd be at the station every week waiting for it. The Tour de France was all over that magazine, too, and here was Kelly, one of our own, in the thick of it. It left a big impression on me.

The Tour de France is cycling's biggest race by far, and every rider dreams of taking part in it. All through the year you'll hear riders saying that they are doing such and such a race as preparation for another; nobody ever says that at the Tour. Every rider arrives with the best form they can have, ready to give everything they have. Anybody who is anybody in cycling rides the Tour de France. That makes the Tour the hardest race of the year – the best of the best doing the best they can.

So, human effort has always been part of the Tour, but TV has made the race even bigger by bringing it into people's homes. It has also brought to life the amazing countryside it goes through. Now that we have information added to our screens – the average speed and the gradients of the mountains – the TV coverage builds the riders into almost super-human athletes. Then there's the fact of 5,000 people – riders, team workers, the press and TV and advertising people – travelling around France for three weeks. The Tour de France is both the focus of each cycling year and a huge show, and that's why it's cycling's biggest race.

Of course, all the attention puts pressure on the competitors, and the pressure starts in a rider's first Tour. Professional cycling teams have 20 or more riders, but only nine from each team are entered into the race, so as well as riding together riders are also competing against the rest of their team to get selected. That means when a young rider is selected he might keep an older one out of the race, and that brings pressure too.

And the pressure only increases when a rider improves or becomes more experienced. Team leaders have to perform because the Tour is crucial to their sponsors. The Tour de France is where more than 80 per cent of marketing opportunities are in cycling, and the focus is increasing. It makes the Tour even more competitive. The top three riders overall used to be the positions to attract attention, now it's the top ten. The other competitions in the race have grown too. Where the first team overall got publicity, now it's the top three. A team lying fourth in the team standings will sacrifice an individual member's overall position to move up to third. It's the same with the green jersey and King of the Mountains.

The Tour is so big and such a pressure cooker that winning it is as much about mental strength as having the right physical abilities. Yes, you have to have the physical tools necessary to win, but there have been riders who have them and who haven't won the Tour de France. A potential winner must aim high and even be a gambler. I hear riders every year who say they are going to do their best. That's not what you should aim for – you go to win and only settle for your best. Second in a race was never any good for me. I never settled for second; I would always try to win. If I was second I could defend that in the bar later and say I could have won, but I never defended second out on the road, I always tried to win.

So that's my take on the Tour de France, on why it's so big, on what it takes to win it and on why it has created the sometimes magnificent, sometimes shocking but always interesting, and always very human, story you'll read about in this book. I hope you enjoy it.

'We run on dynamite'

THE MEN WHO MADE THE TOUR

Newspapers were big business at the turn of the 20th century. There was no TV, no radio, no internet, but the horizons of ordinary people had been extended. The railways and, to a certain extent, the bicycle gave people the chance to travel for recreation and opened their minds to a world outside their own. People wanted to know what was going on in the world and the only way to find out was through reading newspapers.

Sport had changed, too, from something played by wealthy young men for fun to something played by professionals for money. Professional sport had a huge following, and that created sports newspapers. Professional cycling was big in France, so a successful sports newspaper had to cover it in depth.

One way to do it was to get involved in promoting races. The leading sports newspaper in France at the time, *Le Vélo*, had a deal with the French Cycling Federation whereby *Le Vélo* produced the official race calendar. If you wanted to know where a race was and who was in it, you had to buy *Le Vélo*.

That meant its main rival, *L'Auto*, had a smaller share of the cycling market and therefore a smaller circulation. Its editor, Henri Desgrange, had to do something about improving circulation figures, so he and his staff came up with the Tour de France. People were fascinated by ultra-long races and the Tour was the longest by far,

although it was split into stages with several days between each stage for the racers to recover.

THE FIRST TOURS

Sixty pioneer competitors lined up outside the Au Réveil Matin café in a Paris suburb at three o'clock on the afternoon of 1 July 1903. The first stage was from Paris to Lyon, 467 km away. A flag was waved and the field quickly spread out until Maurice Garin won in 17 hours, 45 minutes and 13 seconds, a time he recorded himself because he arrived before the first official.

Five stages later, on 18 July, Garin returned to Paris, the winner of the first Tour de France. His journey wasn't without incident; rural France was quite wild in 1903 and passions about cycling ran high. People had their heroes and some got carried away trying to help their favourite win. There were several ugly incidents in which competitors were held back by rival fans, and some riders were even assaulted.

The Tour's success nearly destroyed it the following year: there was even more sabotage by cycling fans and, at the same time, the racers became so desperate to win that they cheated in quite a spectacular fashion. Hanging on to motor vehicles was commonplace, but some riders even covered vast sections of the route by train.

Some of the cheats were the best racers in the field and that led to the disqualification of the first four finishers in Paris. Scared of fan reprisals, the organizers didn't announce the qualifications until five months after the 1904 Tour had finished.

ABOVE

Le Petit Journal was one of the many magazines that covered pro cycling in 1903.

LEFT

Maurice Garin, who had once been a chimney sweep, won the first ever Tour de France.

'Oh Laffrey! Oh Bayard! Oh Tourmalet! I would be failing in my duty not to proclaim that next to the Galibier you are pale cheap wine. In front of this giant I can do nothing more than raise my hat and salute.'

HENRI DESGRANGE WRITING ABOUT THE COL DU GALIBIER IN 1911

HENRI DESGRANGE

Henri Desgrange is known as the Father of the Tour, although the actual idea and the name of the race came from a member of *L'Auto* staff, a cycling reporter called Géo Lefèvre. Still, it was Desgrange who had the last word, who guided the race through a very stormy start and who shaped it and wrote about it for over 30 years.

Desgrange was an enigma, a man who loved cycling, but didn't seem to like professional cyclists. He admired their endurance and athleticism, but suspected their motivation and seemed to resent the fact that they made money from something he loved and revered.

His attitude brought him into conflict with the racers and sponsors, and it led him to introduce Draconian rules in an effort to thwart any professional trickery that might be going on. To be fair to him, Desgrange was right: a lot of cheating was going on and some of the competitors couldn't be trusted.

Desgrange was a severe man who wrote about cycling in beautiful prose, setting a style of French cycling journalism that can still be detected today. After his death, in 1940, the Tour honoured its founder by building a monument on his favourite mountain, the Col du Galibier.

BELOW

Henri Desgrange being interviewed by pioneer sports broadcaster Georges Briquet.

INTRODUCING THE HIGH MOUNTAINS

The Tour's route was changed in 1905 to minimize sabotage and cheating, and to make it easier to control. It visited wilder places and even climbed up a mountain, the Ballon d'Alsace, to see if racing on such terrain were possible. It was, and climbs like it became a regular part of the Tour, but a *L'Auto* employee, Alphonse Steines, wanted to take the race higher.

He slowly convinced Desgrange to route the Tour through the Pyrenees. In 1910, the race had its first high mountain stage. It began in Luchon and ran for 326 km to Bayonne. The riders had to climb the Col de Peyresourde (1,569 m), the Col d'Aspin (1,489 m), the Col du Tourmalet (2,115 m) and the Col d'Aubisque (1,709 m).

Desgrange built up interest in *L'Auto* by writing about how brave the racers were to tackle such an epic stage, because no-one had ever raced over mountains this high. Secretly, though, he was terrified by the prospect, and would have been even more terrified had he known that Steines had almost died of exposure when he had checked out the route earlier in the year.

Mountain roads were poor in 1910 and the Pyrenees are quite remote even today. Desgrange did what he could. His golden rule was that racers should compete alone and unaided, but on this stage he provided a vehicle to follow and rescue any men who were too tired or whose bikes were too broken to continue. He called it the *voiture balai* (broom wagon) because it swept up after the race. A *voiture balai* still follows the Tour de France, picking up riders who can't complete the race.

The stage was a success. Octave Lapize of France made it to Bayonne in 14 hours and 10 minutes, despite swearing at Steines when he saw him at the summit of one of the climbs. The last man on the stage finished over 7 hours behind Lapize, but nobody got hurt. Newspapers that had criticized the Tour for being reckless with its racers' lives praised it for being the biggest spectacle in sport. The high mountains became a permanent part of the Tour de France.

Taking the race to the Pyrenees was such a success that the Tour felt compelled to visit the Alps in 1911. This allowed the race to expand in scale once more. The highest Alpine passes are a degree up from the Pyrenees, where the most elevated climbs are around the 2,000-m mark. As the century progressed road-building in the Alps pushed up towards 3,000 m and

ABOVE LEFT

Octave Lapize pushes his bike up the steepest slopes of the Col du Tourmalet in 1910.

ABOVE RIGHT

The broom wagon, invented in 1910 for rider safety, has swept up behind the Tour ever since. Here it prepares to take on board a dropped rider in 1963.

the Tour de France would come to use these roads, but in 1911 there was already a giant to be climbed, the Col du Galibier.

Bikes weighed 15 kg (33 lb) back then, compared to just under 7 kg (15 lb) today. The racers had two gears, where modern racers have 20 and sometimes 22. To change gear in 1911 a racer had to stop, remove his rear wheel, turn it around and engage the sprocket on the other side, secure it back in his bike frame and pedal off. Basically, it was one gear for going up and one for going down the mountains. Yet Émile Georget pedalled the 34.8 km of the Galibier, right up to 2,646 m, without walking for one single metre.

The bikes the Tour racers rode were unreliable and the rules Desgrange set to discourage cheating were fearsome. In 1913 the front forks on Frenchman Eugène Christophe's bike broke on the Tourmalet descent. There was no support and no swapping of bikes, so Christophe jogged 14 km down the mountain to a blacksmith's forge. It took him over 4 hours to repair the forks, watched by officials who penalized Christophe by adding 10 minutes to his time because the blacksmith's helper operated the bellows for him (see page 241).

WAR INTERRUPTS THE TOUR

The Tour was ten years old when storm clouds gathered over Europe and World War I brought normal life in much of France to a halt. Hundreds of thousands died, including a number of Tour racers, among them three winners: Lucien Petit-Breton, François Faber and Octave Lapize.

France was decimated by the war, but the Tour started up again as soon as it was over. The 1919 Tour is famous for the terrible road conditions in the north of France... and for the first appearance of the yellow jersey.

Some say the jersey's colour came from the pages of *L'Auto*, which were yellow, but another story holds that Desgrange left the decision that the race leader should wear a distinctive colour late, and the only jerseys available in the quantity and sizes he needed were yellow. Whatever the true story, Eugène Christophe was the first to wear the yellow jersey, but he lost the race on the penultimate day when his forks broke again. Firmin Lambot was the first post-war Tour winner and, in 1920, Philippe Thys of Belgium became the first triple winner of the Tour de France.

TOUGH MEN FOR A TOUGH RACE

The Tour de France is hard today but it bordered on sadistic in its early years. Individual stages got shorter after the very first editions, but their number increased and the rules became increasingly severe. The public loved it. They loved hearing about tough racers who battled for hours in terrible conditions. And about men like the 1921 winner Léon Scieur, who carried his broken wheel strapped to his back for 200 km. He was forced to do so to comply with the rule that said a racer could replace equipment only if, at the end of a stage, he proved the part replaced was broken beyond repair. The wheel left a star-shaped scar on his back that he carried to his grave.

But bike fans also loved the super-talented racers, like the first Italian winner, Ottavio Bottecchia (1924 and 1925), who treated the Tour as though he was out for a Sunday afternoon spin and sang snatches of opera as he raced along the road.

Most of all, though, people were in awe of the racers' physical prowess, their ability to suffer and bounce back and their sheer endurance. However, the riders' suffering went deeper than the public understood, a fact hidden by the style of journalism surrounding the

PHILIPPE THYS

How many Tours would Thys have won if it hadn't been for World War I? Even Henri Desgrange wrote after Thys' third victory, 'France is not unaware that, without the war, the crack rider from Anderlecht would be celebrating not his third Tour, but his fifth or sixth.' And Desgrange was not a man to give compliments easily.

Thys won the 1912, 1913 and 1920 Tours. He competed in 1919 but, like many riders that year, he'd been too busy trying to stay alive during the war to train. Thys was so out of condition he didn't make it through the first stage. He dominated in 1920, taking the yellow jersey on stage 2 and keeping it until the end. It was more than 30 years before Thys' record was equalled and over 40 before somebody beat it.

RIGHT
The first triple winner of the Tour, alone and leading in 1913.

FAR RIGHT
Philippe Thys takes the Tour winner's bouquet in 1913.

Tour. How hard the Tour really was, and what the racers did to survive it, didn't emerge until 1924. And it did so out of a protest against the rules.

COCAINE FOR OUR EYES

Henri Pélissier was a talented racer with a fiery temper who won the 1923 Tour. He didn't like Henri Desgrange and the feeling was mutual. In those days the stages started early in the morning, when it could be very cold and racers often set off with two jerseys on, getting rid of one when things warmed up a bit. But the rules said they had to carry the other jersey with them, and when Desgrange found Pélissier hadn't complied he gave him a time penalty at the end of a stage.

Pélissier was upset, but worse was to come next morning when a race official lifted Pélissier's jersey to check what he was wearing underneath. It was an affront and Pélissier grumbled along the road to the first town, then stopped and went into a café followed by two of his team-mates. A famous journalist, Albert Londres, was following the 1924 Tour so, when he heard that the defending champion had left the race, he

tracked Pélissier down to the station café in Coutances. What the racer told him (see picture, opposite) shocked France when it was published. It didn't damage the Tour, though; instead it generated even more interest.

DECIDING THE RULES

Desgrange was in almost constant conflict with the riders and their teams, who were sponsored by commercial concerns. He often felt that there was a conspiracy to rob the Tour of its sporting purity in favour of commercial gain. This led him to change how the race was decided several times.

The Tour de France was always a stage race, but sometimes the winner was the rider who completed the whole route in the least time, and in other Tours it was the rider who amassed the highest number of points awarded for placings on each stage. Desgrange eventually settled on a quickest-time format, but in 1930 he announced that the Tour would invite national, rather than commercial, teams and it was up to each country's cycling authority to pick the best pro racers to represent their nation.

Desgrange didn't even let the riders race on their sponsors' bikes. Instead, he bought 150 of the same brand of bike, had them all painted yellow and every rider had to use one. This proved expensive and, where the commercially sponsored teams had paid their own bills, such as those for hotels, the Tour had to pay for the national teams. The race needed sponsorship, but no names could be placed on the bikes or riders' clothing, so Desgrange introduced the publicity caravan in which companies pay for places in a cavalcade that precedes the Tour along the whole of its route.

France dominated the first years of national teams, winning from 1930–1934, but a Belgian, Romain Maes, put a stop to their run when he took the yellow jersey on the first stage of the 1935 Tour and kept it until the end. Only three other racers have done the same: Ottavio Bottecchia (Italy) in 1924, Nicolas Frantz (Luxembourg) in 1928 and Jacques Anquetil (France) in 1961.

The 1938 Tour was won by another rider whose career was affected by war, Gino Bartali of Italy. His country did not send a team in 1939 and he didn't get another chance to ride the Tour until 1948, when he won again.

ABOVE
Gino Bartali winning stage 7, Aix-les-Bains to Grenoble, in 1937.

GINO BARTALI

Patriotic, brave, talented and super strong are just a few of the words that have been used to describe Gino Bartali. The Tuscan racer won his second Tour in 1948 in response to the call of his prime minister after communist party leader, Palmiro Togliatti, had been shot. The country was in turmoil, so the Italian prime minister asked Bartali to give Italy something to focus on and celebrate, and the Tuscan champion delivered.

During World War II, Bartali worked for the Resistance, using his training rides as cover to deliver forged documents that helped smuggle Jews out of Italy to safety in neutral countries. When the authorities became suspicious and arrested him, Bartali told them nothing. Instead, when he was released he got even more involved and physically helped many people escape from the Nazis and from the fascists in his own country.

Bartali's later cycling career was characterized by his rivalry with a younger countryman, Fausto Coppi. Bartali represented an older Italy, a religious country and one tied down by dogma from the past. Coppi was young Italy, new Italy. He also became the best racing cyclist the world had ever seen up to that time.

RIGHT

Albert Londres (far right) takes notes while Henri Pélissier (seated left with his elbow on the table) lifts the lid on doping and suffering in the 1924 Tour.

BELOW

Fausto Coppi leads Gino Bartali on a mountains stage of the 1949 Tour.

'There, look, this is what we use to get through the Tour. Cocaine for our eyes, chloroform to rub on our gums, pills for strength. We run on dynamite.'

HENRI PÉLISSIER SHOWS JOURNALIST ALBERT LONDRES THE CONTENTS OF HIS POCKETS IN AN INTERVIEW AT THE STATION CAFÉ IN COUTANCES DURING THE 1924 TOUR DE FRANCE

THE TOUR IN THE 1940S

The Tour de France was suspended for the duration of the war. The Nazi occupiers asked the new race director, Jacques Goddet, who had taken the reins from Henri Desgrange in 1936, to organize it for them, but he wouldn't. A former colleague at *L'Auto*, Jean Leulliot, put on a race called the Circuit de France, in which some Tour riders were bullied into taking part by the Gestapo, but it was a poor imitation of the Tour.

Goddet organized the Grand Prix de Tour de France in 1943 and 1944, but he stressed in his editorials that it wasn't the Tour. It didn't help him when the Allies freed Paris in 1944. They closed down *L'Auto* but allowed Goddet to set up a new sports daily, called *L'Équipe*. It is world famous today but wasn't entirely trusted in the beginning, so together with another

newspaper, *Le Parisien*, *L'Équipe* put on a dry run for the Tour, called Monaco–Paris, in 1946, then announced a full-scale Tour de France for 1947.

The 1947 Tour was a very homemade affair with fans giving up their petrol and food rations to make the race work. It was exciting though. René Vietto, yet another good rider who had the best part of his career taken away by war, led until three days to go. Vietto was a great climber but a poor time triallist, and stage 19 in 1947 was 139 km, the longest individual time trial there's ever been in the Tour de France.

Vietto lost the lead and, at the age of 34, he was doomed to be one of the best bike racers never to win the Tour de France. Pierre Brambilla took over but the race was far from finished. A late attack on the final day gave the Tour to a feisty little rider from Brittany

called Jean Robic. Robic looked awkward on a bike and was awkward when he rode it. It's said that he broke every bone in his body because of the number of crashes he had during his career.

By the end of the 1940s the Tour de France was established again and it was known throughout the world. Its winners were legends, but cycling was about to see its first superstar. Italians called Fausto Coppi 'Il Campionissimo', the Champion of Champions. He won the 1949 and 1952 Tours and many other races, but it wasn't so much what Coppi won, as the margin that he won by. And his life off the bike made Coppi famous too. He was one of the first sports stars who provoked serious debate in newspapers and occupied the gossip columns as much as he did the sports pages.

FAUSTO COPPI

There are some who say that Fausto Coppi is the greatest racing cyclist ever. Even the man who most agree holds that title, Eddy Merckx, points out that Coppi was winning big races before World War II and asks, 'How many races would he have won if it hadn't been for those six years?'

Ungainly looking off it, Coppi was a genius on a bike. He seemed to stroke, rather than push, his pedals around. He started life as a poor boy running errands and became one of the richest men in sport. Coppi revolutionized cycling and, where the best racers had previously won enough to maybe buy a café or open a bike shop when their racing days were over, the interest in Coppi raised cycling to a point where the top riders became wealthy.

Part of the public's fascination with Coppi stemmed from his controversial love affair with Giulia Locatelli, when they were both married to others. Adultery was forbidden in the Catholic Italy of their time, but it happened when Italy was becoming more secular.

Fausto and Giulia loved each other, and they had a child, and many people supported them because of it.

Coppi probably raced longer than he should have and he never had great health anyway. He decided at the age of 40 that he would end his career in 1960, but fell ill during a racing tour of what is now Burkina Faso at the end of 1959. His doctors said Coppi had the flu, but he actually had malaria and died on 2 January 1960.

BELOW
Fausto Coppi closes the gap on early leader, Jean Robic, on the Alpe d'Huez in 1952. It was the first time the Tour visited this iconic mountain.

17

'WE RUN ON DYNAMITE'

'He seems to caress rather than grip the handlebars, while his torso appears fixed to the saddle. His long legs extend to the pedals with the joints of a gazelle, and at the end of each pedal stroke his ankle flexes gracefully'.

THE 1930 AND 1932 TOUR WINNER, ANDRÉ LEDUCQ, WRITING ABOUT FAUSTO COPPI IN *MIROIR DES SPORTS* MAGAZINE

SOIGNEURS AND SCIENCE

Cycling was also becoming scientific. Coppi was one of the first racers to use interval training and some elements of his preparation were prescribed by doctors. He also used the services of a growing band of men called *soigneurs* to look after him at races. *Soigneur* is the French word for carer. A good *soigneur* is similar to a physical therapist, but in the early days of their existence they were as likely to be charlatans or drug pushers as real experts. Coppi's *soigneur*, a blind man called Biagio Cavanna, was an expert. So was Raymond Le Bert. He helped Louison Bobet to win three consecutive Tours in 1953, 1954 and 1955 – the first person ever to do so.

'Louison would beat himself up for a week for wanting a beer, drink it, then beat himself up for another for doing so.'

FELLOW RACER RAPHAËL GÉMINIANI TALKING ABOUT BOBET'S LEGENDARY SELF-DISCIPLINE

LOUISON BOBET

Louison Bobet applied science to the way he trained and raced. He wasn't a cycling natural in the way that Coppi was, but he was a strong athlete who chose cycling and made himself good at it. Bobet was absolutely meticulous, even to the point of refusing to wear the yellow jersey in one Tour because it had man-made fibres in it. Bobet believed that fine wool, which is what cycling jerseys were made from at the time, allowed him to sweat and cool his body properly. The Tour had to have some special woollen jerseys made for him.

Bobet applied the same approach to diet and led a monk-like existence when he was training. He was also a very hard taskmaster who could push himself to the limit. He won his final Tour in 1955 with an audacious move on Mont Ventoux, when his French team-mates rode hard all the way to the foot of the giant climb, then Bobet attacked to gain a lead. Bobet wasn't a natural climber but he flogged his body up the Ventoux in terrible heat and held his lead down the other side, and on into the finish in Avignon. Later that day his brother Jean, who was also a racer, found Bobet alone in a darkened hotel room collapsed with fatigue.

Bobet invested the money he won in a successful business career and he lived in style. He had an interest in science and gained a pilot's licence. Towards the end of his career he sometimes travelled to races in his own light aircraft.

LEFT
Bobet suffers in terrible heat on the arduous slopes of Mont Ventoux to win the third Tour of his hat-trick in 1955.

THE TOUR IN THE 1950S

Bobet's victories followed on from Coppi in 1952. Ferdy Kübler won in 1950, with a style that looked as though he was having a fight with his bike, and Hugo Koblet won in 1951 without appearing to break into a sweat or have a hair out of place.

The Tour de France has always sought out new mountains, the higher and harder the better. Many of the most familiar names today appeared for the first time in the 1950s. Mont Ventoux was added in 1951, and the first visits in 1952 to the Alpe d'Huez and the Puy-de-Dôme gave Coppi two of his finest moments of his career.

ROGER WALKOWIAK

Occasionally somebody wins the Tour without winning a stage. And sometimes the best racers let a lesser light get too much of an early lead and cannot catch him. But only once has the Tour been won by someone who never won a stage in any Tour de France. It was in 1956 and that rider was Roger Walkowiak.

Bobet was ill and didn't start the Tour, so the French team didn't have an obvious leader. Cycling was a very European sport back in the days of national teams and there weren't enough countries in Western Europe to fill the Tour if they each sent only one ten-man team. So some of the bigger countries sent a B team as well, some of the smaller countries combined with others to field a team, and France supplied several teams from around its regions.

Walkowiak raced the 1956 Tour for the combined team from the north-east and centre of France and was part of a group of 31 that gained a lot of time on stage 7. The closest favourites to him – André Darrigade and Gilbert Bauvin of the French A team – were 11 and 12 minutes respectively behind. Darrigade eventually took the yellow jersey from Walkowiak. Darrigade was a sprinter but Walkowiak could climb.

He became inspired and, despite some other favourites, like Belgium's Jan Adriaenssens, making good their earlier losses, Walkowiak took the lead back in the Alps and kept it to the finish in Paris. The French team got a terrible reception at the Parc des Princes stadium, where the Tour used to finish, but they bounced back the following year with a new leader.

Jacques Anquetil won the 1957 Tour and went on to become the first five-times winner in 1964. He was a superb time triallist who could climb almost as well as the best and that is a deadly combination in the Tour de France.

He was another rider, like Fausto Coppi, who transcended his sport. After a difficult follow-up to his first win, when two great climbers – 'The Angel of the Mountains', Charly Gaul, and 'The Eagle of Toledo', Federico Bahamontes – won the 1958 and 1959 Tours, Anquetil took over in the 1960s and dominated. He also became a major figure in his country and beyond because, like Coppi, he came to represent social change.

'WE RUN ON DYNAMITE'

OPPOSITE

Raymond Le Bert mixing magic in a bottle for Bobet in 1953.

BELOW

Roger Walkowiak doggedly defends the yellow jersey on the road to Lyon in 1956.

ANQUETIL VS POULIDOR

At the same time, a rivalry grew between Jacques Anquetil and Raymond Poulidor that divided France. They shared the same start in life but, where Anquetil spent money on the good things and was a flamboyant character, Poulidor stayed true to his peasant roots and lived a comfortable, but not flashy, life when he started earning well. Their attitude represented two sides of 1960s France. Anquetil was the new France: technology-led and a place where anyone could do anything, no matter where they came from. Poulidor was old France: agricultural France, where people stayed in their home area and were content with what they had.

It wasn't really a sporting contest, though. Poulidor was strong but Anquetil was stronger, not that he always had to prove it. The Tour de France is won with

'Prepare yourself Raymond, you are about to be overtaken by a jet plane.'

POULIDOR'S MANAGER INFORMING HIM THAT ANQUETIL WAS ABOUT TO CLOSE A 2-MINUTE GAP AND CATCH HIM IN A TIME TRIAL

brains as well as brawn and Anquetil always out-thought his rival. Poulidor and his long-time manager, Antonin Magne, didn't really grasp modern racing tactics, but Anquetil and his manager, Raphaël Géminiani, did.

Anquetil continued in the Tour until 1966, when he again managed to thwart Poulidor, causing him to lose a Tour he could have won in favour of Lucien Aimar, one of Anquetil's team-mates. The public felt sorry for Poulidor, who often won more support, even though Anquetil won the race. Anquetil never understood the sympathy for the underdog, but a winner never will.

Whereas Anquetil was called 'Maître Jacques' or 'Monsieur Chrono', Poulidor was dubbed 'L'Éternal Second' quite early in his career and that nickname somehow summed it up. He finished second in three Tours and third in five, but he never won the race. He never wore the yellow jersey even for a single day. The end of Anquetil's dominance didn't help Poulidor either because he had unfortunate crashes in 1967 and 1968. Then in 1969 a rider debuted whom neither Poulidor nor anyone else stood a chance of beating when he was in anything close to form – Eddy Merckx.

JACQUES ANQUETIL

As early as his first Tour de France victory, Anquetil was known as 'Maître Jacques'. He came from humble beginnings but seemed the equal to any challenge, whether in sport or in life. As well as being very confident, Anquetil had a naturally questioning nature. He didn't accept the strict rules that Louison Bobet and many other cyclists lived by; Anquetil enjoyed life too much for that.

He ate and drank what he wanted and it didn't seem to harm him – or his performance – at all. Anquetil also enjoyed the trappings of his success. He and his glamorous wife lived in a beautiful home on the banks of the Seine outside Rouen and they were often

pictured there in popular, as well as cycling, magazines. Later they moved to an even grander château.

Anquetil followed his 1957 Tour win with victory in 1961, when he led from the first day until the last, then again in 1962, 1963 and 1964. During that time the Tour succumbed to pressure from companies that sponsored professional cycling teams and it reverted to trade, rather than national, teams in 1962.

RIGHT
Anquetil celebrates his record-setting fifth but final Tour victory at the Parc des Princes, Paris, in 1964.

EDDY MERCKX

Merckx was nicknamed 'The Cannibal' during his first Tour. He is widely accepted as being the greatest ever road-racing cyclist because no-one has matched, or probably ever will match, the breadth and number of his victories. He was an insatiable winner who simply ate up the opposition.

In the 1969 Tour Eddy Merckx was the best he would ever be. He won every classification, the mountains, points and the yellow jersey, and he won by almost 18 minutes. He attacked for the sheer fun of it, even when he had a comfortable lead but, shortly after the Tour, he crashed in an exhibition race, injured his back and was never the same again.

He won four more Tours and many, many more races, but it wasn't the Eddy Merckx of 1969.

In fact he nearly lost the 1971 Tour to Luis Ocaña of Spain. Ocaña was a great climber who could also time trial. He attacked in the Alps when Merckx had the yellow jersey and took it from him by many minutes. Merckx fought back and gained time, but not at a rate that would have seen him win in Paris. Then Ocaña crashed out of the Tour and Merckx carried on to win.

Merckx puts his difficult 1971 Tour down to not rehabilitating his injuries sufficiently and he set about doing so straightaway and was stronger after that. His reign ended in 1975 when he was beaten by Bernard

Thévenet of France. Merckx was punched by a spectator in that Tour – some say accidentally, some say deliberately – and a few days later he crashed and broke a cheekbone (see page 266). He could have dropped out but he fought on to the first-ever finish of the Tour on the Champs-Élysées in Paris and, because he did so, the public warmed to him as never before.

BELOW
Eddy Merckx taking it easy, briefly, during his total annihilation of the 1969 Tour de France.

ABOVE
Relentless, dedicated, fast and strong,
Merckx had everything and built the
best record of any male professional
cyclist ever.

KING OF THE MOUNTAINS

The Tour was especially mountainous in 1976, which gave a man whom many say is the best climber in its history the chance to win. Lucien van Impe took that chance with both hands. He won in style too, with one incredible day in the Pyrenees that outclassed the field.

There have been many great Kings of the Mountains, a title that first appeared in the 1933 Tour. Climbers are special. They are usually small, always thin and appear to sprout wings when the road goes uphill. It's as if the laws of gravity don't apply to them in the same way as they do to others, and true climbers attack in the worst places with killing turns of speed that break their rivals' legs.

There have been many such men. Vicente Trueba, 'The Flea of Torrelavega', was the first. Many of the great Tour de France winners are top climbers too; Gino Bartali, Fausto Coppi and Eddy Merckx all won mountains titles as well as the Tour. But here we are talking about the true specialists, men like Charly Gaul, Federico Bahamontes, Julio Jiménez, Lucien van Impe, Luis Herrera and Richard Virenque.

Not all of them won the Tour, but some did. However, no specialist climber can compete with a man who is good at everything, and the next dominant force in the Tour was just that. It was a Frenchman, Bernard Hinault, who won five Tours between 1978 and 1985. The years in which he didn't win it was because he was suffering from injury. Joop Zoetemelk won in 1980 and Laurent Fignon in 1983 and 1984, although even Hinault would have had a fight on his hands to beat Fignon in 1984, such was the way Fignon raced then.

THE TOUR GOES GLOBAL

Bikes changed during the 1980s and so did the way bike racers trained. Sports scientists began to understand the processes involved in athletic performance, and how to train riders with precision.

At the same time technicians were studying cycling and coming up with ways of making bikes more efficient and faster. Aerodynamic bikes, skinsuits and aerodynamic helmets began to be used in time trials. The clipless pedal was perfected and bikes got lighter.

Cycling was also becoming a worldwide sport. Reforms in communist Eastern Europe saw good cyclists from those countries take part in the Tour de France when they hadn't been allowed to before. The Australian and British presence grew in the Tour as well, and the first American took part in 1981, while a growing

'As long as I breathe, I will attack.'

BERNARD HINAULT TALKING ABOUT HIS STYLE OF RACING IN 1986

LEFT
Lucien van Impe in the King of the Mountains polka dot jersey attacking to win the 1976 Tour.

24

'WE RUN ON DYNAMITE'

ABOVE

Bernard Hinault in his final yellow jersey, followed by Greg LeMond, during the 1985 Tour.

BELOW RIGHT

Hinault was the last 'patron' of the peloton.

BERNARD HINAULT

Born in Brittany, where many French cycling champions come from, Hinault was a talented, proud and uncompromising bike racer. In many ways he was the last of the old school, the last champion who attacked when it felt right and not necessarily when it was right.

The change came, not because modern racers lack bravery, because they don't. It is just that everyone is better trained now so timing an attack is crucial. Many of the changes that made modern bike racing what it is today occurred during Hinault's era. Hinault used the latest training methods and equipment, but he was the last old-style 'patron' of the peloton, as the main group of riders is called.

Hinault's era saw the old feudal system in cycling begin to change. Wages for the average racer began to rise, and riders didn't depend so much on valuable contracts for exhibition races to boost their income, contracts that were often in the gift of the patron and a few of the best riders and their agents.

Hinault helped bring these changes about. His team went out of its way to recruit a raw talent from America and, after serving his apprenticeship, Greg LeMond helped Hinault win his final Tour de France. LeMond would revolutionize cycling even more.

GREG LEMOND

When the first Europeans saw a teenage LeMond race in Belgium towards the end of the 1970s they knew they were watching the next great Tour champion. He rose quickly through the ranks, funded by enthusiasts at first but later by Bernard Hinault's team when he signed for them at the age of 19.

LeMond was third in the 1984 Tour, second in 1985, then he won in 1986, but during that time his friendship with Hinault turned sour. It didn't matter because Hinault stopped racing at the end of 1986 and it looked like LeMond would have cycling – and the Tour de France – all to himself. But, instead, he was shot in a hunting accident.

It took LeMond two and half years to get back, during which time it seemed that he never would. And even when he returned and won the Tour de France twice, LeMond was never the same racer again.

His second win in 1989 was unexpected. It came in the last minute, literally, and is the closest ever victory margin at 8 seconds. Much of the time he gained was due to his use of a new advance in cycling aerodynamics – aerobars – which are designed to reduce aerodynamic drag. Nobody else used the concept then, but everybody does now.

Later the same year LeMond became world champion and he won the Tour again in 1990, but he had to race conservatively to do it. His body was still peppered with shot from the accident, which was too dangerous to remove, and low-level lead poisoning slowly choked the rest of his career.

RIGHT
Greg LeMond brought many things to the Tour, including broader and deeper sponsorship, and the appliance of science.

ABOVE
Alberto Contador celebrates winning the
2010 Tour, a title he ultimately lost when
he was found guilty of doping in 2012.

ABOVE
Richard Virenque holds his head as he
comes to terms with the doping secrets
of his team being made public in 1998.

number of Colombian riders took part throughout the decade. The Tour de France was going global.

The international flavour of the Tour grew even stronger in 1987 when Stephen Roche won for Ireland. The sponsors changed too. LeMond's first Tour victory spiked interest that was already growing in America. Coca-Cola replaced Perrier as the Tour's official drink as the race stepped onto a larger stage as one of the world's top sporting events.

THE UGLY FACE OF THE TOUR

But the Tour wasn't without its problems, and one of the biggest was doping. From the day that Henri Pélissier made his revelations in 1924, little glimpses of an undercurrent in the Tour had been seen at the surface. There was Tom Simpson's death in 1967 (see page 262), various disqualifications and time penalties for positive dope tests, and there was Michel Pollentier in 1978. He was thrown off the Tour when a doctor supervising a drugs test found that the Belgian was trying to pass off someone else's urine as his own.

Doping – or at least the suspicion of it – raised its head again in 1988. The Tour winner, Pedro Delgado, tested positive for probenecid, a substance that sports people had used as a masking agent for anabolic steroids. He denied any wrong-doing, and it has to be said that the tests taken from him the day before and day after his positive test were clear, which would have been unlikely to happen if he'd been up to no good.

How the positive test occurred remains a mystery. Delgado escaped sanction because probenecid was on the International Olympic Committee's banned list, but not on the list of banned substances of cycling's governing body, the Union Cycliste Internationale (UCI). The Tour is run under UCI rules. Still, doping had poked through again, giving a hint of what was happening inside the fabric of the Tour. It would emerge again ten years later in an almost disastrous way.

Delgado was supported in 1988 by a young team-mate called Miguel Indurain. He was a very strong racer and a valuable team member because he was good on the flat roads. In reality, though, he was more than that; he was a diamond in the rough, one his team manager had already spotted had more talent than Delgado. He just needed polishing.

Although Indurain competed at a time when doping was a big problem in the Tour de France, he wasn't involved in any doping scandals and hasn't been

27 'WE RUN ON DYNAMITE'

subsequently. He did once test positive for a substance called salbutalmol, but it was accepted that the drug had come from a nasal inhaler he'd used and no sanction was given.

Bjarne Riis was the man who toppled Indurain in 1996 to give Denmark, and the whole of Scandinavia, its first win. Then in 1997 he had to stand aside while his young team-mate, Jan Ullrich, won Germany's first Tour. But something really didn't look right, and what it was became clear in 1998.

The Festina team car was stopped by customs officials while crossing from Belgium into France on its way to the start of the Tour in Ireland. On board was a large supply of performance-enhancing drugs (PEDs). The man driving the car, Festina's *soigneur* Willy Voet, admitted everything. Festina had an institutionalized doping programme and the

probability was that other teams had the same. Also it later came to light that individuals or small groups of riders were being 'prepared' by doctors using PEDs (see pages 196–197 and 278).

The shockwaves nearly killed the Tour de France. Years later Bjarne Riis admitted he had taken the most popular PED at the time, the blood-booster EPO, and Jan Ullrich was found guilty of doping in 2012. There was also speculation that the 1998 winner, Marco Pantani, had used EPO too, but this was never proven. The Tour's next big winner, Lance Armstrong, was stripped of his titles by the USADA, but this didn't occur until 2012.

Despite the fact that professional cycling was still feeling the ramifications of 1998 and the Festina affair (the doping scandal that marred that year's Tour), the first post-Armstrong Tour in 2006 saw its winner,

Floyd Landis, stripped of the title for doping. And the winner in 2007 and 2009, Alberto Contador, lost his 2010 title for a similar reason. However, through this time there has been a shift in the collective will of cycling.

The Omertà (code of silence), whereby doping was never spoken about, has gone. Even if they didn't dope, professional racers were reluctant to speak out against it, because to do so was held to damage the sport. It was the big pro secret, part of being in the brotherhood, but the secret is out now and cycling and the Tour de France are healthier for it.

There will still be scandals; something going so far back and being so ingrained does not just go away. The pressure must be kept up, though. Thorough, up-to-date and accurate drugs testing, especially away from races, must be continued and any cases that ensue should be prosecuted thoroughly, swiftly and fairly.

OPPOSITE

American Floyd Landis on his way to victory in 2006. He was disqualified for doping shortly after the Tour.

RIGHT

Despite a history of cheating and lying, the Tour de France proved too beautiful to die, and is more popular today than ever.

LANCE ARMSTRONG

RIGHT
Armstrong's intense need for victory is clear in his eyes.

The American was a prodigy long before he won the Tour de France. A pro triathlete when he was 16, Armstrong became the 1993 professional world road race champion in cycling at the age of 21. He continued winning races that suited his stocky and powerful body until 1996, when he was diagnosed with testicular cancer.

Things looked bad but Armstrong survived, not only returning to health, but returning to competitive cycling and resuming his professional sports career. This time he'd lost the swimmer's shoulders he had developed as a young triathlete. His body was leaner and more efficient and Armstrong had developed the hunger to prove himself in the Tour de France.

He won an unprecedented seven Tours in a row by being the best time triallist and the best climber and he was backed by the most powerful team. It was a brutal but efficient way to win and, in the light of the doping that was going on in the race, fingers began to be pointed at Armstrong.

Accusations were investigated by cycling authorities, and even the FBI, and in 2012 Armstrong gave up the fight and declared that he would no longer defend himself against the charges put against him by the USADA, who subsequently stripped him of his seven titles.

Lance Armstrong is an amazing athlete and a formidable person. His story boosted the Tour de France's worldwide profile. His work in the cancer community means a great deal to a great many. His love of cycling runs so deep that he came back at the age of 38 to race in the 2009 Tour, when he finished third, and in the 2010 Tour.

'Through my illness I learned rejection. I was written off. That was the moment I thought, okay, game on. No prisoners. Everybody's going down.'

LANCE ARMSTRONG TALKING ABOUT HIS MOTIVATION TO WIN THE TOUR DE FRANCE

MIGUEL INDURAIN

To become a Tour legend the young Spanish farmer's son had to lose weight. When he did that and kept his power, Miguel Indurain turned into a Tour de France phenomenon. He improved through 1989, won a mountains stage in 1990, then won every Tour from 1991 to 1995. He was the first man to win five in a row.

Indurain was a superb time triallist who won by stunning margins. His weight loss also allowed him to climb well and, although he never did anything spectacular in the mountains, he never looked in trouble and no-one ever took much time away from him. Indurain had it all really.

He was also liked by his fellow pros, although not so much by the press. His fellows admired Indurain's quiet dignity. They liked the fact that he didn't try to kill them in the mountains as well as the time trials,

like Eddy Merckx and Bernard Hinault did before him and Lance Armstrong would do after. The press was unimpressed for the same reasons. Indurain never gave them deep and revealing quotes, he never had a colourful outburst and the way he raced was quite unspectacular, although it was deadly efficient.

But Indurain also had a strength that eventually proved his weakness. He seemed to be solar-powered – no matter how hot it got, Indurain just soaked it up and converted the heat into power. The Tour de France takes place in July so heat was what Indurain always got. No-one knew that he wasn't the same racer when it was cold.

But the 1996 Tour was cold. One stage in the mountains had to be shortened because the passes were unsafe because of snow and ice. Indurain hated

it. Before the Tour he looked like a winner. During the Tour his body creaked and groaned like a broken machine and he finished a battered but valiant 11th. A few months later Indurain left cycling for good.

'It was like being passed by a rocket, it was frightening. It's not possible to go that fast, maybe he is an extra-terrestrial.'

LAURENT FIGNON ON BEING CAUGHT BY INDURAIN DURING A TOUR TIME TRIAL IN 1992, WHEN FIGNON HAD STARTED 6 MINUTES AHEAD OF HIM

RIGHT
Miguel Indurain winning the stage to Luz Ardiden in 1990.

Mark Cavendish is defeated by Germany's Andre Greipel on stage 5 of the 2012 Tour de France. Greipel, who fellow pro racers have christened 'The Gorilla', is one of the few sprinters who can get the better of Cavendish.

The jersey winners line up together on the final stage of the 2012 Tour. Tejay Van Garderen is in white, Bradley Wiggins in yellow, Peter Sagan in green and Thomas Voeckler in the polka-dot jersey.

The Tour de France hasn't come away unscathed. There will always be a feeling, after 1998, that those close to the race must have known what was happening and should have done more. However, the Tour is as popular now as it has ever been and that popularity has spread around the globe.

ONE HUNDRED TOURS
The Tour de France is the biggest annual sporting event in the world – 10–15 million spectators stand by the road to watch the race pass, each year, and many millions more watch it on the television. The Tour goes out to 190 countries, 60 of which receive live transmission.

There is no sporting event like the Tour de France. A sporting contest that combines athleticism and bravery with cutting-edge technical advances, as cycling does, will always be popular. Set that against the backdrop of one of the most beautiful countries in the world, with its Pyrenean and Alpine splendour, and you have a winner.

As I write in 2012, there have been one hundred Tours and all of them have been spectacular. No doubt there will be one hundred more.

The 100 greatest stages

1903

Garin beats the officials

PARIS > LYON

At 3.14pm on 1 July 1903 59 riders set off on the 467 km to Lyon. Some of the best athletes of the day were there, including Hyppolyte Aucouturier, Jean Fischer and Léon Georget. However, Maurice Garin, a two-time winner of Paris–Roubaix and a winner of Bordeaux–Paris and Paris–Brest–Paris, was the man to beat.

Garin later described the start as 'chaotic, turbulent'. While his key rivals attacked from the off only to fade later in the race, Garin marked the leaders and kept a steady tempo. The heat that day was unbearable and the first riders abandoned after 50 km. At around 9pm, Fischer was disqualified for drafting behind a car. By the following morning, Aucouturier had abandoned because of stomach cramp. Then Georget

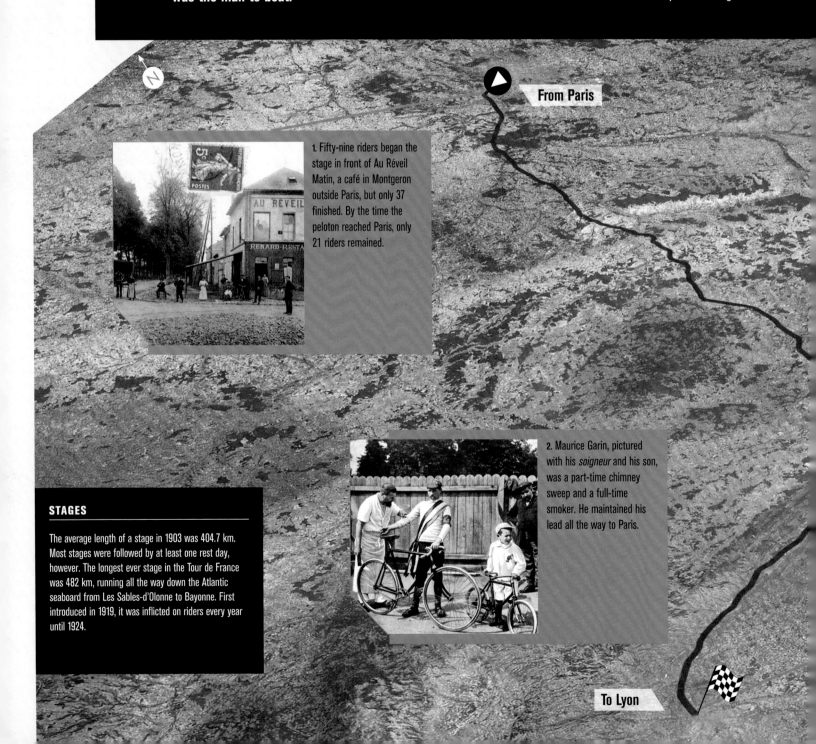

From Paris

1. Fifty-nine riders began the stage in front of Au Réveil Matin, a café in Montgeron outside Paris, but only 37 finished. By the time the peloton reached Paris, only 21 riders remained.

2. Maurice Garin, pictured with his *soigneur* and his son, was a part-time chimney sweep and a full-time smoker. He maintained his lead all the way to Paris.

STAGES

The average length of a stage in 1903 was 404.7 km. Most stages were followed by at least one rest day, however. The longest ever stage in the Tour de France was 482 km, running all the way down the Atlantic seaboard from Les Sables-d'Olonne to Bayonne. First introduced in 1919, it was inflicted on riders every year until 1924.

To Lyon

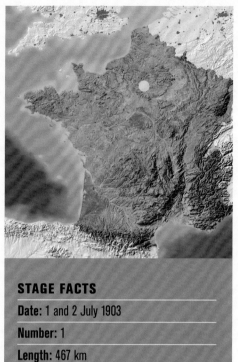

punctured, leaving Garin and a young protégé of his, Émile Pagie, in the lead.

On the outskirts of Lyon Garin soloed away to win the stage, 'bounding like a cat over the cobblestones', according to Géo Lefèvre, *L'Auto's* special correspondent and race director, followed by Pagie just under a minute later. Lefèvre should have been there to witness the event. Instead, chasing the riders in an express train, he arrived to discover, 'thousands on the quai de Vaise, shouting, applauding and thronging around two figures white with dust. It was them! They'd just finished, had boarded a car and were making off in the direction from which I'd just arrived.'

STAGE FACTS

Date: 1 and 2 July 1903

Number: 1

Length: 467 km

3. Bikes weighed more than 10 or 15 kg (22–33 lb), had no gears and were ridden on mainly unpaved roads. Yet Garin still managed to maintain an average speed of 35 km/hour.

4. Garin reached the finish faster than *L'Auto*'s Géo Lefèvre, who had taken an express train.

'We all looked after ourselves – *c'est la guerre* – as far as Fontainebleau! [Claude] Chapperon, [Paul] Trippier, Georget and Aucouturier attacked relentlessly. They were after my scalp, that much was obvious – but they weren't having it!'
MAURICE GARIN

AFTER STAGE 1

1 Maurice Garin (Fra)
2 Émile Pagie (Fra)
at 0'55"
3 Léon Georget (Fra)
at 34'59"

Mob malice

LYON > MARSEILLE

The 1904 Tour de France was riven with scandal: riders cheated by taking lifts in cars and trains, bike frames were sabotaged and nails were scattered on the roads. On the first stage, Maurice Garin, in the lead, was nearly driven off the road by a car and was threatened with death by its passengers.

Having passed Saint-Étienne on stage 2, around 3 am, the peloton was heading up the Col de la République. This is an account by some riders of what happened next: 'At the top the climb, [Antoine] Fauré suddenly accelerates and advances by two or three bike lengths. We raise our heads to see, 50 m ahead, a group of a hundred individuals forming a hedge on either side of the road. They are armed with clubs and stones. Fauré continues

1. Roads strewn with nails or broken glass were a common feature of this Tour. In some cases fans helped clear the debris away.

2. Despite the numerous check points, both official – like the one shown here – and secret, cheating was widespread, with some riders hitching lifts in cars and trains.

From Lyon

Saint-Étienne

Col de la République

To Marseille

resolutely and passes; the clubs are raised for those behind... Maurice Garin receives four simultaneous blows... César Garin receives two blows, one to the nape of his neck, the other to the back; [Auguste] Daumain is knocked over, his knee wounded; he is able to climb back on and escape. As for [Giovanni] Gerbi, he is literally knocked senseless.'

The crowd was dispersed by pistol shots fired by Géo Lefèvre, in a car behind. Fauré, the local meant to benefit from the attacks, lurked near the back of the peloton for the rest of the stage, which was won by Hippolyte Aucouturier.

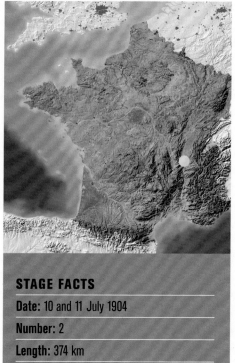

YOUNG AND OLD

Henri Cornet, aged 19 in 1904, is the youngest winner of the Tour de France. The next youngest is Romain Maes, aged 21 in 1935. The oldest winner is Firmin Lambot, aged 36 in 1922.

STAGE FACTS

Date: 10 and 11 July 1904
Number: 2
Length: 374 km

'The Tour is finished and I am very afraid that its second edition will be its last. It will have been killed by its own success, driven out of control by blind passion, by violence and filthy suspicions worthy only of ignorant and dishonourable men.'
HENRI DESGRANGE

3. Garin won the Tour but by November he and another 11 riders had all been disqualified and the fifth-placed Henri Cornet (pictured) declared victor.

4. After yet more attacks on stage 3, Maurice Garin (pictured) commented, 'If I'm not murdered before Paris, I'll win the Tour again.'

BEFORE STAGE 2 BEFORE DISQUALIFICATIONS	**AFTER STAGE 2** BEFORE DISQUALIFICATIONS
1 Maurice Garin (Fra)	1 Maurice Garin (Fra)
2 Lucien Pothier (Fra) at 0'24"	2 Lucien Pothier (Fra) at 0'24"
3 Pierre Chevalier (Fra) at 19'54"	3 César Garin (Fra) at 1h 4'54"
FINAL OFFICIAL GENERAL CLASSIFICATION	FINAL OFFICIAL GENERAL CLASSIFICATION
1 Michel Frédérick (Swi)	1 Émile Lombard (Bel)
2 Giovanni Gerbi (Ita) at 5'35"	2 Antoine Fauré (Ita) at 57'30"
3 François Beaugendre (Fra) at 27'00"	3 François Beaugendre (Fra) at 1h 21'28"

1905

The first of the mountains

NANCY > BESANÇON

Henri Desgrange created a much longer route in 1905, with 11 stages rather than six, which were shorter and easier to control. Skulduggery was not eliminated, however: nails strewn across roads in stage 1 meant only 15 participants crossed the line in Nancy. Other innovations included riders accumulating points, rather than a time advantage, and the introduction of the first real mountain, the Ballon d'Alsace, featuring gradients of 10%.

Six of the favourites – Henri Cornet, Hippolyte Aucouturier, Louis Trousselier, René Pottier, Émile Georget and Lucien Petit-Breton – reached the foot of the Ballon d'Alsace shortly after 9am, swapped their bikes for frames with better gears and plunged into a battle described by *L'Auto*'s Alphonse Steines

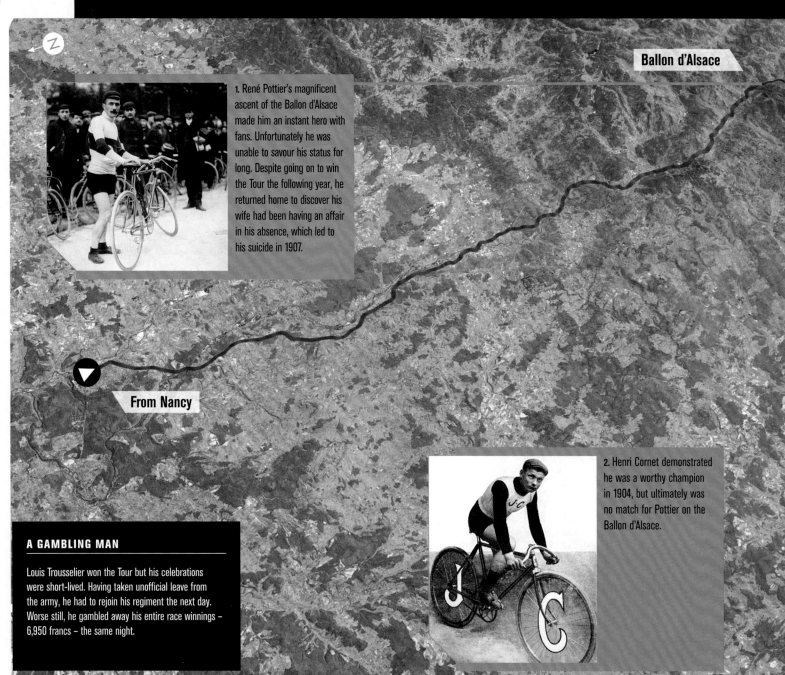

Ballon d'Alsace

1. René Pottier's magnificent ascent of the Ballon d'Alsace made him an instant hero with fans. Unfortunately he was unable to savour his status for long. Despite going on to win the Tour the following year, he returned home to discover his wife had been having an affair in his absence, which led to his suicide in 1907.

From Nancy

2. Henri Cornet demonstrated he was a worthy champion in 1904, but ultimately was no match for Pottier on the Ballon d'Alsace.

A GAMBLING MAN

Louis Trousselier won the Tour but his celebrations were short-lived. Having taken unofficial leave from the army, he had to rejoin his regiment the next day. Worse still, he gambled away his entire race winnings – 6,950 francs – the same night.

as 'a sporting epic'. Cornet initiated the attacks, gradually shaking off his companions to leave only Pottier, who cranked up the pace. While Cornet countered Pottier's first surge, he was unable to respond when Pottier attacked again, leaving Pottier the honour of conquering the Tour's first mountain at an average speed of 20 km/hour.

Following a thrilling descent, Hippolyte Aucouturier eventually overtook Pottier to win the stage, but Pottier's efforts put him in the race lead. The glory didn't last long; the next day Pottier abandoned, troubled by injuries and exhausted by his display of mountain mastery.

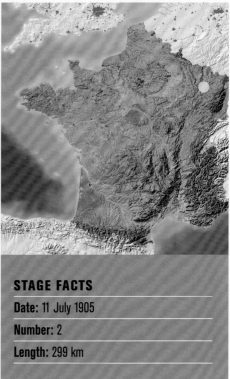

STAGE FACTS

Date: 11 July 1905

Number: 2

Length: 299 km

3. As in the first two Tours, Hippolyte Aucouturier won the second stage in dominating style.

'The climb of the Ballon d'Alsace by the lead group composed of Pottier, Aucouturier, Cornet, Georget and Trousselier is one of the most exciting things I've ever witnessed and confirms after so many others the opinion that man's courage has no limits and that a well-trained athlete can aspire to unimaginable results.' HENRI DESGRANGE

To Besançon

4. Pottier dominated on the Ballon d'Alsace in 1905 and again in 1906, when his strength in the mountains won him the Tour. After Pottier's tragic suicide in 1907, Henri Desgrange erected a monument to his achievements.

BEFORE STAGE 2	AFTER STAGE 2
1 Louis Trousselier (Fra) 1 pt	1 René Pottier (Fra) 7 pts
2 Jean-Baptiste Dortignacq (Fra) 2 pts	2 Hippolyte Aucouturier (Fra) 9 pts
3 René Pottier (Fra) 3 pts	3 Louis Trousselier (Fra) 9 pts

Pottier masters the mountains

GRENOBLE > NICE

René Pottier returned to the Tour as one of the favourites and did not disappoint. In stage 2 he punctured several times – nail scatterers had been at work again – yet managed to rejoin the lead group and win the stage, putting himself in the race lead, where he would remain until the end of the Tour. Dominant over the Ballon d'Alsace again, he had built up a 48-minute margin by the time he reached Dijon 220 km later. He then went on to win the next three stages, generating feverish excitement among fans.

Stage 5 took the race through the Alps, along the road taken by Napoléon on his return from exile, featuring the 1,246-m Col Bayard and the Côte de Laffrey – a short, but sharp, ramp with some sections reaching gradients of 18%. Pottier was leading

1. The riders begin the 1906 Tour de France. Of the 76 starters, only 14 finished. Four riders were disqualified for taking the train while others were victims of punctures.

From Grenoble

Côte de Laffrey

2. Although freewheels existed, riders were still on fixed gear bikes which had become a hindrance with the introduction of mountain descents. Some riders overcame this by resting their feet on pegs welded to the forks, letting the pedals spin independently.

3. The 1906 Tour was raced at the slowest average speed since 1903, a mere 24.460 km/hour. It was not difficult for local fans to ride alongside their heroes for sections of the route.

the Tour by 1 hour when, according to cycling folklore, he stopped at a bar. By the time his first rivals appeared he had enjoyed most of a bottle of wine, but got back on his bike and went on to win the stage by 26 minutes.

Pottier won the 1906 Tour, which was the longest since 1903, featuring more than 4,500 km, compared to the previous year's 3,000. It was also the first time the race had been won by virtue of a rider's climbing skills.

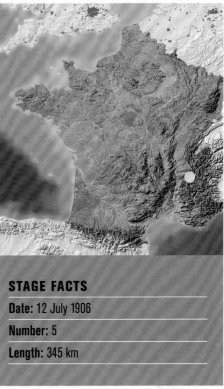

4. René Pottier was the first of the great mountain climbers, winning the Tour through his dominance in the mountains. He rode 650 km in solo breakaways and, with his unusual floppy white hat, was easy to identify.

STAGE FACTS

Date: 12 July 1906

Number: 5

Length: 345 km

'Climbing, you see, is my forte; speeding over the Ballon d'Alsace is much easier for me than writing a newspaper article.'
RENÉ POTTIER

COL BAYARD

Col Bayard, which was first introduced in the Tour in 1905, has featured 25 times in the Tour de France and is classed a category 2 climb. It featured in almost every Tour up to World War II, but has only been used twice since 1947.

Col Bayard

Gap

To Nice

BEFORE STAGE 5	AFTER STAGE 5
1 René Pottier (Fra) 7 pts	1 René Pottier (Fra) 8 pts
2 Georges Passerieu (Fra), Émile Georget (Fra), Lucien Petit-Breton (Fra) 15 pts	2 Georges Passerieu (Fra) 17 pts
	3 Émile Georget (Fra) 20 pts

Penalties and protests

TOULOUSE > BAYONNE

1907 should have been Émile Georget's year. After winning five stages, some featuring epic mountain duels with another emerging star, François Faber, he was dominating the race, and finishing on the top step of the podium in Paris seemed a mere formality. A puncture in stage 9, however, led Georget to swap his bike with that of a team-mate. This was against Tour rules and rival team Alcyon, whose rider Louis Trousselier was in second place, didn't hesitate to report the transgression to race officials.

Georget's penalty was harsh; 45 points were added to his classification, demoting him to third place and rendering overall victory impossible. Alcyon nonetheless considered the sanction insufficiently severe and, even though they were now

1. *L'Auto*'s correspondents were amazed to see Lucien Petit-Breton – shown here at a check point on the 1907 course – riding alone 'as fresh as a rose', yet all the while building a terrific time gap on his rivals.

Tarbes

Pau

From Toulouse

Auch

3. Fans lined the route and thronged the control towns, offering thunderous applause when Petit-Breton appeared.

2. Petit-Breton had a proven talent for punishing solo efforts, having set a world hour record in 1905. Here he is shown leaving a check point in Bordeaux.

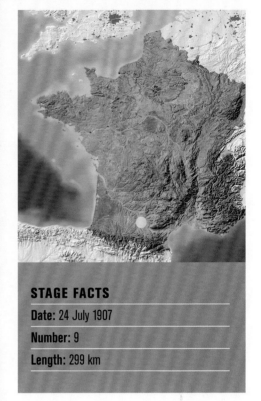

in the lead, they withdrew all their riders, including Trousselier, from the race.

That left Georget's team-mate, Lucien Petit-Breton, in the top spot – which he maintained all the way to Paris. On stage 9 Petit-Breton had put in a performance that perfectly justified his new status. Indeed, he had been the revelation of the day, having simply 'taken flight' after 50 km, eventually riding into Bayonne a staggering 23 minutes ahead of everyone else.

'What can I say,' wrote one of *L'Auto's* correspondents, 'over 250 km we witnessed, amidst an indescribable ovation, a triumphant walkover from Petit-Breton, who with courage and perseverance continued to extend his lead, right until the end.'

STAGE FACTS

Date: 24 July 1907

Number: 9

Length: 299 km

THE ARGENTINE

Lucien Petit-Breton rode under a pseudonym, since his father disapproved of him racing bikes. His real surname was Mazan and he was also known as 'The Argentine', having grown up in Buenos Aires. Petit-Breton was an accomplished track racer and in 1907 was also the first ever winner of Milan–San Remo.

To Bayonne

Peyrehorade

4. Having failed to respond quickly enough when Petit-Breton made his move, Georges Passerieu, Gustave Garrigou and Émile Georget were left to fight over second, third and fourth places respectively in a sprint finish.

'The profile of today's stage and the weather conditions were certainly in my favour, but I'm sure I shall repeat my victory in less favourable conditions.'
PETIT-BRETON AFTER THE RACE. HE WENT ON TO WIN A SECOND STAGE IN HIS HOME TOWN OF NANTES AND RETAINED THE RACE LEAD ALL THE WAY TO PARIS.

BEFORE STAGE 9	AFTER STAGE 9
1 Émile Georget (Fra) 13 pts	1 Émile Georget (Fra) 17.5 pts (He was subsequently penalized)
2 Louis Trousselier (Fra) 29 pts	2 Lucien Petit-Breton (Fra) 37 pts
3 Lucien Petit-Breton (Fra) 36 pts	3 Louis Trousselier (Fra) 40.5 pts

1908

Petit-Breton's triumph

CAEN > PARIS

In 1908 Lucien Petit-Breton's team, Peugeot, boasted the biggest riders of the day, including Émile Georget, who had almost won in 1907; François Faber, the talented mountain climber; Georges Passerieu, who had come second in 1906; Hippolyte Aucouturier, celebrated veteran and multiple stage winner; Jean-Baptiste Dortignacq, a podium finisher and stage winner, and Henri Cornet, the 1904 winner.

Unsurprisingly, Petit-Breton's main rivals were his formidable team-mates. They won every stage, while he took the lead from stage 3 and kept it to the end, winning five stages along the way.

The last stage featured 251 km from Caen to Paris. Despite having an unbeatable points advantage in the general classification,

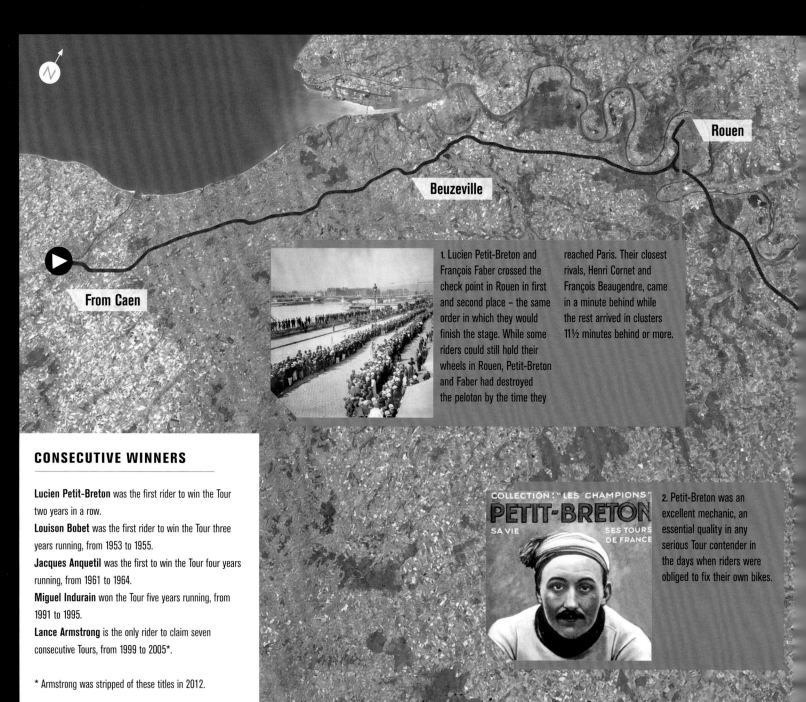

Rouen

Beuzeville

From Caen

1. Lucien Petit-Breton and François Faber crossed the check point in Rouen in first and second place – the same order in which they would finish the stage. While some riders could still hold their wheels in Rouen, Petit-Breton and Faber had destroyed the peloton by the time they reached Paris. Their closest rivals, Henri Cornet and François Beaugendre, came in a minute behind while the rest arrived in clusters 11½ minutes behind or more.

COLLECTION: "LES CHAMPIONS"
PETIT-BRETON
SA VIE   SES TOURS DE FRANCE

2. Petit-Breton was an excellent mechanic, an essential quality in any serious Tour contender in the days when riders were obliged to fix their own bikes.

CONSECUTIVE WINNERS

Lucien Petit-Breton was the first rider to win the Tour two years in a row.

Louison Bobet was the first rider to win the Tour three years running, from 1953 to 1955.

Jacques Anquetil was the first to win the Tour four years running, from 1961 to 1964.

Miguel Indurain won the Tour five years running, from 1991 to 1995.

Lance Armstrong is the only rider to claim seven consecutive Tours, from 1999 to 2005*.

* Armstrong was stripped of these titles in 2012.

Petit-Breton continued to ride aggressively right until the end. After 80 km his blistering pace had reduced the peloton to eight riders, with Paul Duboc, Gustave Garrigou, Henri Cornet, François Faber, Paul Chauvet, Giovanni Gerbi and Eugène Forestier still holding tight; 50 km later they were down to seven. In Mantes, less than 50 km from Paris, they were down to five. Shortly after Versailles Petit-Breton and his team-mate Faber, who was in second place on the general classification, went on the attack again, forcing a gap of several minutes over their pursuers. Together they entered the Parc des Princes velodrome, packed to capacity with an ecstatic crowd, where Petit-Breton won the sprint finish by two bike-lengths over his acolyte.

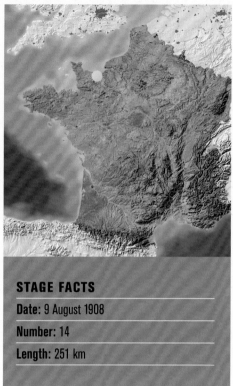

STAGE FACTS

Date: 9 August 1908

Number: 14

Length: 251 km

'I never doubted my victory for one moment. I was marvellously well prepared, I knew I could count on Peugeot and my Lion tyres; in short, I won comfortably enough, even though I met some men who made my life difficult.' LUCIEN PETIT-BRETON

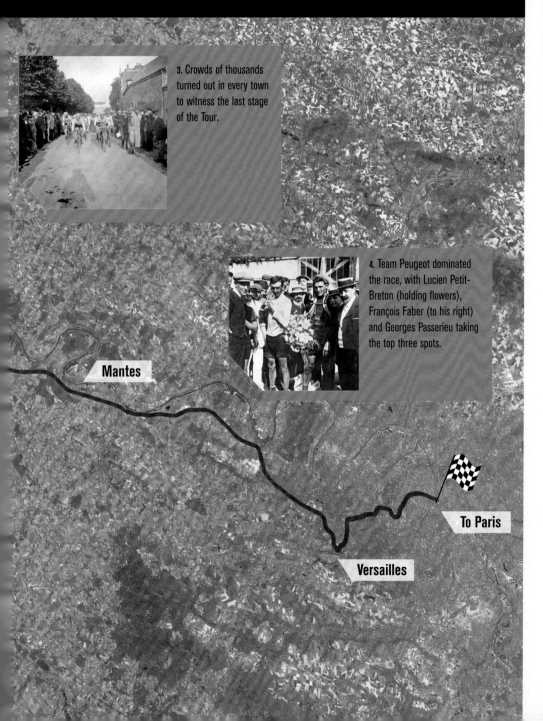

3. Crowds of thousands turned out in every town to witness the last stage of the Tour.

4. Team Peugeot dominated the race, with Lucien Petit-Breton (holding flowers), François Faber (to his right) and Georges Passerieu taking the top three spots.

Mantes

To Paris

Versailles

BEFORE STAGE 14	AFTER STAGE 14
1 Lucien Petit-Breton (Fra) 35 pts	1 Lucien Petit-Breton (Fra) 36 pts
2 François Faber (Lux) 66 pts	2 François Faber (Lux) 68 pts
3 Georges Passerieu (Fra) 70 pts	3 Georges Passerieu (Fra) 75 pts

1909

The indomitable Giant of Colombes

GRENOBLE > NICE

Measuring 1.86 m (6 feet 1 inch) tall, weighing 91 kg (200 lb) and nicknamed 'The Giant of Colombes', 22-year-old François Faber was the tallest and heaviest rider in the peloton. In 1908 Faber had been runner-up to Lucien Petit-Breton, who correctly predicted Faber would become his successor. But who could have foreseen such an electrifying performance? By stage 6 the French were utterly in thrall to this indomitable superman and his Homeric exploits, achieved in the worst weather conditions the Tour had ever seen. With temperatures barely above zero and in the face of driving rain, snow, mud and unsurfaced roads, Faber had simply broken away from the peloton in each of the previous four stages, winning two by margins of more

MAKING HISTORY

François Faber is the only rider in the history of the Tour de France to have won five consecutive stages. In 1930 Charles Pélissier became the first rider to win eight stages in the Tour, although they weren't consecutive. Even more remarkably, he came second on another seven stages the same year, yet he only finished in ninth place, over an hour behind his team-mate André Leducq. Pélissier's eight stage victories in one Tour have only been equalled by Eddy Merckx in 1970 and 1974 and by Freddy Maertens in 1976. Merckx also holds the record for the most Tour stage wins in a career – 34. His closest rivals are Bernard Hinault, who won 28, and Pélissier's team-mate and 1930s heart-throb, Leducq, who won 25.

From Greno

Côte de Laffrey

1. The 'The Giant of Colombes', François Faber, was dominant in the mountains, normally the domain of tiny climbers.

2. Faber is saluted by spectators awed by the enormity of his achievements. He was simply invincible, the archetypal 'hard man' of cycling. In the first six stages he made Tour history with one astonishing stage win after another.

3. The 1909 Tour is reputed to be the hardest in Tour history. Seventy-seven riders abandoned over the first six stages, yet Faber – pictured here in stage 4 of the race – simply ploughed on.

'If *L'Auto*'s classic race has, since its creation, always found the man it needed to remain the most absorbing of all bicycle races, let us recognize, without prejudice, that it has never known a winner more deserving than Faber.' *L'AUTO*

than 30 minutes and, in one case, riding 200 of 398 km on his own. On stage 4 his chain had broken and he ran the final kilometre pushing his bike. On stage 5, climbing the Col de Porte on the way to Grenoble, the wind had been so strong he had been twice blown off his bike and then was knocked down by a horse.

On stage 6 *L'Auto* reported 'he dictated the pace right until the end, producing a final surge 15 km from Nice-la-Belle, which cleanly, indisputably, brought him victory, as if victory no longer wished to recognize anyone but him'.

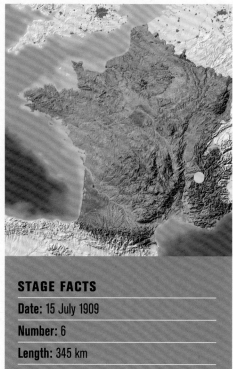

STAGE FACTS

Date: 15 July 1909

Number: 6

Length: 345 km

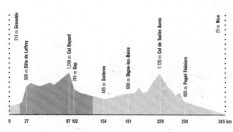

4. Although he lived in the Parisian suburb of Colombes and considered himself French, François Faber was the first rider from Luxembourg to win the Tour.

214 m Grenoble
900 m Côte de Laffrey
1,248 m Col Bayard
745 m Gap
485 m Sisteron
609 m Digne-les-Bains
1,120 m Col de Toutes Aures
400 m Puget-Théniers
25 m Nice

0   27   97 102   154   181   229   234   345 km

BEFORE STAGE 6	AFTER STAGE 6

BEFORE STAGE 6	AFTER STAGE 6
1 François Faber (Lux) 6 pts	**1** François Faber (Lux) 7 pts
2 Gustave Garrigou (Fra) 19 pts	**2** Gustave Garrigou (Fra) 24 pts
3 Cyrille van Hauwaert (Bel) 24 pts	**3** Cyrille van Hauwaert (Bel) 32 pts

Col Bayard

Gap

To Nice

1910

Assassins!

LUCHON > BAYONNE

Alphonse Steines had a record of audacious notions. As one of Henri Desgrange's reporters/race organizers, he had been responsible for sending riders up the Ballon d'Alsace. His brainwave for the 1910 Tour left everyone aghast: a scenic 'detour' through the Pyrenees. On a reconnaissance trip to the Tourmalet, Steines found his taxi blocked by snowdrifts, so he crossed the summit on foot, finally staggering into Barèges at 3am. Then he telegraphed Desgrange: 'Have crossed the Tourmalet. Road very good. Perfectly usable.' Mission accomplished.

By stage 10 the race leader, François Faber, was nursing an injury and losing time to team-mate Octave Lapize. Seeing an opportunity, Lapize went on the attack, followed by another team-mate, Gustave Garrigou. An intense battle ensued with Lapize

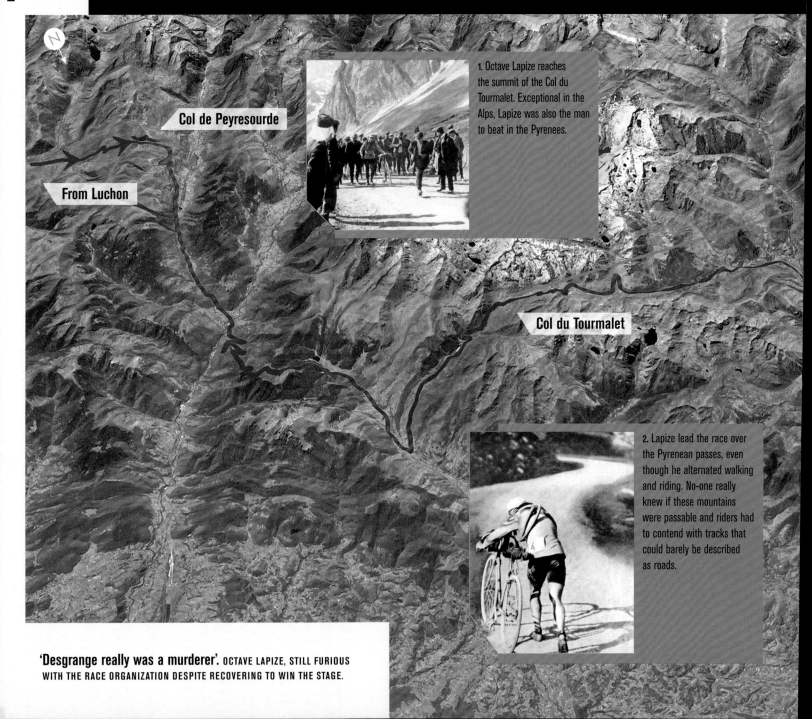

Col de Peyresourde

From Luchon

Col du Tourmalet

1. Octave Lapize reaches the summit of the Col du Tourmalet. Exceptional in the Alps, Lapize was also the man to beat in the Pyrenees.

2. Lapize lead the race over the Pyrenean passes, even though he alternated walking and riding. No-one really knew if these mountains were passable and riders had to contend with tracks that could barely be described as roads.

'Desgrange really was a murderer'. OCTAVE LAPIZE, STILL FURIOUS WITH THE RACE ORGANIZATION DESPITE RECOVERING TO WIN THE STAGE.

crossing the Peyresourde and the Tourmalet first. The pair looked set to dominate the Aubisque when a local rider, François Lafourcade, overtook them. Reaching the summit first, his face contorted with suffering, Lafourcade simply ignored astonished race marshals who asked his name. Lapize, arriving 15 minutes later, was more vocal, '*Vous êtes des assassins!*, 'You are murderers!' he spat, insisting he would abandon at the next check point.

He picked up on the descent, however, and went on to win in Bayonne. Faber came in 10 minutes later, while Garrigou finished eighth, losing 56 minutes. The 1904 winner, Henri Cornet, lost 4½ hours. Only ten riders officially completed the stage.

STAGE FACTS

Date: 21 July 1910

Number: 10

Length: 326 km

3. Garrigou crossed the Tourmalet 500 m behind Lapize. He had adopted a smaller (39 x 19) gear ratio and was the first rider to scale the mountain without dismounting.

Col d'Aubisque

To Bayonne

4. Team-mates and rivals, Lapize, Faber and Garrigou battled all the way to Paris, where they finished in the same order. Here Octave Lapize is photographed receiving his winner's bouquet at the finish of the Tour.

SWEEPING UP

The *voiture balai* (broom wagon) was first introduced in 1910. It was particularly relevant for the many independent riders, who had no team car to pick them and their bikes up when the rigours of the race proved too much. But its primary purpose was to prevent cheating; tired stragglers would no longer have the chance to sneak off and complete the stage by train.

Exceptionally, in the case of stage 10 of the 1910 Tour, conditions on the Pyrenees were so difficult that Henri Desgrange allowed everyone – including those who had taken lifts in cars – to continue the following day.

BEFORE STAGE 10

1 François Faber (Lux)
36 pts

2 Octave Lapize (Fra)
49 pts

3 Cyrille van Hauwaert (Bel)
68 pts

AFTER STAGE 10

1 François Faber (Lux)
36 pts

2 Octave Lapize (Fra)
46 pts

3 Cyrille van Hauwaert (Bel)
73 pts

The Galibier is conquered

CHAMONIX > GRENOBLE

After the sensational Pyrenees in 1910, Henri Desgrange decided a monstrous Alpine summit was needed in 1911. At an altitude of 2,646 m the Galibier was the highest mountain yet attempted, promising a 33-km ascent with a 7% average gradient.

Team Alcyon was dominating the race with Gustave Garrigou and François Faber in first and second place. Stage 5 promised a showdown with their rivals in the La Française team: the climbers Paul Duboc, in third, and Émile Georget, out of contention following a crash, but a troublemaker nonetheless.

'The stage start was amusing: downhill all the way!' Garrigou later reported. 'But soon the fun began, and by fun I refer to the tasteless prank of slipping mountains under the roads of our beautiful country!'

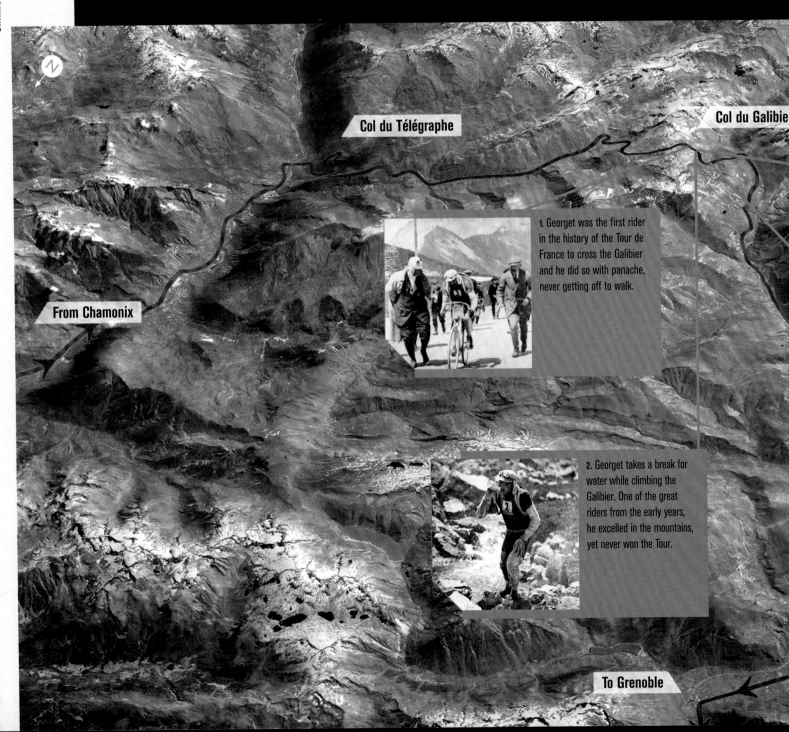

Col du Télégraphe

Col du Galibie

From Chamonix

1. Georget was the first rider in the history of the Tour de France to cross the Galibier and he did so with panache, never getting off to walk.

2. Georget takes a break for water while climbing the Galibier. One of the great riders from the early years, he excelled in the mountains, yet never won the Tour.

To Grenoble

Georget and Duboc went on the attack straightaway, building a 7-minute gap on Garrigou. Yet by the foot of the Télégraphe the race leader had caught up again. Faber, meanwhile, was 45 minutes in arrears, his powerful build making him no match for the scrawny front runners. Georget was first over the Télégraphe and, without dismounting, on an unsurfaced road surrounded by snow, he became the first rider to crest the Galibier, with a 15-minute gap on his rivals.

Georget went on to win the stage. With Duboc, he snapped at Garrigou's heels all the way to Paris, but invincible Garrigou dominated to the end.

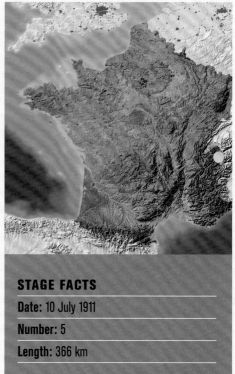

TOUR PEAKS

The Galibier remained the highest summit in the Tour de France until 1938 when the 2,764-m high Iseran was introduced. The highest mountain pass is the 2,802-m Col de la Bonette, first featured in 1962.

STAGE FACTS

Date: 10 July 1911

Number: 5

Length: 366 km

3. Unlike Georget, Garrigou alternated cycling and walking as he ascended the Galibier.

4. 'Very high above us we saw ants advancing; they were our men, nibbling on the monster with the teeth of their pedals,' Henri Desgrange wrote.

'Up there it's bitterly cold, and when Georget passes, having placed his victorious foot on the head of the monster, his moustache full of mucus and food from the last check point, and his jersey filthy with muck from the last stream where, bathed in sweat, he'd wallowed, he turns to us, frightful yet noble, and declares, "Well, that's given you something to think about!"'
HENRI DESGRANGE

BEFORE STAGE 5	AFTER STAGE 5
1 Gustave Garrigou (Fra)	1 Gustave Garrigou (Fra)
10 pts	13 pts
2 François Faber (Lux)	2 François Faber (Lux)
11 pts	23 pts
3 Paul Duboc (Fra)	3 Paul Duboc (Fra)
25 pts	27 pts

1912

Lapize abandons, blames Belgians

PERPIGNAN > LUCHON

The Tour was experiencing a generational shift; punctures and accidents had put most of the big names out of contention and young stars were emerging.

Entering the Pyrenees only two points separated the race leader, 20-year-old Belgian Odile Defraye, from Octave Lapize, the 1910 champion. In third place was young Frenchman Eugène Christophe, who'd already accomplished three astonishing mountain stage wins, one featuring a 315-km solo raid over the Galibier.

Defraye shouldn't even have been in the race as he had crashed descending the Galibier and would have abandoned were it not for Firmin Lambot, a compatriot from a rival team, who had taken pity and shepherded him to the finish.

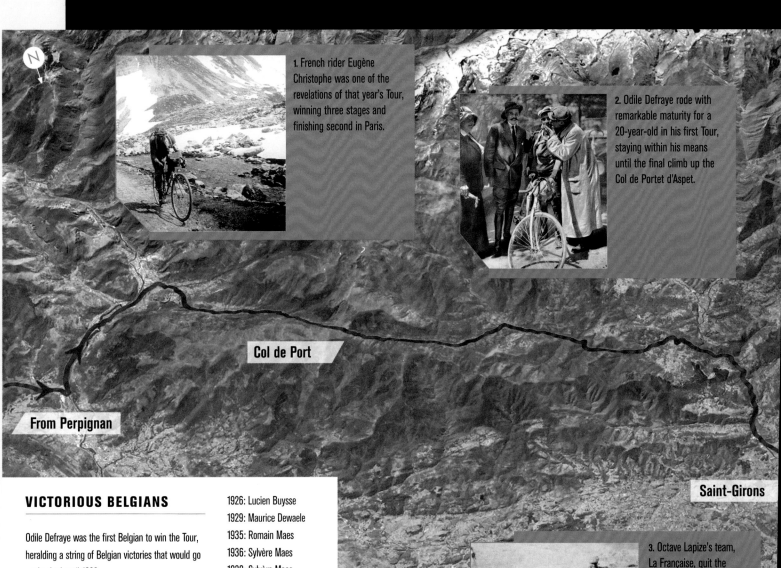

1. French rider Eugène Christophe was one of the revelations of that year's Tour, winning three stages and finishing second in Paris.

2. Odile Defraye rode with remarkable maturity for a 20-year-old in his first Tour, staying within his means until the final climb up the Col de Portet d'Aspet.

Col de Port

From Perpignan

Saint-Girons

3. Octave Lapize's team, La Française, quit the same evening in protest at the Belgians' unchecked violations of the race's rules.

VICTORIOUS BELGIANS

Odile Defraye was the first Belgian to win the Tour, heralding a string of Belgian victories that would go unchecked until 1923:

1913: Philippe Thys
1914: Philippe Thys
1919: Firmin Lambot
1920: Philippe Thys
1921: Léon Scieur
1922: Firmin Lambot

1926: Lucien Buysse
1929: Maurice Dewaele
1935: Romain Maes
1936: Sylvère Maes
1939: Sylvère Maes
1969: Eddy Merckx
1970: Eddy Merckx
1971: Eddy Merckx
1972: Eddy Merckx
1974: Eddy Merckx
1976: Lucien van Impe

In stage 9 Christophe and a young Belgian, Marcel Buysse, attacked early, and roughly halfway through were more than 20 minutes ahead. Another Belgian, Louis Heusghem, now set off in pursuit with a small group that included Lapize and Defraye. Their ferocious pace, and the Col de Port, dramatically reduced the escapees' lead.

On the Col de Portet d'Aspet Defraye accelerated, passing Buysse, now on foot. Reaching the summit with Christophe, whom he then dropped, he went solo into Luchon by 3 minutes. Behind him Lapize abandoned. Wherever Defraye was in the race, there were Belgians to help him, regardless of team loyalties. It was against the rules but, for once, Henri Desgrange paid scant attention.

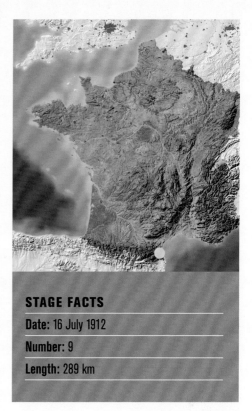

STAGE FACTS

Date: 16 July 1912

Number: 9

Length: 289 km

4. Lapize had won the 1910 Tour on the back of heroic exploits in the Pyrenees. But he was equally capable of abandoning the Tour in despair, even when he had seemingly favourable odds; indeed he only finished one of the six Tours he took part in – a reminder that the Tour is as much a trial of mental as physical endurance.

To Luchon

Col de Portet d'Aspet

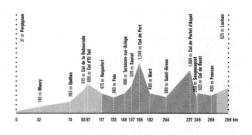

BEFORE STAGE 9	AFTER STAGE 9

BEFORE STAGE 9	AFTER STAGE 9
1 Odile Defraye (Bel) 36 pts	1 Odile Defraye (Bel) 37 pts
2 Octave Lapize (Fra) 38 pts	2 Eugène Christophe (Fra) 57 pts
3 Eugène Christophe (Fra) 55 pts	3 Gustave Garrigou (Fra) 67 pts

'How can you fight in such conditions? Everyone is working for Alcyon! All the Belgians are helping Defraye, whether they're on his team or not. I've had enough and I'm pulling out.' OCTAVE LAPIZE

The Tour is blown in the forge

BAYONNE > LUCHON

The sixth stage of the 1913 Tour took the peloton into the Pyrenees and the epic, 326-km stage included the Cols d'Aubisque, Tourmalet, Aspin and Peyresourde. Eighty-two riders had already abandoned the race.

Eugène Christophe, second on general classification, and his Peugeot team were dominating the Tour. Christophe was in excellent form and the first to crest the Aubisque. He then followed his team-mate Philippe Thys over the Tourmalet.

However, disaster struck when Christophe's fork broke on the descent. He had no choice but to shoulder the bike and run down the mountain to the next village, Sainte-Marie-de-Campan, some 14 km distant, where he found a blacksmith's forge.

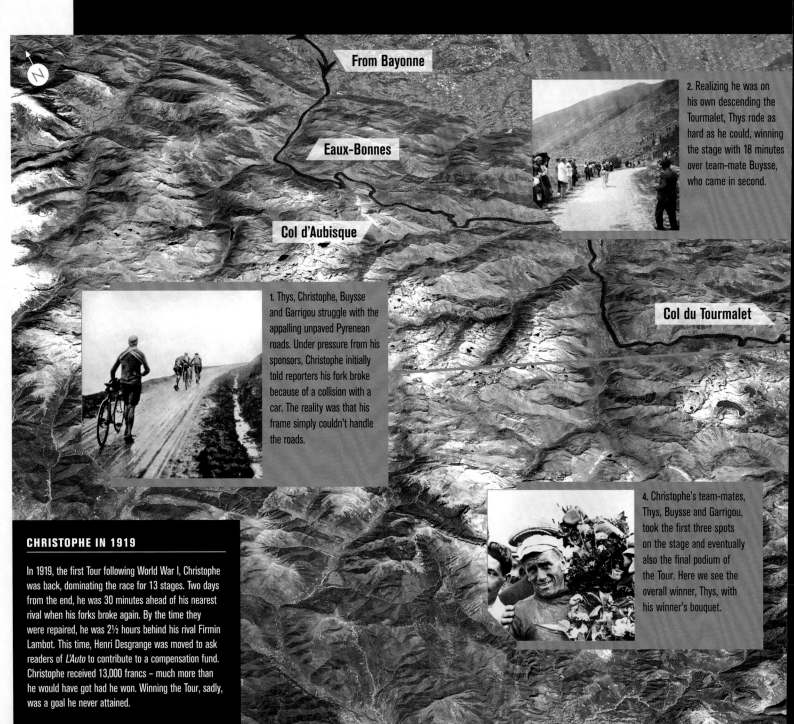

From Bayonne

Eaux-Bonnes

Col d'Aubisque

Col du Tourmalet

2. Realizing he was on his own descending the Tourmalet, Thys rode as hard as he could, winning the stage with 18 minutes over team-mate Buysse, who came in second.

1. Thys, Christophe, Buysse and Garrigou struggle with the appalling unpaved Pyrenean roads. Under pressure from his sponsors, Christophe initially told reporters his fork broke because of a collision with a car. The reality was that his frame simply couldn't handle the roads.

4. Christophe's team-mates, Thys, Buysse and Garrigou, took the first three spots on the stage and eventually also the final podium of the Tour. Here we see the overall winner, Thys, with his winner's bouquet.

CHRISTOPHE IN 1919

In 1919, the first Tour following World War I, Christophe was back, dominating the race for 13 stages. Two days from the end, he was 30 minutes ahead of his nearest rival when his forks broke again. By the time they were repaired, he was 2½ hours behind his rival Firmin Lambot. This time, Henri Desgrange was moved to ask readers of *L'Auto* to contribute to a compensation fund. Christophe received 13,000 francs – much more than he would have got had he won. Winning the Tour, sadly, was a goal he never attained.

Fortunately Christophe was a good mechanic and set to work on repairing his frame. Tour rules stated riders could not accept help with repairs and, as the race commissaires looked on, the blacksmith stood helplessly by, unable to assist the champion.

In the meantime Christophe's team-mates, Philippe Thys, Marcel Buysse and Gustave Garrigou, set the race on fire. By the day's end Thys had won the stage and ridden from fifth place into the overall lead while Buysse and Garrigou completed the top three.

It took Christophe more than 4 hours to repair his bike. He managed to finish the stage within the time cut, but his dreams of Tour de France victory were now shattered.

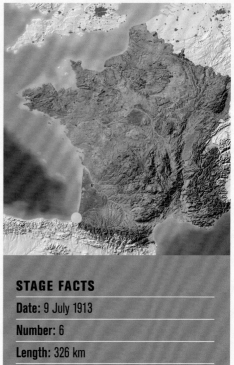

STAGE FACTS

Date: 9 July 1913

Number: 6

Length: 326 km

3. There were no photographers on hand to record Christophe's forge detour, but the event was later immortalized in this painting by Paul Ordner. In addition to the time Christophe lost repairing his bike, Henri Desgrange penalized him a further 10 minutes as, unable to work the blacksmith's bellows alone, he had been forced to ask a young boy to help.

Sainte-Marie-de-Campan

Col d'Aspin

Col de Peyresourde

To Luchon

After 2 hours watching Christophe at the forge, one of the race commissaires asked Desgrange if he could get a sandwich. 'If you're hungry, eat charcoal!' Christophe cried, 'I am your prisoner and you will remain my wardens till the end.'

BEFORE STAGE 6	AFTER STAGE 6
1 Odile Defraye (Bel)	1 Philippe Thys (Bel)
2 Eugène Christophe (Fra) at 4'55"	2 Marcel Buysse (Bel) at 5'58"
3 Marcel Buysse (Bel) at 10'05"	3 Gustave Garrigou (Fra) at 31'36"

Thys destroys favourites

PARIS > LE HAVRE

Shortly before 3am on a hot summer's night, an immense crowd flooded the streets of the Parisian suburb of Saint-Cloud. Only as the race official's car led the peloton to the official start, did spectators reluctantly part.

A race of 388 km lay ahead of the 147 riders. It soon became apparent quite a few weren't in shape. Paul Duboc was dropped from a bunch which he would normally have dominated and Charles Crupelandt – a favourite for the stage – was also under pressure. After Abbeville, roughly halfway through, former Tour winners Louis Trousselier and François Faber lost contact.

Even those responsible for brutal accelerations, like Lucien Petit-Breton, eventually withered in the heat. Continuing at a

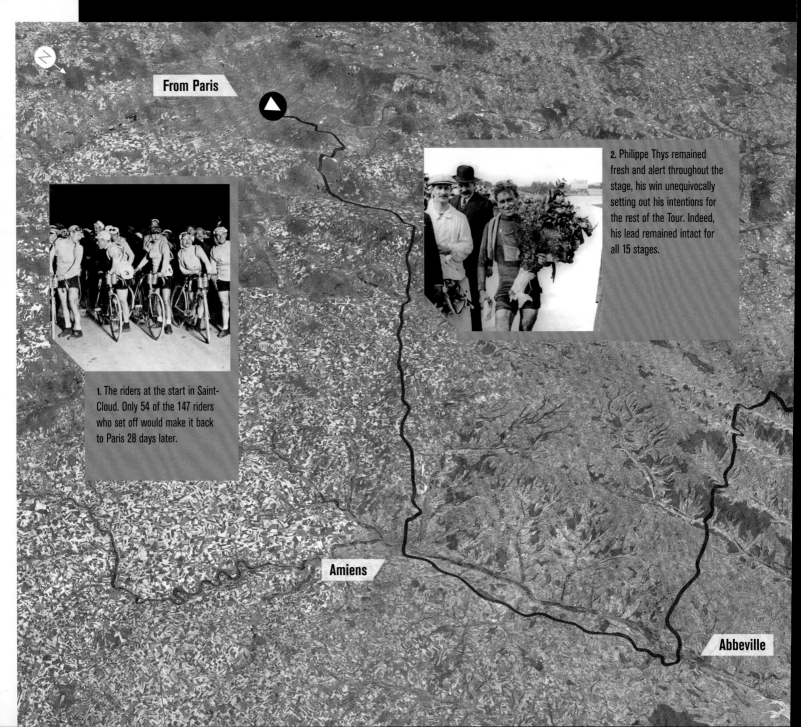

From Paris

1. The riders at the start in Saint-Cloud. Only 54 of the 147 riders who set off would make it back to Paris 28 days later.

2. Philippe Thys remained fresh and alert throughout the stage, his win unequivocally setting out his intentions for the rest of the Tour. Indeed, his lead remained intact for all 15 stages.

Amiens

Abbeville

furious pace, the peloton was shedding riders until, 15 km from the finish, there were only nine left when Octave Lapize punctured and his rivals accelerated. Assuming that was the last they had seen of him, they were astounded when a little later Lapize and a previously dropped Émile Georget re-emerged from a cloud of dust.

In the final sprint Jean Rossius, Gustave Garrigou, Georget and Costante Girardengo were all at the front, but Philippe Thys came up from the side to win by a bike length. The previous year's champion, Thys had set the pace for much of the second half of the race. He was clearly serving notice that 1914 belonged to him.

STAGE FACTS

Date: 28 June 1914

Number: 1

Length: 388 km

THE FALLEN

The Tour had barely finished when its riders went off to fight in World War I. Many would never return. Among those who lost their lives were Lucien Petit-Breton, winner in 1907 and 1908, Octave Lapize, winner in 1910 and François Faber, winner in 1909. Faber proved to be just as heroic in the trenches as he had been on the road, shot by a sniper while rescuing a fellow soldier wounded near enemy lines.

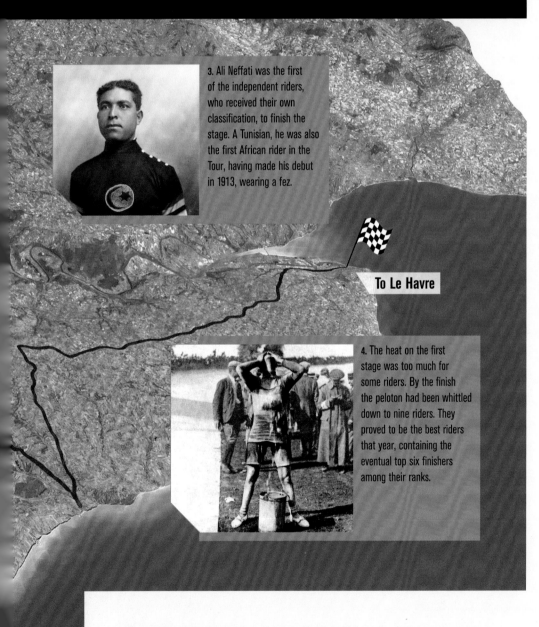

3. Ali Neffati was the first of the independent riders, who received their own classification, to finish the stage. A Tunisian, he was also the first African rider in the Tour, having made his debut in 1913, wearing a fez.

To Le Havre

4. The heat on the first stage was too much for some riders. By the finish the peloton had been whittled down to nine riders. They proved to be the best riders that year, containing the eventual top six finishers among their ranks.

AFTER STAGE 1

1 Philippe Thys (Bel)
at 13h 18'28"
2 Jean Rossius (Fra)
same time
3 Gustave Garrigou (Fra)
same time

'Here I am in first place, and even though the task seems to me to be formidable this year, all my efforts will go towards conserving my first place in the general classification to the end.' PHILIPPE THYS

1919

The first yellow jersey

GRENOBLE > GENEVA

Days after World War I ended Henri Desgrange was already planning the next Tour. It would feature the longest ever stage – 482 km from Les Sables-d'Olonne to Bayonne.

The roads were in appalling condition and so were the riders, who only seven months previously had been fighting in the trenches.

By stage 11 the race had been reduced to 11 riders. Eugène Christophe was in the lead, with Jean Alavoine and Firmin Lambot close behind.

In Grenoble that morning Henri Desgrange had presented Christophe with a yellow jersey – the colour of *L'Auto*'s pages – which would help distinguish him from the other riders in the race. Post-war shortages meant that most sponsors had banded together

From Grenoble

Vizille

1. Eugène Christophe, the stage leader, is given the first-ever yellow jersey to distinguish him from other riders. His closest rivals – Léon Scieur, Jean Alavoine and Firmin Lambot (from left to right) – look on.

2. Léon Scieur was riding in fifth place, almost 3½ hours behind Christophe. He would have been a greater threat to his rivals had he not suffered multiple punctures in the freezing cold on the second stage. Even though his hands were too cold to thread the needle necessary to stitch his tyre back together, a race official was on hand to ensure the woman in whose doorway he sheltered didn't lift a finger to help. Scieur nonetheless continued to ride as if he might win, and finished stage 11 in the same time as Alavoine, Christophe and Lambot.

Aiguebelle

La Chambre

La Grave

Col du Lautaret

Saint-Jean-de Maurienne

Albertville

Col du Galibier

Saint-Michel-de-Maurienne

3. Not content with having won the previous two stages, Barthélémy gave a master class on how to climb the Col du Galibier.

to create one team, La Sportive, whose ubiquitous grey jersey made it hard to distinguish individuals. Christophe, whom the other riders referred to as a canary, was allegedly unimpressed by the honour.

The race that day took riders over the Galibier yet failed to offer the anticipated showdown between Christophe, Alavoine and Lambot. Although they finished in the top five, they took no risks and spent the day marking each other. Instead, it was Honoré Barthélémy who made headlines, winning his third consecutive stage by attacking on the Galibier and riding the last 220 km on his own, finishing 10 minutes ahead of Luigi Lucotti and 15 minutes ahead of Christophe's group.

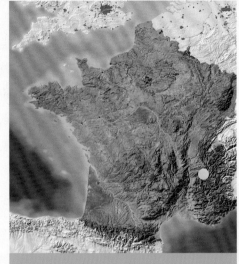

THE YELLOW JERSEY ENIGMA

Was Christophe really the first yellow jersey? Philippe Thys claimed Desgrange asked him to wear a coloured jersey to distinguish him as race leader in 1913, and that his team manager bought a yellow one from a shop a few stages later. There are no newspaper accounts that record the event, however, so the truth remains a mystery.

STAGE FACTS

Date: 19 July 1919

Number: 11

Length: 325 km

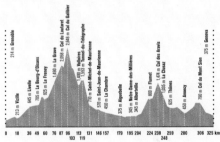

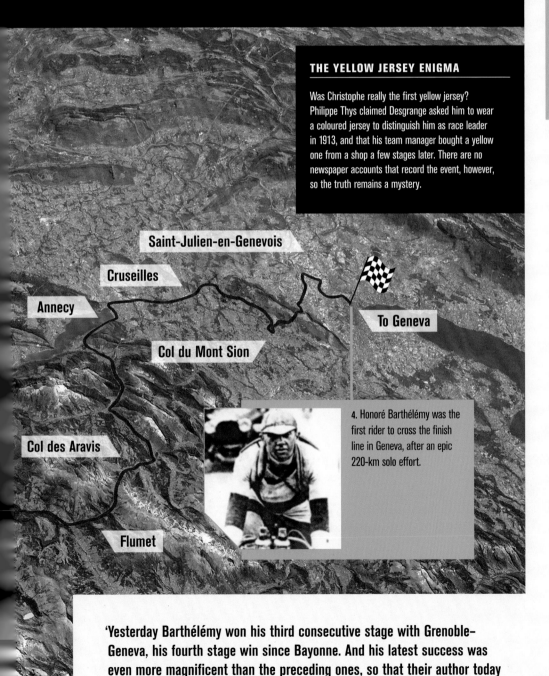

Saint-Julien-en-Genevois

Cruseilles

Annecy

Col du Mont Sion

To Geneva

Col des Aravis

4. Honoré Barthélémy was the first rider to cross the finish line in Geneva, after an epic 220-km solo effort.

Flumet

BEFORE STAGE 11

1 Eugène Christophe (Fra)
2 Firmin Lambot (Bel)
at 23'19"
3 Jean Alavoine (Fra)
at 39'51"

AFTER STAGE 11

1 Eugène Christophe (Fra)
2 Firmin Lambot (Bel)
at 23'19"
3 Jean Alavoine (Fra)
at 39'51"

'Yesterday Barthélémy won his third consecutive stage with Grenoble–Geneva, his fourth stage win since Bayonne. And his latest success was even more magnificent than the preceding ones, so that their author today can be definitely classed among the aces of cycling.' HENRI DESGRANGE

The hell of the north

METZ > DUNKERQUE

Eugène Christophe, the man who might have won the Tour in 1913 had it not been for an accident with his forks, was back and this time his triumph seemed assured. He had led the race for ten stages, there were only two left and he had a 30-minute margin on his nearest rival, Firmin Lambot.

Only 11 riders remained as the race traversed the apocalyptic landscape of post-war northern France. Under dark skies and constant rain the peloton passed through one town after another that had been reduced to rubble. Near Valenciennes, on the same cobbled roads used in the one-day professional Paris–Roubaix bicycle road race, Lambot attacked. Christophe set off after him, but his forks, already damaged in a crash in a previous stage,

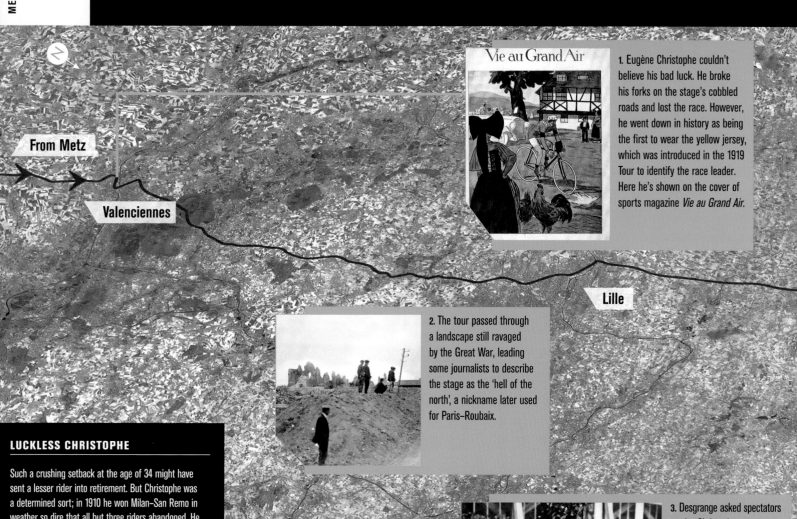

From Metz

Valenciennes

Lille

Vie au Grand Air

1. Eugène Christophe couldn't believe his bad luck. He broke his forks on the stage's cobbled roads and lost the race. However, he went down in history as being the first to wear the yellow jersey, which was introduced in the 1919 Tour to identify the race leader. Here he's shown on the cover of sports magazine *Vie au Grand Air*.

2. The tour passed through a landscape still ravaged by the Great War, leading some journalists to describe the stage as the 'hell of the north', a nickname later used for Paris–Roubaix.

3. Desgrange asked spectators to give Christophe a warm welcome at the end of the race: 'It's a duty for all sports fans that we console him at the finish line on Sunday with our most fervent applause, because I tell you, there has never in the history of our sport been such unfortunate luck as that which burdens Christophe today.'

LUCKLESS CHRISTOPHE

Such a crushing setback at the age of 34 might have sent a lesser rider into retirement. But Christophe was a determined sort; in 1910 he won Milan–San Remo in weather so dire that all but three riders abandoned. He was 40 years old when he rode his final Tour in 1925. Christophe has to be one of the Tour's most unlucky riders. His forks broke yet again in 1922, when he was in third place coming off the Galibier. He might also have won the Tour in 1912 – the year Octave Lapize abandoned in protest at the Belgians' inter-team collusion – had the race lead been calculated by time rather than points, which the Belgians accumulated by sprinting together in stage finishes. Timing-wise Christophe was in the 'lead' all the way to the final stage, when, utterly vexed, he sat up and let a group ride away.

could not withstand the cobbles – and broke yet again. As luck would have it there was a bike factory close by. Bringing his great skills as a mechanic to use – before turning professional Christophe had trained as a locksmith – he repaired his bike, losing 'only' 2½ hours to Lambot. He finished the stage, and the Tour, in third place.

This time Henri Desgrange was moved to ask readers of *L'Auto* to contribute to a compensation fund. Christophe received 13,000 francs – much more than he would have got had he won. That, sadly, was a goal he would never attain.

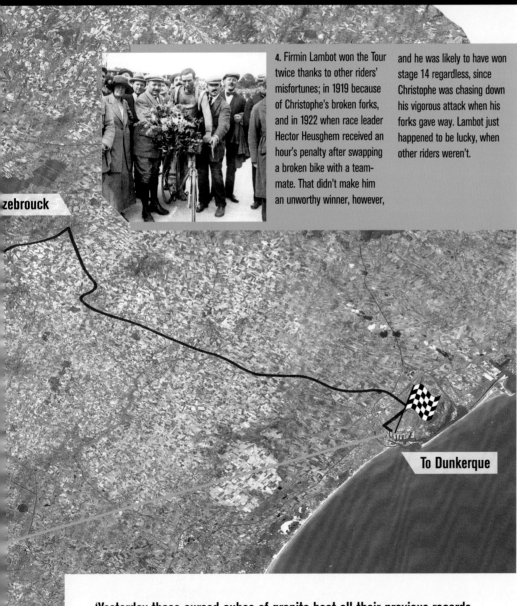

zebrouck

To Dunkerque

4. Firmin Lambot won the Tour twice thanks to other riders' misfortunes; in 1919 because of Christophe's broken forks, and in 1922 when race leader Hector Heusghem received an hour's penalty after swapping a broken bike with a team-mate. That didn't make him an unworthy winner, however, and he was likely to have won stage 14 regardless, since Christophe was chasing down his vigorous attack when his forks gave way. Lambot just happened to be lucky, when other riders weren't.

STAGE FACTS

Date: 25 July 1919

Number: 14

Length: 468 km

BEFORE STAGE 14

1 Eugène Christophe (Fra)
2 Firmin Lambot (Bel)
at 28'05"
3 Jean Alavoine (Fra)
at 49'29"

AFTER STAGE 14

1 Firmin Lambot (Bel)
2 Jean Alavoine (Fra)
at 1h 53'03"
3 Eugène Christophe (Fra)
at 2h 00'53"

'Yesterday those cursed cubes of granite beat all their previous records – and by miles: they went for the best young man in the world, the most serious of our champions.' HENRI DESGRANGE ATTACKS THE COBBLES RESPONSIBLE FOR CHRISTOPHE'S DOWNFALL.

1920

The flint in Barthélémy's eye

PERPIGNAN > AIX-EN-PROVENCE

'The Perpignan stage is always uneventful,' Henri Desgrange reported in 1920, unaware of what had befallen one rider.

The peloton had just completed two brutal Pyrenean stages featuring freezing rain and mud. Stage 8 was long and hot, but at least the road was flat. The pace was fast from the start so that only 11 riders, including Honoré Barthélémy, remained in contention by the time the race reached Arles. Although he posed no threat to the general classification, Barthélémy was the best French rider left in the race. The previous year he had finished fifth and won four stages, three of them in the Alps. When the leaders stopped for a drink at a water fountain in Salon, Hector Heusghem attacked. Efforts to chase him down proved futile,

From Perpignan

Salon-de-Provence

2. Barthélémy leads the peloton through the streets of Bouillargues. Incredibly, after a heavy crash 10 km from the finish, Barthélémy continued to ride despite a broken shoulder, a dislocated wrist and the loss of the sight in one of his eyes.

1. The stage from Perpignan to Aix-en-Provence was frying-pan hot and relatively uneventful until Heusghem attacked while the peloton took a break in Salon.

3. After Hector Heusghem's victory in Aix, a group of seven riders sprinted for second place, with the eventual winner of the 1920 Tour, Philippe Thys, seen here, winning. To his right, Louis Mottiat impedes Joseph van Daele.

only serving to fracture the peloton further, so that Heusghem won with a margin of 8½ minutes.

Meanwhile, 10 km from the finish, Barthélémy had crashed heavily. Badly injured, it took him a moment to realize that a flint had destroyed the sight in one eye. Nevertheless, he completed the stage only 28 minutes behind Heusghem. With a broken shoulder and a dislocated wrist, he continued to ride, finishing each of the remaining stages in the top ten and the Tour itself in eighth place. When he reached the Parc des Princes ecstatic crowds carried him in triumph.

STAGE FACTS

Date: 11 July 1920

Number: 8

Length: 325 km

HONORÉ BARTHÉLÉMY'S GLASS EYE

Tales of riders completing the Tour in recent years despite injuries – Cadel Evans in the yellow jersey riding with a fractured elbow in 2010 or Johnny Hoogerland finishing the Tour in 2011 despite 33 stitches after being thrown into a barbed wire fence – pale in comparison to Honoré Barthélémy's stoicism in 1920.

In spite of having only one eye (and the impact that that would have had on his spatial awareness, essential for cyclists riding in close packs, sprinting or descending), Barthélémy came third in the following year's Tour and continued to race until 1927. He used a glass eye which he took out on dusty stages. The socket would become infected and ooze pus – he once told a journalist, 'My brain's leaking' – and he would fill it with cotton wool. 'It makes no difference to the view but it's softer and I always like a bit of pampering,' he said.

'I spend all the prizes I win on buying new eyes for the ones I lose in races.'
HONORÉ BARTHÉLÉMY ON HIS HANDS AND KNEES AT THE FINISH LINE OF A STAGE LOOKING FOR HIS GLASS EYE.

To Aix-en-Provence

4. Barthélémy came third in the following year's Tour and continued to race until 1927.

BEFORE STAGE 8	AFTER STAGE 8
1 Philippe Thys (Bel)	1 Philippe Thys (Bel)
2 Hector Heusghem (Bel) at 28'14"	2 Hector Heusghem (Bel) at 28'14"
3 Firmin Lambot (Bel) at 1h 20'00"	3 Firmin Lambot (Bel) at 1h 20'00"

1924

Running on dynamite

CHERBOURG > BREST

Henri Pélissier, who had won the 1923 Tour, and his brother Francis were a duo who won stages with great panache and abandoned them in fits of pique.

On the morning of stage 3 an official had lifted Henri's jersey to see if another was hidden underneath. Henri often wore two in the cold

early hours, jettisoning one later – a breach of Tour rules. Outraged, at such insulting treatment, Henri persuaded Francis and team-mate Maurice Ville to abandon in Coutances, where journalist Albert Londres found them in a café.

Londres reported what Henri told him: "'We suffer on the road. But do you want to see how we keep going? Wait…" From his bag he takes a phial. "There, look, this is what we

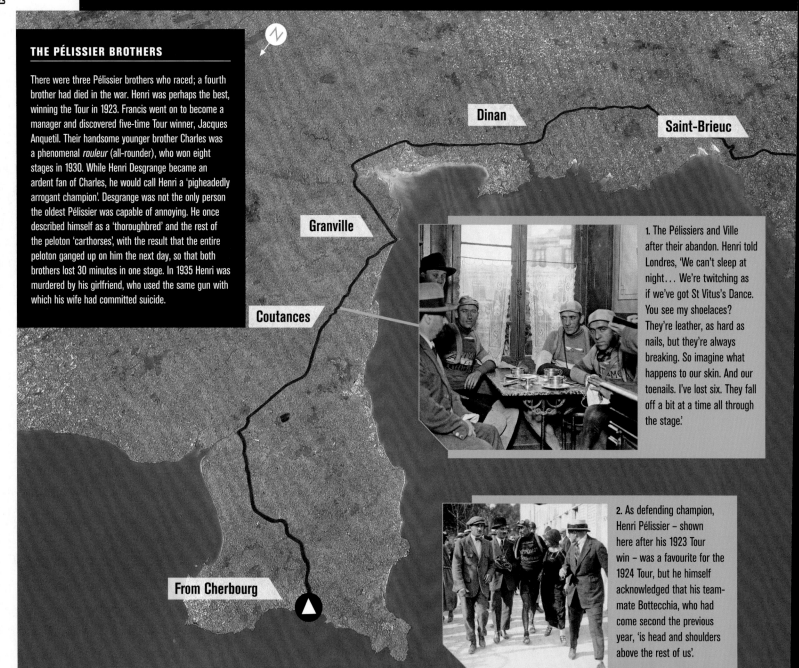

THE PÉLISSIER BROTHERS

There were three Pélissier brothers who raced; a fourth brother had died in the war. Henri was perhaps the best, winning the Tour in 1923. Francis went on to become a manager and discovered five-time Tour winner, Jacques Anquetil. Their handsome younger brother Charles was a phenomenal *rouleur* (all-rounder), who won eight stages in 1930. While Henri Desgrange became an ardent fan of Charles, he would call Henri a 'pigheadedly arrogant champion'. Desgrange was not the only person the oldest Pélissier was capable of annoying. He once described himself as a 'thoroughbred' and the rest of the peloton 'carthorses', with the result that the entire peloton ganged up on him the next day, so that both brothers lost 30 minutes in one stage. In 1935 Henri was murdered by his girlfriend, who used the same gun with which his wife had committed suicide.

Dinan

Saint-Brieuc

Granville

Coutances

1. The Pélissiers and Ville after their abandon. Henri told Londres, 'We can't sleep at night… We're twitching as if we've got St Vitus's Dance. You see my shoelaces? They're leather, as hard as nails, but they're always breaking. So imagine what happens to our skin. And our toenails. I've lost six. They fall off a bit at a time all through the stage.'

From Cherbourg

2. As defending champion, Henri Pélissier – shown here after his 1923 Tour win – was a favourite for the 1924 Tour, but he himself acknowledged that his team-mate Bottecchia, who had come second the previous year, 'is head and shoulders above the rest of us'.

use to get through the Tour. Cocaine for our eyes, chloroform to rub on our gums..."

"'Here,' said Ville, tipping out the contents of his bag, "horse liniment to keep my knees warm. And pills? You want to see the pills?" They got out three boxes apiece.

"In short," said Francis, "we run on dynamite.'"

Londres' article, entitled 'The Convicts of the Route', was the first to reveal doping on the Tour. As the three riders talked to Londres, the peloton apparently took the day off. When Ottavio Bottecchia punctured 18 km from the finish, the bunch was cruising at 21 km/hour and he rejoined with ease. The race concluded in Brest, where 29-year-old Belgian Théophile Beeckman won.

STAGE FACTS

Date: 26 June 1924
Number: 3
Length: 405 km

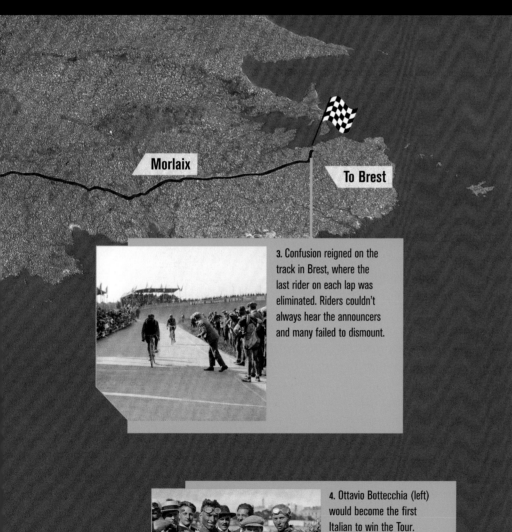

Morlaix   To Brest

3. Confusion reigned on the track in Brest, where the last rider on each lap was eliminated. Riders couldn't always hear the announcers and many failed to dismount.

4. Ottavio Bottecchia (left) would become the first Italian to win the Tour. He was also the first rider to wear the yellow jersey from start to finish.

'If I'm going well, my tyres burst. If my tyres don't burst, I feel like I'm the one who's breathing my last.' JEAN ALAVOINE

BEFORE STAGE 3

1 Ottavio Bottecchia (Ita)
2 Maurice Ville (Fra)
at 2'36"
3 Nicolas Frantz (Bel)
same time

AFTER STAGE 3

1 Ottavio Bottecchia (Ita)
2 Théophile Beeckman (Bel)
same time
3 Nicolas Frantz (Bel)
at 2'36"

1926

The end of Bottecchia's reign

BAYONNE > LUCHON

In 1924 Ottavio Bottecchia had been the first Italian Tour winner. He repeated the feat in 1925, relying heavily on Belgian team-mate, Lucien Buysse, who came second. Would Bottecchia be the first rider to notch three consecutive wins?

Buysse had other ideas. He was 33 years old and it was now or never. Entering the Pyrenees he was in eighth place and another Belgian, Gustaaf van Slembrouck, was in yellow.

From the start, relentless cold rain had turned the unsurfaced roads into rivers of mud on which tyres could gain no traction. Wheels and chains became hopelessly clogged and riders had to urinate on them to clean them, while on the cols visibility was reduced to 30 m.

From Bayonne

Argelès-Gazost

Eaux-Bonnes

Col du Tourmalet

Col d'Aubisque

Barèges

2. Buysse dominated the Pyrenees in rain and mud to ride into the yellow jersey. He was covered in filth and unrecognizable by the time he reached Luchon.

1. In 1924, Bottecchia had been such a dominant climber – even singing while he rode – that Nicolas Frantz, his closet rival, said it would be 'suicidal' to follow him up a mountain pass. 'His pace is so high, so relentless, that we would be suffocated.' Two years later, between Bayonne and Luchon, Bottecchia proved human after all, suffering immensely in the cold and rain.

3. Bottecchia's compatriot Bartolomeo Aimo came second on the stage and eventually finished third. Aimo was the inspiration for one of characters in Ernest Hemingway's *A Farewell to Arms*.

Buysse attacked at the foot of the Aubisque, reaching the summit with a margin of nearly 8 minutes on Bottecchia. Coughing uncontrollably and suffering from terrible backache, Bottecchia, along with many other riders, abandoned before reaching Barèges. All along the route the bikes of riders who could not continue lay propped against walls of houses and inns.

Buysse finally rolled into Luchon more than 17 hours after the race's start with a 25 minute margin over Italian Bartolomeo Aimo and an hour and 50 minutes over van Slembrouck, who would plunge to tenth place on general classification. Buysse was in the yellow and would win the Tour. Bottecchia's reign was over.

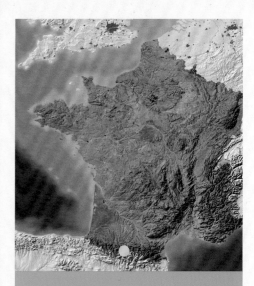

A ladylike way to race

METZ > CHARLEVILLE

In 1928 Nicolas Frantz was untouchable, wearing yellow from beginning to end for his second consecutive victory. Not only was he an excellent climber, he was also consistent, tough and methodical.

Yet, as ever in the early days of the Tour, an accident nearly lost him the yellow jersey.

He damaged his forks on a level crossing 54 km from the start of stage 19 and had to abandon his bike at the next check point, 12 km later. The Alcyon team panicked, their driver insisting the best course was taking Frantz to the nearest Alcyon dealer, but this would have cost at least an hour. Ludovic Feuillet, the team's resourceful and wily manager, quickly found a replacement bike instead.

1. Frantz at the checkpoint in Longuyon with his faulty bike. The new bike would have raised handlebars equipped with a horn, pedals without toe clips, and wooden mudguards. He had had to swap over the wheels from his original bike but, despite all this, less than 15 minutes elapsed between his arrival and departure.

From Metz

Longuyon

Thonne-le-Thil

2. United and totally in control, Alcyon dominated the Tour. Here Maurice Dewaele leads Julien Vervaecke, Nicolas Frantz, Gaston Rebry and Jan Mertens.

3. This was the first Tour to welcome antipodean riders, with one New Zealander and four Australians, led by Hubert Opperman, comprising the Ravat-Wonder team. Opperman was the first to enter the velodrome at Charleville, an essentially ceremonial post-race affair.

'So here is our Frantz setting off again, with a quarter of an hour's delay, on a piece of junk, I'll say no more,' Henri Desgrange reported.

He continued, 'The bike is a girl's frame. There are two mudguards and a rear light, the sort you might find on the back of a locomotive. He looks like a jockey standing on his stirrups and over the remaining 100 km he will valiantly ride at an excellent 27 km an hour.'

Frantz ended up losing 28 minutes to team-mate and second place on general classification, André Leducq, yet his margin had been so dominant he still had 47 minutes to spare.

STAGE FACTS

Date: 12 July 1928

Number: 19

Length: 159 km

YELLOW ALL THE WAY

Riders who have worn the yellow jersey from start to finish:

Ottavio Bottecchia, 1924
Nicolas Frantz, 1928
Romain Maes, 1935

Prior to the yellow jersey, the following riders kept the race lead from start to finish:

Maurice Garin, 1903 and – although he was subsequently disqualified – 1904
Philippe Thys, 1914

'Sparks are going to fly!' ANTONIN MAGNE, RIDING FOR ALLÉLUIA, AT THE START OF THE STAGE.

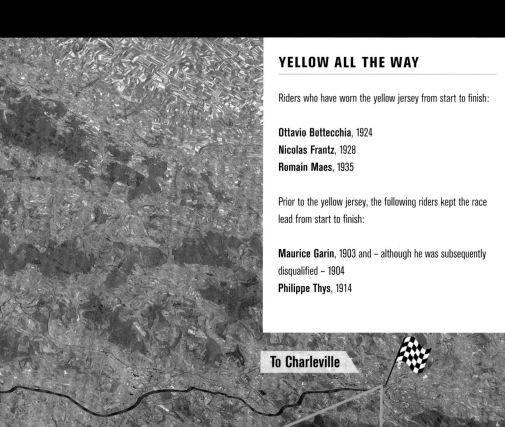

To Charleville

BEFORE STAGE 19

1 Nicolas Frantz (Lux)
2 André Leducq (Fra)
at 1h 15'07"
3 Maurice Dewaele (Bel)
at 1h 27'23"

AFTER STAGE 19

1 Nicolas Frantz (Lux)
2 André Leducq (Fra)
at 47'31"
3 Maurice Dewaele (Bel)
at 53'40"

4. Marcel Huot (left) and his team Alléluia won the stage. In 1928 most of the flat stages were held as team time trials. This brief innovation, which lasted a few years during the 1920s, was eventually done away with when it became clear that only riders on the strongest teams could win the Tour. Talented outsiders with weak teams didn't stand a chance. Alléluia had in fact had a lacklustre Tour and, after a stern reprimand in their team briefing, ended up dominating stage 19.

1929

The triple-headed jersey

LES SABLES-D'OLONNE > BORDEAUX

Maurice Dewaele, second in 1927 and third in 1928, was finally in the yellow jersey. It looked like he would keep it when three riders attacked 100 km from the finish. As the peloton chased them down Dewaele punctured, as did Aimé Déolet, riding in second. By the time the escape was neutralized the peloton had shrunk to 20 riders and Dewaele was far behind, hanging onto his jersey by a mere 18 seconds.

The next casualty was Marcel Bidot, fourth on general classification but with the same time as Déolet and another rider, Aimé Dossche. He had been riding his way into yellow when he crashed into a woman crossing the road, breaking his front wheel.

1. Charles Pélissier, Désiré Louesse and Julien Vervaecke were the architects of an attack that brought them nothing, but changed the race.

2. André Leducq had done much of the work bringing the winning group of five to the finish. A popular and jovial rider, he nonetheless wouldn't hesitate to take yellow off his captain's shoulders – in this case Dewaele – if he could.

Luçon

Marans

Saint-Porchaire

La Rochelle

Saintes

From Les Sables-d'Olonne

3. Leducq, Fontan and Frantz (from left to right) are amused to all be wearing yellow the following morning in Bordeaux.

The peloton reached a level crossing 5 km from the finish where five riders jumped across, 'to the astonishment of onlookers and despite the express train one can hear puffing close by,' *L'Auto* reported. Dossche, in third place, stayed behind. The five escapees contested the final sprint which was won by Nicolas Frantz.

The general classification had been turned on its head and the race hadn't even reached the mountains. More remarkable yet was that three riders from the winning group – Nicolas Frantz, André Leducq and Victor Fontan – would share the yellow jersey, since they all had the same time. It was the only occasion this has happened in the Tour's history.

STAGE FACTS

Date: 6 July 1929
Number: 7
Length: 285 km

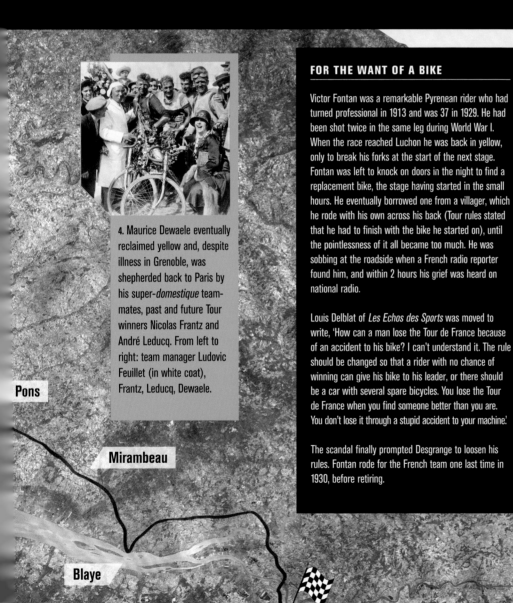

4. Maurice Dewaele eventually reclaimed yellow and, despite illness in Grenoble, was shepherded back to Paris by his super-*domestique* team-mates, past and future Tour winners Nicolas Frantz and André Leducq. From left to right: team manager Ludovic Feuillet (in white coat), Frantz, Leducq, Dewaele.

Pons

Mirambeau

Blaye

To Bordeaux

FOR THE WANT OF A BIKE

Victor Fontan was a remarkable Pyrenean rider who had turned professional in 1913 and was 37 in 1929. He had been shot twice in the same leg during World War I. When the race reached Luchon he was back in yellow, only to break his forks at the start of the next stage. Fontan was left to knock on doors in the night to find a replacement bike, the stage having started in the small hours. He eventually borrowed one from a villager, which he rode with his own across his back (Tour rules stated that he had to finish with the bike he started on), until the pointlessness of it all became too much. He was sobbing at the roadside when a French radio reporter found him, and within 2 hours his grief was heard on national radio.

Louis Delblat of *Les Echos des Sports* was moved to write, 'How can a man lose the Tour de France because of an accident to his bike? I can't understand it. The rule should be changed so that a rider with no chance of winning can give his bike to his leader, or there should be a car with several spare bicycles. You lose the Tour de France when you find someone better than you are. You don't lose it through a stupid accident to your machine'.

The scandal finally prompted Desgrange to loosen his rules. Fontan rode for the French team one last time in 1930, before retiring.

'Evidently, the first place that Frantz has just won and the first place that Leducq won in Cherbourg give both these men a small advantage over Fontan. But Fontan has the right to follow his own tactics at the race finishes, especially when the bunches are so big in sprint finishes that they constitute a danger. And then the rules are so clear, that you can't split hairs. So tomorrow we will have three yellow jerseys.' HENRI DESGRANGE

BEFORE STAGE 7

1 Maurice Dewaele (Bel)
2 Aimé Dossche (Bel),
Aimé Déolet (Bel),
Marcel Bidot (Fra)
at 3'08"

AFTER STAGE 7

1 Nicolas Frantz (Lux), André
Leducq (Fra), Victor Fontan (Fra)
2 Aimé Dossche (Bel)
at 47'31"
3 Gaston Rebry (Bel)
at 0'55"

1930

United France

GRENOBLE > ÉVIAN

In 1930 Henri Desgrange decreed there would only be national teams and independent riders.

For the French, who had last had a national winner in 1923, the new formula certainly worked. By the time the Tour left the Pyrenees the French team was in the lead, with the handsome André Leducq sitting pretty in yellow. Things looked set for a tricolore triumph when Leducq crashed heavily descending the Galibier. Having been knocked almost unconscious, and with injuries to his hands and feet, he nonetheless remounted and set off for the Col du Télégraphe where his pedal, damaged in the crash, now failed and Leducq hit the ground again. A spectator lent him a new one, which his team-mate Marcel Bidot fixed to his bike, but

1. A tearful André Leducq sits by the side of the road in despair, ready to abandon after a second crash. It was a rare moment of anguish for a rider who was normally the joker in the pack, popular with other riders and fans for his cheeky sense of humour. He was also a phenomenal rider, his record of 25 Tour stage wins unchallenged until the arrival of Eddy Merckx.

2. Having almost abandoned the race, André Leducq sets off again after his fall on the Col du Télégraphe, accompanied by team-mate Pierre Magne.

From Grenoble

Col du Galibier

Col du Télégraphe

Saint-Michel-de-Maurienne

To Évian

Leducq was distraught and ready to abandon. His rivals, Learco Guerra and Jef Demuysère, were well aware of the drama unfolding behind and riding like the possessed.

By this point Leducq's other team-mates, including the excellent *rouleur* Charles Pélissier and future Tour winner Antonin Magne and his brother Pierre, had caught up. They persuaded Leducq to get back on his bike, and over the next 75 km put on an extraordinary, improbable pursuit, clawing back the 15 minutes Leducq had lost to his rivals. Not only did they reunite with the front runners in Évian, but Leducq also won the stage in a sprint.

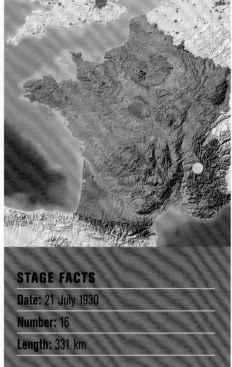

STAGE FACTS

Date: 21 July 1930

Number: 16

Length: 331 km

3. From left to right: Marcel Bidot, Antonin Magne, Pierre Magne, André Leducq and Charles Pélissier savour their triumphant stage win. It was the first year that TSF, French radio, reported from the Tour. The team's exploits made them instant heroes.

4. Everything French fans could wish for – the French team was not only heroic, but also handsome. The team at breakfast, from left to right: Pierre Magne, Victor Fontan, André Leducq, Charles Pélissier, Jules Merviel and Antonin Magne.

BROTHERS ON BIKES

Many of the French riders had siblings who rode, which may have informed their brotherly solidarity. Charles Pélissier's older brother Henri had been the last Frenchman to win the Tour, aided by their other brother, Francis. Antonin and Pierre Magne were on the same team, while Marcel Bidot had a younger brother, Jean, who also raced.

BEFORE STAGE 16	AFTER STAGE 16
1 André Leducq (Fra)	1 André Leducq (Fra)
2 Learco Guerra (Ita)	2 Learco Guerra (Ita)
at 16'13"	at 16'13"
3 Antonin Magne (Fra)	3 Antonin Magne (Fra)
at 18'03"	at 18'03"

'After Leducq was the first to cross the line at the stage finish in Évian, Pierre Magne threw his arms round him and in a voice thick with emotion said, "Leducq, my boy, I think this is the happiest day of my life. Where on earth did you come from?"' HENRI DESGRANGE

1933

The Flea who ruled the mountains

METZ > BELFORT

With the exception of Salvador Cardona's stage win in 1929, Spanish riders had barely made an impact on the Tour. But in 1933 Vicente Trueba, a tiny Cantabrian rider dubbed 'The Flea of Torrelavega', became the first King of the Mountains.

Henri Desgrange had introduced a mountain points competition when it became clear that the best climbers were the smallest and therefore lacked the weight and power necessary to cement uphill gains on descents or on the flat.

On stage 4 the entire 68-man peloton was still intact when it reached the Ballon d'Alsace, the Tour's first mountain, 36 km from the finish. Roger Lapébie attacked together with an independent Italian rider, Giovanni Firpo. The ascent was ragged with riders holding out as long as possible before dismounting to change gear.

KING OF THE MOUNTAINS BY COUNTRY

France: 21 victories
Spain: 16 victories
Italy: 11 victories
Belgium: 11 victories
Colombia: 4 victories
Denmark: 2 victories
Luxembourg: 2 victories
Netherlands: 2 victories
Great Britain: 1 victory
Switzerland: 1 victory

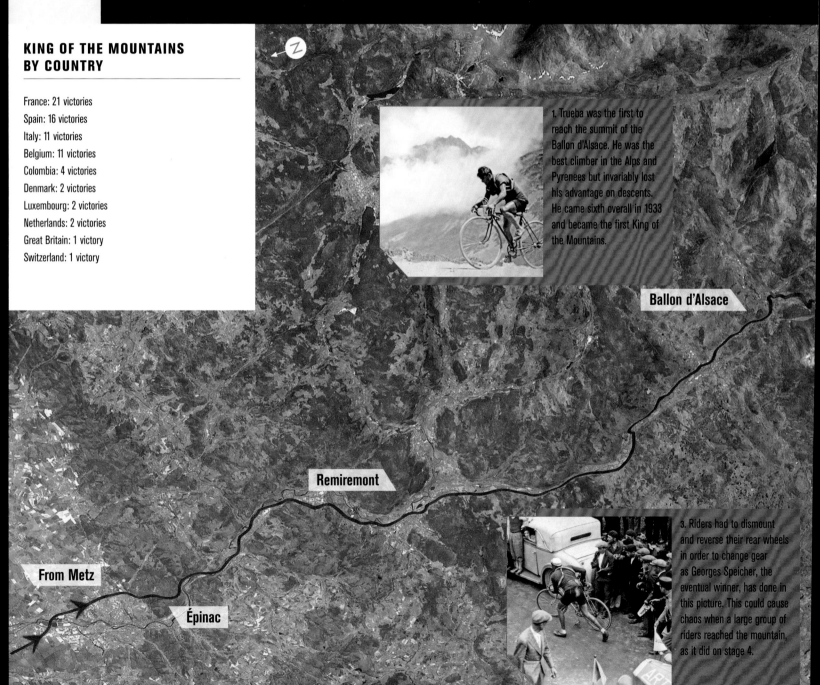

1. Trueba was the first to reach the summit of the Ballon d'Alsace. He was the best climber in the Alps and Pyrenees but invariably lost his advantage on descents. He came sixth overall in 1933 and became the first King of the Mountains.

Ballon d'Alsace

Remiremont

From Metz

Épinac

3. Riders had to dismount and reverse their rear wheels in order to change gear as Georges Speicher, the eventual winner, has done in this picture. This could cause chaos when a large group of riders reached the mountain, as it did on stage 4.

Lapébie was still soldiering on in front when Trueba, an independent rider, zipped past. Desgrange wrote that Trueba resembled a 'thin and suffering Christ, with a stock supply of sickly expressions... Next to him, Lapébie seems as solid, thickset and hefty as an ox.'

Despite being first over the summit with more than 2 minutes on yellow jersey Maurice Archambaud,

Trueba was a terrible descender and lost time on the way down. He was caught, 8 km before the finish, by a chase group of nine which featured Archambaud and Jean Aerts, who won the sprint.

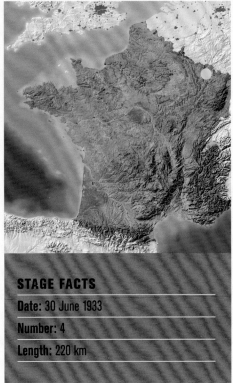

To Belfort

2. Trueba was the archetypal tiny mountain climber, as can be seen in this photograph of him at a level crossing at Bielle in the Pyrenees.

4. In second place on the general classification, Jean Aerts (left) won the sprint into Belfort, ahead of Fernand Cornez (right) and Learco Guerra. In doing so he reduced the gap between himself and Maurice Archambaud, the yellow jersey, by 2 minutes. Vicente Trueba finished in tenth place, but with the same time as Aerts.

STAGE FACTS

Date: 30 June 1933

Number: 4

Length: 220 km

'Vicente needs to take on 50 kilos of ballast, swallow stones on the summit, attach the trunk of a pine tree cut to fit his bike, find something, since he must also descend.' *L'AUTO* CORRESPONDENT

BEFORE STAGE 4	AFTER STAGE 4
1 Maurice Archambaud (Fra)	1 Maurice Archambaud (Fra)
2 Jean Aerts (Bel) at 6'32"	2 Jean Aerts (Bel) at 4'32"
3 Georges Lemaire (Bel) at 7'32"	3 Georges Lemaire (Bel) at 7'32"

KING OF THE MOUNTAINS
Vicente Trueba (Spa)

René Vietto's sacrifice

PERPIGNAN > AX-LES-THERMES

When the 1934 Tour left Paris no-one had heard of 20-year-old René Vietto, riding for the French team. By the time the peloton returned 26 days later, he had become a hero and poster boy for the immense sacrifices made by the loyal *domestique*.

During the first week Vietto lost 40 minutes as the battle for the yellow jersey played out between his team leader, Antonin Magne, and Italian Giuseppe Martano. But when the race hit the Alps Vietto astonished all with his ability to ride with – and drop – the finest climbers. By stage 15 he had won three Alpine stages. As the Tour reached the Pyrenees France was in thrall to the possibility of the former bellboy from Cannes riding into the lead. Then Magne, in the yellow jersey since stage 2, broke

1. In 1934 Henri Desgrange stipulated for the first time that riders could help their team-mates in the event of technical difficulties. He could not have predicted the impact his latest rule would have on the Tour de France. His largesse, in publicity terms, was amply rewarded that year by Vietto's heroism.

2. The boyish Vietto weeps inconsolably as he waits for the team car to replace his front wheel. His sacrifice for his leader Magne meant the end of his ambitions to win.

Mont-Louis

From Perpignan

3. Vietto, who finished fifth, was considered by many the moral victor of the Tour and was allowed to accompany Magne on his final lap of honour in Paris.

his front wheel descending the Col de Puymorens. Martano saw his chance and attacked. Vietto handed over his own wheel to Magne and waited for a replacement, eventually finishing more than 4½ minutes behind the stage winner, team-mate Roger Lapébie. Magne lost only 45 seconds to Martano and was able to maintain his lead.

The following day Magne broke his chain descending the Col de Portet d'Aspet, and Vietto this time relinquished his bike. Vietto's dreams of winning were truly over but, thanks to his efforts, Magne could continue in the yellow jersey all the way to Paris.

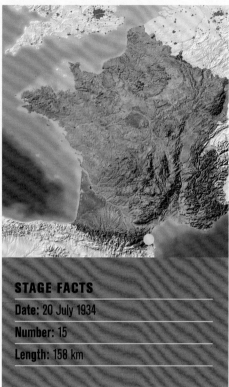

VIETTO'S CAREER

Vietto claimed he could have won the Tour that year. Many considered him a future champion. Instead, up until 2012 he held the strange honour of being the rider to have spent the most days in the yellow jersey – 26 – without ever winning. (That record was finally broken by Fabian Cancellara, whose record in 2012 came to 28 days.) Vietto's career was dogged by ill health, bad luck and a hiatus forced by World War II.

STAGE FACTS

Date: 20 July 1934

Number: 15

Length: 158 km

Bourg-Madame

To Ax-les-Thermes

4. René Vietto with admirers in 1939. His performance in 1934 transformed him from an unknown rider into one of the Tour's stars. Antonin Magne may have won the Tour, but Vietto won fans' hearts.

'That wheel, I didn't give it. It was taken off me. It was a hold-up – I should have made a complaint!' RENÉ VIETTO

BEFORE STAGE 15	AFTER STAGE 15
1 Antonin Magne (Fra)	1 Antonin Magne (Fra)
2 Giuseppe Martano (Ita) at 3'42"	2 Giuseppe Martano (Ita) at 2'57"
3 Félicien Vervaecke (Bel) at 35'31"	3 Félicien Vervaecke (Bel) at 35'17"

KING OF THE MOUNTAINS	KING OF THE MOUNTAINS
Federico Ezquerra (Spa)	Federico Ezquerra (Spa)

Magne wins the 'race of truth'

LA ROCHE-SUR-YON > NANTES (TIME TRIAL)

Henri Desgrange was worried that the final stages of the Tour were getting boring, given the winner was usually decided in the mountains, so in 1934 he introduced the first individual time trial. At 90 km it was much longer than the 50-or-so km of a modern time trial, yet it was the second of two stages that day. After the morning's 81 km to La Roche-sur-Yon, the riders showered, ate and received massages at the velodrome, then set off at 2-minute intervals to the sound of their national anthems.

Antonin Magne had a robust lead over nearest rival Giuseppe Martano but, had it not been for his team-mates, he might not have been in yellow at all. Martano had been snapping at his heels throughout the Tour, until Magne finally put a decisive 15 minutes

INDIVIDUAL TIME TRIALS

The introduction of the individual time trial brought the Tour into the modern era, becoming an indispensable annual ingredient. It is almost impossible to win now without being a good time triallist, just as much as it is essential to ride well in the mountains. The value of individual time trials seems so obvious that it is surprising Henri Desgrange hadn't introduced them earlier, given his distaste for riders drafting, a technique he often tried to ban. Even more surprising is the fact that, for a brief period in the 1920s, nearly every flat stage was run as a team time trial, which had the effect of allowing the strongest team to win which in turn rewarded the wealthiest sponsors, whose machinations in their quest for dominance led Desgrange to introduce national teams in 1930.

1. The three musketeers, Magne, Lapébie and Vietto (from left to right), fool around as they set off for that morning's stage, a road race from La Rochelle to La Roche-sur-Yon. While Magne's triumph in the time trial later that day proved he was a worthy winner, the support of his team-mates was essential to his winning the Tour.

From La Roche-sur-Yon

3. Roger Lapébie finished second, but was arguably the moral victor. Having punctured, he would undoubtedly have lost more time than his final deficit of 1 minute and 16 seconds. His performance moved him into third place on the general classification.

into him on the stage into Tarbes. But Magne broke his bike on two consecutive days in the Pyrenees and without René Vietto's sacrifices – and Vietto and Roger Lapébie depriving Martano of time bonuses with their stage wins – it could have been a very different story.

Any doubts regarding Magne's superiority, however, were erased by his crushing performance in the 'race of truth', which he won. Martano lost a further 11 minutes to Magne while Vietto, in third place, dropped to fourth, reaching Nantes almost 10 minutes behind his captain.

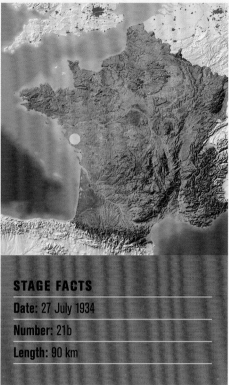

STAGE FACTS

Date: 27 July 1934

Number: 21b

Length: 90 km

2. Magne after his arrival in Nantes. Fearful of losing his yellow jersey, he had ridden all out, barely climbing out of the saddle, and was exhausted by the finish. On his yellow jersey he had sewn the crab of Arcachon, emblem of his cycling club in his adopted home on the south-west coast of France.

To Nantes

4. 'It's not my kind of event,' Vicente Trueba, the Tour's first King of the Mountains, said after the race. He finished 33rd out of 39 riders, reinforcing the cliché that climbers can't time trial.

'This stage of 90 km was too long and I think in future, if one wishes to continue with these experiments, it would be preferable to limit these stages to 50 km.'
ANTONIN MAGNE

BEFORE STAGE 21b	AFTER STAGE 21b
1 Antonin Magne (Fra)	1 Antonin Magne (Fra)
2 Giuseppe Martano (Ita) at 15'34"	2 Giuseppe Martano (Ita) at 26'11"
3 René Vietto (Fra) at 43'05"	3 Roger Lapébie (Fra) at 52'21"
KING OF THE MOUNTAINS René Vietto (Fra)	KING OF THE MOUNTAINS René Vietto (Fra)

Crash kills Cepeda

AIX-LES-BAINS > GRENOBLE

11 July 1935 was a bad day for accidents on the Tour de France. Just beyond Aix-les-Bains a crash involving race vehicles and riders claimed cyclist Antonin Magne, who was second on the general classification and winner of the race in 1931 and 1934. Helped back onto his bike by team-mate André Leducq, he nevertheless abandoned shortly before the summit of the Télégraphe, his right ankle cut all the way to the Achilles tendon.

But there was worse to come. Near Vizille towards the end of the stage, Spanish rider Francisco Cepeda was sweeping through a bend when his tyre peeled off his front wheel. He crashed heavily, fracturing his skull, and was rushed to hospital in Grenoble where he died three days later. It was the first fatal crash on the Tour.

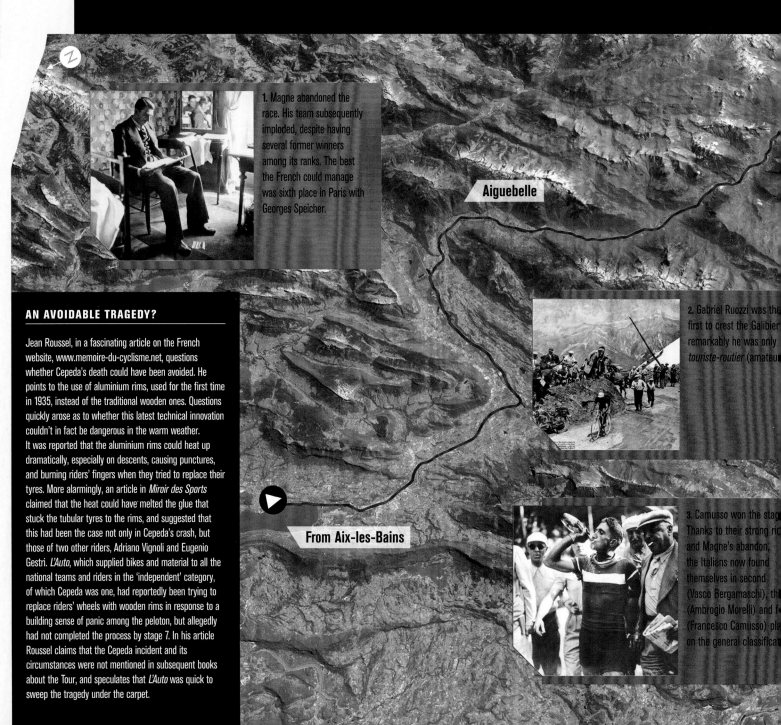

1. Magne abandoned the race. His team subsequently imploded, despite having several former winners among its ranks. The best the French could manage was sixth place in Paris with Georges Speicher.

Aiguebelle

AN AVOIDABLE TRAGEDY?

Jean Roussel, in a fascinating article on the French website, www.memoire-du-cyclisme.net, questions whether Cepeda's death could have been avoided. He points to the use of aluminium rims, used for the first time in 1935, instead of the traditional wooden ones. Questions quickly arose as to whether this latest technical innovation couldn't in fact be dangerous in the warm weather. It was reported that the aluminium rims could heat up dramatically, especially on descents, causing punctures, and burning riders' fingers when they tried to replace their tyres. More alarmingly, an article in *Miroir des Sports* claimed that the heat could have melted the glue that stuck the tubular tyres to the rims, and suggested that this had been the case not only in Cepeda's crash, but those of two other riders, Adriano Vignoli and Eugenio Gestri. *L'Auto*, which supplied bikes and material to all the national teams and riders in the 'independent' category, of which Cepeda was one, had reportedly been trying to replace riders' wheels with wooden rims in response to a building sense of panic among the peloton, but allegedly had not completed the process by stage 7. In his article Roussel claims that the Cepeda incident and its circumstances were not mentioned in subsequent books about the Tour, and speculates that *L'Auto* was quick to sweep the tragedy under the carpet.

From Aix-les-Bains

2. Gabriel Ruozzi was the first to crest the Galibier remarkably he was only *touriste-routier* (amateur

3. Camusso won the stag Thanks to their strong ric and Magne's abandon, the Italians now found themselves in second (Vasco Bergamaschi), th (Ambrogio Morelli) and f (Francesco Camusso) pla on the general classifica

It had also been a strange day of racing, with the biggest surprise being a *touriste-routier* (amateur) dominating on the Galibier. Gabriel Ruozzi from the Côte d'Azur had taken on the monster with another amateur Azuréen, Dante Gianello, and an Italian, Francesco Camusso. Ruozzi crested the summit nearly 2 minutes ahead of Camusso and over 7 minutes ahead of yellow jersey holder Romain Maes.

Ruozzi was a mediocre descender, however, and Camusso overtook him in no time, eventually soloing to victory with nearly 4 minutes. Romain Maes came in nearly 10 minutes later but kept his jersey and his margin remained unchanged.

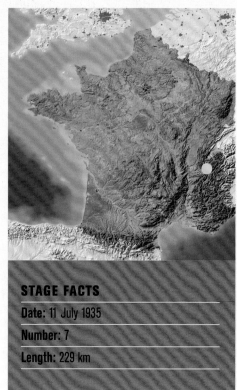

STAGE FACTS

Date: 11 July 1935

Number: 7

Length: 229 km

Saint-Michel-de-Maurienne

Col du Galibier

ourg-d'Oisans

Vizille

To Grenoble

4. Although he sometimes rode for the Spanish team, Cepeda was essentially a very talented amateur who loved racing. From a middle class family of industrialists, he was a municipal judge and ran a successful business with his parents. In 1935 he was participating as an 'independent' – a 'reserve' rider for the Spanish team.

'The news of Cepeda's death caused deep emotions among all Spanish sports fans, because Cepeda was not only a loyal rider, valued by his team-mates, but also a very cultivated man... Cycling was his hobby. On learning that the Spanish would be admitted to the Tour this year, he started training again last winter and was so effective that he recovered his form. He was delighted to be selected, and I can't tell you enough about his attachment to and appreciation of our director, of whom he always spoke with respect. When Canardo, Trueba and Ezquerra deserted the Tour, Cepeda was much affected. "If I had been there," he said, "they would not have abandoned."' *L'AUTO*

BEFORE STAGE 7	AFTER STAGE 7
1 Romain Maes (Bel)	1 Romain Maes (Bel)
2 Antonin Magne (Fra)	2 Vasco Bergamaschi (Ita)
at 4'06"	at 12'05"
3 Vasco Bergamaschi (Ita)	3 Ambrogio Morelli (Ita)
at 12'05"	at 14'19"

KING OF THE MOUNTAINS
Félicien Vervaecke (Bel)

KING OF THE MOUNTAINS
Félicien Vervaecke (Bel)

Partisans, punctures and penalties

PAU > BORDEAUX

Feelings were running high when the Tour came out of the Pyrenees. Stage 16 would pass through the home territory of Roger Lapébie, second placed on the general classification. Only 3 minutes separated him from the Belgian Sylvère Maes, in first place, but it should really have been less.

The previous day, Lapébie had lost 6 minutes 47 seconds to Maes on the Col d'Aspin and had been about to abandon when journalist and future Tour director Félix Lévitan told him Maes was tiring. Lapébie rallied, caught up with the leaders and won the sprint for second place. But the 45-second bonus he gained was rendered meaningless by a 1 minute 30 second penalty for accepting food and being pushed by spectators. Lapébie threatened to leave the race.

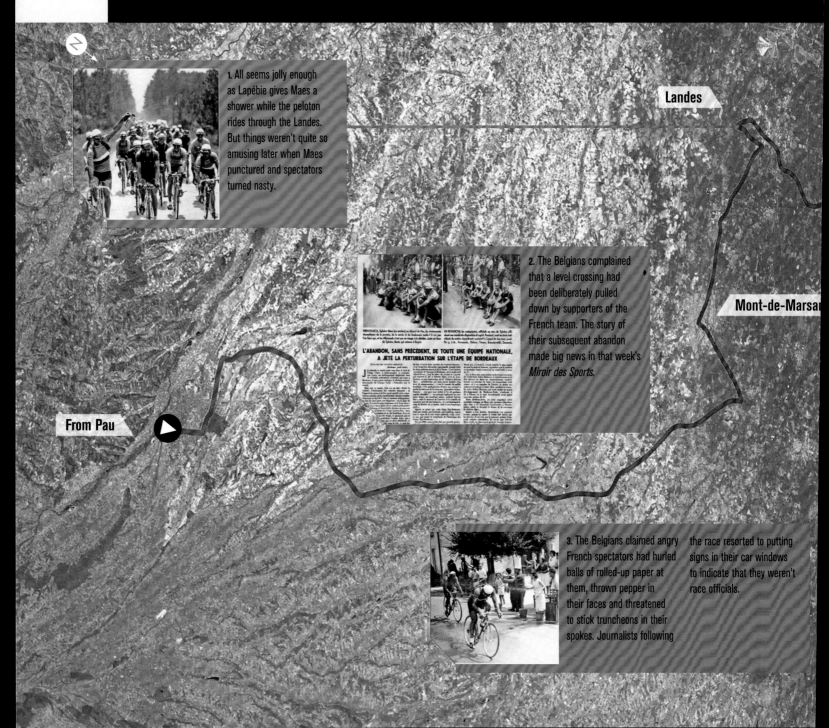

Landes

Mont-de-Marsan

From Pau

1. All seems jolly enough as Lapébie gives Maes a shower while the peloton rides through the Landes. But things weren't quite so amusing later when Maes punctured and spectators turned nasty.

2. The Belgians complained that a level crossing had been deliberately pulled down by supporters of the French team. The story of their subsequent abandon made big news in that week's *Miroir des Sports*.

L'ABANDON, SANS PRÉCÉDENT, DE TOUTE UNE ÉQUIPE NATIONALE, A JETÉ LA PERTURBATION SUR L'ÉTAPE DE BORDEAUX

3. The Belgians claimed angry French spectators had hurled balls of rolled-up paper at them, thrown pepper in their faces and threatened to stick truncheons in their spokes. Journalists following the race resorted to putting signs in their car windows to indicate that they weren't race officials.

The next day was uneventful until Maes punctured and the French attacked. The Belgians were excellent team time triallists, however, and had nearly caught their rivals when they reached a lowered level crossing. Storming into Bordeaux, Lapébie had 1 minute 38 seconds on Maes and looked set to win the stage, when he was outsprinted by fellow Frenchman Paul Chocque. Only 25 seconds now separated the rivals, following Lapébie's time bonus and a 15-second penalty for Maes for drafting.

Discouraged by penalties he considered unfair and unnerved by spectators' aggression, Maes abandoned with his team, leaving Lapébie to win the Tour.

STAGE FACTS

Date: 21 July 1937
Number: 16
Length: 235 km

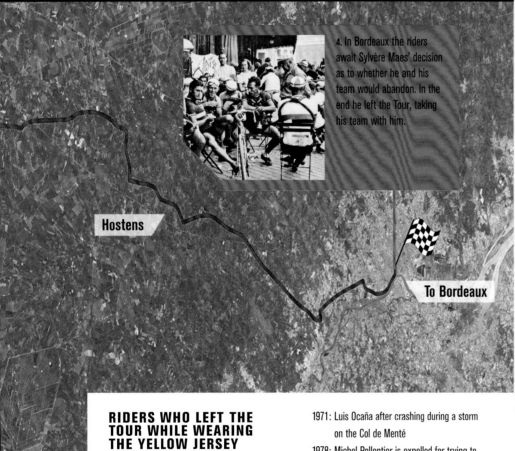

4. In Bordeaux the riders await Sylvère Maes' decision as to whether he and his team would abandon. In the end he left the Tour, taking his team with him.

Hostens

To Bordeaux

'I won't be leaving Bordeaux tomorrow morning with the yellow jersey. I'm a married man and a father. I have no intention of getting torn to pieces on the road, nor to risk the slightest accident. I have made up my mind. I am also profoundly sickened to have been penalized by 15 seconds and I feel discouraged. I really sense there is too much hostility around me. If Roger is the stronger, let him win if he deserves it, but the French public should at least allow the race to be raced freely; they didn't do that today.' SYLVÈRE MAES

RIDERS WHO LEFT THE TOUR WHILE WEARING THE YELLOW JERSEY

1927: Francis Pélissier because of illness
1929: Victor Fontan after his bicycle broke and he was unable to replace it
1937: Sylvère Maes and the Belgian team following time penalties and threats from French fans
1950: Fiorenzo Magni and the Italian team after Gino Bartali was attacked by French thugs
1951: Wim van Est after he plummeted down a ravine on the Aubisque
1956: Bernard van de Kerckhove suffering from sunstroke on the Aubisque

1971: Luis Ocaña after crashing during a storm on the Col de Menté
1978: Michel Pollentier is expelled for trying to cheat a drugs test
1980: Bernard Hinault suffering from knee pain
1983: Pascal Simon after fracturing his shoulder-bone
1991: Rolf Sørensen after fracturing his collar-bone
1996: Stéphane Heulot suffering from tendinitis in his knee
1998: Chris Boardman after injuring his head in a crash
2007: Michael Rasmussen is fired by his team for lying about his pre-race whereabouts

BEFORE STAGE 16	AFTER STAGE 16
1 Sylvère Maes (Bel)	1 Sylvère Maes (Bel)
2 Roger Lapébie (Fra) at 3'03"	2 Roger Lapébie (Fra) at 0'25"
3 Mario Vicini (Ita) at 4'57"	3 Mario Vicini (Ita) at 3'04"
KING OF THE MOUNTAINS Félicien Vervaecke (Bel)	KING OF THE MOUNTAINS Félicien Vervaecke (Bel)

1938

Bartali takes off

DIGNE > BRIANÇON

Gino Bartali, the young Italian star who might have won the Tour de France in 1937 had it not been for a crash, had been battling Belgian Tour veteran, Félicien Vervaecke, through the Pyrenees. But although he kept yo-yoing tantalizingly close, he couldn't dislodge Vervaecke's lead. At the start of stage 14 in Digne-les-Bains he was 1 minute 15 seconds behind his rival. Italy was on tenterhooks; it was 13 years since a native son had won the Tour.

Bartali had ridden cautiously, employing a new tactic that involved staying with the lead group up in the mountains and then sprinting up the summits for time bonuses, a tactic Henri Desgrange deplored.

1. Bartali is the first rider up the Col de Vars, the second mountain of the day. It was on the descent of this climb that he claimed he won the stage, after putting 7 minutes into Vervaecke, who punctured.

2. Bartali was already the virtual yellow jersey after descending the Col de Vars. He entered the history books with his magnificent ascent of the Izoard. Crossing the spectacular amphitheatre of the Casse Déserte, his rivals were nowhere to be seen.

To Briançon

Col d'Iz[oard]

Guillestre

Col de Vars

From Digne

ITALIAN VICTORIES IN THE TOUR

1924: Ottavio Bottecchia
1925: Ottavio Bottecchia
1938: Gino Bartali
1948: Gino Bartali
1949: Fausto Coppi
1952: Fausto Coppi
1960: Gastone Nencini
1965: Felice Gimondi
1998: Marco Pantani

But on 22 July Bartali silenced his critics, riding aggressively from the start. He surged clear of the bunch on the first climb, the Col d'Allos. He was first again over the Vars, where he descended in a frenzy, building an advantage of 7 minutes over Vervaecke and 9 minutes on Victor Cosson. Bartali dropped his last companions, Mario Vicini and Mathias Clemens, 10 km from the summit of the Izoard. On one of the hairpins above the Casse Déserte he turned back to see his team-mate Vicini, nothing but an ant in the distance far below, and waved.

He reached Briançon 17 minutes ahead of Vervaecke, the author of one of the most legendary stage wins in Tour history.

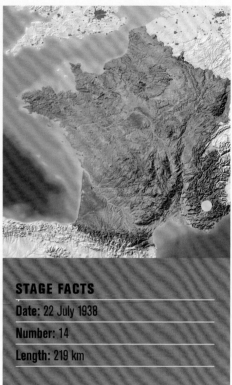

STAGE FACTS
Date: 22 July 1938
Number: 14
Length: 219 km

3. Gino Bartali commented, 'Followers from Turin had flocked to Briançon in their thousands, and there was an explosion of excitement. General Antonelli hugged me and cried for joy, Girardengo was ecstatic and Villa sent telegraphs the length and breadth of Italy.'

'On the Vars, I increased the pace, not to open a big gap, but to have a clear advantage of the group at the top of the descent, where I played my trump card. For it was on the descent from the Vars that I won the Tour de France.' GINO BARTALI

4. Bartali's exploits on stage 14 helped him win the Tour. But he was quick to credit the tactical genius of his *directeur sportif*, the legendary multiple Giro winner, Costante Girardengo, seen here kissing Bartali.

BEFORE STAGE 14	AFTER STAGE 14
1 Félicien Vervaecke (Bel)	1 Gino Bartali (Ita)
2 Gino Bartali (Ita)	2 Mathias Clemens (Lux)
at 1'15"	at 17'45"
3 Mathias Clemens (Lux)	3 Félicien Vervaecke (Bel)
at 6'29"	at 21'30"
KING OF THE MOUNTAINS	KING OF THE MOUNTAINS
Gino Bartali (Ita)	Gino Bartali (Ita)

Sylvère soars on the Iseran

BONNEVAL-SUR-ARC > BOURG-SAINT-MAURICE (TIME TRIAL)

With war clouds on the horizon, the 1939 Tour de France had no Italian, German or Spanish teams and it was left to the French and Belgian teams to fight it out.

René Vietto, the 'boy' who had shown so much promise in 1934, took the yellow jersey on stage 4 and, despite getting bronchitis, held onto it through the Pyrenees. Then in the Alps, Belgian Sylvère Maes launched a searing attack on the Izoard and Vietto fell apart, losing yellow to the tune of 17 minutes.

The next day featured three 'mini' stages: 126 km over the Lautaret, Galibier and Télégraphe; the first-ever mountain time trial of 64 km over the Iseran (at 2,764 m the highest ever peak in the Tour); then a final 104 km into Annecy.

'Who could put into words the suffering inherent in a race against the clock in the mountains? Who could make it comprehensible to people who have never climbed a mountain pass? The physical effort required simply to climb a pass is considerable. The heart beats so fast you feel it's going to burst. Breathing is hard, and breathing becomes increasingly noisy and rapid. Your temples are squeezed in a vice and your legs tremble. But you have to keep on and on, without a moment's respite. Add to that the freezing currents of mountain air that alternate with layers of warm air and make you shiver as if you had a fever. It's a terrifying effort, without compare.' JEAN LEULLIOT, CORRESPONDENT FOR *L'AUTO*.

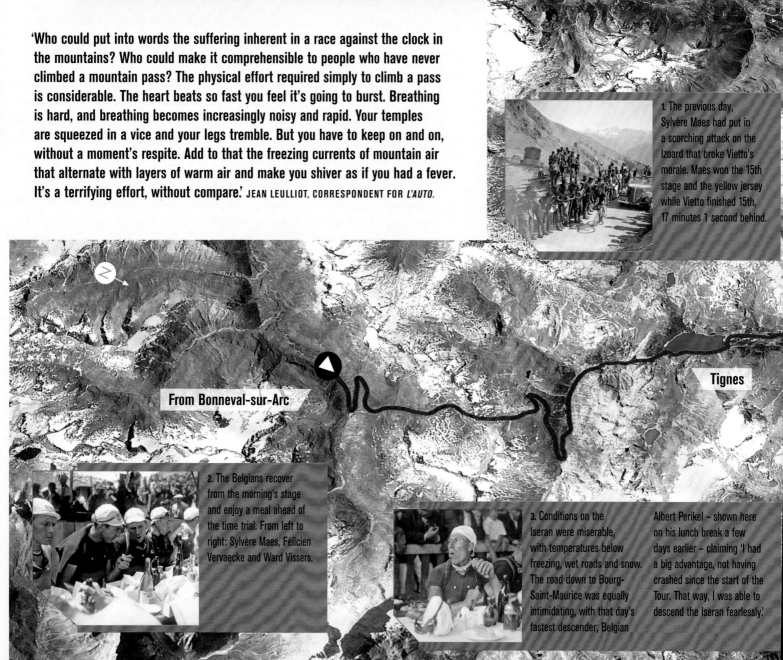

1. The previous day, Sylvère Maes had put in a scorching attack on the Izoard that broke Vietto's morale. Maes won the 15th stage and the yellow jersey while Vietto finished 15th, 17 minutes 1 second behind.

From Bonneval-sur-Arc

Tignes

2. The Belgians recover from the morning's stage and enjoy a meal ahead of the time trial. From left to right: Sylvère Maes, Félicien Vervaecke and Ward Vissers.

3. Conditions on the Iseran were miserable, with temperatures below freezing, wet roads and snow. The road down to Bourg-Saint-Maurice was equally intimidating, with that day's fastest descender, Belgian Albert Perikel – shown here on his lunch break a few days earlier – claiming 'I had a big advantage, not having crashed since the start of the Tour. That way, I was able to descend the Iseran fearlessly.'

Maes approached the time trial as if his life depended on it, blasting up the Iseran – the 14-km climb began straightaway – at an average speed of 16.368 km/hour. He then cemented that advantage on the 50-km descent into Bourg-Saint-Maurice, winning with a margin of 4 minutes over his nearest rival. In the thin air of the Iseran, in freezing wind and -4°C (-25°F) temperatures, Vietto unravelled further, reaching the summit 8 minutes 35 seconds behind Maes. He eventually finished 17th, almost 10 minutes behind.

STAGE FACTS

Date: 27 July 1939

Number: 16b

Length: 64 km

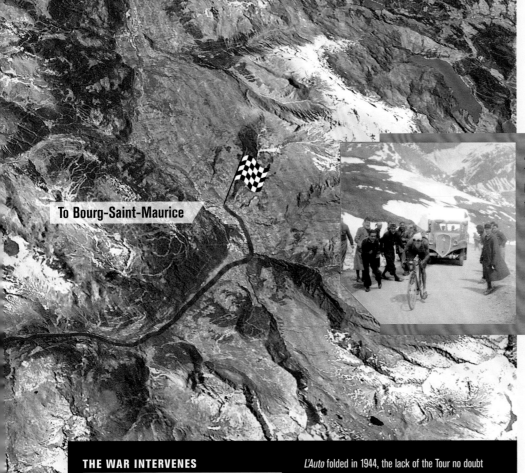

To Bourg-Saint-Maurice

4. Having effectively won the Tour, Maes went on to seal his lead in the first mountain time trial, putting a further 10 minutes into René Vietto.

BEFORE STAGE 16b

1 Sylvère Maes (Bel)
2 René Vietto (Fra)
at 17'12"
3 Lucien Vlaemynck (Bel)
at 27'13"

KING OF THE MOUNTAINS
Sylvère Maes (Bel)

AFTER STAGE 16b

1 Sylvère Maes (Bel)
2 René Vietto (Fra)
at 27'00"
3 Lucien Vlaemynck (Bel)
at 31'16"

KING OF THE MOUNTAINS
Sylvère Maes (Bel)

THE WAR INTERVENES

With the start of World War II, the Tour also witnessed the end of an era. Henri Desgrange died of an illness on 16 August 1940, aged 75, and Jacques Goddet, who had begun running the Tour in 1936, now inherited the race. But while the Germans would have permitted the Tour to continue in occupied France, Goddet decided against it, concerned the Nazis would use it as a publicity stunt. *L'Auto* was renamed *L'Auto-Soldat* and many of its heroes from the 1930s went on to fight. Frenchman Robert Oubron, who had ridden in 1937 and 1938, became a light infantryman and captured German Kurt Stöpel, runner-up behind André Leducq in 1932.

L'Auto folded in 1944, the lack of the Tour no doubt having an impact on sales figures. Jacques Goddet became editor of a new publication, *L'Équipe*.

Racing continued to a surprising degree during the war and, while there was no official Tour de France, there were several 'ersatz' Tours. The war years also saw the emergence of new riders. One of those was Fausto Coppi, who turned professional in 1940 and was allowed to continue racing until 1943 when he was sent to fight in Tunisia and was captured by the British. By then already a legend, one of his jobs in the POW camp was to give haircuts. One recipient was amateur racing cyclist, Len Levesley, thereafter named 'Holy Head' by his friends.

Vietto's trial

VANNES > SAINT-BRIEUC

There were three more stages to go, and René Vietto was in yellow – indeed, he'd spent 15 stages in yellow. Vietto, who might have won the 1939 Tour had he not cracked in the Alps, was, eight years later, dominant again at the age of 33. Stage 19 was a 139-km time trial – the longest in Tour history – with a climb up the Mûr-de-Bretagne.

Eight years is a long time in cycling and during the war new riders had emerged. Vietto may have been in yellow, but a host of hungry young guns was eating up his lead and only 1 minute 34 seconds now separated him from Pierre Brambilla, riding for the Italian team. Knowing time trials weren't his forte, he'd asked a friend, journalist Jean Leulliot, to give him splits. By the time he reached the Mûr-de-Bretagne he had already lost the

THE OTHER SIDE OF RENÉ VIETTO

René Vietto's sacrifices in 1934 had made him a popular champion, and he earned a fortune in post-Tour criteriums (short-course races). He then lost everything to his manager in 1936. Vietto became a bitter man, with strange notions of sacrifice. In the 1947 Tour he'd asked his doctor to remove a toe that had become infected. He then insisted that his own adoring protégé and *domestique*, Apo Lazaridès, do the same. Which, astonishingly, Lazaridès did. Cycling legend has it that Vietto's toe is preserved in formaldehyde in a bar somewhere in Marseille.

After Vietto retired he managed the Helyett team, which Lazaridès joined, only to be insulted and blamed for every misfortune.

In a French TV broadcast from the 1970s, Vietto and Lazaridès were asked to reminisce about riding together in the 1940s. Lazaridès talked of Vietto's toughness, and how he'd told him to 'eat grass' when he was hungry during a long training ride. When the interviewer asked Vietto if this was true, he replied, to Lazaridès giggles, 'With me, to sleep is to die and to eat is to poison yourself.'

1. Impanis was only 22 and in his first year as a professional when he won the stage – his first Tour stage win – with a margin of nearly 5 minutes. Ironically, given his triumph on such an arduous stage, Impanis was not overly keen on suffering; if he could, he was quite happy to dodge training or even racing.

Raphaël Géminiani called him 'the despair of Belgium'. He became an excellent rider in the Classics, the gruelling one-day races held mainly in spring, and his triumphs included Paris–Roubaix, the Tour of Flanders and Paris–Nice in 1960, when he was 35.

Pontiv

From Vannes

2. Throughout the Tour Jean Robic had steadily and consistently clawed his way up the general classification, with standout performances in the Alps and the Pyrenees. He was not the most stylish rider, but he was the most determined. Thanks to his ferocious efforts, he came second on the stage, riding himself from fifth position into third, 2 minutes 58 seconds from yellow.

'It was an uncontroversial defeat. The time gaps on his rivals on the general classification grew ever larger and the steadiness of these losses created an increasingly disquieting situation. This wasn't a Vietto who had set off badly or who was holding back something in reserve, no, it was a rider incapable of going beyond his limits, of being able to react, of surpassing himself.' JACQUES GODDET IN *L'ÉQUIPE*.

yellow jersey – and there were 74 km still to go. But if that wasn't bad enough, he then came across Leuillot, lying on the ground in a pool of blood, having come off his motorbike and fractured his skull. It was too much for Vietto, who finished in 15th place, nearly 15 minutes behind the Belgian winner Raymond Impanis.

In one fell swoop Vietto plunged to fourth place, 5 minutes 6 seconds behind the new yellow jersey Brambilla.

STAGE FACTS

Date: 17 July 1947

Number: 19

Length: 139 km

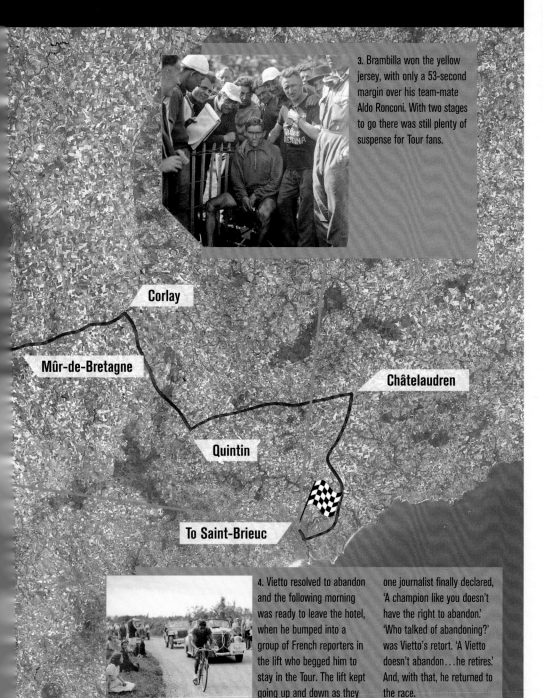

3. Brambilla won the yellow jersey, with only a 53-second margin over his team-mate Aldo Ronconi. With two stages to go there was still plenty of suspense for Tour fans.

Corlay

Mûr-de-Bretagne

Châtelaudren

Quintin

To Saint-Brieuc

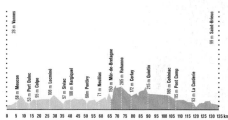

4. Vietto resolved to abandon and the following morning was ready to leave the hotel, when he bumped into a group of French reporters in the lift who begged him to stay in the Tour. The lift kept going up and down as they fought over the buttons, until one journalist finally declared, 'A champion like you doesn't have the right to abandon.' 'Who talked of abandoning?' was Vietto's retort. 'A Vietto doesn't abandon…he retires.' And, with that, he returned to the race.

BEFORE STAGE 19

1 René Vietto (Fra)
2 Pierre Brambilla (Ita)
at 1'34"
3 Aldo Ronconi (Ita)
at 3'55"

KING OF THE MOUNTAINS
Pierre Brambilla (Ita)

AFTER STAGE 19

1 Pierre Brambilla (Ita)
2 Aldo Ronconi (Ita)
at 0'53"
3 Jean Robic (Fra)
at 2'58"

KING OF THE MOUNTAINS
Pierre Brambilla (Ita)

1947

Robic snatches yellow outside Paris

CAEN > PARIS

It is generally acknowledged that no-one attacks the yellow jersey on the final stage of the Tour de France into Paris. But this year, rider Jean Robic had been steadily creeping up the general classification to reach third place, 2 minutes 58 seconds behind Italian Pierre Brambilla. Why should he stop now?

So, after 70 km of racing, Robic attacked on the Côte de Bonsecours outside Rouen. Brambilla quickly bridged the gap and suddenly the two riders were 100 m ahead of the peloton. Then Édouard Fachleitner, a French rider on a rival team, shot past. Robic jumped after him, managing to reconnect shortly before the summit, but Brambilla was unable to respond. Brambilla's team captain Aldo Ronconi, despite having the

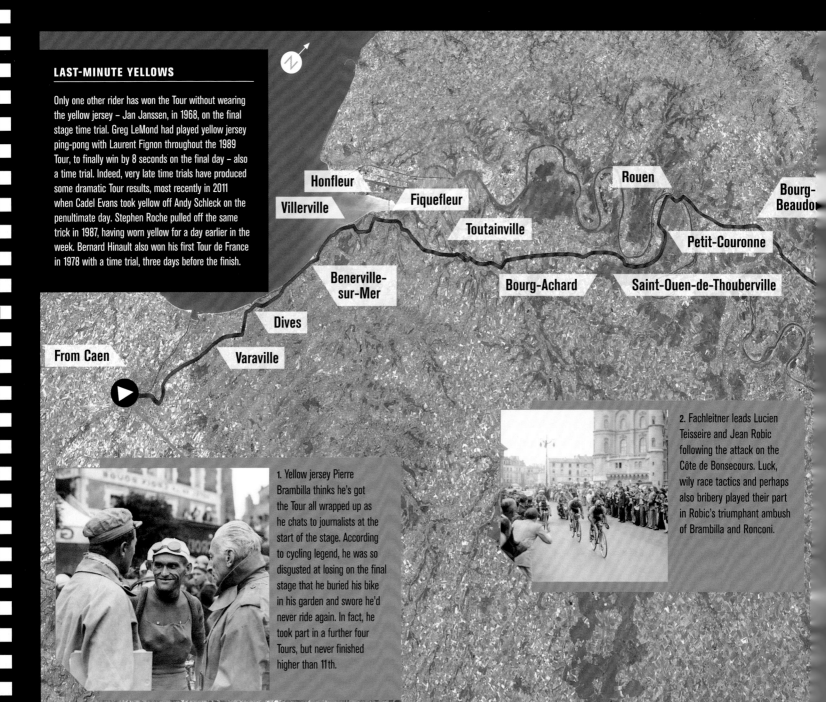

LAST-MINUTE YELLOWS

Only one other rider has won the Tour without wearing the yellow jersey – Jan Janssen, in 1968, on the final stage time trial. Greg LeMond had played yellow jersey ping-pong with Laurent Fignon throughout the 1989 Tour, to finally win by 8 seconds on the final day – also a time trial. Indeed, very late time trials have produced some dramatic Tour results, most recently in 2011 when Cadel Evans took yellow off Andy Schleck on the penultimate day. Stephen Roche pulled off the same trick in 1987, having worn yellow for a day earlier in the week. Bernard Hinault also won his first Tour de France in 1978 with a time trial, three days before the finish.

Honfleur
Villerville
Fiquefleur
Rouen
Bourg-Beaudo[...]
Toutainville
Petit-Couronne
Benerville-sur-Mer
Bourg-Achard
Saint-Ouen-de-Thouberville
Dives
From Caen
Varaville

1. Yellow jersey Pierre Brambilla thinks he's got the Tour all wrapped up as he chats to journalists at the start of the stage. According to cycling legend, he was so disgusted at losing on the final stage that he buried his bike in his garden and swore he'd never ride again. In fact, he took part in a further four Tours, but never finished higher than 11th.

2. Fachleitner leads Lucien Teisseire and Jean Robic following the attack on the Côte de Bonsecours. Luck, wily race tactics and perhaps also bribery played their part in Robic's triumphant ambush of Brambilla and Ronconi.

potential to make a move himself, came loyally to the rescue and, together with Raymond Impanis, they tried to bridge back to the French escape artists, now riding at 50 km/hour. But 25 km later they had made no progress and the French had a gap of 1 minute 45 seconds. The Italians sat up to wait for reinforcements from a peloton which was in no great hurry, with almost every team having escapees in a bunch in front of Robic.

By the time Robic and Fachleitner reached Paris they had built an astonishing gap of 13 minutes on Brambilla, and Robic became the first rider in Tour history to win on the final stage – without ever having worn yellow.

STAGE FACTS

Date: 20 July 1947
Number: 21
Length: 257 km

3. Robic triumphed in the Parc des Princes. He became the first rider to win the Tour never having worn yellow. Robic's nickname 'Bicquet' – literally 'kid' and generally a term of endearment – was used sarcastically, since Robic was stubborn and proud with a talent for losing friends. He was neither a stylish rider nor a handsome one. The fact he was also one of the very rare riders to wear a crash helmet (he'd suffered a concussion in Paris–Roubaix in 1946) did nothing to help his image.

'You can't win the Tour because I won't let you get away. So let's ride together and I'll give you 100,000 francs.' ACCORDING TO TOUR LEGEND, JEAN ROBIC'S PROMISE TO ÉDOUARD FACHLEITNER AS THEY EXTENDED THEIR LEAD ON PIERRE BRAMBILLA.

Suzay

Saint-Clair-sur-Epte

La Chapelle-en-Vexin

Pontoise

4. René Vietto looks devastated, having ended his Tour in fifth place. Unlike Robic, he'd worn yellow for 15 stages. He had come so close to winning, just as in 1939. His performance was all the more remarkable this time, given his age, the intervening war years and the fact that he had undergone several operations on his knees.

Poissy

To Paris

Versailles

BEFORE STAGE 21

1 Pierre Brambilla (Ita)
2 Aldo Ronconi (Ita)
at 0'53"
3 Jean Robic (Fra)
at 2'58"

KING OF THE MOUNTAINS
Pierre Brambilla (Ita)

AFTER STAGE 21

1 Jean Robic (Fra)
2 Édouard Fachleitner (Fra)
at 3'58"
3 Pierre Brambilla (Ita)
at 10'07"

KING OF THE MOUNTAINS
Pierre Brambilla (Ita)

A marriage of convenience

CANNES > BRIANÇON

Gino Bartali and Fausto Coppi were engaged in a rivalry so intense that in 1948 they had preferred to climb off their bikes than risk helping the other to win the world championships.

The question was not if, but when, the pretence of being team-mates would drop and battle commence. On the first Alpine stage Bartali was in ninth place on general classification and Coppi in tenth. Ferdy Kübler, the exciting Swiss hothead in sixth, lit the touch paper for the day's events by attacking early. By the summit of the Col de Vars he had a lead of almost 4 minutes with Bartali, Coppi, Jean Robic, Apo Lazaridès and Stan Ockers in hot pursuit. Then he punctured, was overtaken and his chasers morphed into the day's break.

Castellane

Col d'Allos

From Cannes

1. Ferdy Kübler led the race on the Col de Vars before being plagued with punctures. An excellent climber and time triallist with an impulsive and emotional riding style, he had his day in 1950 when he took home the yellow jersey, along with three stage wins.

2. Kübler despaired after puncturing three times. He eventually ran out of spares and had to wait for his team car – which broke down. 'Who could overlook the fact that if Kübler, once joined by Bartali and Coppi, had managed to stay with them, he would probably be wearing the yellow jersey tonight?', Claude Tillet wrote in L'Équipe. Exhausted and disheartened on the Izoard, Kübler ended up losing 12 minutes on the winners. He was so frustrated with his bad luck that he quit the race the following day.

3. Bartali and Coppi, two of the finest climbers, destroy their rivals as they ascende the Izoard together. The team's strategy for the first day in the Alps had been to ride together in a defensive way, but that had been overturned when Ferdy Kü attacked. 'There was every reason to be alarmed by th buccaneering, dangerous initiative of this devil of a rider', L'Équipe observed.

FIERCE RIVALS

Bartali and Coppi marked one of the great rivalries in cycling history. Bartali never forgave Coppi for winning his first Giro in 1940, when he was supposed to be riding as one of Bartali's domestiques. Bartali even ordered the rest of his team-mates to chase Coppi down on one of the climbs. Five years separated them and, even though their careers overlapped by 20 years, they were essentially from two different generations, Bartali coming of age in the 1930s, Coppi during World War II. Their approach to training and diet reflected these differences – Coppi is credited with being the first rider to pay serious attention to nutrition, whereas Bartali, a Tuscan, liked his hearty regional cuisine, red wine and cigarettes. They were both legends in their own right when they came to the Tour in 1949; Bartali had won in 1938 and 1948 and was hoping to equal Philippe Thys' record of three victories. It was Coppi's first Tour and he had already won that year's Giro. His palmarès included the hour record on the track in 1942 and two further Giro victories, in 1940 and 1947. In 1949 he was untouchable and became the first rider to win the Giro and Tour in the same year.

But Ockers and Lazaridès were slow descending the Vars and Robic had mechanical problems. At the foot of the Izoard Bartali and Coppi suddenly found themselves alone. What did they talk about, as they put 15 minutes into the peloton behind? 'It's my birthday,' Bartali allegedly told Coppi. 'Let's finish together. Tomorrow you'll win the Tour.'

When Bartali punctured less than 10 km from the finish, Coppi waited – and then let Bartali win, without even contesting the sprint. Bartali would take the yellow jersey while Coppi moved into second place, 1 minute 22 seconds behind.

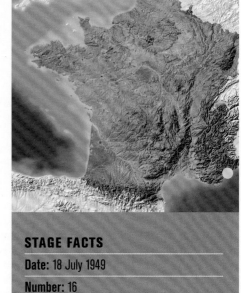

STAGE FACTS

Date: 18 July 1949

Number: 16

Length: 275 km

To Briançon

Guillestre

Barcelonnette

Col de Vars

Col d'Izoard

4. Coppi took the time bonus on the summit of the Izoard, yet he astonished everyone when he waited for Bartali to repair his puncture just a few kilometres from the finish. It was an extraordinary moment that marked the transfer of power from the older to the younger rider. The next day the gloves came off, however, and Coppi would win the Tour.

BEFORE STAGE 16	AFTER STAGE 16
1 Fiorenzo Magni (Ita)	1 Gino Bartali (Ita)
2 Édouard Fachleitner (Fra) at 2'10"	2 Fausto Coppi (Ita) at 1'22"
3 Jacques Marinelli (Fra) at 2'41"	3 Jacques Marinelli (Fra) at 1'24"
KING OF THE MOUNTAINS Fausto Coppi (Ita)	KING OF THE MOUNTAINS Fausto Coppi (Ita)

'The two men, despite their speed, never seemed to be in trouble. We set ourselves the task of comparing them, to watch them climbing side by side, disconnected from the vulgar masses. Bartali more angular, more rhythmic, rocking the bike as he stands on his pedals to increase speed; Coppi feline, hermetically sealed in his thoughts. In the cold rain, the vapour from their breath marked the perfect rhythm of their breathing. No signs of difficulties for either rider. Freed of all exterior preoccupation with their situation, they find themselves in a situation that is abundantly clear. Who will recover best? The Bartali of the Tour is no longer the Bartali of the Giro, who must now be exorcised by the yellow jersey.' JACQUES GODDET IN L'ÉQUIPE.

The Italian revolt

PAU > SAINT-GAUDENS

The Italians were dominating the Tour, having already won four stages. French fans were not amused, given that the key Italian tactic consisted of not helping in breakaways and then winning sprints with fresh legs.

As the 230-km stage crossed the Cols d'Aubisque, du Tourmalet and d'Aspin, spectators hurled abuse, bottle tops and stones at the Italians. Gino Bartali and Jean Robic were near the summit of the Aspin on a road narrowed by onlookers when Bartali tried to dodge an obstruction, only to bring both riders down in the process. Spectators crowded the riders and Bartali later claimed he'd been attacked and threatened with a knife, though commentators suggested he'd over-reacted and that the man wielding the knife had in fact just been making a sandwich and had

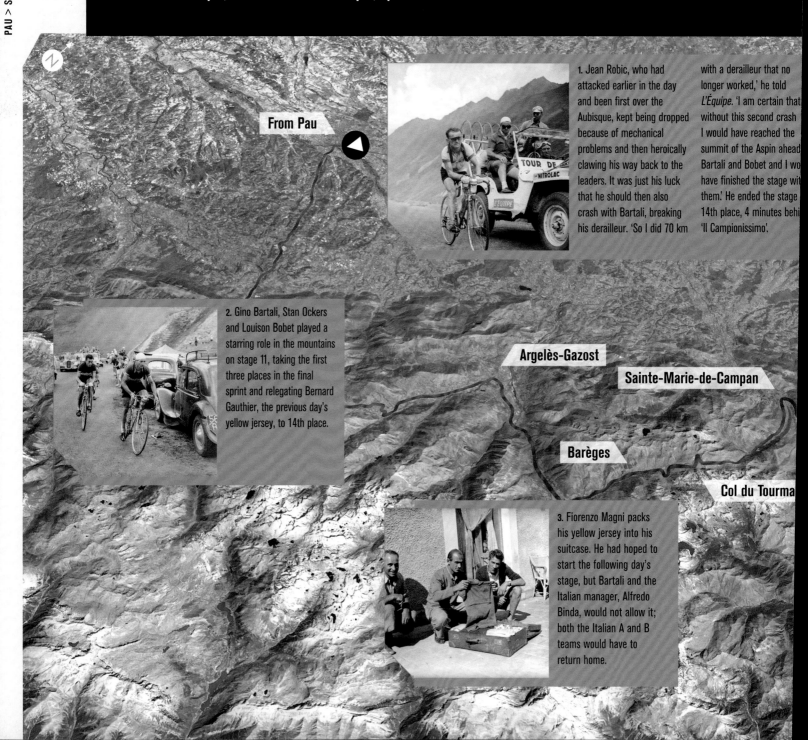

From Pau

1. Jean Robic, who had attacked earlier in the day and been first over the Aubisque, kept being dropped because of mechanical problems and then heroically clawing his way back to the leaders. It was just his luck that he should then also crash with Bartali, breaking his derailleur. 'So I did 70 km with a derailleur that no longer worked,' he told *L'Équipe.* 'I am certain that without this second crash I would have reached the summit of the Aspin ahead [of] Bartali and Bobet and I wo[uld] have finished the stage wit[h] them.' He ended the stage [in] 14th place, 4 minutes behi[nd] 'Il Campionissimo'.

2. Gino Bartali, Stan Ockers and Louison Bobet played a starring role in the mountains on stage 11, taking the first three places in the final sprint and relegating Bernard Gauthier, the previous day's yellow jersey, to 14th place.

Argelès-Gazost

Sainte-Marie-de-Campan

Barèges

Col du Tourma[let]

3. Fiorenzo Magni packs his yellow jersey into his suitcase. He had hoped to start the following day's stage, but Bartali and the Italian manager, Alfredo Binda, would not allow it; both the Italian A and B teams would have to return home.

rushed over to help. This was a view endorsed by Louison Bobet, who witnessed the incident: 'I'm pretty sure that in the time it took me to pass him, Bartali wasn't struck, and I think he mistook as blows what was just an attempt to get him back in the saddle.'

The incident was over in less than half a minute, with race director Jacques Goddet appearing on the scene wielding a walking stick. Bartali won the stage in a sprint involving eight other riders, while his team-mate, Fiorenzo Magni, took the yellow jersey.

Bartali had been shocked by the day's events and, at his insistence, both Italian teams left the Tour. They had already altered the general classification with their ride – their departure turned the tables yet again.

STAGE FACTS

Date: 25 July 1950

Number: 11

Length: 230 km

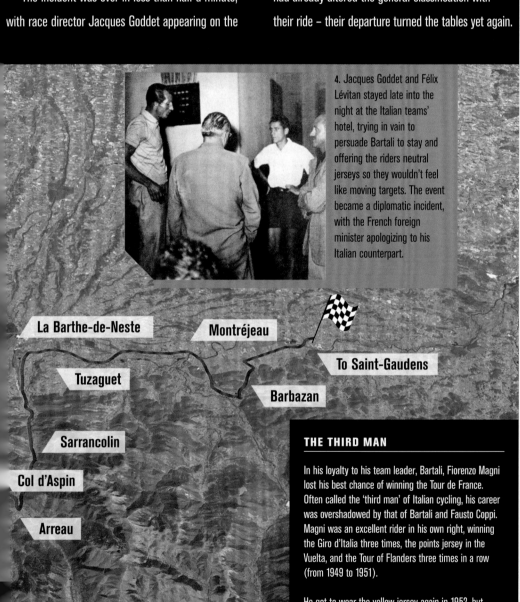

4. Jacques Goddet and Félix Lévitan stayed late into the night at the Italian teams' hotel, trying in vain to persuade Bartali to stay and offering the riders neutral jerseys so they wouldn't feel like moving targets. The event became a diplomatic incident, with the French foreign minister apologizing to his Italian counterpart.

La Barthe-de-Neste

Montréjeau

To Saint-Gaudens

Tuzaguet

Barbazan

Sarrancolin

Col d'Aspin

Arreau

THE THIRD MAN

In his loyalty to his team leader, Bartali, Fiorenzo Magni lost his best chance of winning the Tour de France. Often called the 'third man' of Italian cycling, his career was overshadowed by that of Bartali and Fausto Coppi. Magni was an excellent rider in his own right, winning the Giro d'Italia three times, the points jersey in the Vuelta, and the Tour of Flanders three times in a row (from 1949 to 1951).

He got to wear the yellow jersey again in 1952, but that was when Coppi rode one of his most brilliant races and quickly put Magni's dreams to rest. His bad luck continued in 1952, when he was about to win the world championships when his saddle broke. The following year he was in the lead in the Tour of Lombardy when he was sent down the wrong road, losing the race. He won his final Giro in 1955 when he was 34 and is to this day the oldest winner of the Giro.

'I have no intention of risking my life for a madman, even if he is the last of the species.' GINO BARTALI

BEFORE STAGE 11	AFTER STAGE 11
1 Bernard Gauthier (Fra)	1 Fiorenzo Magni (Ita)
2 Attilio Redolfi (Fra) at 9'20"	2 Ferdy Kübler (Swi) at 2'31"
3 Jean Goldschmit (Lux) at 10'35"	3 Louison Bobet (Fra) at 3'20"

KING OF THE MOUNTAINS	KING OF THE MOUNTAINS
Not available	Louison Bobet (Fra)

PERPIGNAN > NÎMES

1950

The man who raced the wrong way

PERPIGNAN > NÎMES

It was 40°C (104°F) in the shade – what little shade there was. The stretch from Perpignan never had enough trees. It was also the sort of transition stage where nothing would happen on overall rankings but a *domestique* might enjoy a moment of fame. So no-one minded when two Algerians set off up the road, into a headwind,

on the hottest day of the Tour. The peloton was so unconcerned that at one point the Algerians had a margin of 20 minutes and one, Abdel-Khader Zaaf, became virtual yellow jersey on the road.

But 28 km from the finish, Zaaf, who had done most of the work and was intent on winning the stage, collapsed. Spectators tried to revive him, apparently dousing him in wine and bringing him under the shade of a tree.

From Perpignan

Sigean

Narbonne

Béziers

Pézenas

1. Molines and Zaaf dominated the stage in a brief moment of glory for North African cycling. Their team-mates Custodio dos Reis (a Moroccan of Portuguese origin) and Marcel Zelasco (an Algerian) would come first and second the following day. Dos Reis eventually finished the Tour in 26th place.

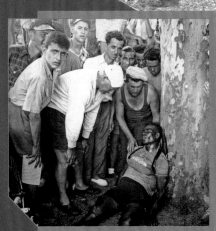

2. Zaaf lies unconscious under a tree, having collapsed in the heat. The following day Zaaf asked if he could ride the missing distance before the next day's stage, and thereby continue the race, but Tour officials refused. The previous day's winner, Belgian Maurice Blomme, had also collapsed from heat stroke, barely 40 m from the race finish.

3. It was so hot in 1950 that two days later, on the stage from Toulon to Menton, riders jumped off their bikes and ran into the sea. 'Surely the riders should have been acquiring, or re-acquiring, the rudiments of their strenuous profession, instead of indulging these carnival antics?' Jacques Goddet groused.

4. Zaaf became a popular figure on post-Tour criteriums and even did an advertising campaign for an alcoholic aperitif called Saint Raphaël. Had he really got drunk on stage 13? He was a devout Muslim who presumably would have avoided alcohol. Sunstroke was clearly a major factor in his collapse, but some have claimed he may also have taken drugs. This, combined with heat, dehydration and exhaustion could have contributed to his collapse and subsequent confusion. As with many Tour myths, the real truth may never be known.

Zaaf regained consciousness, got back on his bike, and started off again – in the wrong direction. He collapsed again and was sent off in an ambulance. Journalists, smelling alcohol, assumed he was drunk. In the meantime his team-mate, 22-year-old Marcel Molines, became the first North African to win a stage in the Tour de France.

Further dramas unfolded behind the Algerians, as Louison Bobet, the main French hope, in second place on the general classification, punctured 30 km from the finish and lost a staggering 10 minutes when Ferdy Kübler and Stan Ockers attacked.

STAGE FACTS

Date: 27 July 1950

Number: 13

Length: 215 km

AFRICA JOINS THE TOUR

In 1950 the Tour introduced its first North African team, with four riders from Algeria and two from Morocco. Since both countries were still French colonies, the riders were officially French and the team counted as one of the French regional teams.

The late 1940s and 50s were a golden age of North African cycling, but with independence a culture of cycling disappeared, perhaps given its associations with French colonialists.

The question is often raised why there aren't any black Africans in the peloton, given the superiority of East African distance runners, whose light physiques and intense endurance capacities should transfer well to cycling. The problem is primarily that of money, terrain and culture. Owning and maintaining racing bikes is impossibly expensive in Africa, suitable roads for training are a rarity and, in a sport where experience and race tactics are essential, there is a dearth of races to allow promising athletes a chance to progress. Despite these odds, in many countries, such as Burkina Faso and Eritrea, cycling is a popular sport and the UCI has been very active over the last decade in developing new races on the continent and supporting promising riders.

'After the Tour everyone wanted to drink a glass of wine with me. I couldn't refuse but I drank far too much.' ABDEL-KHADER ZAAF

BEFORE STAGE 13

1 Ferdy Kübler (Swi)
2 Louison Bobet (Fra)
at 0'49"
3 Raphaël Géminiani (Fra)
at 0'54"

AFTER STAGE 13

1 Ferdy Kübler (Swi)
2 Stan Ockers (Bel)
at 1'06"
3 Pierre Brambilla (Ita)
at 9'01"

KING OF THE MOUNTAINS
Louison Bobet (Fra)

KING OF THE MOUNTAINS
Louison Bobet (Fra)

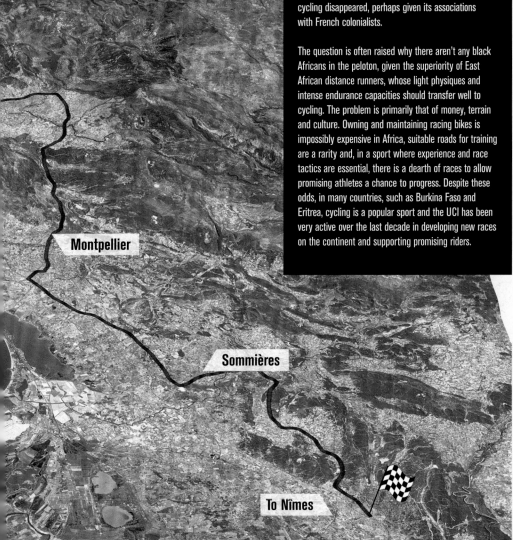

Montpellier

Sommières

To Nîmes

1951

'Le pédalleur de charme'

BRIVE > AGEN

'There's no way of being absolutely sure that we haven't just witnessed, on the smiling roads between Brive and Agen, the greatest exploit of the 1951 tour,' *L'Équipe* commented at the end of stage 11. Hugo Koblet, riding his first Tour, had attacked early on what was supposed to be a quiet rolling stage. With 135 km to go,

he rode with the cool grace of a master time triallist, putting minutes into a peloton which first responded with indifference – although he was in sixth place on the general classification, he was more than 7 minutes behind the yellow jersey – then disbelief, then fury.

Behind him the cream of European cycling, indeed the stars of an era boasting some of the greatest riders ever, worked

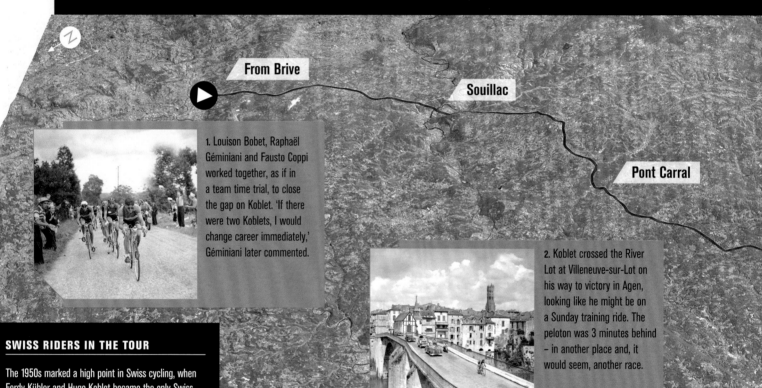

From Brive

Souillac

Pont Carral

1. Louison Bobet, Raphaël Géminiani and Fausto Coppi worked together, as if in a team time trial, to close the gap on Koblet. 'If there were two Koblets, I would change career immediately,' Géminiani later commented.

2. Koblet crossed the River Lot at Villeneuve-sur-Lot on his way to victory in Agen, looking like he might be on a Sunday training ride. The peloton was 3 minutes behind – in another place and, it would seem, another race.

SWISS RIDERS IN THE TOUR

The 1950s marked a high point in Swiss cycling, when Ferdy Kübler and Hugo Koblet became the only Swiss riders to have won the Tour, doing so in two consecutive years, in 1950 (Kübler) and 1951 (Koblet). The first green jersey of the Tour, introduced in 1953, was won by Fritz Schär, a feat Kübler repeated the following year, when Schär finished third. The only Swiss cyclist to have come close to winning since then is Tony Rominger, who came second in 1993 when he was also the only Swiss rider to also take home the polka dot jersey.

Swiss riders have been present at the Tour since its earliest days. Charles Laeser was the first foreign rider to win a stage – in the first edition in 1903. Oscar Egg was another notable rider, winning three stages in 1911.

The only Swiss rider who can equal the panache of Kübler and Koblet, however, is Fabian Cancellara, who to date has won seven stages, including five opening day prologues. In 2012 he finally broke René Vietto's record for a rider who has never won the Tour but worn the yellow jersey for the most days. Vietto's record was 26. Cancellara's, in 2012, was 28.

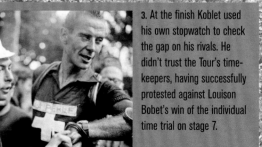

3. At the finish Koblet used his own stopwatch to check the gap on his rivals. He didn't trust the Tour's time-keepers, having successfully protested against Louison Bobet's win of the individual time trial on stage 7.

together yet failed to reel him back. Riding at an average speed of 38.946 km/hour, he won the stage with a margin of 2 minutes and 35 seconds.

'He has achieved something which we had rarely, if ever, seen,' *L'Équipe* reported. 'Not wanting to wait until the high mountains, a great rider has attempted the kind of breakaway normally risked only by riders with a major disadvantage in the general classification and therefore likely to benefit from more or less unanimous tolerance.'

Koblet finished the day in third place and three days later would be in yellow.

STAGE FACTS

Date: 15 July 1951

Number: 11

Length: 177 km

'Up to halfway through the stage, I was pedalling very much below my best. It was only at the end that I hit the gas.' HUGO KOBLET

4. The following morning singer Jacques Grello, writing in *Le Parisien Libéré*, called Koblet, '*le pédalleur de charme*'. Koblet would carry a sponge, comb and bottle of cologne in one of his pockets, so that he could finish stages perfectly groomed. *L'Équipe* called him 'Apollo on a bike', describing a rider who 'rode harmoniously, with suppleness, his elbows with a slight outward flex, his arms absorbing the vibrations coming up from the road.'

Fumel

Saint-Sylvestre-sur-Lot

Caoulet

Villeneuve-sur-Lot

To Agen

BEFORE STAGE 11

1 Roger Lévèque (Fra)
2 Gilbert Bauvin (Fra)
at 0'36"
3 Bernardo Ruiz (Spa)
at 6'14"

KING OF THE MOUNTAINS
Not available

AFTER STAGE 11

1 Roger Lévèque (Fra)
2 Gilbert Bauvin (Fra)
at 0'36"
3 Hugo Koblet (Swi)
at 3'27"

KING OF THE MOUNTAINS
Not available

The flying Dutchman

DAX > TARBES

Wim van Est had won the previous day's stage and, as a result, had become the first Dutchman ever to wear the yellow jersey. He had been racing for only four years and had little experience of mountains. But he was determined to honour yellow and reached the summit of the Col d'Aubisque only a few hundred yards behind the top climbers. When Fiorenzo Magni rode past him, van Est jumped on his wheel.

Riding at speeds of 50–60 km/hour van Est slipped, but climbed back on his bike. 'A few hundred metres further on, he was flung into a dramatic somersault and with his bike, plunged into the ravine, but clambered back up and continued his infernal pursuit,' *L'Équipe* reported.

'I couldn't understand it. I sensed I was cornering badly, I had already fallen and I knew I needed to be careful. But I wanted to keep the jersey so badly. So I really went for it and I went flying. In a flash, I looked death in the eye… the rest, I can't remember so well, there was a great "boom" in my head… then a deathly silence.' WIM VAN EST

From Dax

Oloron-Sainte-Marie

Izeste

Laruns

Col d'Aubisque

Arrens-Marsous

1. Raphaël Géminiani led the day's escapees – Gilbert Bauvin, Edward van Ende, Nello Lauredi and Serafino Biagioni – up the Aubisque. They finished the day together, 9 minutes 15 seconds faster than the rest of the peloton. Biagioni won the stage and Bauvin took yellow.

2. Gino Bartali and Hugo Koblet – two seasoned pros who handled mountains with the respect they were due – climb the Col d'Aubisque. As *L'Équipe* pointed out, the descent of the Aubisque, 'is thought of as the most dangerous of all. On one side of the narrow road there's a wall of rock; on the other, an abyss. The hairpin bends are often disguised by the rock face.' Van Est was defending yellow on a road he had never ridden before, with almost no experience of descents.

'70 METRES DEEP I DROPPED'

Prior to turning professional van Est had smuggled tobacco in his bike and spent several months in prison as a result. He started racing as an amateur in 1946 and was already 28 when he rode the Tour in 1951. He had a long and respectable career, winning the 600-km Bordeaux–Paris race three times.

He won two more stages at the Tour and wore the yellow jersey again in 1955 and 1958. He also won the Tour of Flanders in 1953 and a stage at the Giro the same year, and six Dutch national championship titles in the road race and the individual pursuit.

Following the Tour, van Est made a fortune as the face of a watch advertising campaign that bore the legend '70 metres deep I dropped, my heart stood still but my Pontiac never stopped'.

'His third fall was like a scene from a nightmare,' the newspaper continued. 'Van Est had lurched into the void, between the rock faces of the precipice.' A horrified Roger Decock, riding for the Belgians, stopped to warn others coming down. 'They dismounted and ran over, hearts in their mouths. At the bottom of the ravine, they made out the minuscule figure of the yellow jersey, lying on a rock… there were no signs of life.'

Amazingly, van Est was still alive. He was hauled up to the road and put in an ambulance but tried to get out, and would have clambered back down the ravine to fetch his bike had his manager not intervened.

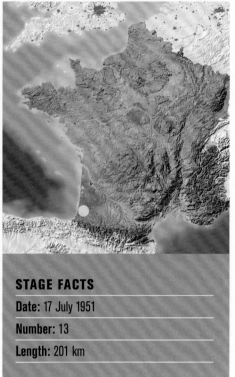

STAGE FACTS

Date: 17 July 1951

Number: 13

Length: 201 km

To Tarbes

3. His team knotted all its spare tyres together to make an impromptu rope to haul van Est back up to the road. The tyres became so stretched they could no longer be used, although it hardly mattered, since the team retired from the Tour.

4. Van Est cries with shock and relief. His team-mate Gerard Peters said van Est had looked like 'a buttercup in the grass' at the bottom of the ravine. This photograph was taken by a Belgian photographer, one of the first people to reach van Est and who, along with his manager and team, helped him out of the ravine.

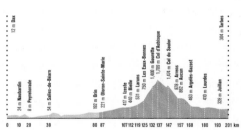

BEFORE STAGE 13

1 Wim van Est (Ned)
2 Georges Meunier (Fra)
at 2'29"
3 Marcel De Mulder (Bel)
at 3'13"

AFTER STAGE 13

1 Gilbert Bauvin (Fra)
2 Serafino Biagioni (Ita)
at 6'18"
3 Raphaël Géminiani (Fra)
same time

KING OF THE MOUNTAINS
Not available

KING OF THE MOUNTAINS
Raphaël Géminiani (Fra)

1952

Coppi leads Tour into modern era

LAUSANNE > ALPE D'HUEZ

Fausto Coppi had won the individual time trial a few days previously and was sitting in fourth place with his _domestique_, Andrea Carrea, in yellow. Stage 10 marked the first stage in the Alps. It also marked the first-ever ascent of the Alpe d'Huez, the first stage finish at altitude, and the first live television broadcast from the Tour.

After an uneventful 251 km where attempts from the likes of Abdel-Khader Zaaf from the North African team were swiftly neutralized by Coppi's Italian battalion, the peloton reached the foot of the Alpe d'Huez. Immediately Jean Robic attacked, with Raphaël Géminiani on his tail and Coppi quickly responding. Géminiani couldn't hold Robic's fierce pace and dropped away. Coppi, meanwhile, took his time with aristocratic ease, reaching

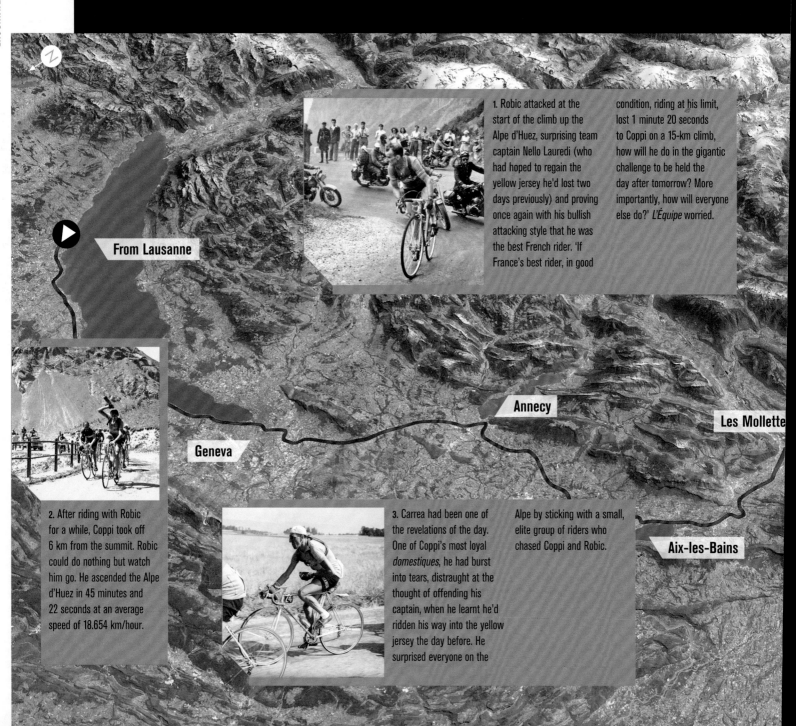

From Lausanne

Geneva

Annecy

Les Mollette

Aix-les-Bains

1. Robic attacked at the start of the climb up the Alpe d'Huez, surprising team captain Nello Lauredi (who had hoped to regain the yellow jersey he'd lost two days previously) and proving once again with his bullish attacking style that he was the best French rider. 'If France's best rider, in good condition, riding at his limit, lost 1 minute 20 seconds to Coppi on a 15-km climb, how will he do in the gigantic challenge to be held the day after tomorrow? More importantly, how will everyone else do?' _L'Équipe_ worried.

2. After riding with Robic for a while, Coppi took off 6 km from the summit. Robic could do nothing but watch him go. He ascended the Alpe d'Huez in 45 minutes and 22 seconds at an average speed of 18.654 km/hour.

3. Carrea had been one of the revelations of the day. One of Coppi's most loyal _domestiques_, he had burst into tears, distraught at the thought of offending his captain, when he learnt he'd ridden his way into the yellow jersey the day before. He surprised everyone on the Alpe by sticking with a small, elite group of riders who chased Coppi and Robic.

Robic after 3 km. Behind, the peloton exploded. Those who tried accelerating too fast, like Jean Le Guilly, were rewarded for their rashness with sudden, brutal exhaustion.

Robic and Coppi rode together until 6 km from the summit, when Coppi rose out of the saddle and steadily drew away, delighting TV viewers who, for the first time, could witness the powerful, inexorable, supple pedalling of the long-limbed 'Campionissimo'. He won the stage with a margin of 1 minute and 20 seconds. He had ridden his way into yellow, but it was just an *aperitivo* for what was to come.

MOUNTAIN STAGE FINISHES

Mountain stage finishes were first introduced to the Tour de France in 1952, with three in one edition; the Alpe d'Huez, Sestriere and the Puy-de-Dôme.

This innovation was perhaps the most significant final ingredient in the creation of a modern Tour, following the introduction of individual time trials in 1934. While the Tour was usually decided in the mountains, and pure climbers had won in the past, pure climbers were seldom rewarded with mountain stage wins if the rest of the peloton had a chance to catch up with them once the final summit had been crested. The introduction of finishes at altitude added a new, essential skill that anyone with general classification ambitions would have to master, and helped tip the balance back in favour of climbers and away from powerful time triallists who could also climb.

Andy Schleck is the most recent pure climber to have won the Tour, awarded to him in 2012 following Alberto Contador's disqualification, for his achievements in 2010. A long time gap separates Schleck from Marco Pantani's win in 1998. Pantani also holds the honour of the fastest ascent up the Alpe d'Huez, in 1997, in 37 minutes and 35 seconds.

STAGE FACTS

Date: 4 July 1952
Number: 10
Length: 266 km

'…it was the French who forced me to go on the attack. Robic escaped right at the start of the climb, Géminiani was following and I couldn't sit on wheels anymore. I took off myself, but again, I didn't expect to climb so well. It was only when I caught up with Robic that I got my confidence. I attacked twice to put him under pressure, then backed off. The third time, however, I sprinted with everything I had in order to drop him.' FAUSTO COPPI

To Alpe d'Huez

Gières

4. The stage finish on the Alpe had a dramatic impact on the peloton and was perfect for television. Perhaps surprisingly, the Alpe did not return to the Tour for another 24 years.

BEFORE STAGE 10	AFTER STAGE 10
1 Andrea Carrea (Ita)	1 Fausto Coppi (Ita)
2 Fiorenzo Magni (Ita) at 1'01"	2 Andrea Carrea (Ita) at 0'05"
3 Nello Lauredi (Fra) at 1'21"	3 Fiorenzo Magni (Ita) at 1'50"
KING OF THE MOUNTAINS Not available	KING OF THE MOUNTAINS Fausto Coppi (Ita)

1952

The 'Eagle of the Summits' soars

BOURG-D'OISANS > SESTRIERE

Fausto Coppi's demonstration of strength on the Alpe d'Huez had awed, but not yet intimidated, his rivals. On stage 11 the French team played plucky adversaries again. This time it was Raphaël Géminiani, with Nello Lauredi (who'd worn the yellow jersey for four stages), Jean Dotto and Lucien Lazaridès who attacked on the Col de la Croix de Fer. By the time they reached the Télégraphe, Géminiani's efforts had reduced the peloton to 15 riders. Then a 20-year-old rider from the West-South West team, Jean Le Guilly, set off on a solo break.

Coppi went on the attack 15 km from the summit of the Galibier. For a few moments Géminiani, Bernardo Ruiz, Stan Ockers and Gino Bartali were able to hold his wheel, but it was pointless.

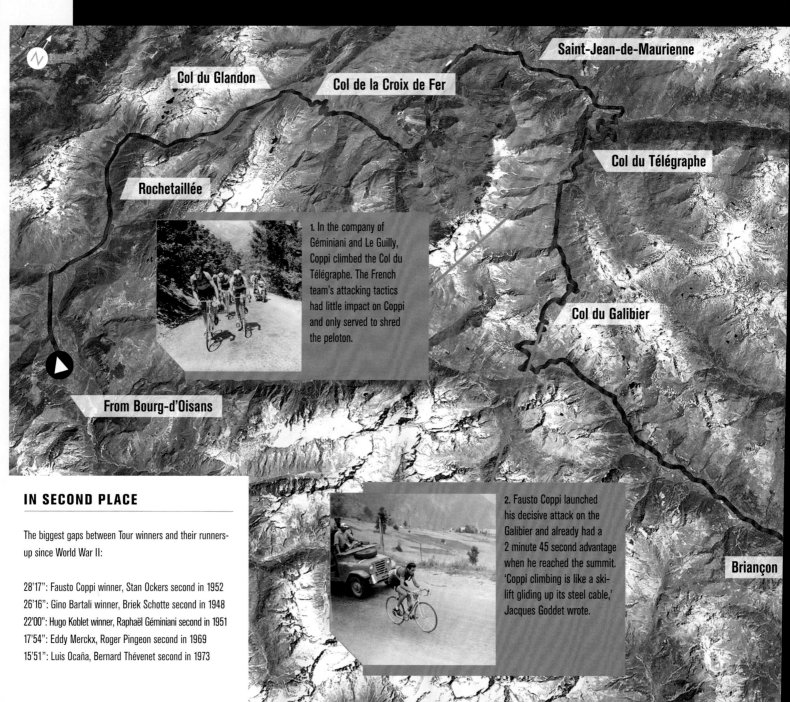

Saint-Jean-de-Maurienne

Col du Glandon

Col de la Croix de Fer

Col du Télégraphe

Rochetaillée

1. In the company of Géminiani and Le Guilly, Coppi climbed the Col du Télégraphe. The French team's attacking tactics had little impact on Coppi and only served to shred the peloton.

Col du Galibier

From Bourg-d'Oisans

Briançon

2. Fausto Coppi launched his decisive attack on the Galibier and already had a 2 minute 45 second advantage when he reached the summit. 'Coppi climbing is like a ski-lift gliding up its steel cable,' Jacques Goddet wrote.

IN SECOND PLACE

The biggest gaps between Tour winners and their runners-up since World War II:

28'17": Fausto Coppi winner, Stan Ockers second in 1952
26'16": Gino Bartali winner, Briek Schotte second in 1948
22'00": Hugo Koblet winner, Raphaël Géminiani second in 1951
17'54": Eddy Merckx, Roger Pingeon second in 1969
15'51": Luis Ocaña, Bernard Thévenet second in 1973

Coppi simply rode away. He came up to Le Guilly, passing him as if he were a roadside marker. By the summit of the Galibier Coppi already had a margin of 2 minutes 45 seconds. He continued alone, crossing the Montgenèvre and riding into Sestriere in Italy, amid rapturous Italian fans, 7 minutes ahead of Ruiz and 10 minutes ahead of Bartali (who came fifth).

In just one stage Coppi – simply in a league of his own – had extended his lead to just under 20 minutes. It was such a dominating performance that the race organizers doubled the prize money for second place.

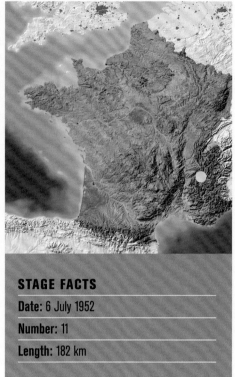

STAGE FACTS

Date: 6 July 1952

Number: 11

Length: 182 km

3. Robic rides alone up to the finish in Sestriere, 4 minutes 30 seconds behind Coppi. He had managed to overtake Ruiz, Ockers and Bartali and, just as in the Alpe d'Huez stage, seemed the only rider who could come close to Coppi. But 10 km from the finish he would puncture. Deciding to pump his tyre rather than change it, he had to repeat the process five times. His manager, Marcel Bidot, had been following Lauredi, but when it became clear Lauredi wasn't doing so well, he tried to catch up with Robic, only to run out of petrol. Robic would finish in seventh place, 11 minutes 24 seconds behind Coppi.

To Sestriere

Montgenèvre

4. 1952 marked a clear turning point for Bartali, who was about to turn 38. *L'Équipe* described his performance on stage 11 as 'the twilight of a god'. Acknowledging he was no longer a rival to his team-mate, Bartali even gave Coppi his wheel when he punctured on a later stage.

'I didn't intend to attack on the Galibier. I wanted to wait for the final climb, and just to try to gain the bonuses at the summit of the Croix de Fer, the Galibier and the Montgenèvre. But the French, particularly Géminiani, roused me with their attacks on the Galibier. I counter-attacked and, since I was feeling very good, I kept going.' FAUSTO COPPI

BEFORE STAGE 11

1 Fausto Coppi (Ita)
2 Andrea Carrea (Ita)
at 0'05"
3 Fiorenzo Magni (Ita)
at 1'50"

AFTER STAGE 11

1 Fausto Coppi (Ita)
2 Alex Close (Bel)
at 19'57"
3 Andrea Carrea (Ita)
at 20'26"

KING OF THE MOUNTAINS
Fausto Coppi (Ita)

KING OF THE MOUNTAINS
Fausto Coppi (Ita)

The Tour goes Dutch

AMSTERDAM > BRASSCHAAT

For the first time in its history the Tour started on foreign soil, from Amsterdam. There were no Italians, the Italian Cycling Federation having refused to authorize a team following a riders' strike at the Giro d'Italia.

It's often said the Tour can be won – or lost – on any stage and so it seemed on stage 1. From the start a remarkable breakaway group of 19 riders formed which contained the race favourites: former Tour winners Ferdy Kübler, Hugo Koblet and Louison Bobet. Working together, the escapees had a gap of 4 minutes 40 seconds by the time they reached Breda, 160 km later.

This was the home town of Dutch rider Wout Wagtmans, who shot off the front to ride 'in the midst of an incredibly dense

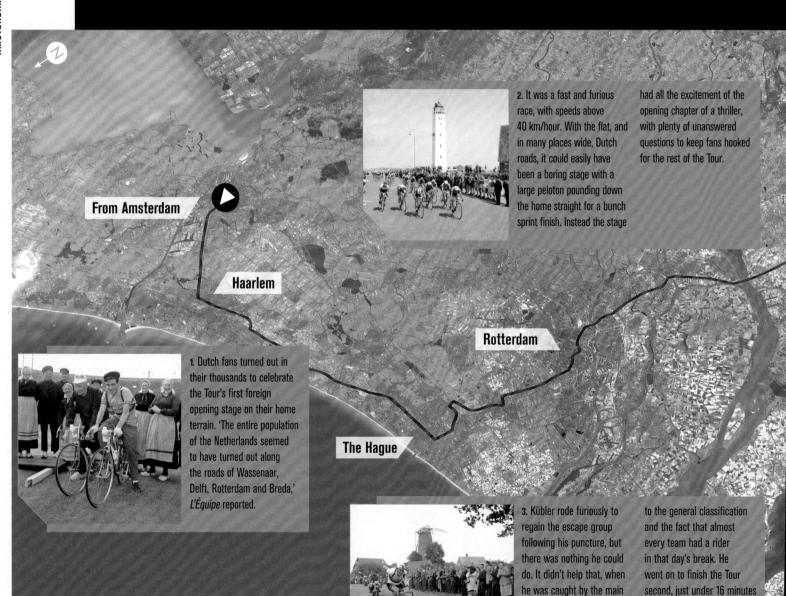

From Amsterdam

Haarlem

Rotterdam

The Hague

2. It was a fast and furious race, with speeds above 40 km/hour. With the flat, and in many places wide, Dutch roads, it could easily have been a boring stage with a large peloton pounding down the home straight for a bunch sprint finish. Instead the stage had all the excitement of the opening chapter of a thriller, with plenty of unanswered questions to keep fans hooked for the rest of the Tour.

1. Dutch fans turned out in their thousands to celebrate the Tour's first foreign opening stage on their home terrain. 'The entire population of the Netherlands seemed to have turned out along the roads of Wassenaar, Delft, Rotterdam and Breda,' *L'Équipe* reported.

3. Kübler rode furiously to regain the escape group following his puncture, but there was nothing he could do. It didn't help that, when he was caught by the main peloton, it was in almost no-one's interest to chase down the breakaway, given the threat that Kübler presented to the general classification and the fact that almost every team had a rider in that day's break. He went on to finish the Tour second, just under 16 minutes behind the eventual winner Louison Bobet.

'Here's something that will make my wife happy if she sees the photo.' WOUT WAGTMANS

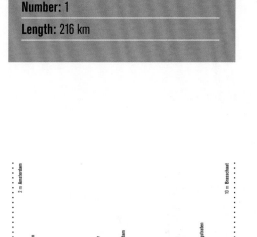

crowd which cheered him as if it were the decisive stage of the Tour', wrote *L'Équipe*. Wagtmans was soon caught but, when the escape group stormed into Brasschaat for the sprint finish, Wagtmans soloed off the front again to win.

The day's big loser was Ferdy Kübler. A key player in the break, he then punctured and was unable to get back to the bunch. He was caught by the main peloton and eventually won the sprint for 22nd place when the peloton came in 9 minutes 4 seconds later. His Tour, it seemed, was already over.

STAGE FACTS

Date: 8 July 1954

Number: 1

Length: 216 km

Breda

Hoogstraten

To Brasschaat

FOREIGN STARTS

The Tour has started in 19 European cities outside France:

1954: Amsterdam, Netherlands
1958: Brussels, Belgium
1965: Cologne, Germany
1973: Scheveningen, Netherlands
1975: Charleroi, Belgium
1978: Leiden, Netherlands'
1980: Frankfurt, Germany
1982: Basle, Switzerland
1987: Berlin, Germany
1989: Luxembourg, Luxembourg
1992: San Sebastián, Spain
1996: 's-Hertogenbosch, Netherlands
1998: Dublin, Ireland
2002: Luxembourg, Luxembourg
2004: Liège, Belgium
2007: London, United Kingdom
2009: Monaco, Monaco
2010: Rotterdam, Netherlands
2012: Liège, Belgium

AFTER STAGE 1

1 Wout Wagtmans (Ned)
2 Gilbert Bauvin (Fra)
at 0'01"
3 Stan Ockers (Bel)
same time

Wout Wagtmans (Ned)

4. Wout Wagtmans looks delighted after he won the first-ever Tour stage on home turf. It was a strong start that had gone precisely according to plan. Five days previously Cees Pellenaers, the Dutch team manager, had said, 'This year our main objective for the first stage is to win it. For the last three months we have been working towards this goal and, if there are no catastrophies, we should be able to challenge the big favourites without the risk of being laughed at.'

Bobet owns the Izoard

GRENOBLE > BRIANÇON

Louison Bobet had finally won the Tour on his sixth attempt in 1953, despite rivalry from within his team. It was on the Izoard that he had shown team-mates – and Tour rivals – who was boss.

In 1954 the Tour went over the Izoard again. This time Bobet was already in the race lead with a gap of approximately 10 minutes on his most dangerous rivals, Swiss riders Fritz Schär, leading the points competition, and Ferdy Kübler, now aged 35.

Spanish climbing ace Federico Bahamontes, riding his first Tour, was first over the Laffrey, in front of Bobet and Jean Le Guilly. The peloton regrouped and, on the Col Bayard, Bahamontes was first across the summit again. The peloton then proceeded to the foot of the Izoard. In the first 4 km Bobet dropped everyone apart from

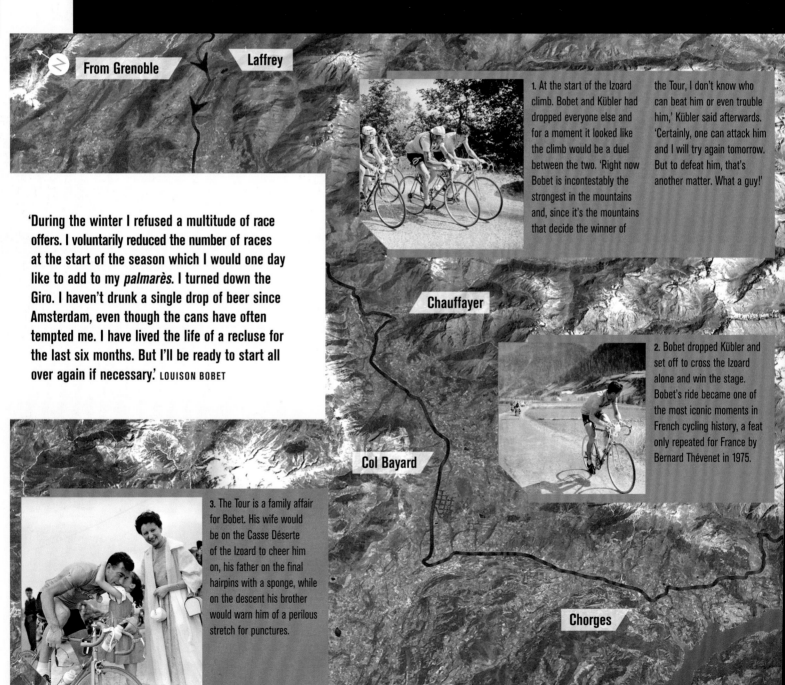

From Grenoble

Laffrey

'During the winter I refused a multitude of race offers. I voluntarily reduced the number of races at the start of the season which I would one day like to add to my *palmarès*. I turned down the Giro. I haven't drunk a single drop of beer since Amsterdam, even though the cans have often tempted me. I have lived the life of a recluse for the last six months. But I'll be ready to start all over again if necessary.' LOUISON BOBET

1. At the start of the Izoard climb. Bobet and Kübler had dropped everyone else and for a moment it looked like the climb would be a duel between the two. 'Right now Bobet is incontestably the strongest in the mountains and, since it's the mountains that decide the winner of the Tour, I don't know who can beat him or even trouble him,' Kübler said afterwards. 'Certainly, one can attack him and I will try again tomorrow. But to defeat him, that's another matter. What a guy!'

Chauffayer

2. Bobet dropped Kübler and set off to cross the Izoard alone and win the stage. Bobet's ride became one of the most iconic moments in French cycling history, a feat only repeated for France by Bernard Thévenet in 1975.

Col Bayard

3. The Tour is a family affair for Bobet. His wife would be on the Casse Déserte of the Izoard to cheer him on, his father on the final hairpins with a sponge, while on the descent his brother would warn him of a perilous stretch for punctures.

Chorges

Kübler and Jean Malléjac. By the time Bobet reached the first hairpin bend that would lead up to the Casse Déserte, he was alone. Yet it was in the 24-km descent into Briançon that Bobet really put time into his rivals.

Bobet's team-mate Raphaël Géminiani, forced to abandon because of injury, had told *L'Équipe* that morning, 'Louison is twice as strong as he was last year. This evening he will win in Briançon in front of Kübler, then he'll win the time trial. And he'll reach the Parc des Princes with a quarter of an hour on the Swiss.' His prediction was correct in every respect. Kübler finished second and moved up into second place on the general classification. Schär came in 16th, losing 8 minutes 2 seconds and dropping to third place.

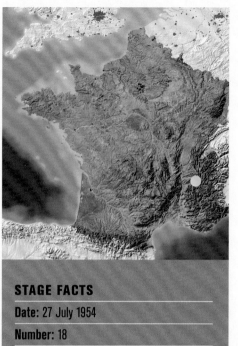

STAGE FACTS

Date: 27 July 1954

Number: 18

Length: 216 km

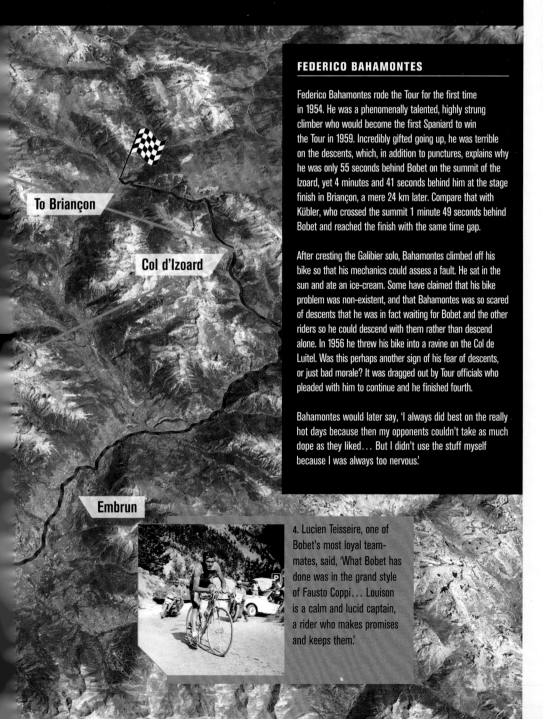

To Briançon

Col d'Izoard

Embrun

FEDERICO BAHAMONTES

Federico Bahamontes rode the Tour for the first time in 1954. He was a phenomenally talented, highly strung climber who would become the first Spaniard to win the Tour in 1959. Incredibly gifted going up, he was terrible on the descents, which, in addition to punctures, explains why he was only 55 seconds behind Bobet on the summit of the Izoard, yet 4 minutes and 41 seconds behind him at the stage finish in Briançon, a mere 24 km later. Compare that with Kübler, who crossed the summit 1 minute 49 seconds behind Bobet and reached the finish with the same time gap.

After cresting the Galibier solo, Bahamontes climbed off his bike so that his mechanics could assess a fault. He sat in the sun and ate an ice-cream. Some have claimed that his bike problem was non-existent, and that Bahamontes was so scared of descents that he was in fact waiting for Bobet and the other riders so he could descend with them rather than descend alone. In 1956 he threw his bike into a ravine on the Col de Luitel. Was this perhaps another sign of his fear of descents, or just bad morale? It was dragged out by Tour officials who pleaded with him to continue and he finished fourth.

Bahamontes would later say, 'I always did best on the really hot days because then my opponents couldn't take as much dope as they liked… But I didn't use the stuff myself because I was always too nervous.'

4. Lucien Teisseire, one of Bobet's most loyal team-mates, said, 'What Bobet has done was in the grand style of Fausto Coppi… Louison is a calm and lucid captain, a rider who makes promises and keeps them.'

BEFORE STAGE 18

1 Louison Bobet (Fra)
2 Fritz Schär (Swi)
at 9'44"
3 Ferdy Kübler (Swi)
at 10'30"

Ferdy Kübler (Swi)

AFTER STAGE 18

1 Louison Bobet (Fra)
2 Ferdy Kübler (Swi)
at 12'49"
3 Fritz Schär (Swi)
at 17'46"

Ferdy Kübler (Swi)

KING OF THE MOUNTAINS
Federico Bahamontes (Spa)

KING OF THE MOUNTAINS
Federico Bahamontes (Spa)

The violent Ventoux

MARSEILLE > AVIGNON

It was all happening on the Mont Ventoux on stage 11 of the 1955 Tour de France. In 40°C (104°F) heat Ferdy Kübler had pushed himself to the point of madness; Jean Malléjac was having seizures by the roadside, his legs still pedalling a phantom bike; Louison Bobet, seeing the Luxembourg climbing sensation Charly Gaul in trouble, had calmly accelerated and was soloing skywards in his world champion's jersey.

Bobet was still in third place, 11½ minutes behind his team-mate Antonin Rolland, but on this stage he made it perfectly clear that this year he would own the Tour de France again, just as he had in 1953 and 1954. At the summit Bobet had 50 seconds on his closest rival, the Belgian Jean Brankart –

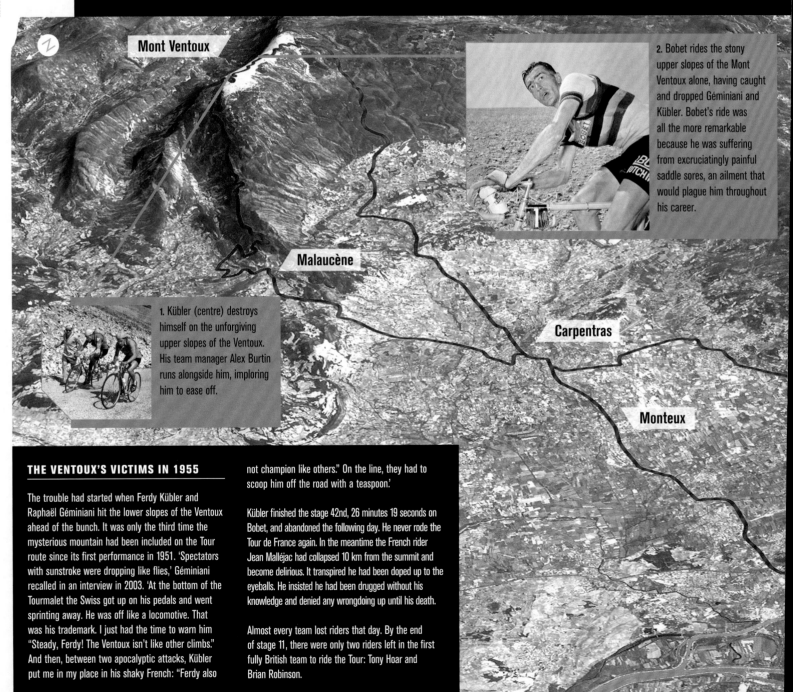

Mont Ventoux

2. Bobet rides the stony upper slopes of the Mont Ventoux alone, having caught and dropped Géminiani and Kübler. Bobet's ride was all the more remarkable because he was suffering from excruciatingly painful saddle sores, an ailment that would plague him throughout his career.

Malaucène

Carpentras

Monteux

1. Kübler (centre) destroys himself on the unforgiving upper slopes of the Ventoux. His team manager Alex Burtin runs alongside him, imploring him to ease off.

THE VENTOUX'S VICTIMS IN 1955

The trouble had started when Ferdy Kübler and Raphaël Géminiani hit the lower slopes of the Ventoux ahead of the bunch. It was only the third time the mysterious mountain had been included on the Tour route since its first performance in 1951. 'Spectators with sunstroke were dropping like flies,' Géminiani recalled in an interview in 2003. 'At the bottom of the Tourmalet the Swiss got up on his pedals and went sprinting away. He was off like a locomotive. That was his trademark. I just had the time to warn him "Steady, Ferdy! The Ventoux isn't like other climbs." And then, between two apocalyptic attacks, Kübler put me in my place in his shaky French: "Ferdy also

not champion like others." On the line, they had to scoop him off the road with a teaspoon.'

Kübler finished the stage 42nd, 26 minutes 19 seconds on Bobet, and abandoned the following day. He never rode the Tour de France again. In the meantime the French rider Jean Malléjac had collapsed 10 km from the summit and become delirious. It transpired he had been doped up to the eyeballs. He insisted he had been drugged without his knowledge and denied any wrongdoing up until his death.

Almost every team lost riders that day. By the end of stage 11, there were only two riders left in the first fully British team to ride the Tour: Tony Hoar and Brian Robinson.

a gap that he maintained all the way to his solo finish, riding the last hour into Avignon as he would have done a time trial.

Brankart came in with a trio of Italians. The remaining key players, including Wout Wagtmans, Antonin Rolland, Raphaël Géminiani and Charly Gaul, came in 5½–6 minutes later.

Bobet had moved into second place, just under 5 minutes behind Rolland. But the Pyrenees were still to come.

STAGE FACTS

Date: 18 July 1955
Number: 11
Length: 198 km

'I don't believe I've ever ridden such a difficult Tour. Every stage is difficult. How I miss the Coppis and the Koblets... with men of that calibre you share responsibility. To be the sole favourite is hard.' LOUISON BOBET

3. The Tour's doctor Pierre Dumas attends to Malléjac, who had collapsed 10 km from the summit.

From Marseille

L'Isle-sur-la-Sorgue

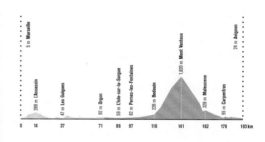

4. Louison Bobet became the first rider to follow Belgian Philippe Thys' record of three Tour victories, gained in 1913, 1914 and 1920. He was also the first person to win the Tour in three consecutive years. Thys, now 65, was invited to the Parc des Princes at the end of the Tour to present Bobet with a bouquet. Bobet and Thys then rode a lap of honour together.

To Avignon

BEFORE STAGE 11	AFTER STAGE 11
1 Antonin Rolland (Fra)	1 Antonin Rolland (Fra)
2 Pasquale Fornara (Ita) at 11'03"	2 Louison Bobet (Fra) at 4'53
3 Louison Bobet (Fra) at 11'33"	3 Pasquale Fornara (Ita) at 6'18"
Wout Wagtmans (Ned)	Wout Wagtmans (Ned)
KING OF THE MOUNTAINS Charly Gaul (Lux)	KING OF THE MOUNTAINS Charly Gaul (Lux)

1956

Walkowiak's lucky break

LORIENT > ANGERS

On 11 July 1956, Roger Walkowiak began the day essentially an unknown, the sort of rider who 'mainly helped others to get the yellow jersey', as he himself put it. By the end of the day he was *in* the yellow jersey – and would eventually win the Tour.

A French rider of Polish origins, he had been included on the regional North East Centre team at the last minute, after its captain Gilbert Bauvin had been promoted to the national team. By stage 7 Walkowiak was in a respectable fifth place on general classification, 7 minutes 18 seconds down on the race leader André Darrigade, thanks to his daily efforts to get into the right breaks. Then he finally picked the plum one, a 31-man express train containing French regional riders, four Dutchmen and six Italians. They crossed

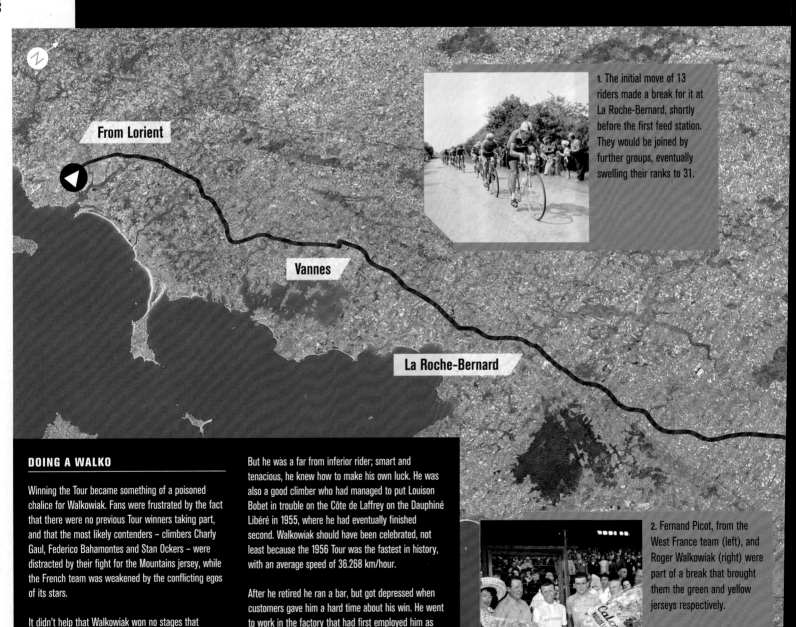

From Lorient

Vannes

La Roche-Bernard

1. The initial move of 13 riders made a break for it at La Roche-Bernard, shortly before the first feed station. They would be joined by further groups, eventually swelling their ranks to 31.

2. Fernand Picot, from the West France team (left), and Roger Walkowiak (right) were part of a break that brought them the green and yellow jerseys respectively.

DOING A WALKO

Winning the Tour became something of a poisoned chalice for Walkowiak. Fans were frustrated by the fact that there were no previous Tour winners taking part, and that the most likely contenders – climbers Charly Gaul, Federico Bahamontes and Stan Ockers – were distracted by their fight for the Mountains jersey, while the French team was weakened by the conflicting egos of its stars.

It didn't help that Walkowiak won no stages that year – indeed he's the only Tour winner never to have won a stage in his career. The phrase 'doing a Walko' soon became a French expression synonymous with succeeding unexpectedly.

But he was a far from inferior rider; smart and tenacious, he knew how to make his own luck. He was also a good climber who had managed to put Louison Bobet in trouble on the Côte de Laffrey on the Dauphiné Libéré in 1955, where he had eventually finished second. Walkowiak should have been celebrated, not least because the 1956 Tour was the fastest in history, with an average speed of 36.268 km/hour.

After he retired he ran a bar, but got depressed when customers gave him a hard time about his win. He went to work in the factory that had first employed him as a young man, and for many years he refused to talk about his victory.

the finish line almost 19 minutes ahead of the yellow jersey.

Initially the French team had chased them, limiting the gap to around 4 minutes. But after approximately 150 km the escapees rocketed away and the Italians set up a sprint train for eventual winner Alessandro Fantini.

Everyone, including Walkowiak, assumed he would be unable to hold onto the jersey with the mountains to come. But he had enough talent, determination and race intelligence – plus a wily, confident team manager – to make the most of his luck.

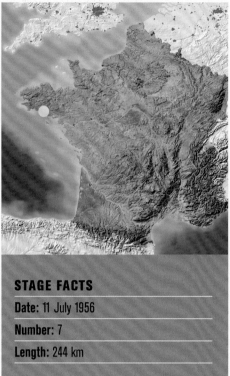

STAGE FACTS

Date: 11 July 1956

Number: 7

Length: 244 km

3. The Italians had big ambitions for the stage, putting six riders in the break. Their sprinter Alessandro Fantini finally won the stage.

Candé

To Angers

Nort-sur-Erdre

4. Walkowiak surprised everyone by eventually arriving in Paris in the yellow jersey. Despite his fresh-faced looks, Walkowiak was already 29 when he won the Tour. His arrival in the Parc des Princes was accompanied by wolf whistles from a crowd that had expected one of the main contenders to win.

'I asked Walkowiak and [Gilbert] Scodeller to respond to the breaks as much as possible. They went beyond my expectations.' SAUVEUR DUCAZEAUX, TEAM MANAGER

BEFORE STAGE 7	AFTER STAGE 7
1 André Darrigade (Fra)	1 Roger Walkowiak (Fra)
2 Daan de Groot (Ned) at 5'13"	2 Fernand Picot (Fra) at 1'22"
3 Leo van der Pluym (Ned) at 5'27"	3 Gilbert Scodeller (Fra) at 2'53"
Daan de Groot (Ned)	Fernand Picot (Fra)
KING OF THE MOUNTAINS Not available	KING OF THE MOUNTAINS Not available

The triumph of Gaul

BRIANÇON > AIX-LES-BAINS

Finally it seemed to be Raphaël Géminiani's year to win the Tour de France, after he had come second in 1951 and had helped Louison Bobet to win three Tours.

Seeking revenge for not being selected for the French national team, Géminiani had waged constant war on his higher-status compatriots

and, at the start of stage 21, was in the yellow jersey, with nearly 4 minutes on his closest rival, Italian Vito Favero.

Stage 21 featured five mountains. Bad weather moved in after the first climb up the Lautaret while punctures wreaked havoc on the descent. On the next climb Charly Gaul, 16 minutes behind on the general classification, decided to attack. Everyone assumed he was simply going for King of the Mountains points. Géminiani

1. Charly Gaul seemed immune to the cold and rain as he summited the Col de Porte. Further down the mountain Jacques Anquetil, the previous year's winner, was falling apart. 'From the first hair pins I think I'm going mad. I am diminished by 60 per cent. Why? I would like to understand. It's as if my lungs were stuffed with cotton. I suffocate,' he said. The following evening he would abandon, suffering from bronchopneumonia.

Grenoble

Col de Porte

Les Seiglières

Rochetaillée

2. The miserable conditions were perfect for the climber from Luxembourg, who suffered on hot stages. His ride had had such a devastating impact on the peloton that race commissars decided not to enforce time limits to eliminate the last riders.

3. Charly Gaul solos into the finish in pouring rain. His gap on Jan Adriaenssens who came second, was sufficient to give enough time for Gaul to shower and change his clothing.

Col du Lautaret

From Briançon

'Charly is a rider like no other. Raphaël loses 14 minutes. I lost 19 minutes and Jacques, who I escorted for a bit, lost 23! Those kinds of gaps aren't made any more, those are the gaps from the pre-war Tours which makes me think Charly is perhaps a rider from the past who has strayed into our times. Actually, I don't think Charly is a man. He's superhuman.' LOUISON BOBET

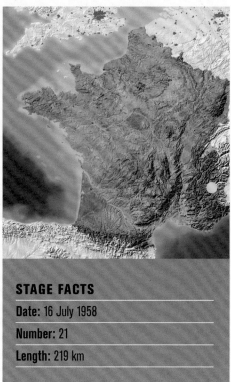

sensed something, however, and, riding with Bobet, tried to catch Gaul. But Bobet wouldn't – or, more likely, couldn't – respond. On the Col de Porte it was Jacques Anquetil's turn to crumble. Then Géminiani, who had depended on Anquetil's pace-making, panicked and forgot to eat, causing a catastrophic hunger knock later.

No-one could respond to Gaul. The peloton broke up entirely, riders working together in twos or threes or simply abandoning in tears. By the race finish Gaul had 8 minutes on the next rider, Jan Adriaenssens, and 14½ on Géminiani. Favero was now in yellow with a 39-second lead. Gaul was in third place just over a minute behind and would win the Tour.

STAGE FACTS

Date: 16 July 1958

Number: 21

Length: 219 km

Chambéry

To Aix-les-Bains

4. Raphaël Géminiani was distraught at losing the yellow jersey. 'All Judases!' he cried, referring in particular to Louison Bobet who failed to help him after the summit of the Luitel. He couldn't see the irony that these were the same riders he'd attacked since the Tour had begun in Belgium.

BEFORE STAGE 21

1 Raphaël Géminiani (Fra)
2 Vito Favero (Ita)
at 3'47"
3 Jacques Anquetil (Fra)
at 7'52"

Jean Graczyk (Fra)

KING OF THE MOUNTAINS
Federico Bahamontes (Spa)

AFTER STAGE 21

1 Vito Favero (Ita)
2 Raphaël Géminiani (Fra)
at 0'39"
3 Charly Gaul (Lux)
at 1'07"

Jean Graczyk (Fra)

KING OF THE MOUNTAINS
Federico Bahamontes (Spa)

ANGEL OF THE MOUNTAINS

Charly Gaul was a brilliant climber, nicknamed 'the Angel of the Mountains' by L'Équipe. Like his compatriot François Faber, who won the Tour in 1909, he excelled in the sort of adverse weather that made even the toughest riders abandon, such as in the 1956 Giro, when 57 riders climbed off their bikes during a blizzard in the Dolomites.

Unusually for a climber, he was also an excellent time triallist, winning all three time trials in the 1958 Tour and even beating the master, Jacques Anquetil (who, it must be said, was unwell and would eventually abandon).

Gaul had the talent to win more Tours, and was certainly the rival everyone watched, but he did not fare well in hot weather and could be dramatically inconsistent, a rider whose grand gestures could be followed by crashing defeats.

He had few friends and often blamed his team-mates for his failures; since Luxembourg was too small to field a national team, Gaul would ride with a mixed bunch of Swiss, Dutch or British riders, whom he accused of riding for themselves. He refused to share his race winnings with them which, of course, didn't help gain him friends.

A fatal momentary mistake

DIJON > PARIS

It had been a Tour with all the excitement of a thriller – crushing setbacks followed by improbable comebacks, and stages won and lost by the sort of intervals associated with pre-war years. The yellow jersey had changed hands right until the time trial on the penultimate stage. It had also been an exhausting Tour, with no rest days, ridden at a record average speed of 36.9 km/hour. The final 320-km stage was also the longest, so the riders could be forgiven for taking things easy. A number of attacks towards the end, however, saw the peloton split in two and a sprint finish contested on the Parc des Princes velodrome.

Coming into the final 200 m, André Darrigade was two bike lengths ahead of the Italian Pierino Baffi and about to win the

1. Charly Gaul preens his hair ahead of the final stage into Paris, proving the cliché that cyclists are rather preoccupied with their looks. Hugo Koblet kept a comb in his pocket so he could smarten up at the end of a stage, while Jacques Anquetil and Raymond Poulidor had lucrative advertising campaigns for hair products.

2. André Darrigade hurtles into the final 200 m of the Parc des Princes velodrome and is about to win the race when he collides with race official Constant Wouters.

From Dijon

Châtillon-sur-Seine

A SPRINTING GREAT

André Darrigade was a phenomenal sprinter who won the World Championship in 1959, the year after his accident. His *palmarès* includes 22 Tour stages and 16 yellow jerseys. His record of winning five opening stages of the Tour was equalled only in 2012 by Fabian Cancellara. In the same year another of Darrigade's records was broken. He had been the most successful sprinter in Tour history with 22 stage wins but Mark Cavendish broke that record, reaching 23 stages.

'My strong point was the bunch sprints, but I'm different to Mark because I could win from breaks too,' he told the *Independent* newspaper in 2012. 'I'd often win from a group of four, five or 10 riders.'

Darrigade's success is perhaps even more remarkable for the fact that, unlike modern sprinters, he had no team or lead-out train working for him. His duties first and foremost were to his team captains, such as Louison Bobet and Jacques Anquetil, and any sprints he won were done entirely on his own.

race. It would be a brilliant complement to his opening stage victory. But an official from the Parc des Princes, Constant Wouters, shooing away photographers too close to the track, had stepped onto it himself. Darrigade slammed right into him and, with horrible impact, their heads collided and both men were thrown into the air. Wouters would die in hospital 11 days later. Darrigade had a cracked skull and broken ribs, but remarkably only needed five stitches and was even able to ride a lap of honour round the track with his team.

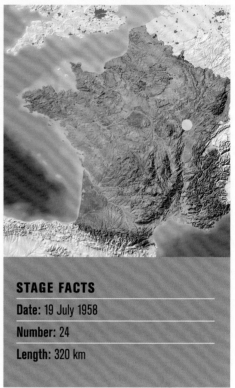

STAGE FACTS

Date: 19 July 1958

Number: 24

Length: 320 km

3. Pierino Baffi – shown here in the Giro d'Italia – won the sprint ahead of the green jersey winner Jean Graczyk. The Italian champion Gastone Nencini came third.

Brie-Comte-Robert

To Paris

4. André Darrigade, after being bandaged and receiving initial stitches, returns to the velodrome where he is supported by Charly Gaul. Despite a fractured skull, he would go on to come third in the World Championships later that year.

'Darrigade was the greatest French sprinter of all time and he'll stay that way for a long time. The mould has been broken. But he wasn't just a sprinter. He was an *animateur* who could start decisive breaks; he destroyed the image of sprinters who just sit on wheels.'
RAPHAËL GÉMINIANI

BEFORE STAGE 24	AFTER STAGE 24
1 Charly Gaul (Lux)	1 Charly Gaul (Lux)
2 Vito Favero (Ita) at 3'10"	2 Vito Favero (Ita) at 3'10"
3 Raphaël Géminiani (Fra) at 3'41"	3 Raphaël Géminiani (Fra) at 3'41"
Jean Graczyk (Fra)	Jean Graczyk (Fra)

KING OF THE MOUNTAINS
Federico Bahamontes (Spa)

KING OF THE MOUNTAINS
Federico Bahamontes (Spa)

1960

Rivière's career ends in ravine

MILLAU > AVIGNON

Roger Rivière was one of the brightest hopes of French cycling, a rival to Jacques Anquetil. In 1960 he won the time trial on stage 2 but it was his team-mate Henry Anglade who took the yellow jersey three days later. On stage 6 Rivière went on the attack with the Italian ace Gastone Nencini and the Belgian Jan Adriaenssens in his wake.

Rivière won the stage but his efforts lost the team its yellow jersey, which now went to the Belgian. Anglade bitterly complained, 'We've just lost the Tour.'

'He'll make mistakes,' Anglade is quoted as saying in *L'Équipe*. 'He'll try to follow Nencini on the descents, and one day it'll go wrong. You saw how close he came to losing control on the Aspin last year.' Anglade was disturbingly prophetic. By stage 14 Rivière

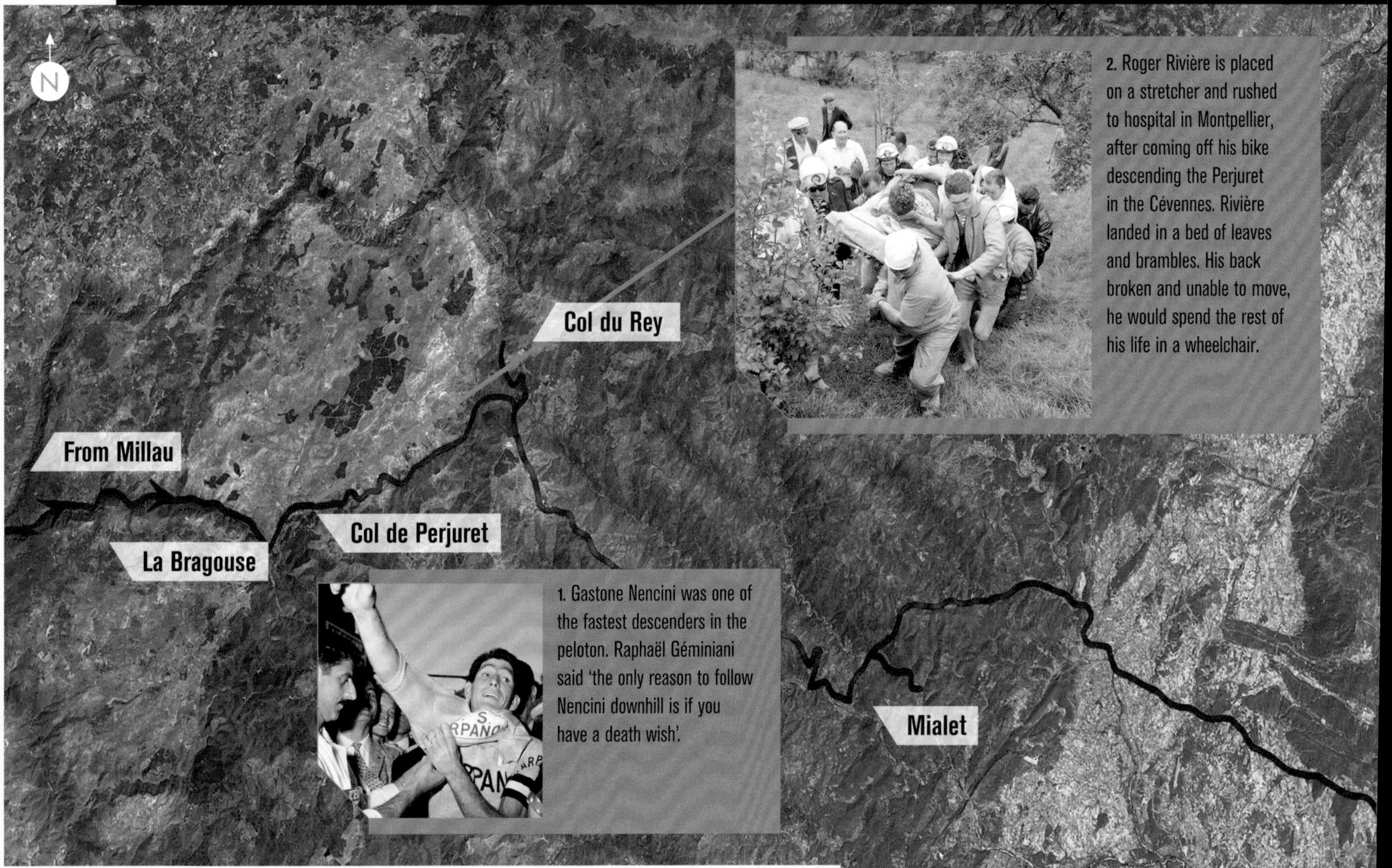

2. Roger Rivière is placed on a stretcher and rushed to hospital in Montpellier, after coming off his bike descending the Perjuret in the Cévennes. Rivière landed in a bed of leaves and brambles. His back broken and unable to move, he would spend the rest of his life in a wheelchair.

1. Gastone Nencini was one of the fastest descenders in the peloton. Raphaël Géminiani said 'the only reason to follow Nencini downhill is if you have a death wish'.

'Roger was going to win the Tour. I've never seen him so relaxed and well rested in a stage race. I had gone to see him in Millau. He was in excellent spirits, and now he's suffering in this room. He doesn't know where to lie. He won't stop repeating, "My back… my back… it hurts!" And then his legs are numb, he can already see himself an invalid in a wheelchair. It's dreadful. He is certain that his career is over, and what am I supposed to say to him?… I'm in the dark, just like he is.' HUGETTE, RIVIÈRE'S WIFE, BEFORE THE DOCTORS CONFIRMED HIS BACK WAS BROKEN.

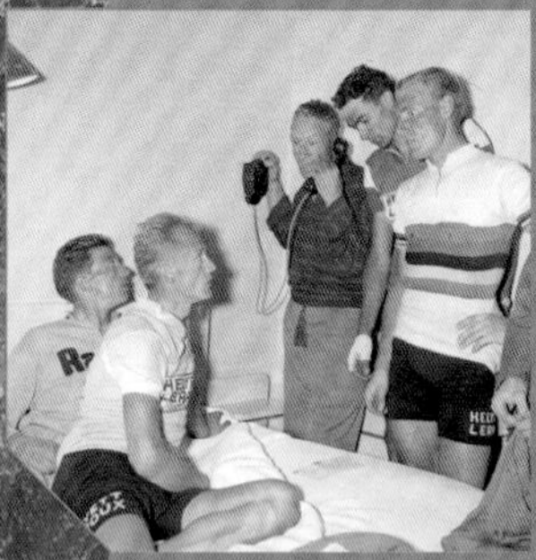

3. Rivière's team-mates (left to right) Pierre Everaert, Jean Graczyck, Louis Rostollan and André Darrigade wait anxiously, while team manager Marcel Bidot rings the hospital for news on Rivière's condition.

was in second place on general classification, 1 minute 38 seconds behind Nencini, now in yellow. If Rivière could avoid losing time on Nencini in the mountains, he was certain to win the Tour on the final time trial.

Nencini was the fastest descender in the peloton, however, an apparently fearless, masterful bike handler; talents Rivière lacked. Coming down the Col de Perjuret in the Cévennes, Rivière failed to pull hard enough on his brakes and flew over a wall into a ravine some 20 m deep. He broke his back and would never walk again.

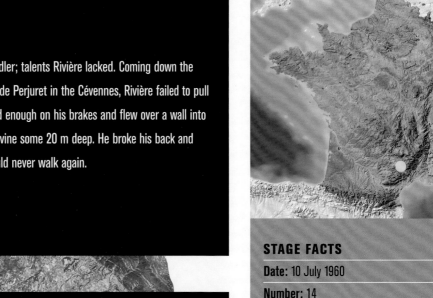

STAGE FACTS

Date: 10 July 1960

Number: 14

Length: 217 km

ROGER RIVIÈRE

Born in Saint-Étienne, Roger Rivière was equally talented on the track and the road. In 1957, the year he turned professional, he set a new hour record which stood for nine years. When he was 19 he beat Jacques Anquetil to win the national pursuit championship and became world pursuit champion three years running, from 1957 to 1959.

Initially he blamed the team mechanic for his accident, claiming the brakes had been incorrectly fitted. When the mechanic protested, the mangled frame of Rivière's bike was examined and the brakes were found to be in perfect working order. Later it transpired that Rivière had taken an opiate called palfium, a powerful painkiller three times the strength of morphine, which would have slowed his reaction time and made it impossible for him to judge how hard – if at all – he pulled on the brakes. Eventually Rivière sold his story to a newspaper, admitting his use of drugs on that stage. He also confessed that he had taken amphetamines and solucamphor when he set the hour record.

He opened a restaurant, then a garage, then a holiday camp, all of which failed, and died of throat cancer at the age of 40.

4. Nencini went on to win the Tour. In Paris he gave his victory bouquet to Marcel Bidot, the French team manager, and asked him to give it to Rivière.

Uzès

Bégude-de-Sare

To Avignon

BEFORE STAGE 14

1 Gastone Nencini (Ita)
2 Roger Rivière (Fra)
at 1'38"
3 Jan Adriaenssens (Bel)
at 2'25"

Jean Graczyk (Fra)

KING OF THE MOUNTAINS
Gastone Nencini (Ita) &
Kurt Gimmi (Swi)

AFTER STAGE 14

1 Gastone Nencini (Ita)
2 Jan Adriaenssens (Bel)
at 2'25"
3 Graziano Battistini (Ita)
at 6'00"

Jean Graczyk (Fra)

KING OF THE MOUNTAINS
Gastone Nencini (Ita)

Maître Jacques rules from the off

ROUEN > VERSAILLES

Jacques Anquetil had won the Tour in 1957 on his first outing. In 1958 he'd caught pneumonia, in 1959 he was distracted by a rivalry with team-mate Roger Rivière and in 1960 he didn't take part. In 1961 he announced to his team that he would take the yellow jersey on the first day and keep it all the way to Paris.

Day 1 consisted of two stages: a 136.5-km road race that began in Anquetil's home town of Rouen, followed by a 28.5-km time trial in Versailles. That morning Anquetil got into a break, at around 50 km, which included his team-mates André Darrigade and Joseph Groussard, and four Italians. Darrigade won the sprint; it was a record fifth time that he'd won the first stage in a Tour. The group finished with a margin of nearly 5 minutes over Anquetil's main rivals.

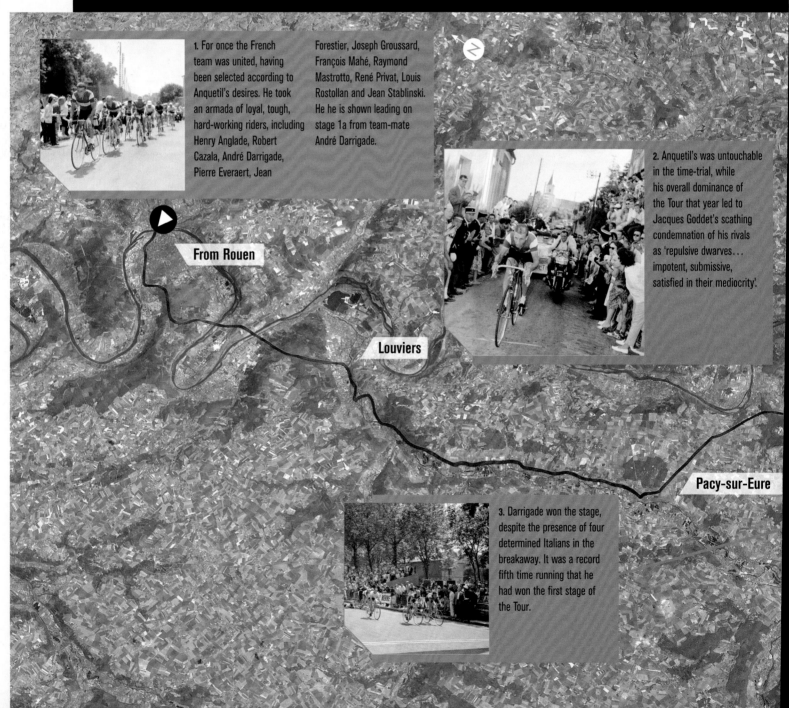

1. For once the French team was united, having been selected according to Anquetil's desires. He took an armada of loyal, tough, hard-working riders, including Henry Anglade, Robert Cazala, André Darrigade, Pierre Everaert, Jean Forestier, Joseph Groussard, François Mahé, Raymond Mastrotto, René Privat, Louis Rostollan and Jean Stablinski. He he is shown leading on stage 1a from team-mate André Darrigade.

From Rouen

Louviers

Pacy-sur-Eure

2. Anquetil's was untouchable in the time-trial, while his overall dominance of the Tour that year led to Jacques Goddet's scathing condemnation of his rivals as 'repulsive dwarves... impotent, submissive, satisfied in their mediocrity'.

3. Darrigade won the stage, despite the presence of four determined Italians in the breakaway. It was a record fifth time running that he had won the first stage of the Tour.

Darrigade's lead didn't last long, however. Anquetil's domination of the time trial that afternoon was so complete that, with an average speed of 43 km/hour, he finished 2½ minutes ahead of the second-place finisher Albert Bouvet.

It was a staggering display of dominance. In just the first day Anquetil had a lead of 4 minutes 46 seconds over the next rider, and more than 8 minutes over his rival Charly Gaul. The Tour was already won.

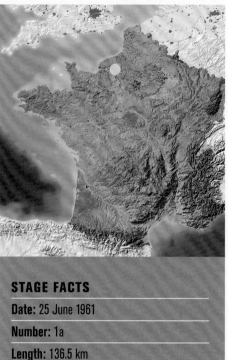

STAGE FACTS

Date: 25 June 1961

Number: 1a

Length: 136.5 km

JACQUES ANQUETIL

Jacques Anquetil was the first rider ever to win five Tours. While he could ride with the best in the mountains, it was said this was primarily thanks to his exceptional capacity to suffer. His speciality was his mastery of the time trial with which he won all his Tours.

While he was a notorious *bon viveur* who paid little heed to diet, he was meticulous in his training and preparation for the race against the clock. He was also a pioneer in developing techniques that reduced wind resistance while maximizing efficiency in pedalling and energy expenditure. He paid attention to the smallest details, from the wind direction (and predicting how it would affect him later in the course) to ensuring he rode on the part of the road most 'polished' by car wheels to minimize rolling resistance.

'You have to know how to cope with and subdue pain, to be deaf to your body's screams. If you can do that to yourself, you can improve your performance by 30 per cent.' JACQUES ANQUETIL

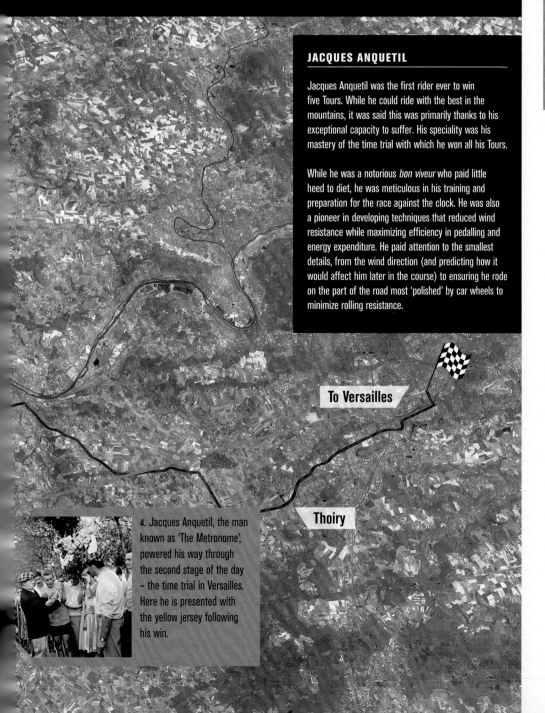

To Versailles

Thoiry

4. Jacques Anquetil, the man known as 'The Metronome', powered his way through the second stage of the day – the time trial in Versailles. Here he is presented with the yellow jersey following his win.

AFTER STAGE 1a

1 André Darrigade (Fra)
2 Mario Minieri (Ita)
at 0'15"
3 Jean Gainche (Fra)
at 0'30"

1962

A British first

PAU > SAINT-GAUDENS

Stage 12 was a 207.5-km epic featuring the Col du Tourmalet, Col d'Aspin and the Col de Peyresourde. Spanish climber Federico Bahamontes was the first to cross all three peaks although, by the summit of the Peyresourde, he had Rolf Wolfshohl and Imerio Massignan for company.

There were 60 km left to Saint-Gaudens, and 1½ minutes behind the trio a formidable chase group contained the likes of Jacques Anquetil, Charly Gaul and Raymond Poulidor, Hans Junkermann, Raymond Mastrotto and Jef Planckaert. Also in the mix was Tom Simpson, a British rider in third place on the general classification. Bahamontes' terrible descending was compounded by a puncture and he was soon overhauled. Massignan held out

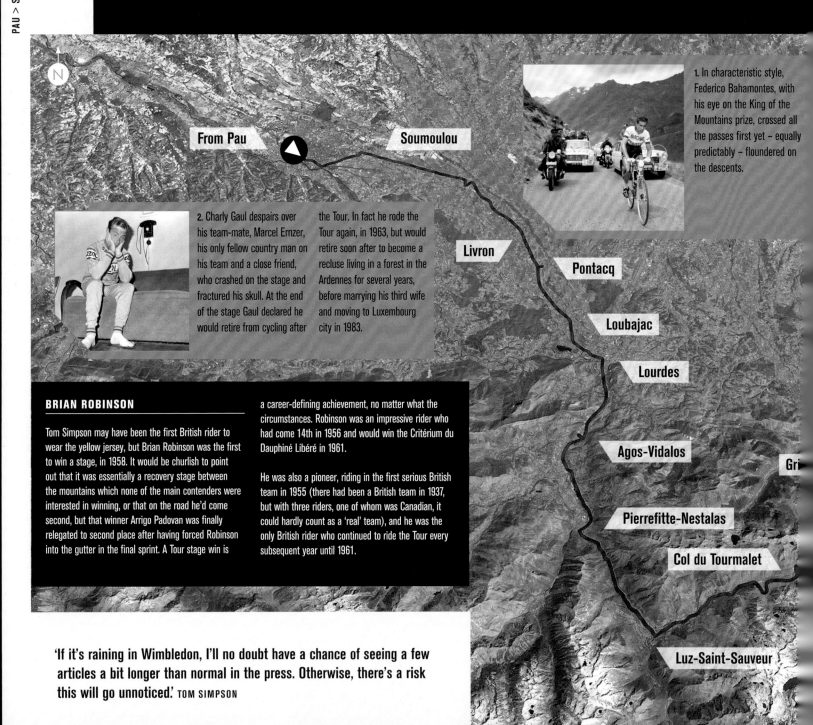

1. In characteristic style, Federico Bahamontes, with his eye on the King of the Mountains prize, crossed all the passes first yet – equally predictably – floundered on the descents.

2. Charly Gaul despairs over his team-mate, Marcel Ernzer, his only fellow country man on his team and a close friend, who crashed on the stage and fractured his skull. At the end of the stage Gaul declared he would retire from cycling after the Tour. In fact he rode the Tour again, in 1963, but would retire soon after to become a recluse living in a forest in the Ardennes for several years, before marrying his third wife and moving to Luxembourg city in 1983.

From Pau

Soumoulou

Livron

Pontacq

Loubajac

Lourdes

Agos-Vidalos

Gri

Pierrefitte-Nestalas

Col du Tourmalet

Luz-Saint-Sauveur

BRIAN ROBINSON

Tom Simpson may have been the first British rider to wear the yellow jersey, but Brian Robinson was the first to win a stage, in 1958. It would be churlish to point out that it was essentially a recovery stage between the mountains which none of the main contenders were interested in winning, or that on the road he'd come second, but that winner Arrigo Padovan was finally relegated to second place after having forced Robinson into the gutter in the final sprint. A Tour stage win is a career-defining achievement, no matter what the circumstances. Robinson was an impressive rider who had come 14th in 1956 and would win the Critérium du Dauphiné Libéré in 1961.

He was also a pioneer, riding in the first serious British team in 1955 (there had been a British team in 1937, but with three riders, one of whom was Canadian, it could hardly count as a 'real' team), and he was the only British rider who continued to ride the Tour every subsequent year until 1961.

'If it's raining in Wimbledon, I'll no doubt have a chance of seeing a few articles a bit longer than normal in the press. Otherwise, there's a risk this will go unnoticed.' TOM SIMPSON

until the last 10 km, while Wolfshohl's valiant battle was neutralized less than 3 km from the end. The stage finished in a 22-man sprint won by Poulidor's team-mate Robert Cazala.

The rest of the field had been torn apart, with the top two riders on that morning's general classification, Willy Schroeders and André Darrigade, finishing almost 9 minutes later. Simpson became the first British rider ever to wear the yellow jersey. He lost it the following day, but went on to finish the Tour in sixth place, another British record. It appeared to be the start of a new era for British cycling.

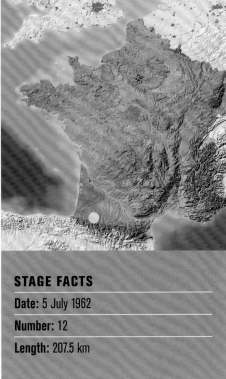

123

1962

STAGE FACTS

Date: 5 July 1962

Number: 12

Length: 207.5 km

4. Simpson poses in the yellow jersey, with the obligatory cup of tea, bowler hat and umbrella. The French were delighted by the novelty of a British yellow jersey, Jacques Goddet speculating that the British press would now pay more attention to what he translated into English as the 'yellow jacket'. He added 'Let us hope that this happy achievement stimulates British cycling, that it will bring fresh blood, and relegate among the mothballs those alpaca blazers that constitute the obligatory race uniform of English velocipedes'.

3. Robert Cazala, one of Raymond Poulidor's strong men, wins the sprint finish ahead of all the top riders of that year's Tour.

To Saint-Gaudens

Loures-Barousse

La Séoube

Col d'Aspin

Cierp

Arreau

Anéran-Camors

Saint-Aventin

Col de Peyresourde

Luchon

BEFORE STAGE 12

1 Willy Schroeders (Bel)
2 André Darrigade (Fra) at 0'45"
3 Tom Simpson (UK) at 1'36"

Rudi Altig (Ger) &
Jean Graczyk (Fra)

KING OF THE MOUNTAINS
Rolf Wolfshohl (Ger)

AFTER STAGE 12

1 Tom Simpson (UK)
2 Albertus Geldermans (Ned) at 0'30"
3 Gilbert Desmet (Bel) at 1'08"

Rudi Altig (Ger) &
Jean Graczyk (Fra)

KING OF THE MOUNTAINS
Federico Bahamontes (Spa)

1962

Staggering heights, crushing lows

JUAN-LES-PINS > BRIANÇON

Time was running out for those with ambitions to win the 1962 Tour de France. Belgian Joseph Planckaert was in the race lead, with Jacques Anquetil just over a minute behind. The other three contenders, Imerio Massignan, Charly Gaul and Raymond Poulidor, were a further 7–9 minutes back.

Stage 18 promised an inaugural outing up the 2,802-m Col de Restefond or Col de la Bonette – 25.8 km of ascent on the highest paved road in France. Federico Bahamontes was the first to summit the Restefond, with 1 minute 45 seconds to spare, over relatively unknown Belgian, Eddy Pauwels, and the favourites a further 2½ minutes back. Despite two punctures and a crash, Pauwels overtook Bahamontes on the descent, then put 4 minutes

1. Bleeding and covered in road rash from two crashes, Eddy Pauwels continued his heroic ride, only to puncture and be overtaken shortly before the final summit of the Izoard.

2. Pauwels crashed for the third time on the Izoard. He is helped on his way by former Tour winner Louison Bobet, who wasn't riding and would shortly announce his official retirement.

3. Planckaert rides defensively, marking Anquetil's every move. With all the favourites finishing in the first group of eight riders, the general classification remained essentially unchanged. The only casualty was Gilbert Desmet, who moved down to fourth place, ceding second to Anquetil.

Isola

Pont de la Manda

From Juan-les-Pins

'Luck wasn't on my side. Think of it – five punctures, three crashes. That was the most disagreeable day of my life, the hardest in my entire career... the sort of day that makes you want to smash your bike.' EDDY PAUWELS

between them cresting the Col de Vars. Another crash left Pauwels with severe road rash on his neck and face yet, remarkably, he increased his lead to 6 minutes 20 seconds with 36.5 km remaining.

Everything unravelled for Pauwels on the Col d'Izoard, however. Puncturing again, he was caught by Bahamontes shortly before the summit.

A third crash cemented his misery and he finished tenth, 1½ minutes behind the winner – who should have been Anquetil, but instead was a sprinter, Émile Daems, the day's revelation. Part of a chase group that featured the favourites, Daems had miraculously made it over the mountains to put his fast-twitch muscles to good use.

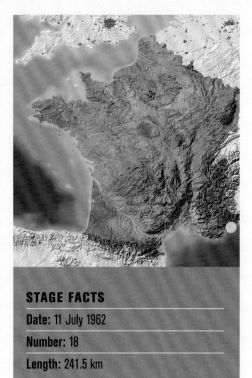

STAGE FACTS

Date: 11 July 1962

Number: 18

Length: 241.5 km

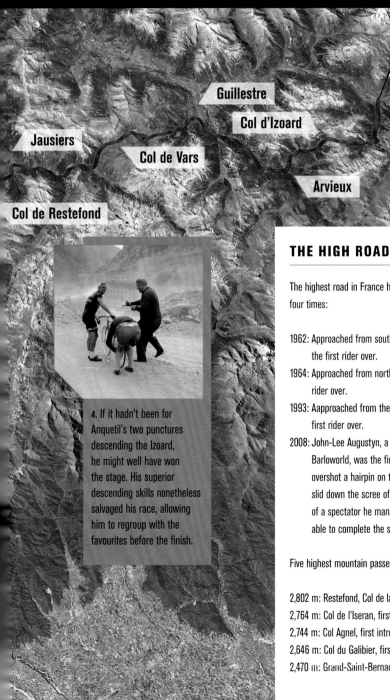

Jausiers

Col de Vars

Col de Restefond

Guillestre

Col d'Izoard

Arvieux

To Briançon

4. If it hadn't been for Anquetil's two punctures descending the Izoard, he might well have won the stage. His superior descending skills nonetheless salvaged his race, allowing him to regroup with the favourites before the finish.

THE HIGH ROAD

The highest road in France has appeared in the Tour only four times:

1962: Approached from south; Federico Bahamontes was the first rider over.

1964: Approached from north; Bahamontes was the first rider over.

1993: Aapproached from the north; Robert Millar was the first rider over.

2008: John-Lee Augustyn, a South African riding for Barloworld, was the first across the summit, but he overshot a hairpin on the descent into Jausiers and slid down the scree of the mountains. With the help of a spectator he managed to climb back up and was able to complete the stage.

Five highest mountain passes in the Tour:

2,802 m: Restefond, Col de la Bonette, first introduced 1962
2,764 m: Col de l'Iseran, first introduced in 1938
2,744 m: Col Agnel, first introduced in 2008
2,646 m: Col du Galibier, first introduced in 1911
2,470 m: Grand-Saint-Bernard, first introduced in 1949

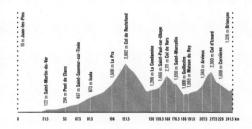

BEFORE STAGE 18

1 Joseph Planckaert (Bel)
2 Gilbert Desmet (Bel)
at 0'50"
3 Jacques Anquetil (Fra)
at 1'08"

Rudi Altig (Ger)

KING OF THE MOUNTAINS
Federico Bahamontes (Spa)

AFTER STAGE 18

1 Joseph Planckaert (Bel)
2 Jacques Anquetil (Fra)
at 1'08"
3 Tom Simpson (UK)
at 3'16"

Rudi Altig (Ger)

KING OF THE MOUNTAINS
Federico Bahamontes (Spa)

A Franco–Irish alliance

JAMBES > ROUBAIX

It was a stage for the hard men of the north – 223.5 km over narrow, paved roads used in the Paris–Brussels and Paris–Roubaix races, with conditions windy and rainy.

After 95 km, a number of escape groups had coalesced into a ten-man band of riders from most of the teams, including Jacques Anquetil's team-mates Jean Stablinski (an ex-miner and a local who, it was said, knew the roads as intimately from below as above), and his brother-in-law Seamus 'Shay' Elliott, an emerging Irish talent. The gap to the peloton kept increasing, from 4 minutes to 7, then 8½.

Responsibility for the chase fell to Anquetil and his remaining team-mates, left out to dry by the other teams, 'whose main preoccupation seems to be to drown Jacques Anquetil…even if

'I pictured my child's face and that gave me strength.' SEAMUS ELLIOTT

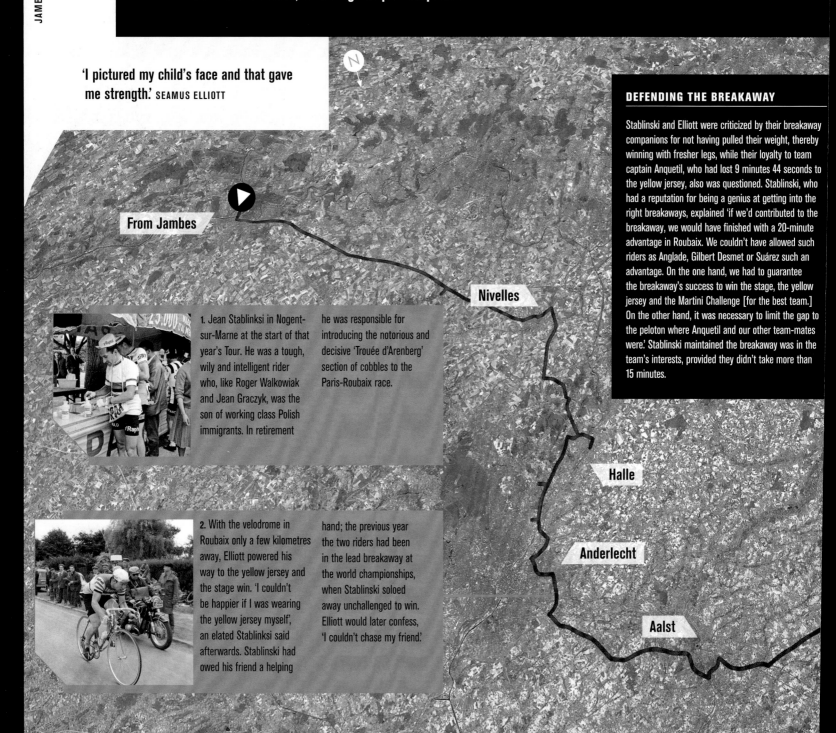

From Jambes

Nivelles

Halle

Anderlecht

Aalst

DEFENDING THE BREAKAWAY

Stablinski and Elliott were criticized by their breakaway companions for not having pulled their weight, thereby winning with fresher legs, while their loyalty to team captain Anquetil, who had lost 9 minutes 44 seconds to the yellow jersey, also was questioned. Stablinski, who had a reputation for being a genius at getting into the right breakaways, explained 'if we'd contributed to the breakaway, we would have finished with a 20-minute advantage in Roubaix. We couldn't have allowed such riders as Anglade, Gilbert Desmet or Suárez such an advantage. On the one hand, we had to guarantee the breakaway's success to win the stage, the yellow jersey and the Martini Challenge [for the best team.] On the other hand, it was necessary to limit the gap to the peloton where Anquetil and our other team-mates were.' Stablinski maintained the breakaway was in the team's interests, provided they didn't take more than 15 minutes.

1. Jean Stablinksi in Nogent-sur-Marne at the start of that year's Tour. He was a tough, wily and intelligent rider who, like Roger Walkowiak and Jean Graczyk, was the son of working class Polish immigrants. In retirement he was responsible for introducing the notorious and decisive 'Trouée d'Arenberg' section of cobbles to the Paris-Roubaix race.

2. With the velodrome in Roubaix only a few kilometres away, Elliott powered his way to the yellow jersey and the stage win. 'I couldn't be happier if I was wearing the yellow jersey myself', an elated Stablinksi said afterwards. Stablinski had owed his friend a helping hand; the previous year the two riders had been in the lead breakaway at the world championships, when Stablinski soloed away unchallenged to win. Elliott would later confess, 'I couldn't chase my friend.'

it means drowning themselves,' Jacques Goddet would comment in *L'Équipe*.

Elliott punctured twice, but both times was shepherded back to the escape group by Stablinski. Then, with 6 km to go, Stablinski initiated the winning move by launching a distracting false attack. With the big guns latched onto 'Stab', Elliott could counterattack and then time trial his way into the Roubaix velodrome to win with 8 minutes 44 seconds over the main peloton. He won the stage and Ireland's first yellow jersey, which he held for the next three days. Stablinski took the sprint for second place 33 seconds later.

STAGE FACTS

Date: 25 June 1963

Number: 3

Length: 223.5 km

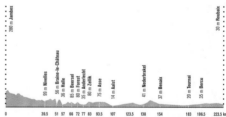

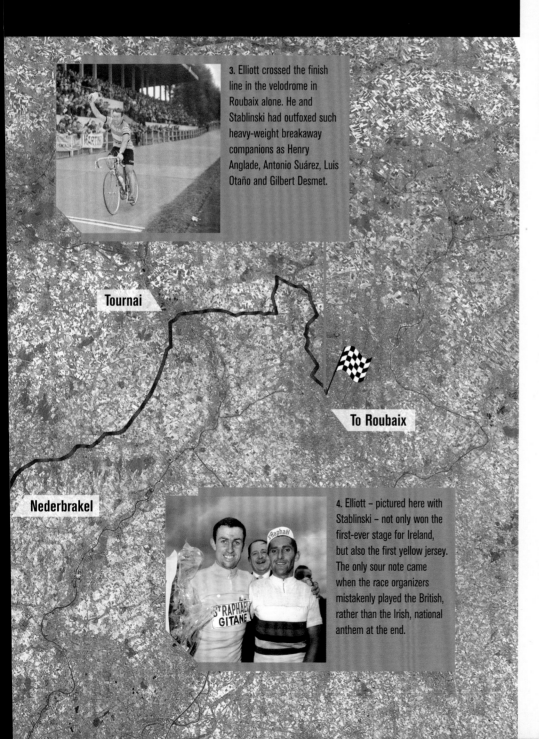

3. Elliott crossed the finish line in the velodrome in Roubaix alone. He and Stablinski had outfoxed such heavy-weight breakaway companions as Henry Anglade, Antonio Suárez, Luis Otaño and Gilbert Desmet.

Tournai

To Roubaix

Nederbrakel

4. Elliott – pictured here with Stablinski – not only won the first-ever stage for Ireland, but also the first yellow jersey. The only sour note came when the race organizers mistakenly played the British, rather than the Irish, national anthem at the end.

BEFORE STAGE 3

1 Eddy Pauwels (Bel)
2 Edgar Sorgeloos (Bel)
at 0'30"
3 Alan Ramsbottom (UK)
at 0'39"

Rik van Looy (Bel)

KING OF THE MOUNTAINS
Not available

AFTER STAGE 3

1 Seamus Elliott (Ire)
2 Henry Anglade (Fra)
at 1'14"
3 Guillaume van Tongerloo (Bel)
at 1'30"

Rik van Looy (Bel)

KING OF THE MOUNTAINS
Not available

1964

The duel on the volcano

BRIVE > PUY-DE-DÔME

Rivalry between Raymond Poulidor, perennial runner-up, and Jacques Anquetil, crusher of all opposition, reached its peak in 1964. Having won a gruelling Giro two weeks before the Tour, Anquetil was exhausted.

Only 56 seconds separated Anquetil's yellow jersey from Poulidor at the start of the stage.

If Poulidor could win or come second, he would also get a bonus of a minute or 30 seconds.

Anquetil feared the stage that would finish on the Puy-de-Dôme, an extinct volcano, featuring 11 km of agonizing climbing. The peloton was in smithereens 5.5 km into the ascent, with only four riders left in front: Federico Bahamontes in third place on general classification, new Spanish star Julio Jiménez in seventh, then

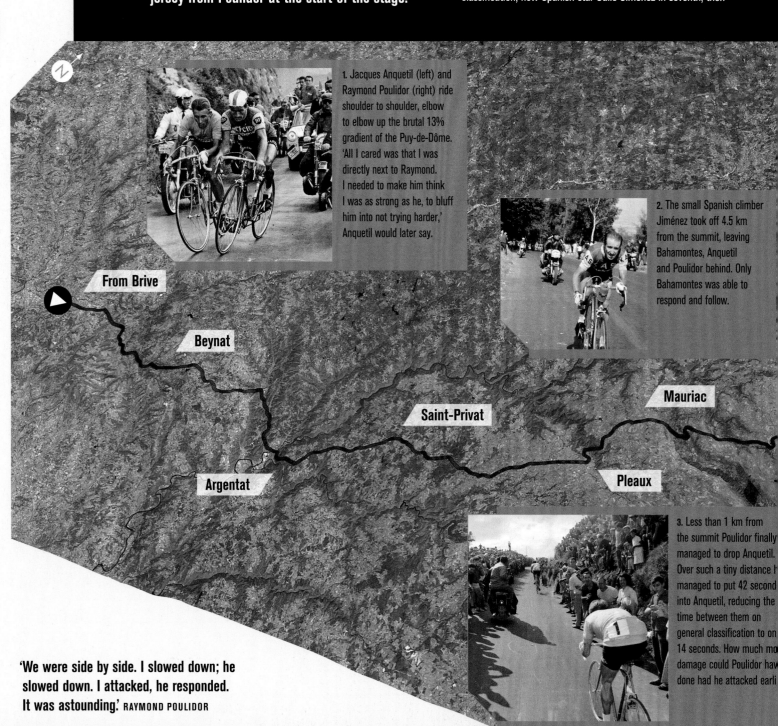

1. Jacques Anquetil (left) and Raymond Poulidor (right) ride shoulder to shoulder, elbow to elbow up the brutal 13% gradient of the Puy-de-Dôme. 'All I cared was that I was directly next to Raymond. I needed to make him think I was as strong as he, to bluff him into not trying harder,' Anquetil would later say.

2. The small Spanish climber Jiménez took off 4.5 km from the summit, leaving Bahamontes, Anquetil and Poulidor behind. Only Bahamontes was able to respond and follow.

3. Less than 1 km from the summit Poulidor finally managed to drop Anquetil. Over such a tiny distance h[e] managed to put 42 second[s] into Anquetil, reducing the time between them on general classification to on[ly] 14 seconds. How much mo[re] damage could Poulidor hav[e] done had he attacked earli[er]

From Brive

Beynat

Saint-Privat

Mauriac

Argentat

Pleaux

'We were side by side. I slowed down; he slowed down. I attacked, he responded. It was astounding.' RAYMOND POULIDOR

Poulidor and Anquetil. When 4.5 km from the summit, Jiménez attacked and was followed by Bahamontes. Poulidor couldn't follow and the Spaniards took the precious bonuses, with Jimenez winning.

Behind, Anquetil and Poulidor were locked in combat. Anquetil did all he could not to concede an inch, while Poulidor was unable to find the oxygen to attack. Finally, 950 m from the summit, Poulidor drew away. When Anquetil reached the finish line, he'd lost 42 seconds to his rival and held onto the yellow jersey by a mere 14.

'I never again felt as bad on a bike,' Poulidor later said, while Anquetil confessed, 'If he had taken the jersey from me, I would have gone home.'

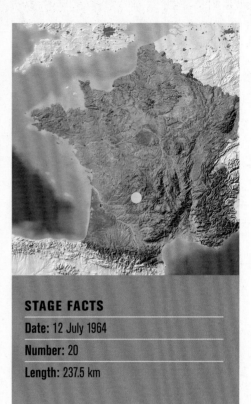

STAGE FACTS

Date: 12 July 1964

Number: 20

Length: 237.5 km

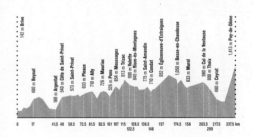

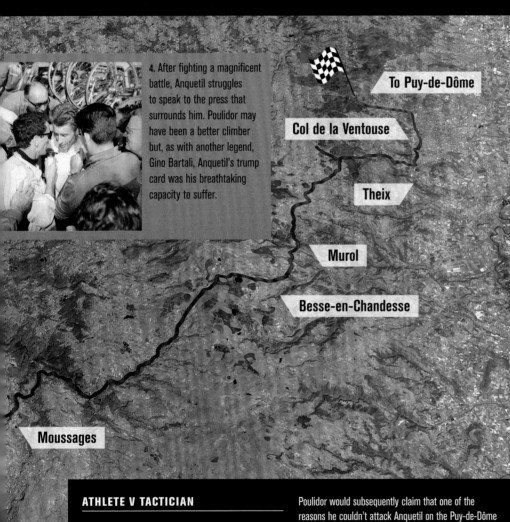

4. After fighting a magnificent battle, Anquetil struggles to speak to the press that surrounds him. Poulidor may have been a better climber but, as with another legend, Gino Bartali, Anquetil's trump card was his breathtaking capacity to suffer.

To Puy-de-Dôme

Col de la Ventouse

Theix

Murol

Besse-en-Chandesse

Moussages

ATHLETE V TACTICIAN

Was Poulidor the superior athlete, Anquetil the superior tactician? In a sport where a rider's mental state can make all the difference between winning and losing – whether it's a question of confidence, a capacity to suffer or the ability to read a race – it has been said that Poulidor's greatest weaknesses were his lack of confidence and tactical nous. Indeed it was his manager, former Tour winner Antonin Magne, who was often the Svengali behind Poulidor's finest moments, whereas Anquetil – despite riding for the wily Raphaël Géminiani – was a masterful, cool-headed tactician in his own right.

Poulidor would subsequently claim that one of the reasons he couldn't attack Anquetil on the Puy-de-Dôme was that he had chosen too big a gear, which wouldn't permit ambushing attacks. Poulidor had also failed to reconnoitre the climb prior to the Tour. But Jacques Goddet, who was behind the riders in a car as they began their ascent, would later say, 'I still think that it was in his head that Pou-Pou [Poulidor] should have changed gears.'

BEFORE STAGE 20

1 Jacques Anquetil (Fra)
2 Raymond Poulidor (Fra)
at 0'56"
3 Federico Bahamontes (Spa)
at 3'31"

Jan Janssen (Ned)

KING OF THE MOUNTAINS
Federico Bahamontes (Spa)

AFTER STAGE 20

1 Jacques Anquetil (Fra)
2 Raymond Poulidor (Fra)
at 0'14"
3 Federico Bahamontes (Spa)
at 1'33"

Jan Janssen (Ned)

KING OF THE MOUNTAINS
Federico Bahamontes (Spa)

'The Phoenix' rises

ROUBAIX > ROUEN

Everyone thought the 1965 Tour would belong to Raymond Poulidor. His arch-rival Jacques Anquetil wasn't taking part; having already won five Tours, Anquetil felt he deserved a break. He didn't hold back, however, from warning that his rival was 'in danger at some point of committing a mistake that will compromise his chances'.

The stage to Rouen saw a breakaway of two riders which struggled into headwinds for 135 km, only to eventually be reabsorbed by the peloton. Instead, the decisive attack came 8 km from the finish when ten riders, including the legendary sprinter André Darrigade, future Tour winner Roger Pingeon and a rising Italian talent, Felice Gimondi, set off. Gimondi launched a lone missile attack on the last kilometre to take a clean win.

THE ETERNAL SECOND

Raymond Poulidor had an astonishingly long career, riding the Tour 14 times and finishing on the podium eight times; even at the age of 40, in 1976, he was able to finish the Tour in third place. His career spanned two eras: that of Jacques Anquetil and that of Eddy Merckx. He has been nicknamed 'The Eternal Second', although other riders have since beaten his three second place finishes, most notably Joop Zoetemelk – who came second six times – and Jan Ullrich, who took second five times. However, both of these riders also won the Tour, which Poulidor never did. Indeed, Poulidor never even wore the yellow jersey.

1. It was a swelteringly hot Tour, which would cause several stars to abandon from sunstroke (it was suspected this was exacerbated by doping) on the later stages in the Pyrenees. For the Spanish rider Esteban Martin, this bucket of water from a group of ardent priestly fans, was probably one of the few blessings on a stage dominated by cobbles, headwinds and heat.

 Frévent

Béthune

From Roubaix

2. Even Gimondi's team had underestimated his potential, including him at the last minute when another rider pulled out. But, aside from two days when the jersey was worn by the Belgian Bernard van de Kerckhove, Gimondi would lead the Tour all the way to the finish.

3. Gimondi takes a gamble and solos into the finish, a 'Campionissimo' in the making. Gimondi had come third in that year's Giro d'Italia, despite fulfilling duties as a domestique, and the previous year had won the Tour de l'Avenir. His was certainly not a talent to be underestimated, as Poulidor discovered.

It was the 22-year-old's first victory in his first year among the professionals. Having come second the previous day, he also took the yellow jersey, with 3 minutes 23 seconds over Poulidor.

Poulidor's mistake was to assume that the rider who would become known as 'The Phoenix' would falter in the mountains. But, apart from two days when he briefly relinquished it, Gimondi kept the yellow jersey for the rest of the Tour, even winning a mountain time trial that Poulidor had also assumed was his.

'I'm as happy as if I had won myself.'
VITTORIO ADORNI, GIMONDI'S CAPTAIN AND WINNER OF THE 1965 GIRO D'ITALIA.

STAGE FACTS
Date: 24 June 1965
Number: 3
Length: 240 km

Abbeville   Buchy   To Rouen

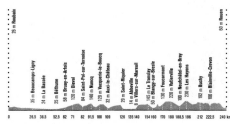

4. Gimondi on the final podium in Paris, three weeks later, with second-placed Raymond Poulidor to the left and third-placed Gianni Motta on the right. No-one had expected the 22-year-old rookie to win the Tour on his first outing. A bright future lay ahead, yet it was his only Tour win – the Giro had greater priority for Gimondi, which he went on to win three times.

BEFORE STAGE 3	AFTER STAGE 3
1 Bernard van de Kerckhove (Bel)	1 Felice Gimondi (Ita)
2 Felice Gimondi (Ita) at 0'53"	2 Bernard van de Kerckhove (Bel) at 0'39"
3 Arie den Hartog (Ned) at 1'18"	3 Cees Haast (Ned) at 1'39"
Bernard van de Kerckhove (Bel)	Felice Gimondi (Ita)
KING OF THE MOUNTAINS Frans Brands (Bel)	KING OF THE MOUNTAINS Frans Brands (Bel)

Errandonea wins first prologue

PROLOGUE: ANGERS

Short prologue time trials had already been introduced on a number of other big cycling races, most notably the Vuelta a España and, initially, Paris–Nice. The idea behind a short opening time trial is that it establishes a hierarchy among the riders right from the beginning of a race – making it more likely, in theory, that riders will attempt to regain time lost in such a test, resulting in more aggressive tactics.

The Tour's very first prologue almost resulted in a long-awaited first appearance in the winning yellow jersey for perennial nearly man Raymond Poulidor, the Eternal Second. The race was being run under national team format again, with Poulidor considered to be France's number one contender. And indeed, he quickly

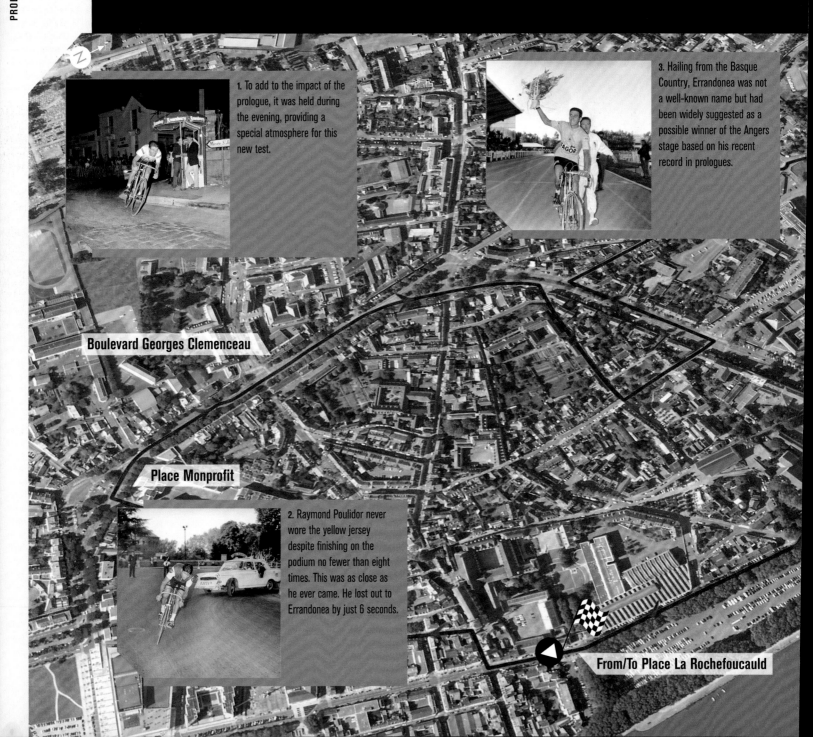

1. To add to the impact of the prologue, it was held during the evening, providing a special atmosphere for this new test.

3. Hailing from the Basque Country, Errandonea was not a well-known name but had been widely suggested as a possible winner of the Angers stage based on his recent record in prologues.

Boulevard Georges Clemenceau

Place Monprofit

2. Raymond Poulidor never wore the yellow jersey despite finishing on the podium no fewer than eight times. This was as close as he ever came. He lost out to Errandonea by just 6 seconds.

From/To Place La Rochefoucauld

asserted himself by beating all of his main rivals in the 5.775-km test in Angers.

However, Poulidor was upstaged by Spaniard José María Errandonea. Although this was only his second Tour appearance – and it turned out to be his last – Errandonea had already established himself as a prologue specialist on the back of wins at the Vuelta and the Tour of Switzerland. He covered the course a second a kilometre faster than Poulidor, much to the dismay of the evening-time crowds in Angers.

Errandonea held the lead for just two days before he abandoned the race suffering, according to *L'Équipe*'s Pierre Chany, from the effects of anthrax.

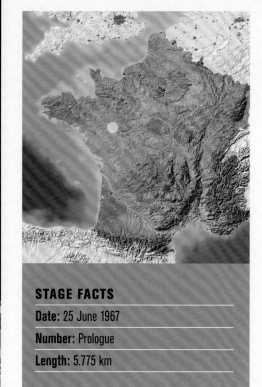

STAGE FACTS

Date: 25 June 1967

Number: Prologue

Length: 5.775 km

Rue du Figuier

Rue Braille

Rue Larrey

Pont de la Haute Chaîne

4. Although far from all of the feedback on the prologue was positive, with one report suggesting that the test didn't fit in with the fantastic nature of the challenge the Tour had always presented, Tour directors Jacques Goddet and Félix Lévitan were very encouraged by events in Angers.

PROLOGUE WINNERS

1967: José María Errandonea (Spa) in Angers
1968: Charly Grosskost (Fra) in Vittel
1969: Rudi Altig (Ger) in Roubaix
1970: Eddy Merckx (Bel) in Limoges
1971: Molteni in Mulhouse – run as team time trial
1972: Eddy Merckx (Bel) in Angers
1973: Joop Zoetemelk (Ned) in Scheveningen
1974: Eddy Merckx (Bel) in Brest
1975: Francesco Moser (Ita) in Charleroi
1976: Freddy Maertens (Bel) in Saint-Jean-de-Monts
1977: Dietrich Thurau (Ger) in Fleurance
1978: Jan Raas (Ned) in Leiden
1979: Gerrie Knetemann (Ned) in Fleurance
1980: Bernard Hinault (Fra) in Frankfurt
1981: Bernard Hinault (Fra) in Nice
1982: Bernard Hinault (Fra) in Basle
1983: Eric Vanderaerden (Bel) in Fontenay-sous-Bois
1984: Bernard Hinault (Fra) in Montreuil-sous-Bois
1985: Bernard Hinault (Fra) in Plumelec
1986: Thierry Marie (Fra) in Boulogne-Billancourt

1987: Jelle Nijdam (Ned) in West Berlin
1989: Erik Breukink (Ned) in Luxembourg
1990: Thierry Marie (Fra) in Futuroscope
1991: Thierry Marie (Fra) in Lyon
1992: Miguel Indurain (Spa) in San Sebastián
1992: Miguel Indurain (Spa) in Le Puy de Fou
1994: Chris Boardman (UK) in Lille
1995: Jacky Durand (Fra) in Saint-Brieuc
1996: Alex Zülle (Swi) in 's-Hertogenbosch
1997: Chris Boardman (UK) in Rouen
1998: Chris Boardman (UK) in Dublin
1999: Lance Armstrong (USA) in Le Puy de Fou
2000: David Millar (UK) in Futuroscope
2001: Christophe Moreau (Fra) in Dunkerque
2002: Lance Armstrong (USA) in Luxembourg
2003: Bradley McGee (Aus) in Paris
2004: Fabian Cancellara (Swi) in Liège
2006: Thor Hushovd (Nor) in Strasbourg
2007: Fabian Cancellara (Swi) in London
2010: Fabian Cancellara (Swi) in Rotterdam
2012: Fabian Cancellara (Swi) in Liège

AFTER PROLOGUE

1 José María Errandonea (Spa)
2 Raymond Poulidor (Fra)
at 0'06"
3 Jan Janssen (Ned)
at 0'10"

José María Errandonea (Spa)

'I thought I would do a good time, but winning the prologue was a real surprise – but a good one.' JOSÉ MARÍA ERRANDONEA

Shadow cast by Simpson's death

MARSEILLE > CARPENTRAS

One of the sport's great personalities and hugely popular among his peers, Tom Simpson believed that the 1967 Tour offered him his best chance ever of taking overall victory. In Marseille, prior to the start of the stage over Mont Ventoux, Simpson still believed, even though he was seventh place, 8 minutes down on race leader Roger Pingeon.

The day started hotter and got hotter, reaching 45°C (113°F). The temperatures were higher still on the road.

Although Simpson did not go with the attack made by Julio Jiménez and Raymond Poulidor on the early slopes of the Ventoux, he was not far behind in a group also containing defending champion Lucien Aimar. Emerging from the trees below Chalet Reynard, where the road enters the Ventoux's

'His gaiety in the peloton made all of us forget the difficult hours required in our job.' ROGER PINGEON

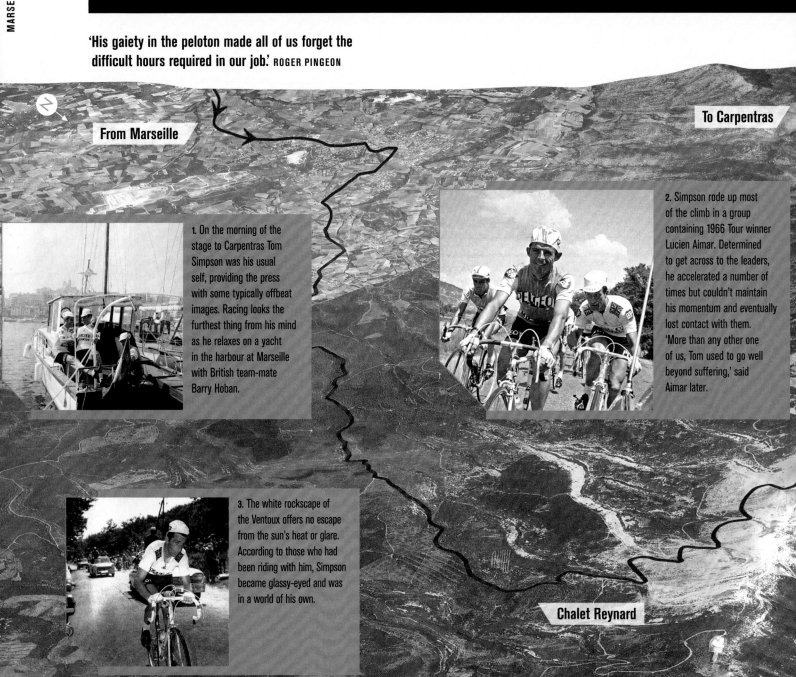

From Marseille

To Carpentras

1. On the morning of the stage to Carpentras Tom Simpson was his usual self, providing the press with some typically offbeat images. Racing looks the furthest thing from his mind as he relaxes on a yacht in the harbour at Marseille with British team-mate Barry Hoban.

2. Simpson rode up most of the climb in a group containing 1966 Tour winner Lucien Aimar. Determined to get across to the leaders, he accelerated a number of times but couldn't maintain his momentum and eventually lost contact with them. 'More than any other one of us, Tom used to go well beyond suffering,' said Aimar later.

3. The white rockscape of the Ventoux offers no escape from the sun's heat or glare. According to those who had been riding with him, Simpson became glassy-eyed and was in a world of his own.

Chalet Reynard

bare moonscape, Simpson attempted to ride away from his group, but couldn't maintain his pace.

Instead, he gradually fell behind them and began to zigzag across the road. With 3 km to the summit, he fell to the ground and was helped back on to his bike by fans at the roadside. Another 350 m on, he fell again. A fan administered mouth-to-mouth resuscitation as Simpson lay at the roadside. The Tour's doctor, Pierre Dumas, was quickly on the scene and continued the treatment. A helicopter was summoned to take the stricken Briton to hospital in Avignon where, at 17.40, his death was confirmed.

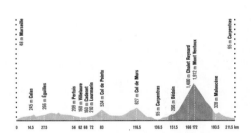

STAGE FACTS

Date: 13 July 1967

Number: 13

Length: 211.5 km

4. Although legend has it that Simpson told those attending to him to 'put me back on my bike', he was barely conscious when he fell to the ground and never came round again. An inquest later revealed he had suffered a cardiac arrest, which was attributed to the heat and the amphetamines he had taken, some of which were found in his jersey pockets.

Mont Ventoux

TRAGIC ENDS FOR TOUR HEROES

Although there have been relatively few fatal incidents on the roads of the Tour de France, a number of renowned Tour performers have died in other events:

Ottavio Bottecchia: Having gone out on a training ride, Italy's 1924 and 1925 Tour winner was found dead at the roadside near Gemona in Italy with a skull fracture (see page 67).

Stan Ockers: Twice the Tour runner-up and points champion in 1956, the Belgian died when he crashed racing behind a Derny motorbike on the Antwerp track in September 1956.

Russell Mockridge: One of Australia's Tour pioneers, he rode and finished the 1955 Tour. He died in 1958 after being hit by a bus before the start of the Tour of Gippsland.

José Samyn: The Frenchman was the youngest rider in the 1967 race and won the stage into Digne. Selected for the French team in 1968, he died a year later from head injuries sustained during a Belgian criterium.

Joaquim Agostinho: Four times a stage winner and twice third overall, the Portuguese died when a dog ran into his wheels during the 1984 Tour of the Algarve.

Antonio Martín: Winner of the best young rider prize at the 1993 Tour, the Spaniard died in Febuary 1994 after being hit by a car while training.

Ricardo Otxoa: The Kelme rider died after he and his brother Javier were hit by a car while training in southern Spain in 2001. Javier Otxoa had won the Hautacam stage at the 2000 Tour. Although he survived, Javier's injuries meant he never raced professionally again, although he has many Paralympic medals.

Andrei Kivilev: Fourth in the 2001 Tour de France, the Kazakh died two years later when he crashed on the Paris–Nice stage into Saint-Étienne, suffering serious head injuries. His death led to the wearing of helmets becoming compulsory.

BEFORE STAGE 13

1 Roger Pingeon (Fra)
2 Désiré Letort (Fra)
at 4'02"
3 Julio Jiménez (Spa)
at 4'57"

Guido Reybrouck (Bel)

KING OF THE MOUNTAINS
Julio Jiménez (Spa)

AFTER STAGE 13

1 Roger Pingeon (Fra)
2 Désiré Letort (Fra)
at 4'05"
3 Julio Jiménez (Spa)
at 5'00"

Franco Bitossi (Ita)

KING OF THE MOUNTAINS
Aurelio González (Spa)

1968

Janssen swoops at the last

MELUN > PARIS (TIME TRIAL)

With Jacques Anquetil now retired from racing and Eddy 'The Cannibal' Merckx still a year away from making his Tour de France debut, the 1968 race was arguably the most open in history. There is certainly no doubt that it was the most open going into the final day of racing, which began with a road stage won by Frenchman

Maurice Izier. The race concluded with a 55.2 km time trial that afternoon into the French capital.

Incredibly, just 2½ minutes separated the leading nine riders. There were a mere 16 seconds between the top three, with Herman van Springel leading the race. The Belgian's most likely challengers were Jan Janssen, lying third, and Ferdinand Bracke, in fourth. Van Springel's compatriot Bracke looked particularly

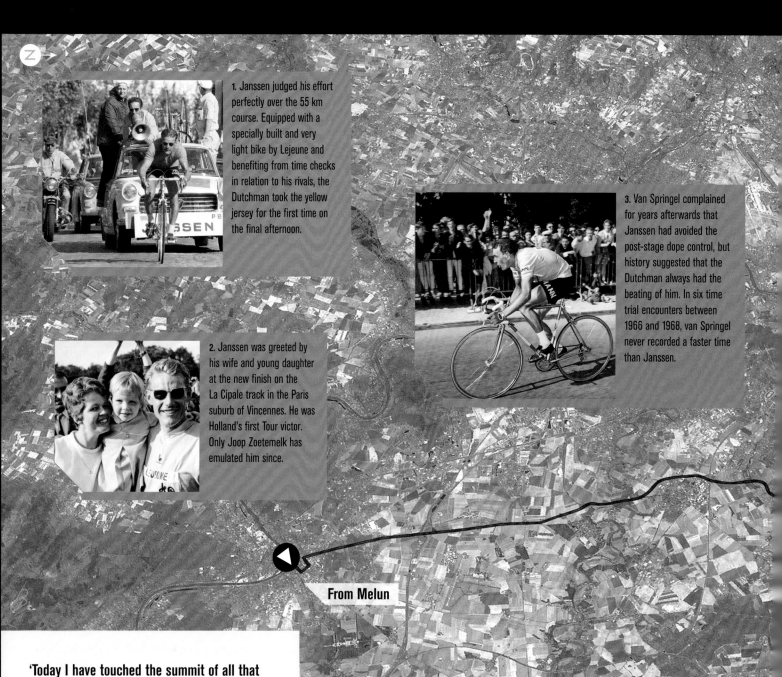

1. Janssen judged his effort perfectly over the 55 km course. Equipped with a specially built and very light bike by Lejeune and benefiting from time checks in relation to his rivals, the Dutchman took the yellow jersey for the first time on the final afternoon.

2. Janssen was greeted by his wife and young daughter at the new finish on the La Cipale track in the Paris suburb of Vincennes. He was Holland's first Tour victor. Only Joop Zoetemelk has emulated him since.

3. Van Springel complained for years afterwards that Janssen had avoided the post-stage dope control, but history suggested that the Dutchman always had the beating of him. In six time trial encounters between 1966 and 1968, van Springel never recorded a faster time than Janssen.

From Melun

'Today I have touched the summit of all that is unimaginable.' JAN JANSSEN

dangerous as he had set a new mark for the world hour record less than a year before.

Bracke went off hard, too hard as it turned out. He quickly faded out of the picture. The time trial became a duel between Belgium A team leader van Springel and Holland's Janssen. At halfway, Janssen had trimmed van Springel's lead back to 2 seconds,

but the Dutchman was riding a canny time trial. He had measured his effort with the aim of riding harder during the second half of the test.

The tactic worked perfectly. At the line, he was almost a minute faster. The stage was his, but, more importantly, so was the Tour.

STAGE FACTS

Date: 21 July 1968

Number: 22b

Length: 55.2 km

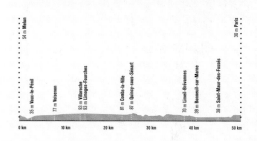

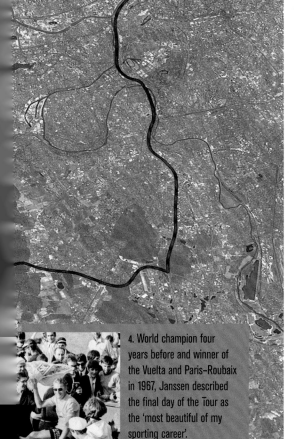

To Paris

4. World champion four years before and winner of the Vuelta and Paris–Roubaix in 1967, Janssen described the final day of the Tour as the 'most beautiful of my sporting career'.

TOUR TURNAROUNDS

1919: Race leader Eugène Christophe's forks break on the penultimate stage. He loses almost 2½ hours and the title to Firmin Lambot.

1947: Jean Robic's attack on the final stage into Paris enables him to take the yellow jersey from Pierre Brambilla.

1962: A minute down on Joseph Planckaert going into the final time trial at Lyon, Jacques Anquetil is worried. But he beats the Belgian by 5 minutes to take the lead.

1968: Jan Janssen's victory in the time trial on the final afternoon boosts him from third to first.

1971: Heavily defeated by Luis Ocaña in the Alps, Eddy Merckx inherits the lead in the Pyrenees when the Spaniard crashes out in a violent thunderstorm.

1987: At the end of the Tour with the most wears of the yellow jersey, Stephen Roche clinches it by beating Pedro Delgado in the Dijon time trial on the penultimate day.

1989: 50 seconds down on Laurent Fignon going into the final time trial, Greg LeMond beats the Frenchman by 8 seconds to win the closest Tour ever.

1998: 3 minutes down on Jan Ullrich heading for Les Deux Alpes, Marco Pantani beats the German by 9 minutes.

2006: Beaten to the yellow jersey by Floyd Landis in the final time trial, Óscar Pereiro is awarded the title after Landis tests positive.

2010: Andy Schleck equals Alberto Contador in the mountains and runs him close in the final time trial. He is awarded the title two years later as a result of the Spaniard's disqualification.

2011: A minute down on Andy Schleck going into the Grenoble time trial on the penultimate stage, Cadel Evans gains 2½ minutes to take the title.

BEFORE STAGE 22b

1 Herman Van Springel (Bel)
2 Gregorio San Miguel (Spa)
at 0'12"
3 Jan Janssen (Ned)
at 0'16"

Franco Bitossi (Ita)

KING OF THE MOUNTAINS
Aurelio González (Spa)

AFTER STAGE 22b

1 Jan Janssen (Ned)
2 Herman Van Springel (Bel)
at 0'38"
3 Ferdinand Bracke (Bel)
at 3'03"

Franco Bitossi (Ita)

KING OF THE MOUNTAINS
Aurelio González (Spa)

Merckx's greatest day

LUCHON > MOURENX

Eddy Merckx admitted to journalists later that he had no plan of attack for what would become one of the greatest days in his career and in Tour de France history. He added that if he saw a chance to attack he would always take it, but no-one could have foreseen that opportunity coming 140 km from the finish.

Already 8 minutes clear of second-placed Roger Pingeon, Merckx had no need to attack, but he revealed later that he was fired by anger. A couple of days earlier, Martin van den Bossche, his main lieutenant in the mountains, had revealed that he was moving to another team for the following year. Merckx felt let down, especially as the news had come to him right in the middle of the Tour.

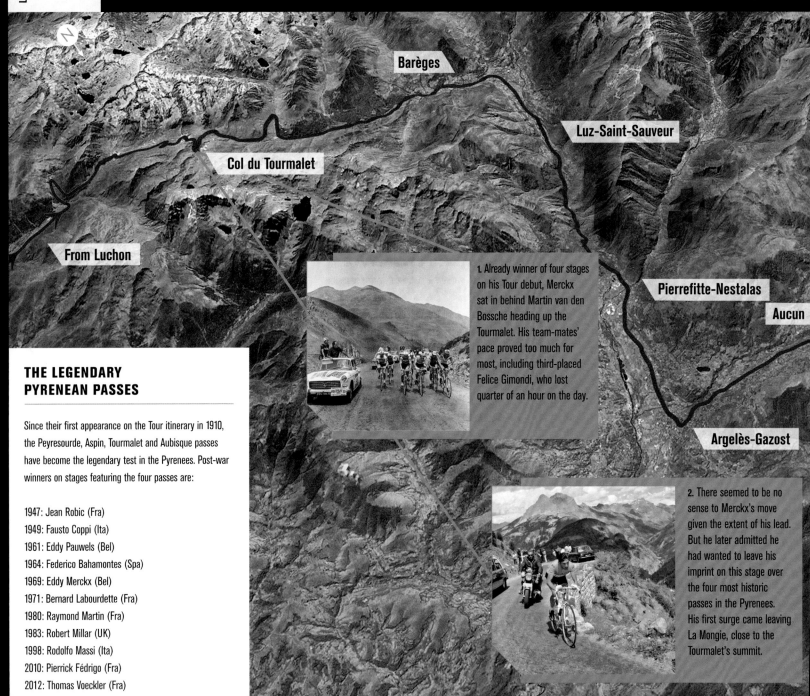

Barèges

Luz-Saint-Sauveur

Col du Tourmalet

From Luchon

Pierrefitte-Nestalas

Aucun

1. Already winner of four stages on his Tour debut, Merckx sat in behind Martin van den Bossche heading up the Tourmalet. His team-mates' pace proved too much for most, including third-placed Felice Gimondi, who lost quarter of an hour on the day.

THE LEGENDARY PYRENEAN PASSES

Since their first appearance on the Tour itinerary in 1910, the Peyresourde, Aspin, Tourmalet and Aubisque passes have become the legendary test in the Pyrenees. Post-war winners on stages featuring the four passes are:

1947: Jean Robic (Fra)
1949: Fausto Coppi (Ita)
1961: Eddy Pauwels (Bel)
1964: Federico Bahamontes (Spa)
1969: Eddy Merckx (Bel)
1971: Bernard Labourdette (Fra)
1980: Raymond Martin (Fra)
1983: Robert Millar (UK)
1998: Rodolfo Massi (Ita)
2010: Pierrick Fédrigo (Fra)
2012: Thomas Voeckler (Fra)

Argelès-Gazost

2. There seemed to be no sense to Merckx's move given the extent of his lead. But he later admitted he had wanted to leave his imprint on this stage over the four most historic passes in the Pyrenees. His first surge came leaving La Mongie, close to the Tourmalet's summit.

After crossing the Peyresourde and Aspin, the lead group was only nine-strong approaching the summit of the Tourmalet. Van den Bossche was leading and most expected Merckx to allow his team-mate the honour of being the first to crest the pass. However, a kilometre below the summit, Merckx surged clear, apparently to confirm his lead in the mountains competition.

Merckx descended alone and went through the feed station in the valley. He expected the group to come back up to him, but when it didn't he pressed on. His lead stretched going over the Soulor and Aubisque. By the finish it was 8 minutes. 'Merckxissimo!' proclaimed *L'Équipe*.

STAGE FACTS

Date: 15 July 1969

Number: 17

Length: 214.5 km

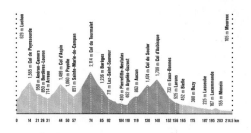

Col du Soulor

4. From the summit of the Aubisque, Merckx had still to cover 75 km into the finish at Mourenx. With 15 km remaining he told his team director, Guillaume Driessens: 'I'm dead, I don't think I'm going to be able to finish.' Driessens replied: 'The others behind are more dead than you are!'

Laruns

Col d'Aubisque

To Mourenx

3. Huge crowds were at the roadside to see what was to become one of the Tour's greatest exploits. Merckx rode the final 140 km alone, steadily gaining time on his rivals. By the time he reached the summit of the Aubisque he was 7 minutes clear.

'Even though I was exhausted at the finish, I am happy to have achieved something that will be remembered, I think...' EDDY MERCKX

BEFORE STAGE 17

1 Eddy Merckx (Bel)
2 Roger Pingeon (Fra)
at 8'21"
3 Felice Gimondi (Ita)
at 9'29'

Eddy Merckx (Bel)

KING OF THE MOUNTAINS
Eddy Merckx (Bel)

AFTER STAGE 17

1 Eddy Merckx (Bel)
2 Roger Pingeon (Fra)
at 16'18"
3 Raymond Poulidor (Fra)
at 20'43"

Eddy Merckx (Bel)

KING OF THE MOUNTAINS
Eddy Merckx (Bel)

Ocaña trounces Merckx

GRENOBLE > ORCIÈRES-MERLETTE

Having struggled heading into Grenoble the previous day, Eddy Merckx didn't look at his all-conquering best. Certainly, several of his key rivals wasted little time before attacking on a shortish stage through the Alps to the resort of Orcières Merlette. Just 13 km had passed when Joaquim Agostinho accelerated away on the Côte de Laffrey, and Luis

Ocaña, Lucien van Impe and race leader Joop Zoetemelk quickly joined him. Merckx remained in the bunch, either unwilling or unable to respond.

With the sun beating down relentlessly, Ocaña looked the strongest of the lead quartet and underlined that when he accelerated away on his own on the early slopes of the Col de Noyer. At the top his lead over Merckx in the peloton was more

1. On the attack from the very first kilometres of the stage with Joaquim Agostinho, Joop Zoetemelk and Lucien van Impe, Luis Ocaña accelerated clear of this trio on the day's penultimate climb, the Col de Noyer.

2. Climbing to Orcières-Merlette, Ocaña gets the latest information from the blackboard man. Not only was he set to take one of the most stunning mountain victories in Tour history, but he also gained enough time to put him almost out of sight of his rivals.

3. Merckx tried to get some assistance from other riders in the bunch, but few were willing or able to help him. In the end, he was forced to lead the pursuit himself, as Ocaña's Bic team-mates sat on his wheel.

From Grenoble
Laffrey
Saint-Théoffrey
Pierre-Châtel
Les Égâts
La Salle-en-Beaumon
La Mure

'Today Ocaña brought us to heel like El Cordobes brings bulls to heel in the arena.' EDDY MERCKX

than 5 minutes. The Belgian tried to encourage other teams to chase but, given past beatings he had handed out, few heeded his call. Many, it seemed, wanted to see 'The Cannibal' suffer.

Although he was on his own, Ocaña continued to extend his lead as Merckx drove on the front of what remained of the peloton several minutes behind. His back rounded, his legs pumping steadily, the Spaniard never faltered. At the finish, he was almost 6 minutes clear of van Impe, with Merckx home the best part of 9 minutes down. Ocaña had handed Merckx the heaviest defeat of his career.

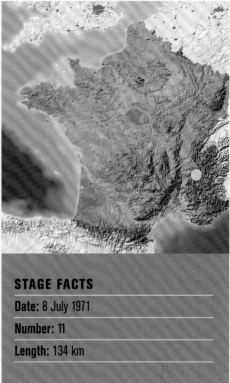

THE FASTEST TOURS

Despite Ocaña's later abandon, the 1971 race was at that point the fastest in the race's history by some distance, as Eddy Merckx's average speed of 38.084 km/hour beat the previous best mark of 37.317 km/hour set by Jacques Anquetil in 1962. The record speed has been improved on several occasions since:

38.960 km/hour set by Bernard Hinault in 1981
39.504 km/hour set by Miguel Indurain in 1992
39.983 km/hour set by Marco Pantani in 1998
40.789 km/hour set by Óscar Pereiro in 2006

STAGE FACTS

Date: 8 July 1971

Number: 11

Length: 134 km

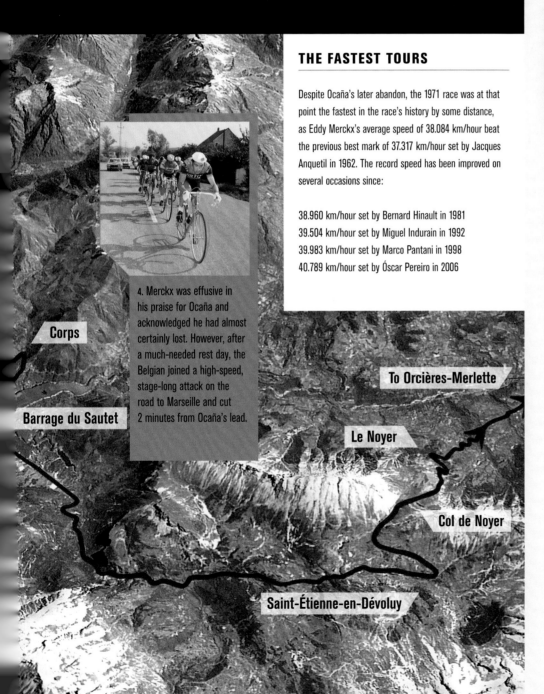

4. Merckx was effusive in his praise for Ocaña and acknowledged he had almost certainly lost. However, after a much-needed rest day, the Belgian joined a high-speed, stage-long attack on the road to Marseille and cut 2 minutes from Ocaña's lead.

Corps

Barrage du Sautet

To Orcières-Merlette

Le Noyer

Col de Noyer

Saint-Étienne-en-Dévoluy

BEFORE STAGE 11

1 Joop Zoetemelk (Ned)
2 Luis Ocaña (Spa)
   at 0'01"
3 Gösta Pettersson (Swe)
   at 0'40"

Cyrille Guimard (Fra)

KING OF THE MOUNTAINS
Joop Zoetemelk (Ned)

AFTER STAGE 11

1 Luis Ocaña (Spa)
2 Joop Zoetemelk (Ned)
   at 8'43"
3 Lucien van Impe (Bel)
   at 9'20"

Cyrille Guimard (Fra)

KING OF THE MOUNTAINS
Joop Zoetemelk (Ned)

Ocaña's blackest day

REVEL > LUCHON

With 7 minutes on the great Eddy Merckx and apparently coasting to what would have been only Spain's second Tour success, Luis Ocaña fell victim to matters well beyond his control as the race headed for Luchon. The stage started in baking conditions that became more threatening as the riders went deeper into the Pyrenees.

Several riders had gone clear early on, including Spanish climber José Manuel Fuente, who led over the Portet d'Aspet, then the Col de Menté. By that point, a violent storm had engulfed the riders. Hail and torrential rain washed stones and mud into the road ahead of them. Descending the Menté, Fuente went over the parapet. He was pulled back up with a spare inner tube and continued on to victory.

TOUR DE FRANCE MEMORIALS

There are numerous memorials remembering great names, great exploits and also tragedies at the Tour de France, including one to Luis Ocaña on the bend where his Tour hopes ended on the Col de Menté. Others remembered include:

Tom Simpson: A stone and steps were erected in his memory at the place where he collapsed on Mont Ventoux in 1967.
Fabio Casartelli: A stone memorial marks the place where the Italian died on the Portet d'Aspet in 1995.
Fausto Coppi and Louison Bobet: There are busts of both riders on the Col d'Izoard.
Henri Desgrange: The Tour founder is remembered with a stone memorial a kilometre below the summit of the Galibier.
Jacques Goddet and Octave Lapize: A sculpture of a rider in action pays tribute to the former Tour director on the summit of the Tourmalet. Another statue pays tribute to Octave Lapize, winner of the first stage in the Pyrenees.
Wim van Est: A plaque marks the spot where Holland's first yellow jersey crashed off the road between the Aubisque and Soulor.
René Pottier: Twice the first man to the top of the Ballon d'Alsace, a memorial was raised in his honour on that summit after he committed suicide in 1907.
Eugène Christophe: A plaque on the old forge in Sainte-Marie-de-Campan marks the spot where the Frenchman welded his forks after crashing on the Tourmalet in 1913.
Laurent Fignon: A memorial was unveiled to the two-time Tour winner in Créteil, home of his first club.

1. Luis Ocaña had the measure of Eddy Merckx going into this stage and never looked troubled until the weather changed. Merckx persistently tried to attack on the way up the Col de Menté, but Ocaña responded with ease each time.

2. The first sign of the danger ahead came when the stage leader, José Manuel Fuente, crashed off the road as he descended the Menté in the storm. The Spaniard remounted and finished more than 6 minutes clear at the finish.

Col de Menté

Col de Portet d'Aspet

From Revel

Meanwhile, having failed to drop Ocaña on the same climb, Merckx went all out on the descent only to lose control on a hairpin and hit the rock wall on the corner of the bend. As spectators rushed to help Merckx, Ocaña tried to avoid them and also crashed.

Both men were quickly back up. However, as Ocaña prepared to remount, Joop Zoetemelk came sliding down into the same corner and hurtled into the Spaniard. Two more riders also crashed into Ocaña. He lay battered and semi-conscious at the roadside, unable to continue, his Tour de France hopes shattered.

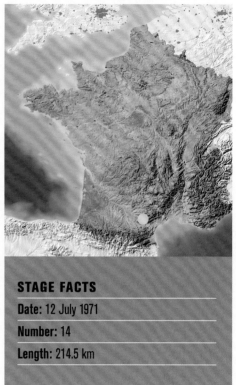

STAGE FACTS

Date: 12 July 1971

Number: 14

Length: 214.5 km

To Luchon

Saint-Béat

Boutx

4. Merckx admitted that he felt the Tour had been lost and, out of respect for Ocaña, he refused to accept the yellow jersey on the podium that night or to wear it on the stage the following day. Later in the race he visited Ocaña at home as he recovered from his injuries.

3. Ocaña's downfall was instigated when Merckx crashed, but it was only when Joop Zoetemelk and then two more riders hit Ocaña as he was standing at the roadside that he sustained the injuries that put him out of the race. 'I couldn't avoid him,' Zoetemelk said later.

'I felt like I was going to die. I thought about my father, my wife and my children.' LUIS OCAÑA

BEFORE STAGE 14	AFTER STAGE 14

BEFORE STAGE 14	AFTER STAGE 14
1 Luis Ocaña (Spa)	1 Eddy Merckx (Bel)
2 Eddy Merckx (Bel) at 7'23"	2 Joop Zoetemelk (Ned) at 2'21"
3 Joop Zoetemelk (Ned) at 9'26"	3 Lucien van Impe (Bel) at 2'51"

Cyrille Guimard (Fra)	Cyrille Guimard (Fra)

KING OF THE MOUNTAINS	KING OF THE MOUNTAINS
Joop Zoetemelk (Ned)	Lucien van Impe (Bel)

1974

The Tour heads to Britain

PLYMOUTH > PLYMOUTH

The Tour de France's first excursion outside mainland Europe took it to Plymouth, Great Britain, in 1974. The local council there was hoping that the race's visit would boost tourist numbers and help to publicize the port's ferry link with Brittany, which had been launched the year before.

However, the stage did not prove a particular success. That was due to a number of factors, not least Britain's lack of experience in hosting top-class bike races and a clear lack of knowledge and enthusiasm among British sports fans, most of whom appeared to be more interested in the football World Cup taking place at the same time in West Germany, even though England weren't involved in it.

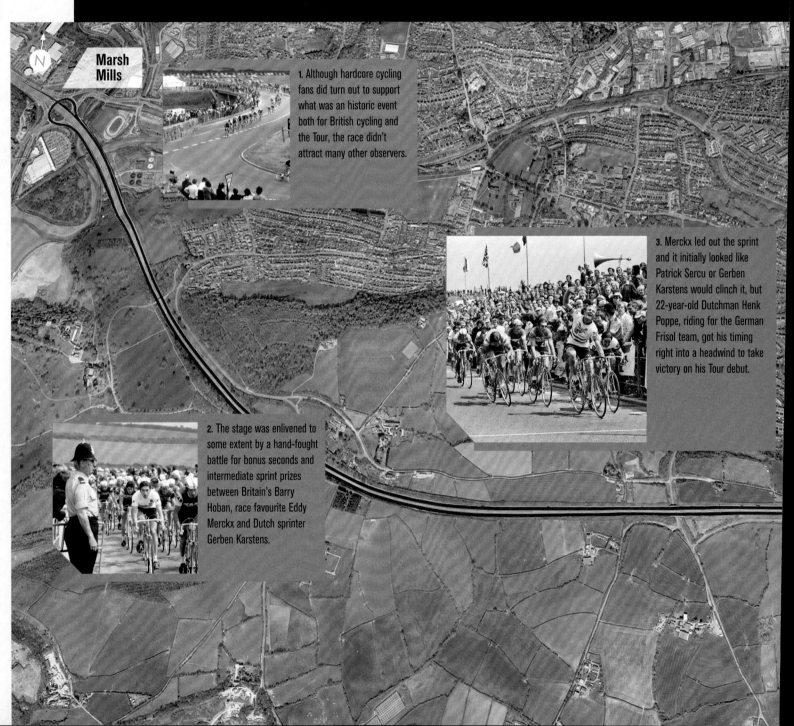

Marsh Mills

1. Although hardcore cycling fans did turn out to support what was an historic event both for British cycling and the Tour, the race didn't attract many other observers.

3. Merckx led out the sprint and it initially looked like Patrick Sercu or Gerben Karstens would clinch it, but 22-year-old Dutchman Henk Poppe, riding for the German Frisol team, got his timing right into a headwind to take victory on his Tour debut.

2. The stage was enlivened to some extent by a hand-fought battle for bonus seconds and intermediate sprint prizes between Britain's Barry Hoban, race favourite Eddy Merckx and Dutch sprinter Gerben Karstens.

The course selected for the stage probably didn't help matters, either. Legend has it that the riders raced on the recently completed Plympton bypass, which hadn't then been opened to cars. However, the road, in fact, had been opened and it required permission from the Department of the Environment to close it again for the day.

Having started in Plymouth, the route took the riders onto the bypass, where they completed 14 laps of an 11.7-km circuit in front of relatively few spectators and with little of the Tour's traditional festival spirit. It was perhaps fitting that hitherto unheralded Dutchman Henk Poppe won the stage. It was his only major victory.

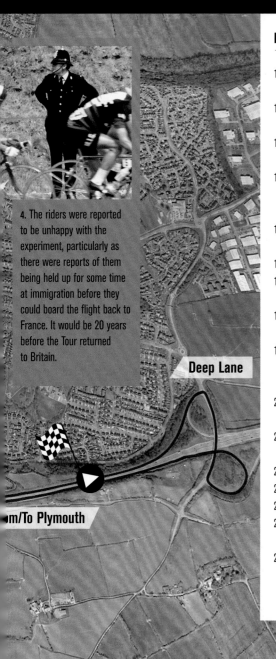

4. The riders were reported to be unhappy with the experiment, particularly as there were reports of them being held up for some time at immigration before they could board the flight back to France. It would be 20 years before the Tour returned to Britain.

Deep Lane

...m/To Plymouth

BRITAIN'S TOUR HIGHS AND LOWS

1955: Brian Robinson is the first British rider to finish the Tour, in 29th place.

1958: Robinson becomes the first Briton to win a Tour stage in Brest.

1962: Tom Simpson is the first Briton to lead the Tour, finishing a career-best sixth.

1967: Simpson collapses on Mont Ventoux and later dies. Barry Hoban wins the stage the following day as the peloton pays tribute.

1974: The Tour makes its first visit to Britain for the stage in Plymouth.

1975: Hoban wins his eighth Tour stage.

1984: Robert Millar wins the King of the Mountains title and is fourth overall, the best finish by a Briton.

1987: ANC-Halfords are the first British team to start the Tour. They fold soon after it.

1994: Chris Boardman takes the first of three prologue wins in Lille. After huge crowds turn out to watch two stages in southern England, Sean Yates leads the race for a day.

2003: David Millar wins the Tour's final time trial but is banned at the end of the year after admitting EPO use.

2007: Millions turn out to watch the Tour's Grand Départ in London and the following day's stage to Canterbury.

2008: New sensation Mark Cavendish wins four bunch sprints.

2009: Bradley Wiggins equals Robert Millar's fourth place finish.

2010: Team Sky line up in their first Tour de France.

2011: Cavendish takes his number of stage wins to 20 in just four years.

2012: Bradley Wiggins wins the Tour, Chris Froome finishes second and British riders win seven stages between them.

STAGE FACTS

Date: 29 June 1974

Number: 2

Length: 163.7 km

'It was perfectly well organized but without any emotion worthy of mention.'
SPANISH NEWSPAPER, *EL MUNDO DEPORTIVO*

BEFORE STAGE 2

1 Joseph Bruyère (Bel)
2 Eddy Merckx (Bel)
at 0'16"
3 Herman van Springel (Bel)
at 0'26"

Joseph Bruyère (Bel)

KING OF THE MOUNTAINS
Lucien van Impe (Bel)

AFTER STAGE 2

1 Joseph Bruyère (Fra)
2 Eddy Merckx (Bel)
at 0'10"
3 Gerben Karstens (Ned)
at 0'22"

Gerben Karstens (Ned)

KING OF THE MOUNTAINS
Lucien van Impe (Bel)

Merckx attacks, then cracks

NICE > PRA LOUP

When Eddy Merckx set out from Nice on the crucial mountain stage to Pra Loup, there was no indication that 'The Cannibal' was starting his final day in the yellow jersey. As he sought to take a record-breaking sixth victory, Merckx had steadily distanced all of his rivals until only Bernard Thévenet remained within range of the Belgian.

However, Merckx's chances had received a blow – quite literally – on stage 14. Just short of the summit finish on the Puy-de-Dôme, a spectator had punched Merkcx in the kidneys as he passed by. Merckx had struggled on to finish, but needed painkillers prior to the Pra Loup stage that followed two days later.

On the third of the day's five climbs, the Col des Champs, Thévenet took the fight to Merckx, attacking six times, only to be

1. Two days before the stage, Merckx was punched by a fan who jumped out of the crowd about 200 m short of the finish on the Puy-de-Dôme. Some of those watching said that the blow had been accidental. Whether it was or not, it led to the Belgian's rapid decline.

2. Merckx looked strong for most of the stage to Pra Loup and must have felt good, too, as he attacked near the summit of the Col d'Allos and looked all set for victory.

3. Just 4 km remained when Merckx began to falter. Felice Gimondi was the first to pass him. Crucially, Thévenet was the next to pass by, urged on by Peugeot team director Maurice de Muer, who told him: 'Go Bernard, he's struggling, he's cooked!'

To Pra Loup

La Foux d'Allos

Col d'Allos

Colmars

'I tried everything and I lost. I don't think I will win this Tour. It's finished.' EDDY MERCKX AT PRA LOUP

chased down on each occasion. The Col d'Allos followed. A kilometre from the top, Merckx surged clear, leaving his rivals struggling behind. The Tour, it seemed, had been decided.

Thévenet admitted later that his only thought then was limiting his losses, so was as surprised as anyone when he began to gain rapidly on Merckx on the final ascent. As the Frenchman went by, Merckx could not respond. His legs had gone, perhaps due to the medication he had taken. Thévenet pressed home his advantage, turning a 58-second deficit into a 58-second lead. Merckx's era had ended.

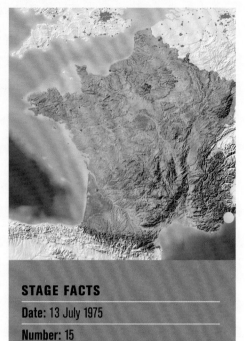

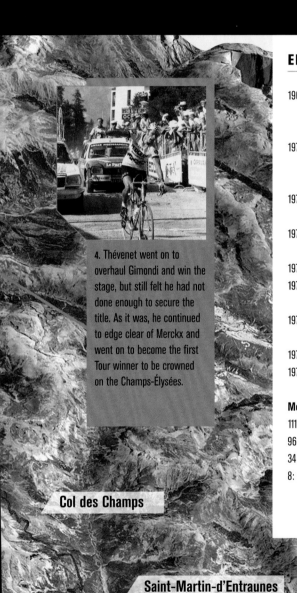

4. Thévenet went on to overhaul Gimondi and win the stage, but still felt he had not done enough to secure the title. As it was, he continued to edge clear of Merckx and went on to become the first Tour winner to be crowned on the Champs-Élysées.

Col des Champs

Saint-Martin-d'Entraunes

From Nice

EDDY MERCKX'S TOUR RECORD

1969: First overall, six stage wins, points winner, King of the Mountains winner, combination classification winner, combativity award winner

1970: First overall, eight stage wins, King of the Mountains winner, combination classification winner, combativity award winner

1971: First overall, four stage wins, points winner, combination classification winner

1972: First overall, six stage wins, points winner, combination classification winner

1973: Did not start

1974: First overall, eight stage wins, combination classification winner, combativity award winner

1975: Second overall, two stage wins and second place for the King of the Mountains

1976: Did not start

1977: Sixth overall

Merckx's Tour statistics

111: Stages in the yellow jersey

96: Days in the yellow jersey

34: Stage victories

8: Stage victories in the 1970 and 1974 Tours, equalling the record set by Charles Pélissier

STAGE FACTS

Date: 13 July 1975

Number: 15

Length: 217.5 km

BEFORE STAGE 15

1 Eddy Merckx (Bel)
2 Bernard Thévenet (Fra)
at 0'58"
3 Joop Zoetemelk (Ned)
at 3'54"

Rik van Linden (Bel)

Lucien van Impe (Bel)

Francesco Moser (Ita)

AFTER STAGE 15

1 Bernard Thévenet (Fra)
2 Eddy Merckx (Bel)
at 0'58"
3 Joop Zoetemelk (Ned)
at 4'08"

Rik van Linden (Bel)

Lucien van Impe (Bel)

Francesco Moser (Ita)

1976

Van Impe in his prime

SAINT-GAUDENS > SAINT-LARY-SOULAN

Although winner of the King of the Mountains title on three occasions, Lucien van Impe had never looked a likely winner of the overall title until Cyrille Guimard took over as manager of the Gitane team. Heading into the Pyrenees, Guimard had advised van Impe to hold back and not pursue Peugeot's Raymond Delisle, because of a strong headwind.

Two days further into the race, Guimard unveiled the next part of his tactical gameplan. With several riders already on the attack on the tough stage to Pla d'Adet above Saint-Lary-Soulan, Guimard ordered van Impe to attack 3 km from the summit of the Col du Portillon. Race leader Delisle and van Impe's main rival, Joop Zoetemelk, held back, believing the move to be too premature.

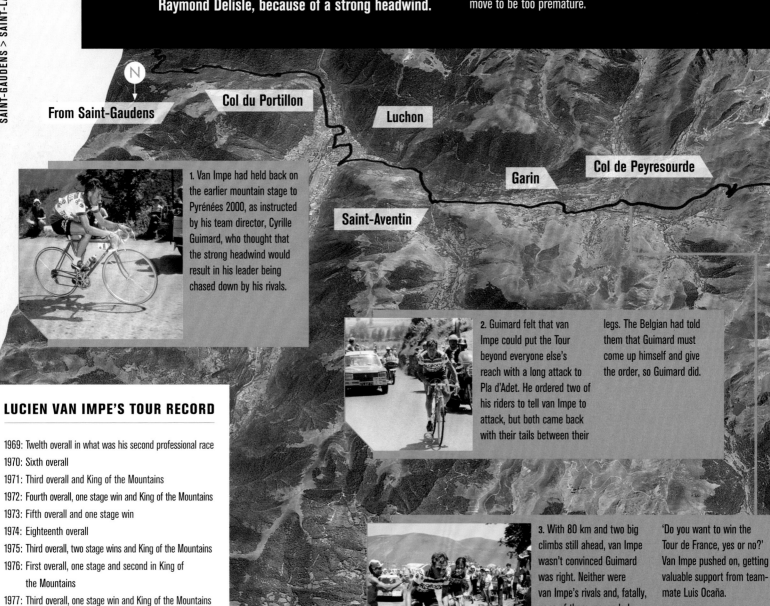

From Saint-Gaudens

Col du Portillon

Luchon

Col de Peyresourde

Garin

Saint-Aventin

1. Van Impe had held back on the earlier mountain stage to Pyrénées 2000, as instructed by his team director, Cyrille Guimard, who thought that the strong headwind would result in his leader being chased down by his rivals.

2. Guimard felt that van Impe could put the Tour beyond everyone else's reach with a long attack to Pla d'Adet. He ordered two of his riders to tell van Impe to attack, but both came back with their tails between their legs. The Belgian had told them that Guimard must come up himself and give the order, so Guimard did.

3. With 80 km and two big climbs still ahead, van Impe wasn't convinced Guimard was right. Neither were van Impe's rivals and, fatally, none of them responded immediately. Heading towards the Peyresourde, Guimard told van Impe he was 2 minutes up and asked: 'Do you want to win the Tour de France, yes or no?' Van Impe pushed on, getting valuable support from team-mate Luis Ocaña.

LUCIEN VAN IMPE'S TOUR RECORD

1969: Twelfth overall in what was his second professional race
1970: Sixth overall
1971: Third overall and King of the Mountains
1972: Fourth overall, one stage win and King of the Mountains
1973: Fifth overall and one stage win
1974: Eighteenth overall
1975: Third overall, two stage wins and King of the Mountains
1976: First overall, one stage and second in King of the Mountains
1977: Third overall, one stage win and King of the Mountains
1978: Ninth overall
1979: Eleventh overall and one stage win
1980: Sixteenth overall
1981: Second overall, one stage win and King of the Mountains
1983: Fourth overall, one stage win and King of the Mountains
1985: Twenty-seventh overall

The Bernard Hinault years – the last champion of the old school 1976–1988

Climbing the Peyresourde, van Impe pressed on, joining lone leader Luis Ocaña. Pitched into the middle of the battle for the yellow jersey, Ocaña decided to repay Zoetemelk for what the Spaniard viewed as the Dutchman's lack of assistance during Ocaña's many battles with Eddy Merckx. He set a scorching pace on the long run off the Peyresourde to the final climb, happily scuppering his own chances of success.

Again displaying the climbing skills that would win him six King of the Mountains titles, the flyweight van Impe flew up the final climb, where he finished more than 3 minutes clear of Zoetemelk. Thanks to Guimard, the yellow jersey was his.

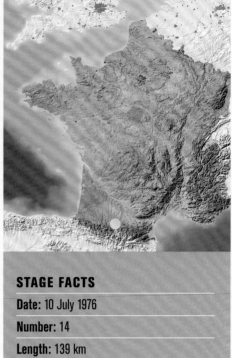

STAGE FACTS

Date: 10 July 1976

Number: 14

Length: 139 km

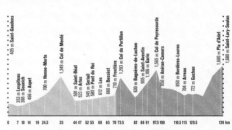

4. Van Impe's offensive turned the race upside down. Zoetemelk was the rider still within range of him in the overall standings, but even the Dutchman was too far back to repair the damage that van Impe had inflicted on everyone.

To Saint-Lary-Soulan

Pla d'Adet

Anéran-Camors

Bordères-Louron

Guchen

Arreau

'If you haven't got a good team around you, all is lost. But I feel reassured that for the first time ever I am starting the Tour de France with the aim of winning it.' LUCIEN VAN IMPE

BEFORE STAGE 14

1 Raymond Delisle (Fra)
2 Lucien van Impe (Bel)
at 2'41"
3 Joop Zoetemelk (Ned)
at 2'47"

Freddy Maertens (Bel)

Giancarlo Bellini (Ita)

Alain Meslet (Fra)

AFTER STAGE 14

1 Lucien van Impe (Bel)
2 Joop Zoetemelk (Ned)
at 3'18"
3 Raymond Delisle (Fra)
at 9'27"

Freddy Maertens (Bel)

Lucien van Impe (Bel)

Alain Meslet (Fra)

Eight wins for Maertens!

PARIS CHAMPS-ÉLYSÉES (TIME TRIAL)

Already the winner of a host of titles during the first half of the season, including victory in Amstel Gold, Gent-Wevelgem and no fewer than six stages in Paris–Nice, Belgian sprinter Freddy Maertens raised his performance to another level at the Tour. His triumph in the prologue time trial in Saint-Jean-de-Monts put him in the yellow jersey, which he held for another eight days, during which he claimed another three victories.

In the final five days of the race Maertens added another four stage wins to his collection, placing him alongside Charles Pélissier (1930) and Eddy Merckx (1970 and 1974) as a new member of the elite band of riders to win eight stages during a single edition of the Tour.

From/To Place de la Concorde

Rond-point des Champs-Élysées

2. Maertens held the yellow jersey as far as the Alpe d'Huez, where he was succeeded by compatriot Lucien van Impe. But his grip on the green points jersey was unbreakable.

1. Maertens' incredible run of success began when he won the opening two stages of the race, highlighting his principal strengths in the process. First he claimed the prologue time trial in Saint-Jean-de-Monts, then he took the bunch sprint in Angers.

3. The Belgian won the final short time trial of the race by no fewer than 11 seconds from Joop Zoetemelk. He would go on to win the world title later in the year and claim an incredible 13 stages as he romped to victory in the 1997 Vuelta a España.

'When I saw the finish I would start my sprint and then make sure no-one came past. I was strong.' FREDDY MAERTENS

Maertens' final success came on the Tour's last day, which was split into two stages: a short 6 km time trial on the Champs-Élysées in the morning followed by the traditional circuit race in the same location in the afternoon. The power-packed Maertens was 2 seconds a kilometre faster than anyone else in the time trial.

In the afternoon, Maertens' Flandria team rode full bore in order to make things difficult for their leader's rivals. However, they were outwitted by Raleigh's Gerben Karstens, who was set up by Jan Raas and managed to hold off Maertens as he went all out for a ninth win.

STAGE FACTS

Date: 18 July 1976

Number: 22a

Length: 6 km

MOST STAGE WINS IN ONE TOUR

Eight: Charles Pélissier (1930), Eddy Merckx (1970, 1974), Freddy Maertens (1976)

Seven: Gino Bartali (1948), Bernard Hinault (1979)

Six: Émile Georget (1907), François Faber (1909), Marcel Buysse (1913), Jean Aerts (1933), Eddy Merckx (1969), Eddy Merckx (1972), Luis Ocaña (1973), Mark Cavendish (2009)

Five: Louis Trousselier (1905), René Pottier (1906), Lucien Petit-Breton (1908), Philippe Thys (1922), André Leducq (1929, 1932), Learco Guerra (1933), Roger Lapébie (1934), Fausto Coppi (1952), Dietrich Thurau (1977), Bernard Hinault (1981), Freddy Maertens (1981), Laurent Fignon (1984), Mark Cavendish (2010, 2011)

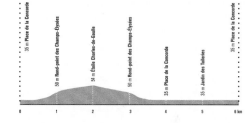

Champs-Élysées

Place Charles de Gaulle

BEFORE STAGE 22a	AFTER STAGE 22a
1 Lucien Van Impe (Bel)	1 Lucien Van Impe (Bel)
2 Joop Zoetemelk (Ned) at 4'21"	2 Joop Zoetemelk (Ned) at 4'14"
3 Raymond Delisle (Fra) at 12'15"	3 Raymond Poulidor (Fra) at 12'08"
Freddy Maertens (Bel)	Freddy Maertens (Bel)
Giancarlo Bellini (Ita)	Giancarlo Bellini (Ita)
Enrique Martínez Heredia (Spa)	Enrique Martínez Heredia (Spa)

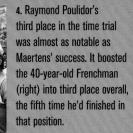

4. Raymond Poulidor's third place in the time trial was almost as notable as Maertens' success. It boosted the 40-year-old Frenchman (right) into third place overall, the fifth time he'd finished in that position.

1978

Hinault leads riders' strike

TARBES > VALENCE D'AGEN

During the 1970s, split stages featured increasingly on the Tour route, to the consternation of the riders. In 1977, they had gone on strike during Paris–Nice to protest about the late finishes and early starts that were often the result of running stages with two, or even three, sections during one day. A year on, they repeated their action at the Tour.

The riders hadn't got to bed until 11pm after the stage into Saint-Lary-Soulan. The following morning, they had to get up at 4.30am to transfer to Tarbes for a 7.30am start. The protest began with the peloton riding at just 25 km/hour, although not all of the riders supported the action. French champion Bernard Hinault remonstrated with those who didn't and eventually all of the riders fell into line.

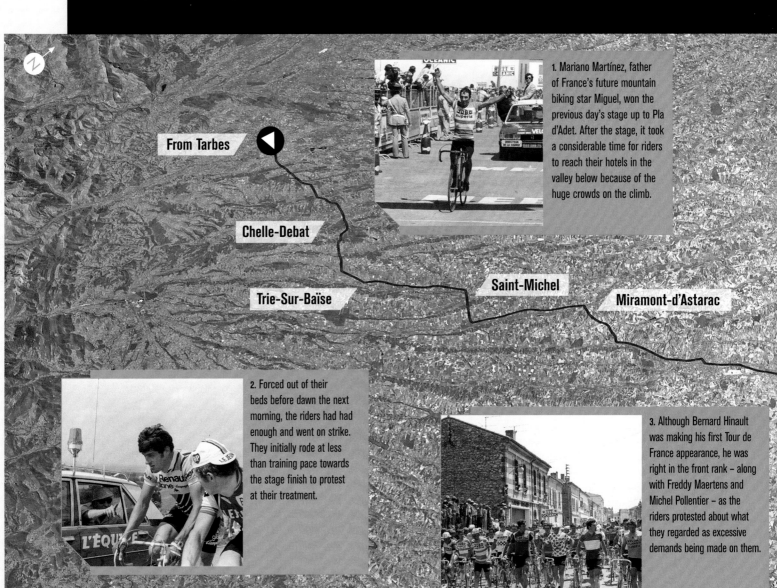

From Tarbes

Chelle-Debat

Trie-Sur-Baïse

Saint-Michel

Miramont-d'Astarac

1. Mariano Martínez, father of France's future mountain biking star Miguel, won the previous day's stage up to Pla d'Adet. After the stage, it took a considerable time for riders to reach their hotels in the valley below because of the huge crowds on the climb.

2. Forced out of their beds before dawn the next morning, the riders had had enough and went on strike. They initially rode at less than training pace towards the stage finish to protest at their treatment.

3. Although Bernard Hinault was making his first Tour de France appearance, he was right in the front rank – along with Freddy Maertens and Michel Pollentier – as the riders protested about what they regarded as excessive demands being made on them.

'We're not circus beasts on display from town to town... We're not asking for more money but simply a bit more consideration.' ANDRÉ CHALMEL

Negotiations between the riders and Tour organizers failed to resolve the issue and, coming into the finish at Valence d'Agen, the whole field halted 50 m short of the finishing line and refused to continue. Despite the watching crowd whistling their disapproval and further talks with organizers, the stage was annulled.

In the longer term, the protest did result in more consideration being given to the riders' need for rest and recuperation. Split stages gradually disappeared almost totally from the race as race organizers realized that less is more in terms of the payments demanded for hosting stages.

STAGE FACTS

Date: 12 July 1978

Number: 12a

Length: 158 km

DEBUTANTS WHO WON THE TOUR

1903: Maurice Garin (Fra)
1904: Henri Cornet (Fra)
1905: Louis Trousselier (Fra)
1947: Jean Robic (Fra)
1949: Fausto Coppi (Ita)
1957: Jacques Anquetil (Fra)
1965: Felice Gimondi (Ita)
1978: Bernard Hinault (Fra)
1983: Laurent Fignon (Fra)

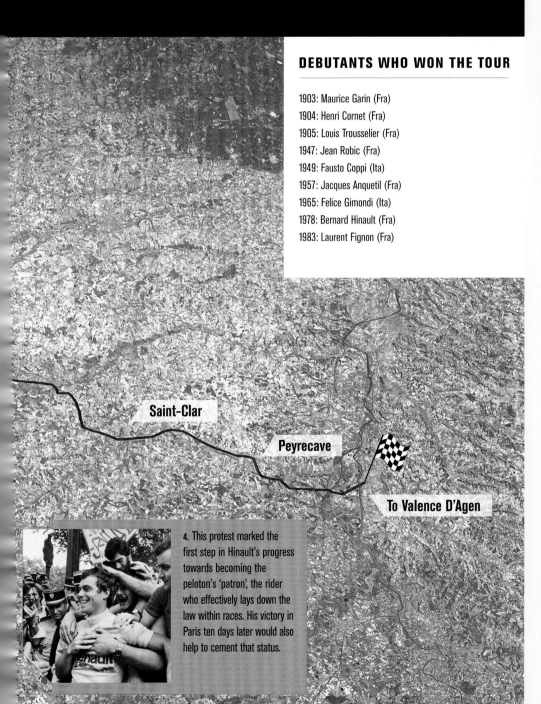

Saint-Clar

Peyrecave

To Valence D'Agen

4. This protest marked the first step in Hinault's progress towards becoming the peloton's 'patron', the rider who effectively lays down the law within races. His victory in Paris ten days later would also help to cement that status.

BEFORE STAGE 12a	AFTER STAGE 12a
1 Joseph Bruyère (Bel)	1 Joseph Bruyère (Bel)
2 Bernard Hinault (Fra) at 1'05"	2 Bernard Hinault (Fra) at 1'05"
3 Joop Zoetemelk (Ned) at 1'58"	3 Joop Zoetemelk (Ned) at 1'58"
Freddy Maertens (Bel)	Freddy Maertens (Bel)
Michel Pollentier (Bel)	Michel Pollentier (Bel)

Henk Lubberding (Ned)	Henk Lubberding (Ned)

1978

Pollentier caught at dope control

SAINT-ÉTIENNE > ALPE D'HUEZ

Within the space of 2 hours, what should have been the greatest day of Michel Pollentier's professional cycling career turned into a nightmare from which the Belgian never really recovered. Lying in fourth position overall and wearing the King of the Mountains jersey on the road to the Alpe d'Huez, Pollentier attacked towards the top of the Col de Luitel in order to consolidate his lead in the mountains competition.

Noticing that no-one had followed him, Pollentier pressed on down to the descent to the foot of the Alpe d'Huez and started up the climb more than 3 minutes up on Bernard Hinault, Joop Zoetemelk and Hennie Kuiper. This gap was enough to guarantee him the stage win and with it the yellow

A BRIEF HISTORY OF DOPING

1924: In an interview with journalist Albert Londres, Henri Pélissier talks of widespread drug-taking, including the use of cocaine and chloroform.

1955: Jean Malléjac collapses 10 km from the summit of Mont Ventoux and is taken to hospital. Malléjac denied wrongdoing up until his death and claimed he was drugged against his will. Tour doctor Pierre Dumas says he will call for a charge of 'attempted murder' against whoever supplied Malléjac with drugs.

1966: Drug testing is introduced at the Tour de France. The riders strike in protest.

1967: Tom Simpson collapses and dies on Mont Ventoux. Amphetamine use is partly to blame.

1978: Race leader Michel Pollentier is one of two riders kicked off the race for trying to cheat the dope control.

1998: The discovery of doping products in a Festina team car being driven to the Tour start by team *soigneur* Willy Voet leads to the Festina affair.

2006: The Puerto blood-doping inquiry leads to several riders, including favourites Jan Ullrich and Ivan Basso, being forced to miss the start of the Tour. Race winner Floyd Landis is stripped of the title after testing positive for testosterone.

2007: A number of riders test positive, including stage winner Alexander Vinokourov.

2010: Race winner Alberto Contador is stripped of the title after a positive test for clenbuterol.

2012: Several former riders on the Motorola and US Postal teams tell a US Anti-Doping Agency investigation that seven-time Tour winner Lance Armstrong consistently took EPO and other doping products during his reign as Tour champion and encouraged other riders to follow suit. The investigation resulted in Armstrong being stripped of all his Tour titles by the UCI in 2012.

From Saint-Étienne

Gières

Uriage-les-Bains

Col du Luitel

Séchilienne

1. Pollentier was renowned for his lack of style on the bike, as he twisted from side to side with his elbows and knees sticking out. But he was a very effective performer, and never more so than on the stage to the Alpe d'Huez.

3. Pollentier claimed that half of the riders in the race were using 'products', although he refused to say what they were when pressed on the issue. He returned to the Tour in the following three seasons but didn't finish the race on any of those occasions.

jersey when previous incumbent Joseph Bruyère came in a whole 12 minutes later.

Pollentier presented himself at the dope control caravan 2 hours after winning the stage. The two riders who had been selected for random tests were tested first. The second of them, Frenchman Antoine Gutierrez, was found trying to cheat the control, having fitted a rubber pouch containing untainted urine under his arm.

The official then asked Pollentier to lift his shirt and discovered that the Belgian had a similar device fitted under his arm. Immediately disqualified from the race, Pollentier was also handed a 2-month ban.

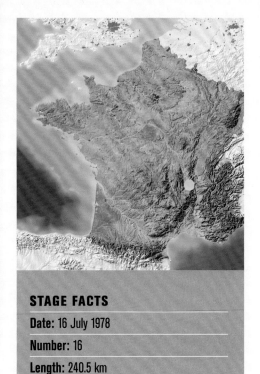

STAGE FACTS

Date: 16 July 1978

Number: 16

Length: 240.5 km

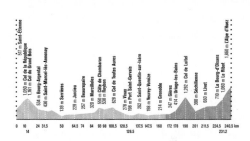

2. The Belgian took the yellow jersey on the famous summit, but only ever got to wear it on the post-stage podium. Within hours he was would leave the race in disgrace.

To Alpe d'Huez

Huez-en-Oisans

Livet

Bourg-d'Oisans

4. Joop Zoetemelk started the next stage in the yellow jersey, but knew that he would need to extend his lead over young French champion Bernard Hinault in order to hang on to it. In the end, the Dutchman yielded as Hinault claimed his first title.

BEFORE STAGE 16	AFTER STAGE 16

1 Joseph Bruyère (Bel)	1 Joop Zoetemelk (Ned)
2 Joop Zoetemelk (Ned) at 1'03"	2 Bernard Hinault (Fra) at 0'14"
3 Bernard Hinault (Fra) at 1'50"	3 Hennie Kuiper (Ned) at 5'31"

Freddy Maertens (Bel) | Freddy Maertens (Bel)

Michel Pollentier (Bel) | Mariano Martínez (Fra)

Henk Lubberding (Ned) | Henk Lubberding (Ned)

'That should have been the finest day of my career. Unhappily, it will be one of the saddest.' MICHEL POLLENTIER IN A LETTER OF APOLOGY TO THE TOUR ORGANIZERS.

1979

Duel on the Champs-Élysées

LE PERREUX-SUR-MARNE > PARIS CHAMPS-ÉLYSÉES

Although tradition has it that the Tour's final stage finish on the Champs-Élysées has been the domain of the sprinters, there have been some exceptions. The most notable occurred in 1979, following an attack on a climb in the Vallée de Chevreuse by second-placed Joop Zoetemelk. Race leader Bernard Hinault was quick to respond to the Dutchman, then countered with an attack of his own. This seemed like nothing more than a bit of cat and mouse between the Tour's two outstanding performers, but it became much more when Hinault persisted with his attack. Forced to chase, Zoetemelk caught the Frenchman 5 km later. However, rather than sit up and wait for the bunch, the two rivals began to coordinate their efforts heading into Paris.

1. Hinault already had the race sewn up heading into the final two stages, which appeared to suit the sprinters. However, he was too strong for the rest in Nogent-sur-Marne on the penultimate day, when second-placed Marc Demeyer described him as 'a beast'.

2. Zoetemelk had tried throughout the race to put Hinault on the back foot, attacking persistently in the mountains. He continued in that same style on the final stage through the Vallée de Chevreuse.

3. The two rivals caused a sensation when they rode into Paris together and continued with their joint offensive in front of the packed crowds on the Champs-Élysées.

4. Hinault was too strong for Zoetemelk in the final sprint. It not only provided Hinault with his seventh stage win of the race, but also confirmed his victory in the points competition. He also finished second in the mountains competition and third in the intermediate sprints contest, while his Renault team topped that classification.

Jouy-en-Josas

Châteaufort

Dampierre

Chevreuse

From Le-Perreux-sur-Marne

When the pair reached the city their advantage was a minute. That lead continued to stretch as they drove hard up and down the Champs-Élysées, while the bunch failed to mount a concerted chase behind them.

Coming into the finish, Zoetemelk led out the sprint from 150 m, but could not hold off Hinault, who surged by to claim his seventh stage win as he retained his title in commanding fashion.

Zoetemelk later received a 10-minute penalty after testing positive for steroids but, such was the difference between the Dutchman, Hinault and the rest, that he still finished 13 minutes clear of third-placed Joaquim Agostinho.

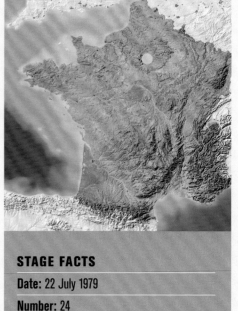

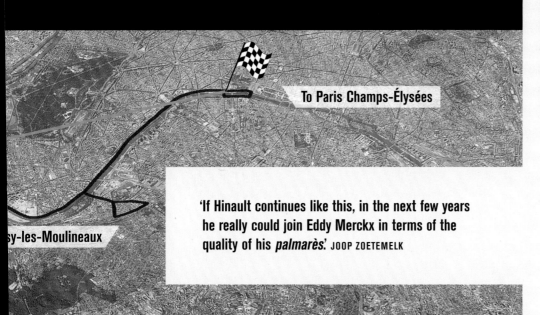

To Paris Champs-Élysées

sy-les-Moulineaux

'If Hinault continues like this, in the next few years he really could join Eddy Merckx in terms of the quality of his *palmarès*.' JOOP ZOETEMELK

STAGE FACTS

Date: 22 July 1979

Number: 24

Length: 180.3 km

WINNERS ON THE CHAMPS-ÉLYSÉES

1975: Walter Godefroot (Bel)
1976: Gerben Karstens (Ned)
1977: Alain Meslet (Fra)
1978: Gerrie Knetemann (Ned)
1979: Bernard Hinault (Fra)
1980: Pol Verschuere (Bel)
1981: Freddy Maertens (Bel)
1982: Bernard Hinault (Fra)
1983: Gilbert Glaus (Swi)
1984: Eric Vanderaerden (Bel)
1985: Rudy Matthijs (Bel)
1986: Guido Bontempi (Ita)
1987: Jeff Pierce (USA)
1988: Jean-Paul van Poppel (Ned)
1989: Greg LeMond (USA)
1990: Johan Museeuw (Bel)
1991: Dmitri Konyshev (Rus)
1992: Olaf Ludwig (Ger)

1993: Djamolidine Abdoujaparov (Uzb)
1994: Eddy Seigneur (Fra)
1995: Djamolidine Abdoujaparov (Uzb)
1996: Fabio Baldato (Ita)
1997: Nicola Minali (Ita)
1998: Tom Steels (Bel)
1999: Robbie McEwen (Aus)
2000: Stefano Zanini (Ita)
2001: Ján Svorada (Cze)
2002: Robbie McEwen (Aus)
2003: Jean-Patrick Nazon (Fra)
2004: Tom Boonen (Bel)
2005: Alexander Vinokourov (Kaz)
2006: Thor Hushovd (Nor)
2007: Daniele Bennati (Ita)
2008: Gert Steegmans (Bel)
2009: Mark Cavendish (UK)
2010: Mark Cavendish (UK)
2011: Mark Cavendish (UK)
2012: Mark Cavendish (UK)

BEFORE STAGE 24	AFTER STAGE 24
1 Bernard Hinault (Fra) 2 Joop Zoetemelk (Ned) at 3'07" 3 Joaquim Agostinho (Por) at 24'35"	1 Bernard Hinault (Fra) 2 Joop Zoetemelk (Ned) at 13'07" 3 Joaquim Agostinho (Por) at 26'53"
Bernard Hinault (Fra)	Bernard Hinault (Fra)
Giovanni Battaglin (Ita)	Giovanni Battaglin (Ita)
Jean-René Bernaudeau (Fra)	Jean-René Bernaudeau (Fra)

Crocked Hinault's moonlight flit

AGEN > PAU

Bernard Hinault always did things his own way when he was racing, and that included quitting the 1980 Tour de France when he was wearing the yellow jersey. Winner of three stages in the first half of the race, Hinault looked to be in control as he took the yellow jersey in a long mid-race time trial. However, he was only fifth that day and admitted to journalists that he'd been struggling with tendinitis in his right knee.

The weather had been dismal during that first half of the race, which certainly contributed to Hinault's injury. It was widely felt, though, that once the Tour reached the heat of the south of France, he would stroll to a third consecutive victory. However, Hinault realized on the road to Pau that he wasn't even going to

JOOP ZOETEMELK'S TOUR RECORD

Prior to the 2012 Tour, Joop Zoetemelk held the record for the most Tour appearances jointly with George Hincapie, both having ridden 16. The American now has 17 to his credit, although Zoetemelk can still claim the record for the most Tour finishes, as he completed all of his 16.

1970: Second
1971: Second
1972: Fifth
1973: Fourth and one stage win
1975: Fourth and one stage win
1976: Second and three stage wins
1977: Eighth and one stage win
1978: Second and one stage win
1979: Second and one stage win
1980: First and two stage wins
1981: Fourth
1982: Second
1983: Twenty-third
1984: Thirtieth
1985: Twelfth
1986: Twenty-fourth

2. After the finish in Pau, Hinault confirmed that he had no thoughts of leaving the race even though he had already decided to quit. In one radio interview he said he was planning to attack on the Aubisque the next day, but the race left Pau without him. He told *L'Équipe* later he 'didn't have the courage to face a press conference'.

Fleurance

Miradoux

Vic-Fezensac

1. Hinault appeared to be struggling to some extent with his knee, most obviously in the 52 km time trial at Laplume, where he only managed to finish fifth. But he was adamant he was going to press on no matter what.

3. After Hinault had slipp[ed] away in the night, Cyrille Guimard faced journalist[s] who didn't hide their an[ger] at apparently having bee[n] misled by the Tour de France's biggest star.

From Agen

reach the Pyrenees. He later admitted that he decided at the 50 km mark of the stage between Agen and Pau that he was going to quit. This being Hinault, though, quitting wasn't as straightforward as it would be for most riders.

Following the stage, Hinault insisted he was going to continue but hours later he slipped out of Hotel Continental in Pau and was spirited away as Renault team director Cyrille Guimard broke the news to the press. As the race moved on, it emerged that Hinault had taken refuge at the Lourdes home of team-mate Hubert Arbes.

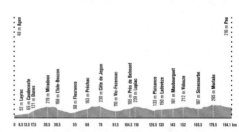

4. Hinault was reunited with his wife, Martine, and son, Michael, at Hubert Arbes' house. Once the press had tracked him down there, he said he was turning his sights towards the World Championships at Sallanches in the French Alps, which he won in typically dominating fashion.

STAGE FACTS

Date: 9 July 1980

Number: 12

Length: 194.1 km

BEFORE STAGE 12	AFTER STAGE 12 (AND HINAULT'S ABANDON)

1 Bernard Hinault (Fra)	1 Joop Zoetemelk (Ned)
2 Joop Zoetemelk (Ned) at 0'21"	2 Rudy Pévenage (Bel) at 1'08"
3 Rudy Pévenage (Bel) at 1'29"	3 Hennie Kuiper (Ned) at 1'10"

Rudy Pévenage (Bel) — Rudy Pévenage (Bel)

Not available — Not available

Not available — Not available

Plaisance

Simacourbe

To Pau

'I'm a man like any other. I've got limits. I could have started in Pau but I would have had to stop on the first climb and watch the peloton riding away from me. There was no question of that.' BERNARD HINAULT

1981

Anderson takes yellow for Oz

SAINT-GAUDENS > SAINT-LARY-SOULAN

The 1981 race would end up in a crushing victory for Bernard Hinault over his rivals, who never looked up to the job of challenging the Frenchman as he cruised towards his third Tour success. Instead, the most persistent challenge came from young Australian Phil Anderson, who was making his Tour debut.

Anderson came to the fore on the one and only stage in the Pyrenees, which finished at Pla d'Adet, above Saint-Lary-Soulan. After a couple of smaller climbs, the leaders reached the Col de Peyresourde, where Hinault upped the pace and quickly decimated his rivals. By the time he reached the summit, the Frenchmen had just two riders with him, Teka's Alberto Fernández and Peugeot's Anderson.

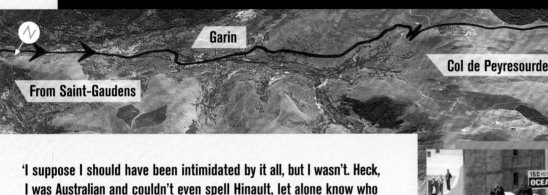

From Saint-Gaudens

Garin

Col de Peyresourde

Bordères-Louron

'I suppose I should have been intimidated by it all, but I wasn't. Heck, I was Australian and couldn't even spell Hinault, let alone know who he was.' PHIL ANDERSON

1. Michel Laurent and Jean-René Bernaudeau were expected to be Peugeot's leaders, but it was 23-year-old Australian Phil Anderson – pictured here behind Bernard Hinault – who stood out as the French team's star performer on the stage to Pla d'Adet.

AUSTRALIA'S TOUR HIGHS

1981: Phil Anderson becomes the first Australian to wear the yellow jersey.

1982: Anderson becomes Australia's first stage winner, finishes fifth and takes the best young rider title.

1997: Neil Stephens becomes Australia's second stage winner in Colmar.

1998: Stuart O'Grady wins in Grenoble and holds the yellow jersey for three days.

1999: Robbie McEwen wins the final stage in Paris.

2001: O'Grady holds the yellow jersey for five days.

2002: After winning in Reims, McEwen wraps up the points title with another victory on the Champs-Élysées; Bradley McGee takes the Avranches stage.

2003: Bradley McGee wins the prologue in the centenary Tour and holds yellow for three days; after winning a stage in Sedan, Baden Cooke goes on to take the points title when he pips compatriot McEwen on the line in Paris.

2004: McEwen takes two stage wins and a second points title; O'Grady takes the stage into Chartres.

2005: McEwen takes three stages.

2006: McEwen takes three stages and a third points title; Cadel Evans finishes fourth overall.

2007: McEwen wins his final Tour stage in Canterbury; Evans wins the time trial in Albi and finishes second overall.

2008: Simon Gerrans takes an unexpected mountains win at Prato Nevoso; Evans holds the yellow jersey for five days and finishes second overall.

2010: Evans holds the yellow jersey for one day.

2011: Evans wins on the Mûr-de-Bretagne and takes the overall title.

2012: GreenEDGE is the first Australian team to start the Tour.

3. Anderson – pictured here with Bernard Hinault – has been succeeded by another four Australians over the subsequent three decades: Robbie McEwen, Stuart O'Grady, Bradley McGee and Cadel Evans.

On the drop into the valley below, another three riders joined this trio: Claude Criquielion, Marino Lejarreta and Lucien van Impe. Belgian veteran van Impe, who would claim the King of the Mountains title and second place overall in Paris, attacked on the final climb with 5 km to the finish and went on to take victory on the day.

Hinault dropped three of the other riders, but could not shake the dogged Anderson, who stuck with the Frenchman all the way to the line. This largely unexpected performance put him in the yellow jersey, making him the first Australian to savour this honour.

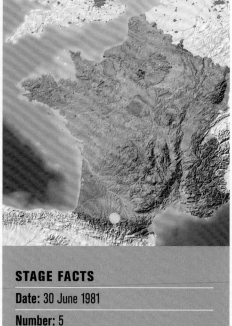

STAGE FACTS

Date: 30 June 1981

Number: 5

Length: 117.5 km

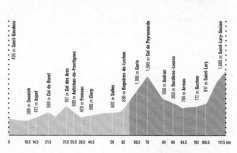

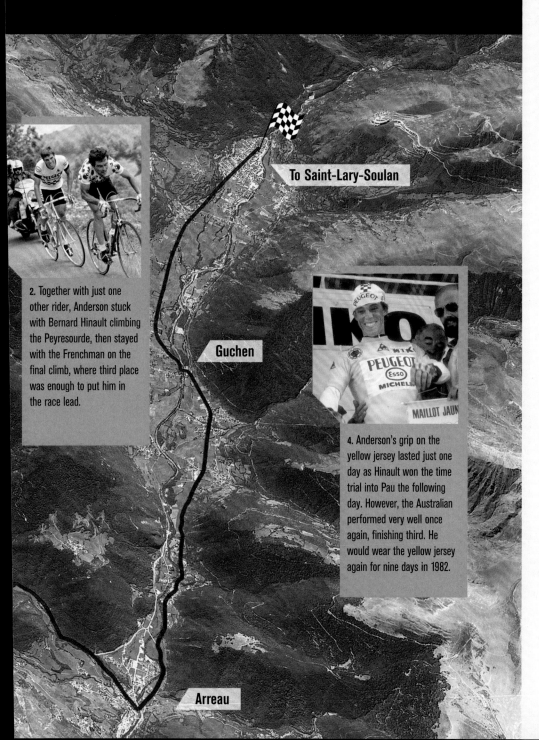

To Saint-Lary-Soulan

2. Together with just one other rider, Anderson stuck with Bernard Hinault climbing the Peyresourde, then stayed with the Frenchman on the final climb, where third place was enough to put him in the race lead.

Guchen

4. Anderson's grip on the yellow jersey lasted just one day as Hinault won the time trial into Pau the following day. However, the Australian performed very well once again, finishing third. He would wear the yellow jersey again for nine days in 1982.

Arreau

BEFORE STAGE 5	AFTER STAGE 5
1 Gerrie Knetemann (Ned)	1 Phil Anderson (Aus)
2 Ludo Peeters (Ned)	2 Bernard Hinault (Fra)
at 0'01"	at 0'17"
3 Joop Zoetemelk (Ned)	3 Jostein Wilmann (Nor)
at 0'16"	at 3'08"
Freddy Maertens (Bel)	Freddy Maertens (Bel)
Not available	Lucien van Impe (Bel)
Peter Winnen (Ned)	Phil Anderson (Aus)

1983

Disaster strikes Simon

LUCHON > FLEURANCE

What should have been a routine 'transition' day as the Tour left the Pyrenees in 1983 provided the turning point in the race. The day before, Peugeot's Pascal Simon had claimed the yellow jersey with a performance of such superiority that it seemed unlikely anyone would challenge him for the title.

Stage 11 didn't present any notable difficulties. However, with 37 km covered, Simon's hopes fell apart. His downfall began when Joaquim Agostinho attacked. Simon's team-mate Bernard Bourreau started to chase on the front of the peloton and clashed with Agostinho's team-mate Jonathan Boyer. Bourreau went down. Simon, who was on his wheel, couldn't avoid Bourreau and crashed too, landing heavily on his left shoulder.

From Luchon

1. Fignon felt that he and Simon were well matched in time trials but conceded that his Peugeot rival was far superior in the mountains, based on Simon's impressive performance into Luchon, where he claimed the yellow jersey.

2. On the evening of his crash, Simon admitted he had wondered whether he would get through the stage. Asked what he felt his chances were of reaching Paris, he replied: 'About one in a hundred.'

3. After a week of agonizing struggle, Simon finally yielded on the road to the Alpe d'Huez, fully aware that there was no chance of him remaining in contention on such a tough climb.

Montréjeau

'Our doctor has told me that I can hang on to the jersey. But perhaps he has told me that just to keep my spirits up.' PASCAL SIMON

It was obvious that the race leader was in a lot of pain, but he struggled on to the finish. That evening an X-ray revealed a broken shoulder-blade. With a clear lead, Simon bravely pressed on, his team-mates setting the pace each day, while their leader's rivals awaited his inevitable fate. He lost 3 minutes to Laurent Fignon in a time trial up the Puy-de-Dôme.

Two days later, after a week in yellow, Simon could bear the pain no longer. He abandoned on the road to the Alpe d'Huez, where Fignon inherited the yellow jersey. While Fignon rode on to claim victory on his Tour debut, Simon never again achieved this level at the Tour.

STAGE FACTS

Date: 12 July 1983

Number: 11

Length: 177 km

4. Once in the yellow jersey, Fignon rode almost untroubled all the way into the capital guided by masterful Renault team director Cyrille Guimard.

Fleurance

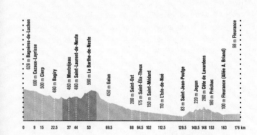

BEFORE STAGE 11

1 Pascal Simon (Fra)
2 Laurent Fignon (Fra)
at 4'22"
3 Jean-René Bernaudeau (Fra)
at 5'34"

Sean Kelly (Ire)

Patricinio Jiménez (Col)

Laurent Fignon (Fra)

AFTER STAGE 11

1 Pascal Simon (Fra)
2 Laurent Fignon (Fra)
at 4'22"
3 Jean-René Bernaudeau (Fra)
at 5'34"

Sean Kelly (Ire)

Patricinio Jiménez (Col)

Laurent Fignon (Fra)

YELLOW JERSEYS BY COUNTRY

France tops the list of yellow jersey-wearers by nation, with Eugène Christophe having the honour of being France's first recipient of the famous tunic and the Tour's first ever yellow jersey-wearer, on stage 11 in 1919. The rider who first wore the yellow jersey for each country and the year it was worn appears in brackets:

86: France (Eugène Christophe in 1919)
55: Belgium (Firmin Lambot in 1919)
24: Italy (Ottavio Bottecchia in 1923)
17: Holland (Wim van Est in 1951)
13: Germany (Kurt Stöpel in 1932)

11: Spain (Miguel Poblet in 1955)
9: Switzerland (Paul Egli in 1936); Luxembourg (Nicolas Frantz in 1927)
5: Denmark (Kim Andersen in 1983); Australia (Phil Anderson) in 1981
4: Great Britain (Tom Simpson in 1962)
3: Ireland (Seamus Elliott in 1963); United States (Greg LeMond in 1986)
2: Canada (Alex Stieda in 1986)
1: Austria (Max Bulla in 1931); Colombia (Victor Hugo Peña in 2003); Estonia (Jaan Kirsipuu in 1999), Norway (Thor Hushovd in 2006); Poland (Lech Piasecki in 1987); Portugal (Acácio da Silva in 1989); Russia (Evgeni Berzin in 1996); Ukraine (Serhiy Honchar in 2006)

1984

Haughty Fignon downs Hinault

GRENOBLE > ALPE D'HUEZ

Winner of the Tour the previous year when Bernard Hinault had been injured, Laurent Fignon was in even better shape in 1984 when Hinault returned to the race looking for his fifth title. The French champion had won the previous day's time trial and went into the Alpe d'Huez stage looking to finish off his rivals, Hinault included.

Backed into a corner by his compatriot's superiority, Hinault lived up to his nickname of 'The Badger' by attacking persistently. He went first on the Col du Coq, then again on the Laffrey pass, only to see Fignon ride away from him in the company of Colombian climber Luis Herrera.

Approaching the Alpe d'Huez, Hinault was one of a group that got across to the two leaders. Rather than catching his breath,

1. Hinault refused to yield without pushing himself as hard as he could. He attacked early on in the Alpe d'Huez stage. On the Col de Laffrey he tried to get away on no fewer than five occasions, but couldn't respond to Fignon's counterattack with Luis Herrera.

Col du Coq

Saint-Joseph-de-Rivière

Col de la Placette

Voreppe

Saint-Égrève

From Grenoble

3. Herrera left the two Frenchmen to their duel and pressed on alone towards the summit of the famous climb. His victory was the first ever by a Colombian rider and the first by an amateur in the modern era.

COLOMBIAN TOUR SUCCESSES

1983: Edgar Corredor is 16th when Colombia's Varta team debuts.

1984: Luis Herrera wins at the Alpe d'Huez, Rafael Acevedo is 12th.

1985: Herrera wins at Avoriaz and Saint-Étienne, finishes seventh and wins King of the Mountains title; Fabio Parra win at Lans-en-Vercors and finishes eighth.

1987: Herrera finishes fifth and wins King of the Mountains title, Parra sixth.

1988: Parra wins at Morzine and finishes third.

1993: Oliverio Rincón wins at Andorra, Álvaro Mejía finishes fourth.

1994: Nelson Rodríguez wins at Val Thorens.

1995: Hernán Buenahora is tenth.

1996: Chepe González wins at Valence.

2000: Santiago Botero wins at Briançon, finishes seventh and wins King of the Mountains title.

2001: Félix Cárdenas wins at Ax-les-Thermes.

2002: Botero wins at Lorient and Les Deux Alpes and finishes fourth.

2003: Víctor Hugo Peña is the first Colombian to wear the yellow jersey.

2007: Mauricio Soler wins at Briançon and wins King of the Mountains title.

2. Hinault managed to get across to the two leaders before the Alpe d'Huez and didn't hesitate in making another attack. Fignon and Herrera caught and passed him on the early ramps of the climb.

Hinault powered on, stomping on the pedals with a belligerent show of force.

He led by 26 seconds heading onto the Alpe's initial ramps, but his non-stop attacks began to take their toll. First Herrera and then Fignon passed him. Herrera found his best rhythm and rode away from Fignon to claim his country's first Tour success.

Defeat on the day mattered little to Fignon, whose rivals were scattered down the mountainside below him. Hinault insisted that he would attack all the way to the Champs-Élysées but, such was Fignon's dominance, he countered Hinault's attacks and cantered to victory.

STAGE FACTS

Date: 16 July 1984

Number: 17

Length: 151 km

To Alpe d'Huez

Livet

Vizille

Côte de Laffrey

4. Second place on the day was enough to put Fignon into the yellow jersey at the expense of his Renault team-mate Vincent Barteau. Crucially, his lead on Hinault was now almost 6 minutes.

BEFORE STAGE 17	AFTER STAGE 17
1 Vincent Barteau (Fra)	1 Laurent Fignon (Fra)
2 Laurent Fignon (Fra) at 6'29"	2 Vincent Barteau (Fra) at 4'22"
3 Bernard Hinault (Fra) at 9'15"	3 Bernard Hinault (Fra) at 5'41"
Jacques Hanegraaf (Ned)	Jacques Hanegraaf (Ned)
Jean-René Bernaudeau (Fra)	Robert Millar (UK)
Vincent Barteau (Fra)	Vincent Barteau (Fra)

'When I saw him attacking, it really made me laugh. Honestly, I laughed. His attitude is absurd. When you get dropped the very least you can do is to take advantage of the situation by recovering your resources. But Bernard has got too much pride.' LAURENT FIGNON

North America's first yellow

NANTERRE > SCEAUX

1986

A well-known biblical quote has it that 'the last shall be first'. On the second day of the 1986 Tour that unlikely occurrence played out when Canada's Alex Stieda, numerically the last rider in the race as he was wearing number 210, captured the yellow, and indeed all of the other race jerseys, thanks to a short-lived raid.

Having finished 21st in the opening prologue, just 12 seconds down on winner Thierry Marie, Stieda, riding for the American 7-Eleven team that was making its debut in the race, attacked going into the first intermediate sprint. Having grabbed that prize and the bonus seconds on offer, the Canadian pressed on, building a lead of almost 2 minutes as he led the way through a couple more sprints, collecting more prizes and even more bonus seconds.

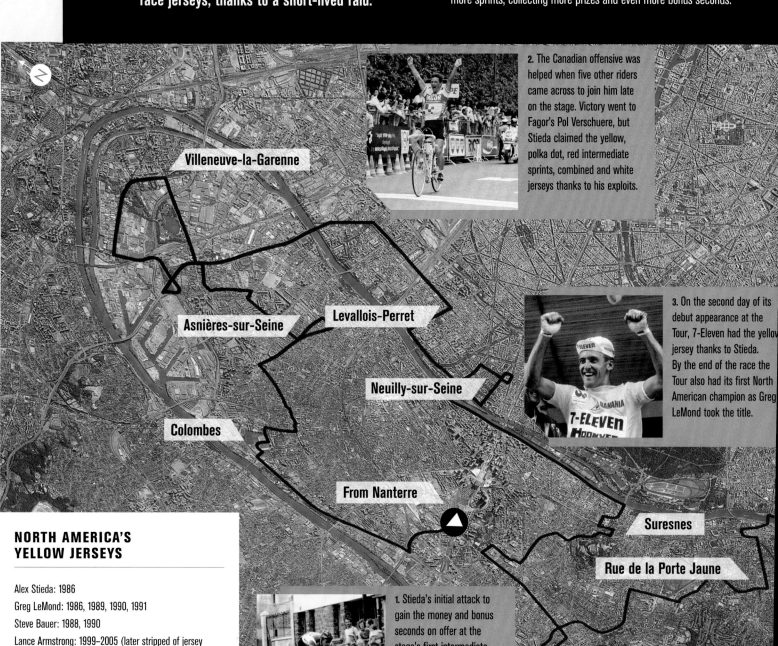

Villeneuve-la-Garenne

Asnières-sur-Seine

Levallois-Perret

Neuilly-sur-Seine

Colombes

From Nanterre

Suresnes

Rue de la Porte Jaune

Rueil-Malmaison

2. The Canadian offensive was helped when five other riders came across to join him late on the stage. Victory went to Fagor's Pol Verschuere, but Stieda claimed the yellow, polka dot, red intermediate sprints, combined and white jerseys thanks to his exploits.

3. On the second day of its debut appearance at the Tour, 7-Eleven had the yellow jersey thanks to Stieda. By the end of the race the Tour also had its first North American champion as Greg LeMond took the title.

1. Stieda's initial attack to gain the money and bonus seconds on offer at the stage's first intermediate sprint took on much more significance when he pressed on and gained more time at subsequent sprints.

NORTH AMERICA'S YELLOW JERSEYS

Alex Stieda: 1986
Greg LeMond: 1986, 1989, 1990, 1991
Steve Bauer: 1988, 1990
Lance Armstrong: 1999–2005 (later stripped of jersey for doping)
David Zabriskie: 2005
George Hincapie: 2006
Floyd Landis: 2006 (later disqualified for doping)

With 16 of the stage's 85 km still remaining, Stieda was caught up by five other riders, who were all interested in contesting the stage victory. Realizing that if he could stick with them and finish ahead of the bunch he would take the yellow jersey, the Canadian clung on. Although he finished fifth of the five on the line, the time he gained gave him the race lead. However, he kept the lead for only a matter of hours as 7-Eleven finished 20th in the time trial that same afternoon.

STAGE FACTS

Date: 5 July 1986

Number: 1

Length: 85 km

'After a few kilometres I noodled up the side of the road and just took off... The yellow jersey was totally unpredicted and our whole team was really thrilled.' ALEX STIEDA

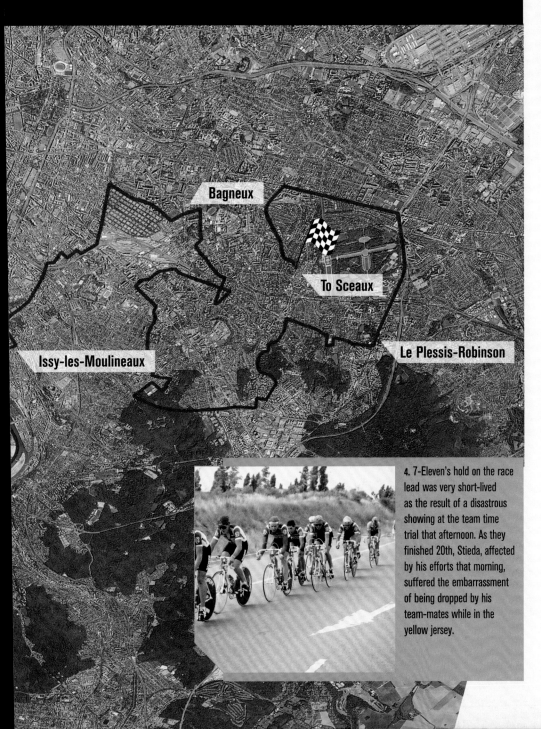

Bagneux

To Sceaux

Issy-les-Moulineaux

Le Plessis-Robinson

4. 7-Eleven's hold on the race lead was very short-lived as the result of a disastrous showing at the team time trial that afternoon. As they finished 20th, Stieda, affected by his efforts that morning, suffered the embarrassment of being dropped by his team-mates while in the yellow jersey.

BEFORE STAGE 1	AFTER STAGE 1
1 Thierry Marie (Fra)	1 Alex Stieda (Can)
2 Eric Vanderaerden (Bel) same time	2 Eric Vanderaerden (Bel) at 0'08"
3 Bernard Hinault (Fra) at 0'02"	3 Steve Bauer (Can) at 0'22"
Thierry Marie (Fra)	Pol Verschuere (Ned)
(polka dot jersey)	(polka dot jersey)
Not awarded	Alex Stieda (Can)
Jesús Blanco Villar (Spa)	Alex Stieda (Can)

Hinault's kamikaze attack

PAU > SUPERBAGNÈRES

On the previous stage, Bernard Hinault had again been in his prime. Having publicly committed himself to help La Vie Claire team-mate Greg LeMond's challenge for the yellow jersey, Hinault had gone on the attack with Pedro Delgado. Delgado took the stage but the real winner was Hinault, now more than 5 minutes up on LeMond in second.

Rather than sit back and defend the yellow jersey, Hinault went on the attack again on the next stage to Superbagnères. He made his move on the descent off the Col du Tourmalet, gaining a remarkable 90 seconds. He pressed on over the Aspin and joined lone breakaway Dominique Arnaud on the climb of the Peyresourde. Despite his best efforts, Arnaud couldn't cope with Hinault's rhythm for long.

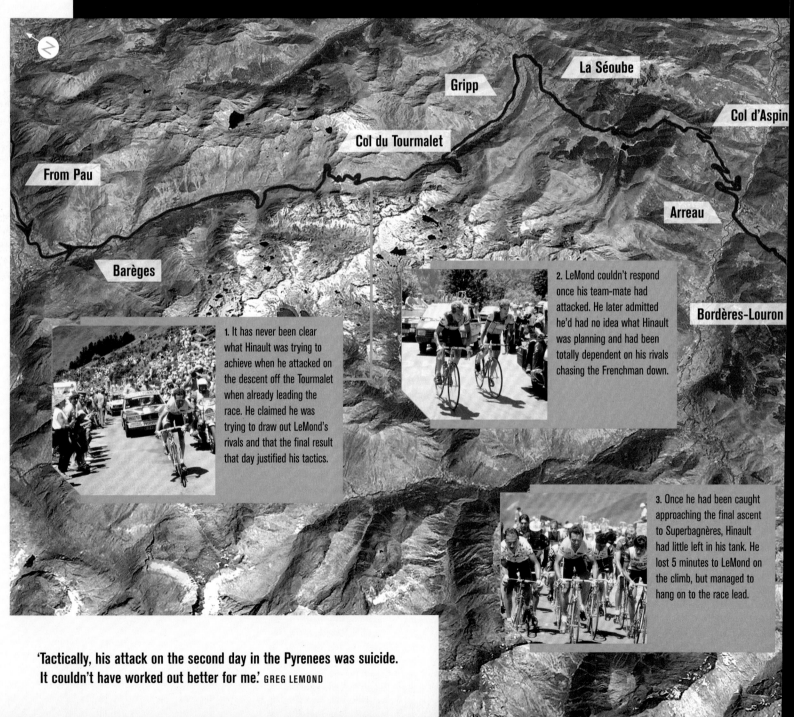

La Séoube

Gripp

Col d'Aspin

Col du Tourmalet

From Pau

Arreau

Barèges

Bordères-Louron

1. It has never been clear what Hinault was trying to achieve when he attacked on the descent off the Tourmalet when already leading the race. He claimed he was trying to draw out LeMond's rivals and that the final result that day justified his tactics.

2. LeMond couldn't respond once his team-mate had attacked. He later admitted he'd had no idea what Hinault was planning and had been totally dependent on his rivals chasing the Frenchman down.

3. Once he had been caught approaching the final ascent to Superbagnères, Hinault had little left in his tank. He lost 5 minutes to LeMond on the climb, but managed to hang on to the race lead.

'Tactically, his attack on the second day in the Pyrenees was suicide. It couldn't have worked out better for me.' GREG LEMOND

But, feeling the effects of the previous day's efforts, Hinault began to wilt too. His rivals were only 25 seconds down crossing the Peyresourde and caught him on the descent. His reserves almost spent, Hinault could not follow their pace on the final climb.

His team-mate Andy Hampsten made the first move to win the stage and was then joined by LeMond, who had accelerated away from rivals. Knowing that he had the perfect opportunity to regain time on Hinault and to assert himself as La Vie Claire's leader, LeMond went on alone. At the finish, Hinault hung on narrowly to the yellow jersey, but the momentum was now with LeMond.

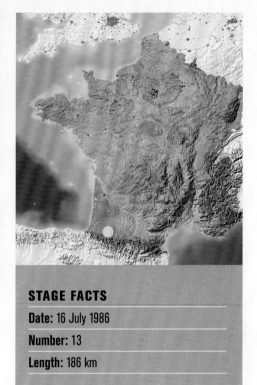

STAGE FACTS

Date: 16 July 1986

Number: 13

Length: 186 km

BERNARD HINAULT'S TOUR RECORD

1978: First and three stage wins

1979: First, points champion and seven stages wins

1980: Three stage wins, abandoned after stage 12 because of tendinitis in his knee

1981: First, four stage wins, combativity prize and combined competition winner

1982: First, four stage wins, combined competition winner

1983: Did not start

1984: Second, one stage win, combativity prize

1985: First and two stage wins

1986: Second, three stage wins, King of the Mountains, combativity prize

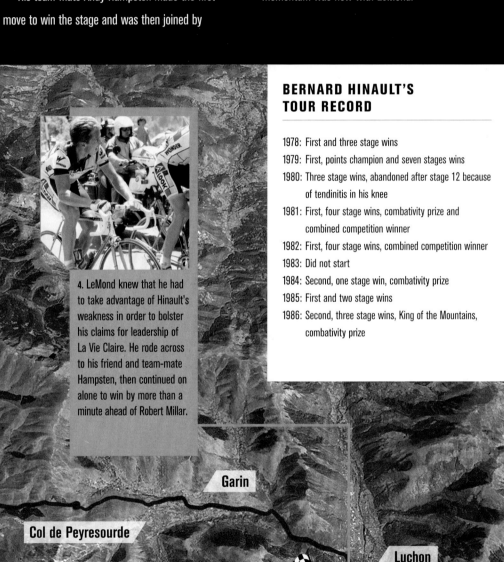

4. LeMond knew that he had to take advantage of Hinault's weakness in order to bolster his claims for leadership of La Vie Claire. He rode across to his friend and team-mate Hampsten, then continued on alone to win by more than a minute ahead of Robert Millar.

Garin

Col de Peyresourde

Luchon

To Superbagnères

BEFORE STAGE 13	AFTER STAGE 13
1 Bernard Hinault (Fra)	1 Bernard Hinault (Fra)
2 Greg LeMond (USA)	2 Greg LeMond (USA)
at 5'25"	at 0'40"
3 Urs Zimmermann (Swi)	3 Urs Zimmermann (Swi)
at 6'22"	at 2'58"
Eric Vanderaerden (Bel)	Eric Vanderaerden (Bel)
Ronan Pensec (Fra)	Robert Millar (UK)
Jean-François Bernard (Fra)	Andy Hampsten (USA)

1986

Hand in hand on the Alpe

BRIANÇON > ALPE D'HUEZ

This stage is one of the Tour's most legendary. The previous day, Greg LeMond had taken the yellow jersey from team-mate and defending champion Bernard Hinault, who had treatment on a calf injury that evening. However, if Hinault was struggling, there was little sign of it in his performance the next day in tandem with LeMond.

Descending off the Col du Galibier, the first of the day's three big climbs, Hinault attacked along with La Vie Claire team-mate Steve Bauer. With Urs Zimmermann – who was in second position overall – on his wheel, LeMond conferred with team director Paul Koechli, and then made his move on the descent into the Vallée de la Maurienne, where he joined Hinault and Bauer at the front of the race.

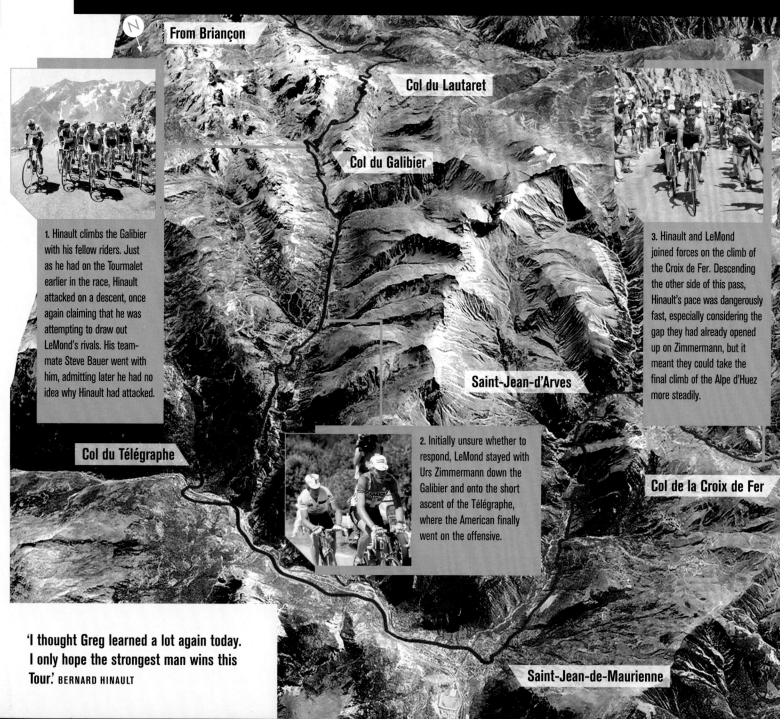

From Briançon

Col du Lautaret

Col du Galibier

1. Hinault climbs the Galibier with his fellow riders. Just as he had on the Tourmalet earlier in the race, Hinault attacked on a descent, once again claiming that he was attempting to draw out LeMond's rivals. His team-mate Steve Bauer went with him, admitting later he had no idea why Hinault had attacked.

3. Hinault and LeMond joined forces on the climb of the Croix de Fer. Descending the other side of this pass, Hinault's pace was dangerously fast, especially considering the gap they had already opened up on Zimmermann, but it meant they could take the final climb of the Alpe d'Huez more steadily.

Saint-Jean-d'Arves

Col du Télégraphe

2. Initially unsure whether to respond, LeMond stayed with Urs Zimmermann down the Galibier and onto the short ascent of the Télégraphe, where the American finally went on the offensive.

Col de la Croix de Fer

'I thought Greg learned a lot again today. I only hope the strongest man wins this Tour.' BERNARD HINAULT

Saint-Jean-de-Maurienne

Bauer worked flat out to the foot of the Croix de Fer, then fell back, leaving his two leaders to continue with their breakaway on this second big climb. At the summit, their advantage over Zimmermann was almost 3 minutes. This stretched further as Hinault set a terrifying pace down the other side, reaching speeds in excess of 100 km/hour.

At the foot of the Alpe d'Huez, their advantage was 5 minutes. Heading up, Hinault set the pace, appearing to shepherd his younger team-mate. The pair reached the summit together and crossed the line hand in hand. Both had won, Hinault taking the stage as LeMond took a huge step towards the Tour de France title.

Bourg-d'Oisans

Huez-en-Oisans

To Alpe d'Huez

Le Rivier d'Allemont

4. The image of LeMond and Hinault crossing the line together was one for the ages. They had seen off all of their rivals and, at the same time, the baton of Tour champion had passed between them, Hinault handing it on to his younger team-mate.

STAGE FACTS

Date: 21 July 1986

Number: 18

Length: 162.5 km

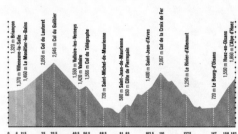

BEFORE STAGE 18

1 Greg LeMond (USA)
2 Urs Zimmermann (Swi)
at 2'24"
3 Bernard Hinault (Fra)
at 2'47"

Eric Vanderaerden (Bel)

Robert Millar (UK)

Andy Hampsten (USA)

AFTER STAGE 18

1 Greg LeMond (USA)
2 Bernard Hinault (Fra)
at 2'45"
3 Urs Zimmermann (Swi)
at 7'41"

Eric Vanderaerden (Bel)

Greg LeMond (USA)

Andy Hampsten (USA)

SPEEDING UP THE ALPE D'HUEZ

A look at the time taken by the stage winner to climb the Alpe d'Huez shows how rapidly speeds increased in the 1990s and early 2000s, and how they have slowed again.

1952: Fausto Coppi 45'22"
1986: Bernard Hinault 48'00"
1989: Gert-Jan Theunisse 45'20"
1991: Gianni Bugno 39'44"
1995: Marco Pantani 38'04"
1997: Marco Pantani 37'35"

2001: Lance Armstrong 38'01"*
2003: Iban Mayo 39'06"
2004: Lance Armstrong 37'36"
2006: Fränk Schleck 40'46"
2008: Carlos Sastre 39'31"
2011: Pierre Rolland 41'57"

Bernard hits heights, then stumbles

CARPENTRAS > MONT VENTOUX (TIME TRIAL)

The 1987 Tour fell between two eras of domination. Bernard Hinault had retired the year before, Greg LeMond was out of racing because of injuries and Miguel Indurain was yet to emerge. This resulted in a much more open race, with as many as ten riders marked as possible winners.

Heading into the time trial that finished on Mont Ventoux, little more than 3 minutes covered the four riders at the top of the overall classification: Charly Mottet, Jean-François Bernard, Stephen Roche and Pedro Delgado. Fastest on the initial rolling section to the foot of the Ventoux on a low-profile bike, Bernard then switched to a lightweight climbing bike and steadily increased his advantage.

1. Although tipped to perform well in the 36.5 km Ventoux time trial, Bernard surpassed everyone's expectations. Unlike his rivals, he opted for a low-profile bike for the initial rolling section of the course, gaining important time on them.

2. Delgado later admitted he had considered riding two different bikes and swapping between them at the foot of the Ventoux, but decided against it because it would cost him 15 seconds. Bernard, though, felt that the change was justified and there was no doubt he was right.

3. The following day on stage 19, and having been slowed by a puncture, Bernard was in the wrong place at the wrong time when his rivals upped the pace heading through the feed station on the road to Villard-de-Lans. Although he gave his all in trying to get back up to them, his stint in yellow lasted just one day.

Bédoin

From Carpentras

Les Bruns

'It was an incredible mess. It was impossible to get through between all the *soigneurs* and *musettes*... The road was completely packed.' JEAN-FRANÇOIS BERNARD

Tipped by Hinault himself as his successor, Bernard beat everyone out of sight. Delgado lost almost 2 minutes, Roche more than 2 and Mottet almost 4. Bernard had, it seemed, shown himself to be the strongest man in the race.

However, his fortunes changed completely the next day. It was a tricky stage through the Vercors mountain massif and Bernard punctured. At the same time, his rivals were massing on the front of the bunch. As Bernard tried to recover, they accelerated and Bernard's Tour hopes disappeared. He lost more than 4 minutes, dropping from first to fourth, as Roche and Delgado emerged as the real favourites.

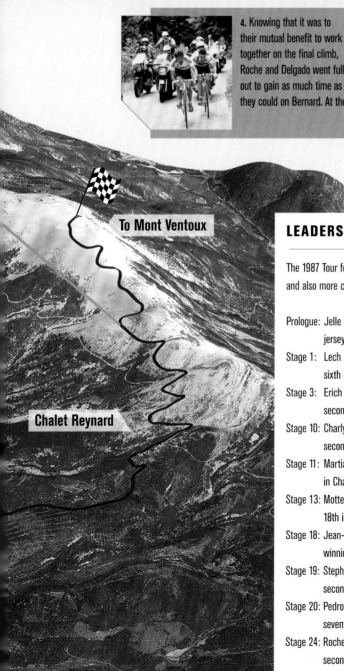

To Mont Ventoux

Chalet Reynard

4. Knowing that it was to their mutual benefit to work together on the final climb, Roche and Delgado went full out to gain as much time as they could on Bernard. At the finish in Villard-de-Lans, the Spaniard took the stage and the Irishman the yellow jersey.

STAGE FACTS

Date: 19 July 1987

Number: 18

Length: 36.5 km

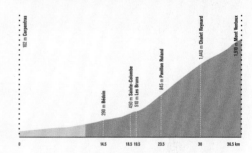

LEADERS GALORE

The 1987 Tour featured more race leaders than any other and also more changes of lead:

Prologue: Jelle Nijdam (Ned) won it and took the yellow jersey in Berlin.

Stage 1: Lech Piasecki (Pol) took yellow after finishing sixth in Berlin.

Stage 3: Erich Maechler (Swi) took yellow after finishing second in Stuttgart.

Stage 10: Charly Mottet (Fra) took yellow after finishing second in the Futuroscope time trial.

Stage 11: Martial Gayant (Fra) took yellow after winning in Chaumeil.

Stage 13: Mottet regained the yellow jersey after finishing 18th in Pau.

Stage 18: Jean-François Bernard (Fra) took yellow after winning on Mont Ventoux.

Stage 19: Stephen Roche (Ire) took yellow after finishing second in Villard-de-Lans.

Stage 20: Pedro Delgado (Spa) took yellow after finishing seventh on the Alpe d'Huez.

Stage 24: Roche regained the yellow jersey after finishing second in the Dijon time trial.

BEFORE STAGE 18

1 Charly Mottet (Fra)
2 Jean-François Bernard (Fra)
at 1'11"
3 Stephen Roche (Ire)
at 1'26"

Jean-Paul van Poppel (Ned)

Luis Herrera (Col)

Raúl Alcalá (Mex)

AFTER STAGE 18

1 Jean-François Bernard (Fra)
2 Stephen Roche (Ire)
at 2'34"
3 Charly Mottet (Fra)
at 2'47"

Jean-Paul van Poppel (Ned)

Luis Herrera (Col)

Raúl Alcalá (Mex)

1987

Roche digs deep

BOURG-D'OISANS > LA PLAGNE

The 1987 Tour was the most open for years. Bernard Hinault had retired the previous season, while defending champion Greg LeMond was missing as a result of injuries.

As the race started in Berlin, up to a dozen riders were being talked up as potential winners. By the time the race had reached the crucial stages in the Alps, two men had emerged as the strongest. Ireland's Stephen Roche had come to the Tour straight from winning the Giro d'Italia, but it looked likely that Spain's Pedro Delgado was going to thwart Roche at the Tour.

Much the better climber, Delgado had taken the yellow jersey from Roche at the Alpe d'Huez, but his lead was a mere 25 seconds. With a time trial still to come, where Roche was

LUCKY NUMBER?

Each year the defending champion is allocated race number 1, while team leaders are traditionally given the first slot in their respective lists of riders, making them easier to pick out on the road. Tour legend has it that the number 51 is the 'winningest' race number after 1, based on a number of high-profile victories by riders bearing that number:

– Eddy Merckx in 1969
– Luis Ocaña in 1973
– Bernard Thévenet in 1975
– Bernard Hinault in 1978

However, riders wearing 11 have taken more victories, notably in recent years:

– Lucien van Impe in 1976
– Joop Zoetemelk in 1980
– Bernard Hinault in 1985
– Stephen Roche in 1987
– Carlos Sastre in 2008
– Andy Schleck in 2010

1. Noticing that Delgado had no team-mates with him coming off the Galibier, Roche attacked approaching the Madeleine and joined the lead breakaway. But his new companions wouldn't work with him and Delgado's team regrouped and chased him down.

2. Roche knew that Delgado would attack when they reached the early ramps on the climb up to La Plagne and that he would be unable to follow the Spaniard. His plan was to allow Delgado some leeway, then counter nearer to the top.

Aigueblanche

Celliers

Moûtiers

Col de la Madeleine

From Bourg-d'Oisans

sure to gain time on him, it was essential that Delgado press home his advantage at La Plagne.

Roche decided attack was the best form of defence and made a surprise move 60 km from the finish. It failed. Caught approaching the last climb, the Irishman looked cooked, especially when Delgado attacked as the road rose again. Roche gathered

himself, tried to manage his losses, then gave all he had in the final 4 km. He cut a deficit of 90 seconds down to just 4. Crossing the line, he collapsed and was given oxygen. But he had saved his Tour hopes.

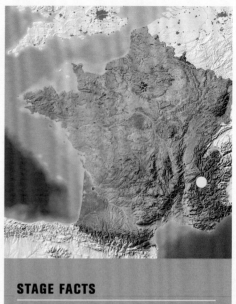

Aime

To La Plagne

'I'm OK. But no woman for me this evening.'
STEPHEN ROCHE WHEN ASKED AS HE LAY IN AN AMBULANCE HOW HE WAS.

STAGE FACTS

Date: 22 July 1987

Number: 21

Length: 185.5 km

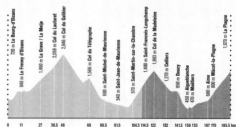

3. When Delgado finished, everyone thought he had the Tour won, but Roche emerged almost immediately to come in just 4 seconds down, much to everyone's surprise. Roche couldn't speak at the finish and was laid out at the foot of the press gantry, where the medical team gave him oxygen. He admitted later that his biggest concern was the structure behind him collapsing as photographers battled to get his picture.

4. Roche was determined to undermine Delgado's confidence heading into the crucial time trial at Dijon. In the following stage he gained a few vital seconds on the Spaniard following a daredevil descent into Morzine, hoping that it would underline the feeling that momentum was with him. The Irishman then reclaimed the yellow jersey in Dijon, where he beat Delgado by a minute. With just the final stage to negotiate, the title was almost his.

BEFORE STAGE 21

1 Pedro Delgado (Spa)
2 Stephen Roche (Ire)
at 0'25"
3 Jean-François Bernard (Fra)
at 2'02"

Jean-Paul van Poppel (Ned)

Luis Herrera (Col)

Raúl Alcalá (Mex)

AFTER STAGE 21

1 Pedro Delgado (Spa)
2 Stephen Roche (Ire)
at 0'39"
3 Charly Mottet (Fra)
at 3'12"

Jean-Paul van Poppel (Ned)

Luis Herrera (Col)

Raúl Alcalá (Mex)

A mere 8 seconds!

VERSAILLES > PARIS CHAMPS-ÉLYSÉES (TIME TRIAL)

The Tour of 1989 produced an epic duel between two former winners: Greg LeMond and Laurent Fignon. LeMond took the lead in the first long time trial, Fignon snatched the yellow jersey at Superbagnères, LeMond regained it in the second trial, only for Fignon to grab it again on the Alpe d'Huez.

Going into the final time trial, Fignon led his rival by 50 seconds. Over a course of 24.5 km it looked likely to be enough. Surely LeMond couldn't gain 2 seconds a kilometre on his rival?

However, unbeknown to most, Fignon was struggling with a painful saddle sore. LeMond, meanwhile, had the confidence of knowing he'd beaten the Frenchman in two previous time trials.

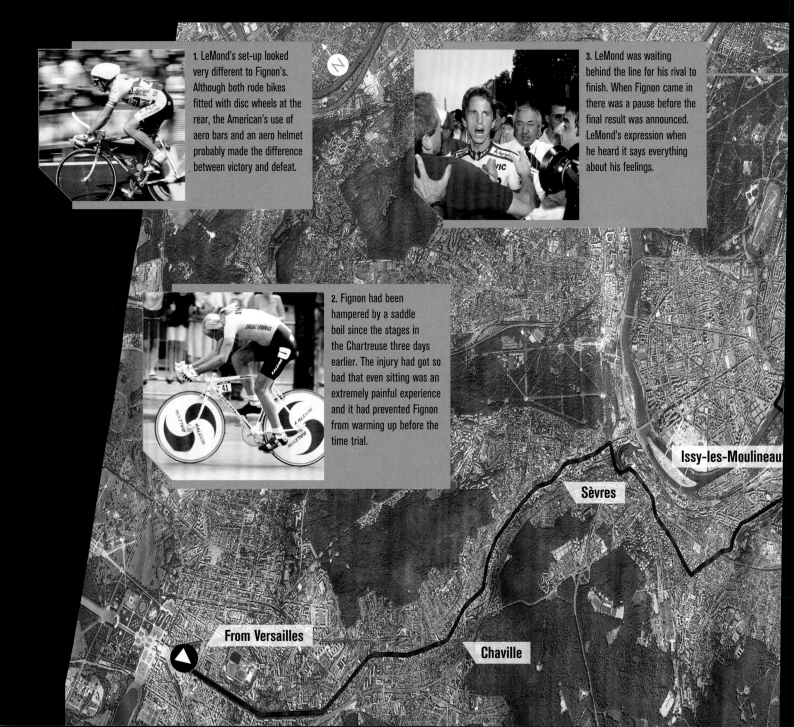

1. LeMond's set-up looked very different to Fignon's. Although both rode bikes fitted with disc wheels at the rear, the American's use of aero bars and an aero helmet probably made the difference between victory and defeat.

3. LeMond was waiting behind the line for his rival to finish. When Fignon came in there was a pause before the final result was announced. LeMond's expression when he heard it says everything about his feelings.

2. Fignon had been hampered by a saddle boil since the stages in the Chartreuse three days earlier. The injury had got so bad that even sitting was an extremely painful experience and it had prevented Fignon from warming up before the time trial.

Issy-les-Moulineau

Sèvres

From Versailles

Chaville

He was also set to use an aero helmet and aero bars, technology developed in triathlon but still little used on the road.

At halfway, LeMond had chipped 24 seconds off Fignon's lead. At 18 km, the Frenchman's advantage was just 15 seconds. As he sped up to the finish on the Champs-Élysées, Fignon still held a narrow lead. But it slipped away from him over those final few hundred metres. LeMond had won the Tour by a mere 8 seconds, the closest victory in the race's history. Two years on from a life-threatening shooting accident and after being written off by many, the American was a Tour winner for the second time.

STAGE FACTS

Date: 23 July 1989

Number: 21

Length: 24.5 km

To Paris Champs-Élysées

Cours-la-Reine

Place de la Concorde

4. The two men's expressions on the podium tell the story of the final day. The final distance between them was estimated to be 82 m at the end of 3,285 km.

THE TOUR'S CLOSEST WINNING MARGINS

8 seconds: Greg LeMond beat Laurent Fignon in 1989.

23 seconds: Alberto Contador beat Cadel Evans in 2007.

32 seconds: Óscar Pereiro beat Andreas Klöden in 2006.

38 seconds: Jan Janssen beat Herman van Springel in 1968.

40 seconds: Stephen Roche beat Pedro Delgado in 1987.

48 seconds: Bernard Thévenet beat Hennie Kuiper in 1977.

55 seconds: Jacques Anquetil beat Raymond Poulidor in 1964.

58 seconds: Carlos Sastre beat Cadel Evans in 2008.

'There are a thousand places where I have lost this Tour and also a thousand places where Greg has won it.' LAURENT FIGNON

BEFORE STAGE 21

1 Laurent Fignon (Fra)
2 Greg LeMond (USA)
at 0'50"
3 Pedro Delgado (Spa)
at 2'28"

Sean Kelly (Ire)

Gert-Jan Theunisse (Ned)

Fabrice Philipot (Fra)

AFTER STAGE 21

1 Greg LeMond (USA)
2 Laurent Fignon (Fra)
at 0'08"
3 Pedro Delgado (Spa)
at 3'34"

Sean Kelly (Ire)

Gert-Jan Theunisse (Ned)

Fabrice Philipot (Fra)

1990

The longest pursuit in history

FUTUROSCOPE > FUTUROSCOPE

Most long breakaways come to nothing, but occasionally one changes the whole complexion of a stage race. The second day featured a split stage, a short road stage in the morning and a team time trial in the afternoon. With the contenders focusing on the latter, there was a big opportunity for lesser names in that morning stage.

The break started when Claudio Chiappucci broke clear after 6 km to take the points at the top of the race's first climb. Ronan Pensec, Steve Bauer and Frans Maassen joined the Italian. The peloton idled as the quartet pressed on.

Their advantage ballooned to more than 10 minutes. When PDM's riders went to the front to chase, their team director ordered them to ease off. Like many, he viewed the team time trial as critical.

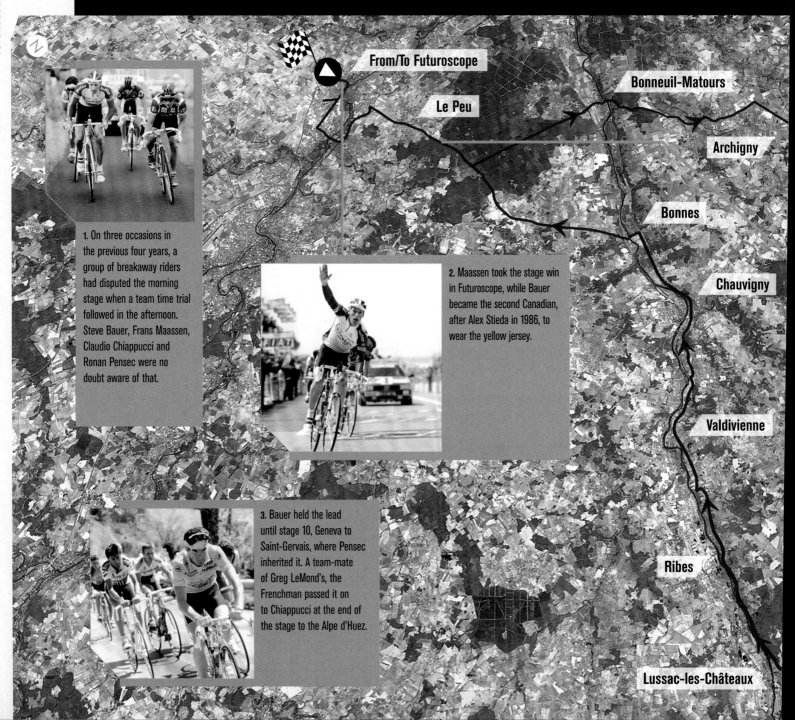

From/To Futuroscope

Le Peu

Bonneuil-Matours

Archigny

Bonnes

Chauvigny

Valdivienne

Ribes

Lussac-les-Châteaux

1. On three occasions in the previous four years, a group of breakaway riders had disputed the morning stage when a team time trial followed in the afternoon. Steve Bauer, Frans Maassen, Claudio Chiappucci and Ronan Pensec were no doubt aware of that.

2. Maassen took the stage win in Futuroscope, while Bauer became the second Canadian, after Alex Stieda in 1986, to wear the yellow jersey.

3. Bauer held the lead until stage 10, Geneva to Saint-Gervais, where Pensec inherited it. A team-mate of Greg LeMond's, the Frenchman passed it on to Chiappucci at the end of the stage to the Alpe d'Huez.

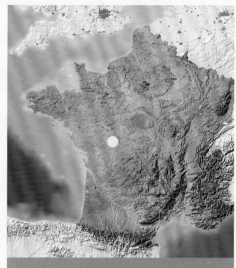

In fact, the peloton had good reason to be nervous about three of them. Maassen was no great shakes as a climber, but he took the stage win, more than 10 minutes up on the bunch. However, Bauer had finished fourth overall two years before, Pensec was strong in the mountains and Chiappucci had just won the mountains title at the Giro d'Italia. All three wore yellow. Chiappucci's tenure only ended in the time trial on the penultimate day when Greg LeMond finally ended the long pursuit of the stage 1 breakaways.

STAGE FACTS

Date: 1 July 1990

Number: 1

Length: 138.5 km

GREG LEMOND'S TOUR CAREER

1984 (Renault): Third and best young rider on Tour debut in support of team leader Laurent Fignon

1985 (La Vie Claire): Second, winner of stage 21 time trial at Lac de Vassivière and combined jersey

1986 (La Vie Claire): First, winner of stage 13 at Superbagnères and combined jersey

1987 (Toshiba): Unable to defend title after sustaining serious gunshot injuries in a hunting accident

1988 (PDM): Did not start

1989 (ADR): First, winner of stage 5 time trial at Rennes, stage 19 at Aix-les-Bains and stage 21 time trial in Paris

1990 (Z): First

1991 (Z): Seventh

1992 (Z): Abandoned stage 14

1993 (GAN): Did not start

1994 (GAN): Abandoned stage 6

'The team that sets the pace in the morning is sure to pay for it in the afternoon.' CASTORAMA'S GÉRARD RUÉ

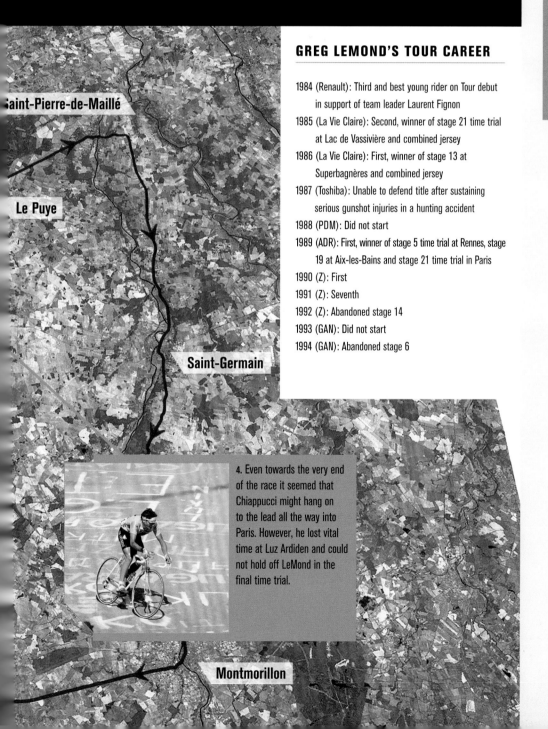

Saint-Pierre-de-Maillé

Le Puye

Saint-Germain

4. Even towards the very end of the race it seemed that Chiappucci might hang on to the lead all the way into Paris. However, he lost vital time at Luz Ardiden and could not hold off LeMond in the final time trial.

Montmorillon

BEFORE STAGE 1	AFTER STAGE 1
1 Thierry Marie (Fra) 2 Greg LeMond (USA) at 0'04" 3 Raúl Alcalá (Mex) at 0'10"	1 Steve Bauer (Can) 2 Frans Maassen (Ned) at 0'02" 3 Claudio Chiappucci (Ita) at 0'09"
Thierry Marie (Fra)	Frans Maassen (Ned)
Not awarded	Claudio Chiappucci (Ita)
Not available	Not available

Indurain takes LeMond's mantle

JACA > VAL LOURON

When Greg LeMond lost his yellow jersey to Luc Leblanc at Jaca, it seemed a temporary blip in LeMond's progress towards a fourth Tour victory. LeMond looked sure to regain the lead on the following day's summit finish at Val Louron. Heading over the Col du Pourtalet and the Col d'Aubisque, LeMond looked comfortable.

He looked equally serene on the Col du Tourmalet until the final kilometre of the climb. As the summit approached, LeMond gradually slipped off the back of the group. His deficit on the seven riders ahead of him was only 17 seconds at the summit. Speeding down the descent through La Mongie, LeMond regained contact, only to realize that Miguel Indurain had attacked and gone.

1. LeMond had held the yellow jersey for four days, having come a close second to Indurain in a long time trial at Alençon. Nothing suggested then that his quest for a hat-trick of Tour titles would come to nothing.

'This year I've got such confidence in my time trialling that I've got the sensation that that ability can protect me from everything else.' MIGUEL INDURAIN

2. Heading towards the summit of the Tourmalet, Indurain asked his team director which riders appeared to be struggling the group. 'Leblanc. LeMo as well I think,' José Migu Echavarri told him. Indura answered immediately wit an injection of pace that LeMond could not respon

From Jaca

Col du Soulor

Argelès-Gazost

Arrens-Marsous

Pierrefitte-Nestalas

Luz-Saint-Sauveur

1991 – AN INCIDENT-PACKED TOUR

France's Thierry Marie won the prologue, then claimed a second victory in Le Havre with the second longest solo break in Tour history – 234 km!

Mauro Ribeiro's victory in Rennes made him the first Brazilian to win a Tour stage.

Djamolidine Abdoujaparov took two stages and the points title but is best remembered for a spectacular crash on the final day that sent him somersaulting up the Champs-Élysées.

Rolf Sørensen had to quit the race when in the yellow jersey after hitting a traffic island coming into the finish on stage 5, breaking his collar-bone.

Colombia's Álvaro Mejía won the white jersey, going on to finish fourth overall two years later.

Charly Mottet won back-to-back stages, a flat stage into Saint-Herblain, then a mountain stage in Jaca.

The PDM team quit the race after what was said to be either a mystery virus or food poisoning swept through the team during the first week.

Tri-spoke wheels appeared on the Tour for the first time.

Italian riders won five consecutive stages between Val Louron and the Alpe d'Huez.

Heading towards the Aspin, Claudio Chiappucci attacked too, joining the Spaniard. From that point on, the two rivals worked together knowing that it was for their mutual benefit. LeMond was the reigning champion and this was their chance to distance him.

On the ascent to Val Louron Indurain and Chiappucci had good reason to press hard. The Spaniard knew that the yellow jersey would be his, while the Italian had the prospect of a career-defining win. Between them, they blitzed their rivals, none more so than LeMond, who trailed in more than 7 minutes behind them. The baton had passed from the American to Indurain, whose Tour de France reign was about to begin.

181

1991

STAGE FACTS

Date: 19 July 1991

Number: 13

Length: 232 km

3. Indurain and Chiappucci coordinated their efforts all the way into the finish, knowing that they were both set to benefit from distancing all of their rivals. Their own personal battle could wait for another day.

4. As if to underline the changing of the guard, Indurain's main challenge came, not from one of the established Tour contenders, but from another Italian, Gianni Bugno, who would win the stage at the Alpe d'Huez and finish second overall.

Col du Tourmalet

Col d'Aspin

La Mongie

To Val Louron

BEFORE STAGE 13	AFTER STAGE 13
1 Luc Leblanc (Fra)	1 Miguel Indurain (Spa)
2 Greg LeMond (USA) at 2'35"	2 Charly Mottet (Fra) at 3'00"
3 Charly Mottet (Fra) at 3'52"	3 Gianni Bugno (Ita) at 3'10"
Djamolidine Abdoujaparov (Uzb)	Djamolidine Abdoujaparov (Uzb)
Pascal Richard (Swi)	Claudio Chiappucci (Ita)
Not available	Not available

1992

Indurain steamrollers his rivals

LUXEMBOURG (TIME TRIAL)

Undoubtedly the Tour's most impressive time triallist since Jacques Anquetil, Miguel Indurain first demonstrated his phenomenal ability in 'the race of truth' in Luxembourg. Already winner of the prologue time trial in San Sebastián, Indurain went into the stage 12th on general classification and well down on some of his key rivals.

There was little surprise when Indurain set the quickest times through the intermediate check points, but as he came towards the line it became clear that something special was taking place. Indurain caught and passed Laurent Fignon, who had started the test 6 minutes before him. The Spaniard's time was 3 minutes faster than that of the next man, his Banesto team-mate Armand de Las Cuevas.

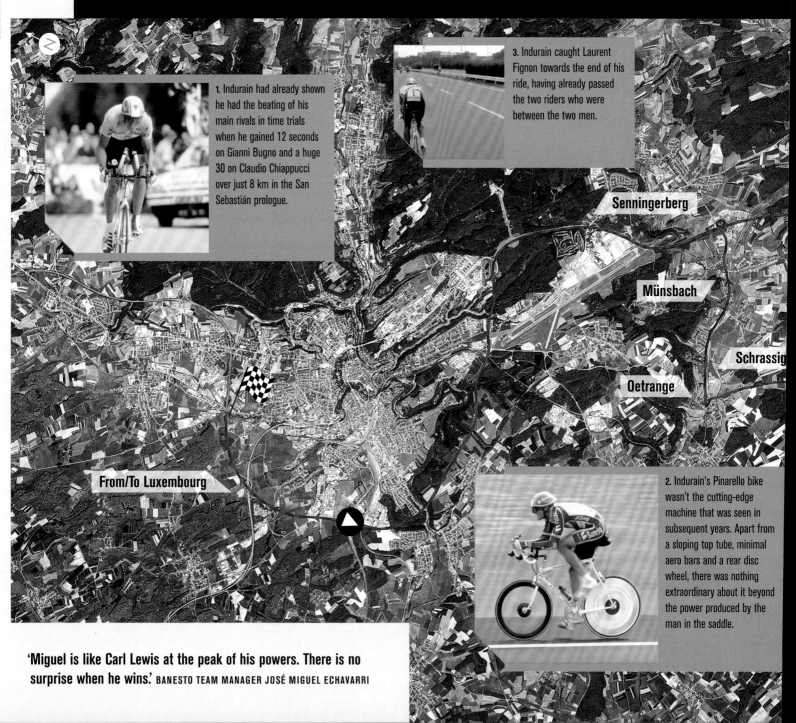

1. Indurain had already shown he had the beating of his main rivals in time trials when he gained 12 seconds on Gianni Bugno and a huge 30 on Claudio Chiappucci over just 8 km in the San Sebastián prologue.

3. Indurain caught Laurent Fignon towards the end of his ride, having already passed the two riders who were between the two men.

Senningerberg

Münsbach

Schrassig

Oetrange

From/To Luxembourg

2. Indurain's Pinarello bike wasn't the cutting-edge machine that was seen in subsequent years. Apart from a sloping top tube, minimal aero bars and a rear disc wheel, there was nothing extraordinary about it beyond the power produced by the man in the saddle.

'Miguel is like Carl Lewis at the peak of his powers. There is no surprise when he wins.' BANESTO TEAM MANAGER JOSÉ MIGUEL ECHAVARRI

Among the riders following Indurain were Gianni Bugno, Greg LeMond, Richard Virenque, Stephen Roche and Claudio Chiappucci. None of them got inside the mark set by de Las Cuevas. Indeed, 1991 Tour runner-up Bugno was the only one to lose less than 4 minutes. LeMond and Roche lost 4 minutes, Chiappucci more than 5 minutes and Virenque in excess of 10 minutes as Indurain completed the course at an average speed of 49.046 km/hour.

He jumped over all his rivals into second place and, in doing so, created a template for his Tour hegemony – crush his rivals in the time trials then control them in the mountains.

STAGE FACTS

Date: 13 July 1992

Number: 9

Length: 65 km

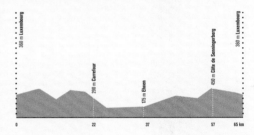

Machtum

Ahn

Ehnen

Canach

Lenningen

4. The Spaniard completed a hat-trick of time trial victories in 1992 when he won the final test over 64 km between Tours and Blois. Bugno was an impressive second, just 40 seconds down, but the rest were once again minutes back.

BEFORE STAGE 9

1 Pascal Lino (Fra)
2 Jens Heppner (Ger)
 at 2'51"
3 Jesper Skibby (Den)
 at 2'54"

Laurent Jalabert (Fra)

Richard Virenque (Fra)

Yvon Ledanois (Fra)

AFTER STAGE 9

1 Pascal Lino (Fra)
2 Miguel Indurain (Spa)
 at 1'27"
3 Jesper Skibby (Den)
 at 3'47"

Laurent Jalabert (Fra)

Richard Virenque (Fra)

Yvon Ledanois (Fra)

MIGUEL INDURAIN'S CAREER IN NUMBERS

1: Team – started with Reynolds, which then became Banesto

2: Tour de France/Giro d'Italia doubles

5: Tour de France victories

10: Tour de France time trial victories

12: Tour de France stage wins (including time trials)

13: Number of seasons in pro peloton

42: Number of time trial victories and his resting heart rate

53.040: Distance in kilometres when he set a new mark for the hour record in 1994

60: Days in the yellow jersey

99: Career victories

Sensation at Sestriere

SAINT-GERVAIS > SESTRIERE

Second in 1990, third in 1991, Claudio Chiappucci went into the 1992 Tour saying that he couldn't win because the race's two long time trials would suit Miguel Indurain. However, Chiappucci added that he would leave an indelible mark on the race, and this was the day that he did it, the toughest of the race.

It featured five big climbs, concluding with a final ascent to Sestriere, where an estimated 150,000 tifosi were waiting to acclaim 'Il Diablo'. He didn't disappoint. He led over the Saisies, then joined a group of 11 riders on the climb of the Cormet de Roselend, where he was first to the summit again.

On the ascent of the Iseran, the biggest climb in the race, he went clear on his own. He had covered 125 km and had

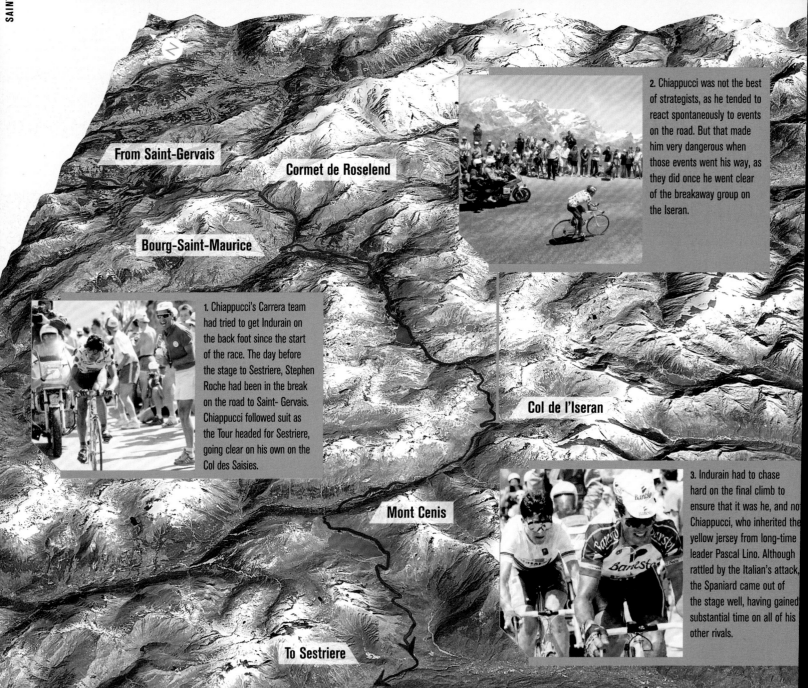

From Saint-Gervais

Cormet de Roselend

Bourg-Saint-Maurice

2. Chiappucci was not the best of strategists, as he tended to react spontaneously to events on the road. But that made him very dangerous when those events went his way, as they did once he went clear of the breakaway group on the Iseran.

1. Chiappucci's Carrera team had tried to get Indurain on the back foot since the start of the race. The day before the stage to Sestriere, Stephen Roche had been in the break on the road to Saint- Gervais. Chiappucci followed suit as the Tour headed for Sestriere, going clear on his own on the Col des Saisies.

Col de l'Iseran

Mont Cenis

3. Indurain had to chase hard on the final climb to ensure that it was he, and not Chiappucci, who inherited the yellow jersey from long-time leader Pascal Lino. Although rattled by the Italian's attack, the Spaniard came out of the stage well, having gained substantial time on all of his other rivals.

To Sestriere

another 125 km to the finish. It seemed the ultimate kamikaze move. At the summit of Mont Cenis he led by 5 minutes. The unthinkable was becoming possible. Already in the polka dot jersey, Chiappucci now had yellow in his sights.

Indurain had to counter and did so on the final climb. As Chiappucci started to tire, Indurain chipped away at his lead and did enough to secure the yellow jersey. But the glory all went to the Italian, who had pulled off a victory worthy of Coppi and Merckx in their heyday.

ITALY'S KING OF THE MOUNTAINS

1938: Gino Bartali
1948: Gino Bartali
1949: Fausto Coppi
1952: Fausto Coppi
1957: Gastone Nencini
1960: Imerio Massignan
1961: Imerio Massignan

1976: Giancarlo Bellini
1979: Giovanni Battaglin
1991: Claudio Chiappucci
1992: Claudio Chiappucci
2009: Franco Pellizotti. His victory was subsequently removed from the race's roll of honour as his biological passport indicated irregular blood values.

STAGE FACTS

Date: 18 July 1992
Number: 13
Length: 254.5 km

4. At the finish Chiappucci had achieved something that had not been seen at the Tour for many years. His 125 km solo break was compared to the victory taken by his hero, Fausto Coppi, after his 140 km solo break to the same summit 40 years before.

BEFORE STAGE 13

1 Pascal Lino (Fra)
2 Miguel Indurain (Spa) at 1'27"
3 Stephen Roche (Ire) at 1'58"

Johan Museeuw (Bel)

Claudio Chiappucci (Ita)

Yvon Ledanois (Fra)

AFTER STAGE 13

1 Miguel Indurain (Spa)
2 Claudio Chiappucci (Ita) at 1'42"
3 Gianni Bugno (Ita) at 4'20"

Johan Museeuw (Bel)

Claudio Chiappucci (Ita)

Eddy Bouwmans (Ned)

'When I heard that Indurain had dropped Bugno and was chasing me, I felt like I was two Chiappuccis, three Chiappuccis combined – a cooperative of Chiappuccis.' CLAUDIO CHIAPPUCCI

Armstrong announces himself

CHÂLONS-SUR-MARNE > VERDUN

Although he was the youngest rider on the race, and perhaps because of this, few people were interested in Lance Armstrong when he made his Tour debut in 1993. The race was in the midst of the Indurain era, and most eyes were focused on the Spaniard ahead of the following day's key Lac de Madine time trial as the peloton headed towards Verdun.

However, a few kilometres from the finish, 1987 Tour de France winner Stephen Roche instigated a break on the descent off the Côte de Douaumont, and five riders went across to join him. Among them was Motorola's Armstrong. He may have been wearing the Stars and Stripes jersey as the recently crowned American national champion, but few observers rated his chances against the more experienced campaigners in the

From Châlons-sur-Marne

Sivry-sur-Meuse

1. Armstrong went to the 1993 Tour de France looking to gain experience on his debut in the race and hoping to win a stage. He achieved both goals.

2. Although he may not have been favoured by many for the stage win when he got into the break late on, Armstrong already had eight wins to his credit that season and was in super form.

Bras-sur-Meuse

3. At the line, Armstrong flung his chest out and his arms high. He was not even 22, but he had already shown himself on the biggest cycling stage of all.

Douaumont

To Verdun

'No, I'll be the first Lance Armstrong.'
ARMSTRONG WHEN ASKED IF HE WOULD BE THE
SECOND GREG LEMOND.

break: Raúl Alcalá, Ronan Pensec, Dominique Arnould, Giancarlo Perini and Roche.

Coming into the finish, Armstrong was most concerned about Arnould. As the sprint for the stage win began with the young American fourth in line, he outwitted his French rival by squeezing through the narrow gap between Pensec and the right-hand barriers. There was room for Arnould to follow, but not enough to overtake.

Armstrong surged through the gap and out into the open, flinging his arms high in the air to celebrate his first Tour stage win. No-one could have guessed how many wins and what drama and controversy was to follow...

187

1993

STAGE FACTS

Date: 11 July 1993

Number: 8

Length: 184.5 km

4. Armstrong didn't start stage 12, having struggled in the Lac de Madine time trial and the stages in the Alps that followed in his success. Little more than a month later, though, he took the chance to repeat that joyous victory celebration when he claimed the world title in Oslo.

BEFORE STAGE 8   **AFTER STAGE 8**

1 Johan Museeuw (Bel)   1 Johan Museeuw (Bel)
2 Álvaro Mejía (Col)   2 Álvaro Mejía (Col)
at 0'39"   at 0'39"
3 Bjarne Riis (Den)   3 Mario Cipollini (Ita)
at 1'11"   at 1'07"

Mario Cipollini (Ita)   Mario Cipollini (Ita)

Bjarne Riis (Den)   Davide Cassani (Ita)

Wilfried Nelissen (Bel)   Wilfried Nelissen (Bel)

MULTIPLE TOUR WINNERS ON THEIR DEBUT

1905: Lucien Petit-Breton finished fifth overall.

1911: Firmin Lambot finished 11th overall.

1912: Philippe Thys finished sixth overall.

1923: Ottavio Bottecchia won one stage and finished second overall.

1924: Nicolas Frantz won two stages and finished second overall.

1927: André Leducq won three stages and finished fourth overall.

1927: Antonin Magne won one stage and finished sixth overall.

1934: Sylvère Maes won one stage and finished eighth overall.

1937: Gino Bartali abandoned.

1947: Louison Bobet abandoned.

1949: Fausto Coppi won three stages and the overall title.

1957: Jacques Anquetil won four stages and the overall title.

1969: Eddy Merckx won six stages and the overall title.

1970: Bernard Thévenet won one stage and finished 35th overall.

1978: Bernard Hinault won three stages and the overall title.

1983: Laurent Fignon won one stage and the overall title.

1984: Greg LeMond won the best young rider title and finished third overall.

1985: Miguel Indurain abandoned.

1993: Lance Armstrong won one stage and abandoned.

2005: Alberto Contador finished 30th overall.

1995

Jalabert's great escape

SAINT-ÉTIENNE > MENDE

Laurent Jalabert later admitted that he had been seized by a moment of madness when he attacked just 24 km into this 222.5 km stage with Dario Bottaro. The pair were soon joined by Melcior Mauri, Jalabert's ONCE team-mate. Having considered easing off, the trio persisted with the attack.

The break still seemed unlikely to amount to much until three more riders came across to join the leading trio, including a third ONCE rider, Neil Stephens. Now there was hope for them. Their advantage over the yellow jersey group of Miguel Indurain ballooned to more than 10 minutes. Incredibly, Jalabert was now the leader.

While Mauri and Stephens rode themselves into the ground for their leader, Indurain instructed all of his Banesto *domestiques* to

LAURENT JALABERT AT THE TOUR

1991: Tour debut for Toshiba, 71st overall

1992: First year with ONCE, 34th overall, a stage win in Brussels, points champion

1993: Abandoned on stage 17

1994: Abandoned on stage 2 after crashing into a policeman in the finishing straight at Armentières

1995: Fourth overall, a stage in Mende, points champion, two days in the yellow jersey

1996: Abandoned on stage 10 because of stomach problems

1997: 43rd overall

1998: In the wake of the Festina affair, ONCE and the other Spanish teams quit the race on stage 17

1999: Decided not to ride the Tour after finishing fourth and winning the points title at the Giro d'Italia

2000: 54th overall and two days in the yellow jersey

2001: Now with CSC, he finished 19th overall, won the stages in Verdun and Colmar and the King of the Mountains title, voted the race's most aggressive rider

2002: 42nd overall, won King of the Mountains title

From Saint-Étienne

Saint-Bonnet-le-Château

Saint-Paulien

1. Jalabert had already spent two days in the yellow jersey during the first week of the race. He lost the lead approaching the stage 4 finish in Le Havre when the peloton went into a roundabout too quickly and the Frenchman was one of several riders to crash.

2. Jalabert revealed that the arrival of Neil Stephens in the break made all the difference as the three ONCE riders could achieve something by combining their efforts with those of their three breakaway companions.

'I would be lying if I said I hadn't dreamed of the yellow jersey. It would have been incredible to return to my home roads tomorrow with the yellow jersey on my back.' LAURENT JALABERT

chase. It was widely reported that when Banesto's riders failed to cut the gap quickly enough he also called in favours from riders on other teams.

As the lead group sped into Mende it was certain that one of them would win the stage which concluded with a steep climb to the plateau above the town. Wearing the green jersey of points leader,

Jalabert made his final move, pressing on alone to take the most glorious win of his career. Indurain saved his yellow jersey, but had never faced such danger during his five-year domination of the Tour.

STAGE FACTS

Date: 14 July 1995

Number: 12

Length: 222.5 km

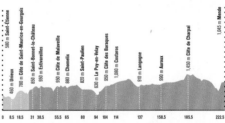

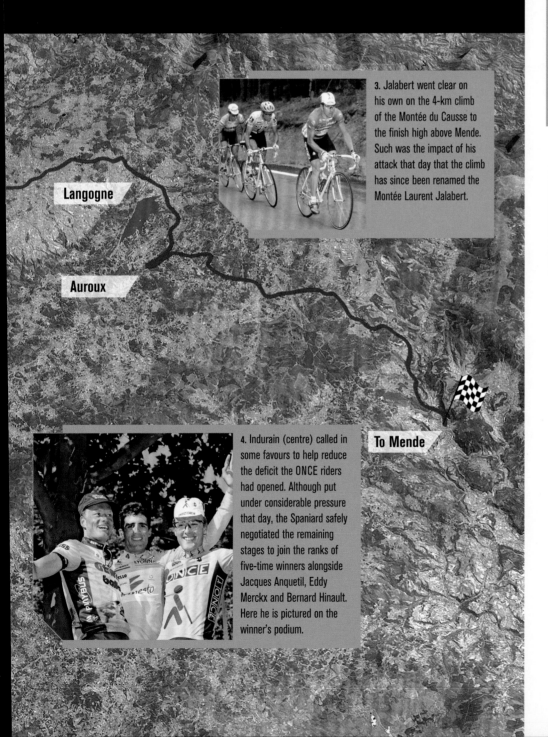

Langogne

Auroux

3. Jalabert went clear on his own on the 4-km climb of the Montée du Causse to the finish high above Mende. Such was the impact of his attack that day that the climb has since been renamed the Montée Laurent Jalabert.

To Mende

4. Indurain (centre) called in some favours to help reduce the deficit the ONCE riders had opened. Although put under considerable pressure that day, the Spaniard safely negotiated the remaining stages to join the ranks of five-time winners alongside Jacques Anquetil, Eddy Merckx and Bernard Hinault. Here he is pictured on the winner's podium.

BEFORE STAGE 12	AFTER STAGE 12
1 Miguel Indurain (Spa)	1 Miguel Indurain (Spa)
2 Alex Zülle (Swi) at 2'27"	2 Alex Zülle (Swi) at 2'44"
3 Bjarne Riis (Den) at 6'00"	3 Laurent Jalabert (Fra) at 3'35"
Laurent Jalabert (Fra)	Laurent Jalabert (Fra)
Richard Virenque (Fra)	Richard Virenque (Fra)
Marco Pantani (Ita)	Marco Pantani (Ita)

Tragedy hits the Tour

SAINT-GIRONS > CAUTERETS

The 1995 Tour would be decided over three stages in the Pyrenees. The second stage, a long day to Cauterets, featured six climbs. The first, the Portet d'Aspet, became the scene for one of the race's most tragic moments.

Heading over the summit, the pace was steady rather than frenetic. Just a few hairpins down from the top, Radio Tour announced that a number of riders had crashed. 'Motorola, Museeuw, Perini' was the message delivered to the following cars.

The Motorola rider was 1992 Olympic champion Fabio Casartelli. Helmetless, like most other riders in the field, the Italian had landed heavily on his head and was lying unmoving in the road as blood ran from his wounds. Nearby, Frenchman

Saint-Lary

Col de Portet d'Aspet

Orgibet

Augirein

From Saint-Girons

1. No-one was able to say exactly what had caused Casartelli to crash. It is believed that two riders crashed in front of the Italian, who usually wore a helmet. His team doctor suggested that he hadn't put it on that morning because of the heat and the long climb beyond the Portet d'Aspet.

2. The Tour was in shock the next morning. The whole peloton lined up at the start in Tarbes to pay silent tribute to Casartelli, with Motorola's riders and team staff in the front rank.

3. The peloton rode the whole stage together until Motorola's riders moved of the front to lead the Tour i Pau. Casartelli's compatrio and friend Andrea Peron led the Motorola riders ove the line.

Dante Rezze had gone off the edge of the road and dropped 12 m into a ravine. Race followers struggled to retrieve him.

However, Casartelli's condition was causing the most concern. Already in a coma, he was transferred to hospital by helicopter. Although resuscitated three times, the 24-year-old's head injuries were too serious to save him. He died before Richard Virenque led the race into Cauterets, the Frenchman, like many others, finding out Casartelli's fate only after the finish.

The next day's stage was neutralized as a mark of respect. Coming into the finish in Pau, Casartelli's team-mates moved ahead of the bunch and crossed the line abreast.

STAGE FACTS

Date: 18 July 1995

Number: 15

Length: 206 km

DEATHS ON THE TOUR

1910: France's Adolphe Hélière died while swimming in the Mediterranean on a rest day.

1934: A motorcyclist died during a demonstration to entertain fans before the race's arrival in La Roche-sur-Yon.

1935: Spain's Francisco Cepeda died after crashing into a ravine on the Galibier.

1957: Motorcyclist René Wagner and journalist Alex Virot died when their bike crashed off a mountain road in the Pyrenees.

1958: Race official Constant Wouters died after stepping into the path of French sprinter André Darrigade at the finish in Paris' Parc des Princes.

1964: Twenty people died when a supply van hit a bridge in the Dordogne.

1967: Britain's Tom Simpson died of heart failure climbing Mont Ventoux.

1995: Fabio Casartelli died after crashing on the descent of the Col de Portet d'Aspet.

'I could tell it was a serious injury. Casartelli had cuts that were bleeding badly. We did everything in the best conditions and as fast as we could.' TOUR DOCTOR GÉRARD PORTE

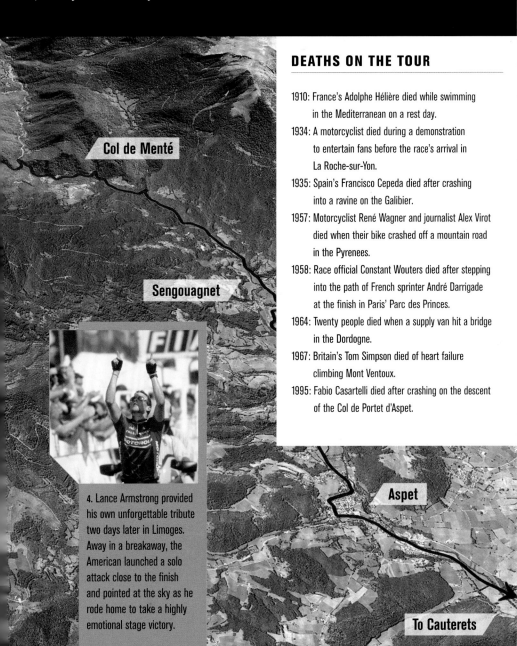

Col de Menté

Sengouagnet

Aspet

To Cauterets

4. Lance Armstrong provided his own unforgettable tribute two days later in Limoges. Away in a breakaway, the American launched a solo attack close to the finish and pointed at the sky as he rode home to take a highly emotional stage victory.

BEFORE STAGE 15	AFTER STAGE 15
1 Miguel Indurain (Spa)	1 Miguel Indurain (Spa)
2 Alex Zülle (Swi)	2 Alex Zülle (Swi)
at 2'46"	at 2'46"
3 Laurent Jalabert (Fra)	3 Bjarne Riis (Den)
at 4'28"	at 5'59"
Laurent Jalabert (Fra)	Frédéric Moncassin (Fra)
Richard Virenque (Fra)	Richard Virenque (Fra)
Marco Pantani (Ita)	Marco Pantani (Ita)

1996

The end nears for Indurain

CHAMBÉRY > LES ARCS

The Tour de France's first day in the high mountains tends to throw up surprises, but rarely has it produced a day like this one in 1996. Going into it, France's Stéphane Heulot held the yellow jersey, but the real contenders were gathering, with five-time champion Miguel Indurain heavily tipped to lead them.

A tone of unpredictability was set when French hope Laurent Jalabert dropped off the pace on the first climb, the Madeleine. Ascending the Cormet de Roselend, Heulot too fell off the pace, his face contorted in agony due to tendinitis in his knee. After much stopping and starting, Heulot quit the race in tears.

There was more drama heading off this climb when Johan Bruyneel skidded, plunging off the road and into a ravine. The

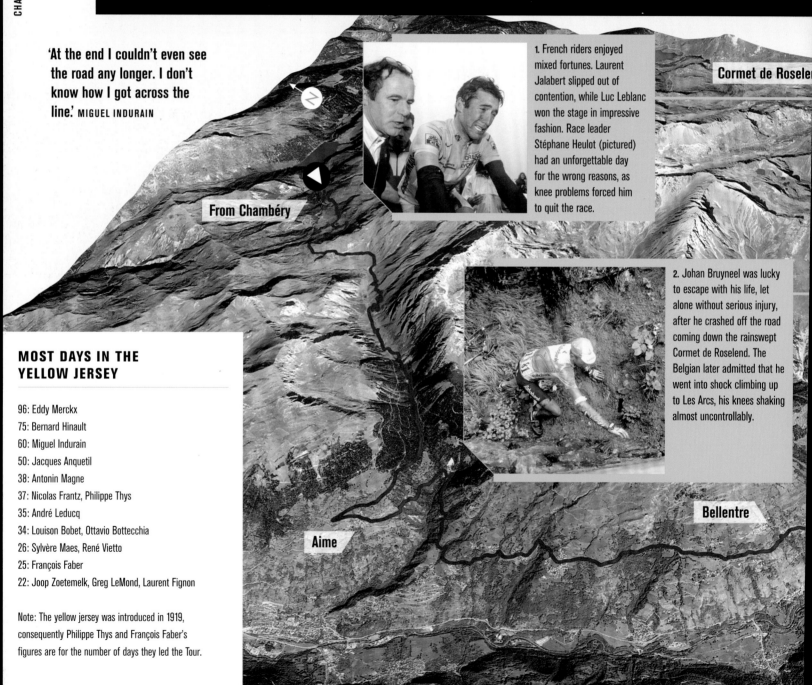

'At the end I couldn't even see the road any longer. I don't know how I got across the line.' MIGUEL INDURAIN

From Chambéry

Cormet de Roseler

1. French riders enjoyed mixed fortunes. Laurent Jalabert slipped out of contention, while Luc Leblanc won the stage in impressive fashion. Race leader Stéphane Heulot (pictured) had an unforgettable day for the wrong reasons, as knee problems forced him to quit the race.

2. Johan Bruyneel was lucky to escape with his life, let alone without serious injury, after he crashed off the road coming down the rainswept Cormet de Roselend. The Belgian later admitted that he went into shock climbing up to Les Arcs, his knees shaking almost uncontrollably.

Bellentre

Aime

MOST DAYS IN THE YELLOW JERSEY

96: Eddy Merckx
75: Bernard Hinault
60: Miguel Indurain
50: Jacques Anquetil
38: Antonin Magne
37: Nicolas Frantz, Philippe Thys
35: André Leducq
34: Louison Bobet, Ottavio Bottecchia
26: Sylvère Maes, René Vietto
25: François Faber
22: Joop Zoetemelk, Greg LeMond, Laurent Fignon

Note: The yellow jersey was introduced in 1919, consequently Philippe Thys and François Faber's figures are for the number of days they led the Tour.

The Lance Armstrong era 1996–2005

Belgian clambered back up to the road and continued relatively unscathed. Alex Zülle, riding almost blind with rain coating his glasses, crashed twice but also finished.

However, the most stunning incident still lay ahead. Indurain later admitted that he had felt so good starting the climb to Les Arcs that he almost attacked, but decided to hold back. With less than 4 km to the finish, Indurain slipped back through the lead group. Was he bluffing? Dropping back to his team car for instructions? His rivals realized that the champion was spent. He lost more than 4 minutes. The Spaniard's reign was coming to an end.

STAGE FACTS

Date: 6 July 1996

Number: 7

Length: 200 km

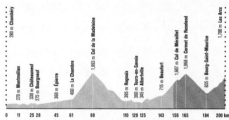

3. Indurain looked comfortable enough heading towards Les Arcs, riding towards the front of the group as Telekom riders set the pace.

4. Although he later said that he had taken on plenty of food and drink, Indurain ran out of juice less than 4 km from Les Arcs. He was insistent he could turn things around in the Val-d'Isère time trial that followed, but fifth place in that test only underlined his decline. He finished 11th overall in Paris.

To Les Arcs

BEFORE STAGE 7

1 Stéphane Heulot (Fra)
2 Mariano Piccoli (Ita)
at 0'20"
3 Alex Zülle (Swi)
at 4'05"

Frédéric Moncassin (Fra)

Léon van Bon (Ned)

Jan Ullrich (Ger)

AFTER STAGE 7

1 Evgeni Berzin (Rus)
2 Abraham Olano (Spa)
same time
3 Tony Rominger (Swi)
at 0'07"

Frédéric Moncassin (Fra)

Richard Virenque (Fra)

Jan Ullrich (Ger)

1997

Ullrich comes of age

LUCHON > ANDORRA ARCALÍS

In finishing as runner-up in 1996 to Bjarne Riis, Jan Ullrich suggested that he was destined for greatness. A year on, that suggestion became reality when the German rode away from the whole Tour field on a brutally tough day in the Pyrenees.

It covered more than 250 km, with four big passes before the final climb to Andorra Arcalís.

Ullrich went into it the best placed of the main contenders but was still nominally playing second fiddle to Riis. The previous day, he had kept a close watch on Richard Virenque and Marco Pantani, but it was evident that Riis was struggling. Would Ullrich be let off the leash?

Prior to the stage Telekom had decided to get Ullrich to set a rapid pace on the final climb to slim down the lead group.

1. Ullrich's orders were to keep the pace high for defending champion Bjarne Riis and he carried them out faithfully. However, it's clear from the picture that the young German is not at his limit while the ashen-faced Riis appears to have reached his.

2. Born in Rostock, Ullrich was regarded as a prodigy as he came up through the East German sporting system. Signed by Telekom in 1994, he said his idol was five-time Tour champion Miguel Indurain and his performance at Arcalís certainly compared with the powerful Spaniard's best days.

Port d'Envalira

Col d'Ordino

Canillo

From Luchon

Soldeu

4. Although Ullrich came under attack from Festina on a stage through the Vosges mountains, he was so far ahead that his overall victory was never in doubt. He all but sealed it when he romped to victory in the Saint-Étienne time trial, catching and passing Richard Virenque, who had started 3 minutes before him.

'I made the break, then looked back and saw no one coming with me so I thought, "This is it", and pressed on.' JAN ULLRICH

Riis would then make his move. Heading onto the long climb up to Arcalís, Ullrich went to the front to set the pace as planned. Although he later said he had not been riding flat out, no-one could stay on the German's wheel.

Looking back, Ullrich realized that he had a gap and pressed on, but now he was flat out. Although his advantage was only a minute on Virenque and Pantani, the rest of the field was scattered. The Tour had a new king, set to win the race at just 23.

3. Riis was among the first to congratulate his young team-mate after he had received the yellow jersey for the first time. After Arcalís, their roles switched as Riis became Ullrich's loyal lieutenant.

To Arcalís

Ordino

STAGE FACTS

Date: 15 July 1997

Number: 10

Length: 252.5 km

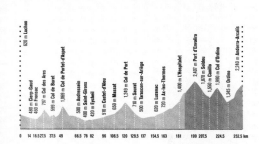

	BEFORE STAGE 10	AFTER STAGE 10
	1 Cédric Vasseur (Fra) 2 Jan Ullrich (Ger) at 0'13" 3 Abraham Olano (Spa) at 1'14"	1 Jan Ullrich (Ger) 2 Richard Virenque (Fra) at 2'58" 3 Abraham Olano (Spa) at 4'46"
	Erik Zabel (Ger)	Erik Zabel (Ger)
	Laurent Brochard (Fra)	Laurent Brochard (Fra)

	Jan Ullrich (Ger)	Jan Ullrich (Ger)

JAN ULLRICH'S RISE AND FALL

1996: Second and best young rider on his Tour debut, one stage win

1997: First and best young rider, two stage wins

1998: Second and best young rider, three stage wins

1999: Missed Tour because of injuries sustained in a crash

2000: Second

2001: Second

2002: Missed Tour after testing positive for amphetamines during an injury lay-off. He claimed he had taken ecstasy in a nightclub. Contract with Telekom ended.

2003: Second, one stage win riding for Bianchi

2004: Fourth on his return to what was now the T-Mobile team

2005: Third, although his results from May 2005 were later annulled by the Court of Arbitration for Sport (CAS) because of a doping offence

2006: Prevented from starting the Tour on the eve of the race after being implicated in the Puerto blood-doping investigation

2012: Found guilty of a doping offence by the CAS and admitted contact with Eufemiano Fuentes, the doctor at the centre of the Puerto investigation

1998

Scandal rocks the Tour

MEYRIGNAC-L'ÉGLISE > CORRÈZE (TIME TRIAL)

It was quite simply the biggest doping scandal in the history of the Tour. What became known as the Festina affair began when police stopped Willy Voet, a *soigneur* on the Festina team, on the Belgian–French border. A search of his team car turned up 400 doping products. Although Voet was detained, Festina's riders and team management were not implicated initially. That changed when the team's director Bruno Roussel and doctor Eric Ryckaert were taken into custody when the race returned to France from Ireland. The team's riders continued, protesting the lack of evidence, while Tour director Jean-Marie Leblanc announced he had no reason to eject them from the race.

However, after Roussel revealed to the authorities that riders were being doped under the supervision of some of the team's

FESTINA AFFAIR TIMELINE

8 July: Willy Voet stopped by police on French–Belgian border.

10 July: Voet charged with 'importing banned products'.

11 July: Tour starts in Dublin, Chris Boardman wins prologue.

14 July: Voet's lawyer says his client was acting on team orders.

15 July: Festina director Bruno Roussel and doctor Eric Ryckaert are detained.

17 July: Roussel reveals Festina systematically doped most of their riders. The team is excluded from the Tour.

23 July: Festina's Laurent Brochard, Laurent Dufaux, Armin Meier and Alex Zülle admit doping.

24 July: Tour peloton delays start of stage 12 in protest at media coverage.

29 July: The riders stage a sit-down strike. The ONCE, Banesto and Riso Scotti teams quit the race.

30 July: Kelme and Vitalicio Seguros teams quit the race. King of the Mountains Rodolfo Massi is taken into custody.

31 July: TVM's riders fail to start the stage.

2 August: Marco Pantani wins the Tour in Paris. Only 96 riders finish the race.

From Meyrignac-L'Église

1. The Festina affair exploded when *soigneur* Willy Voet, who was driving from Belgium to the Tour start in Dublin, was found in possession of an arsenal of doping products, including the blood-booster EPO and anabolic steroids. A police search of Festina's team headquarters turned up more banned products.

Sarran

2. For a time Festina riders were distanced from the scandal, but that changed when Festina directeur sportif Bruno Roussel (pictured) and doctor Eric Ryckaert were taken into custody. Roussel admitted the team had funded its own doping programme, explaining that it was the best way to control what the riders were taking and thereby guarantee their good health.

Vitrac-sur-Montane

management, Leblanc immediately acted. At 10.50pm on the night before the first major time trial, Leblanc excluded the Festina riders from the race. The next morning, they appeared at an impromptu press conference and again protested the lack of charges or witnesses against them. Subsequently interviewed by the police, several of the riders admitted doping.

The Tour continued, although Jan Ullrich's victory in the Corrèze time trial was little more than a footnote as the affair widened. Several teams abandoned the race in protest at police actions, mountains leader Rodolfo Massi was arrested on doping charges and one stage was abandoned after the peloton staged a sit-down strike.

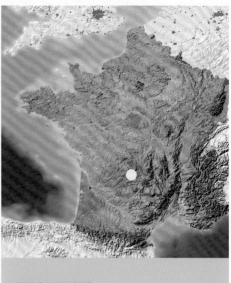

STAGE FACTS

Date: 18 July 1998

Number: 7

Length: 58 km

To Corrèze

Égletons

3. Following the stage finish in Brive, Tour director Jean-Marie Leblanc became aware of further revelations stemming from the police's investigation in Lille. That evening, he called a press conference to announce that the race jury had come to the 'unavoidable' decision to exclude Festina's riders from the race.

4. Despite their exclusion, Festina's riders gathered in Chez Gillou café near the stage start the following morning. Dressed in team kit apparently in expectation that they still might be allowed to ride, they protested the lack of charges or witnesses against them. Team leader Richard Virenque departed in tears. Many months later, he would finally admit his involvement in doping, but claimed that he had no choice.

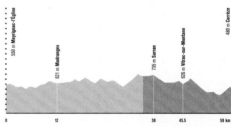

BEFORE STAGE 7	AFTER STAGE 7

1 Stuart O'Grady (Aus)
2 George Hincapie (USA) at 0'09"
3 Bo Hamburger (Den) at 0'13"

1 Jan Ullrich (Ger)
2 Bo Hamburger (Den) at 1'18"
3 Bobby Julich (Spa) at 1'18"

Erik Zabel (Ger)

Erik Zabel (Ger)

Pascal Hervé (Fra)

Stefano Zanini (Ita)

Stuart O'Grady (Aus)

Stuart O'Grady (Aus)

'I wonder what this Tour de France is going to be like without us, without this Festina team that has brought so much to the race in recent years.' RICHARD VIRENQUE

1998

Regal Pantani humbles Ullrich

GRENOBLE > LES DEUX ALPES

Although it was easy to forget that there was a race taking place in light of the Festina affair, Tour director Jean-Marie Leblanc insisted that the show must go on. Heading into the Alps, defending champion Jan Ullrich held a narrow, but seemingly comfortable lead. With a long time trial to come, he was odds-on for a second victory.

After losing lots of time during the first half of the race, Marco Pantani had climbed his way back into contention in the Pyrenees, but still needed to produce something extraordinary to unseat Ullrich. The stage to Les Deux Alpes offered his best opportunity. With 5.5 km to the summit of the Galibier, Pantani made his move, while Ullrich sat tight with the other contenders. After all, there were still 48 km to the finish.

1. Pantani makes his move on the Galibier as his rivals stick together in the grim conditions either unable to respond or feeling that the Italian had attacked too soon. By the summit he was almost 3 minutes up on them.

From Grenoble

To Les Deux Alpes

2. Wearing his trademark bandanna and with his glasses perched on his head, 'Il Pirata' drove himself relentlessly on climbing up to Les Deux Alpes, knowing that with a long time trial still to come he had to gain as much time on Ullrich as possible.

3. The Italian's staggering performance briefly diverted attention away from the ructions caused by the Festina affair. His gain of almost 9 minutes on Ullrich was almost unthinkable in the modern era.

Crossing the summit, Pantani had almost wiped out his deficit of 3 minutes 11 seconds on the German. He had time to stop, put on a raincoat and wait for six other riders to join him on the long descent. It was a canny move as, after Ullrich had punctured, Pantani's lead on him was 4 minutes as he turned up towards Les Deux Alpes.

Aboard the lightest frame in the race, Pantani pressed on alone. On the 9-km climb he gained another 30 seconds/km on the floundering Ullrich. He had pulled off the seemingly impossible.

STAGE FACTS

Date: 27 July 1998

Number: 15

Length: 189 km

Col de la
Croix de Fer

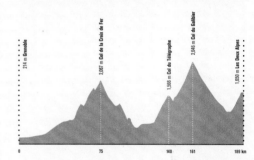

4. Determined to redeem his image at the very least, Ullrich went on the attack the next day on the Madeleine, trying to break the Italian who had taken the yellow jersey from him. But Pantani proved unshakeable, as the two men rode away from the rest of the field. Ullrich ultimately won the day's sprint, but Pantani was still right on his wheel.

Col du Télégraphe

Col du Galibier

ITALIAN JERSEY WINNERS

Italians have won the Tour title on no fewer than nine occasions, putting them fourth in the all-time list behind France (36), Belgium (18) and Spain (12). Surprisingly, though, the Tour's green jersey has only been claimed by an Italian rider on two occasions: by Franco Bitossi in 1968 and Alessandro Petacchi in 2010. Italy has fared considerably better when it comes to the mountains title. It stands third in the all-time list behind France (21) and Spain (17), thanks to victories by:

Gino Bartali: 1938 and 1948
Fausto Coppi: 1949 and 1952
Gastone Nencini: 1957
Imerio Massignan: 1960 and 1961

Giancarlo Bellini: 1976
Giovanni Battaglin: 1979
Claudio Chiappucci: 1991 and 1992
Franco Pellizotti: 2009

BEFORE STAGE 15

1 Jan Ullrich (Ger)
2 Bobby Julich (USA)
at 1'11"
3 Laurent Jalabert (Fra)
at 3'01"

Erik Zabel (Ger)

Rodolfo Massi (Ita)

Jan Ullrich (Ger)

AFTER STAGE 15

1 Marco Pantani (Ita)
2 Bobby Julich (USA)
at 3'53"
3 Fernando Escartín (Spa)
at 4'14"

Erik Zabel (Ger)

Rodolfo Massi (Ita)

Jan Ullrich (Ger)

'I knew Pantani was dangerous but I didn't think he could do what he did today. He made us all look silly.' BOBBY JULICH

1999

Fastest stage in history

LAVAL > BLOIS

Mario Cipollini's four consecutive stage victories during the first week of the 1999 race pushed his total number of Tour wins past his stack of nicknames. Dubbed 'SuperMario', 'The Lion King' and 'Mousse-olini' among others, the Italian's run of success began with success on the fastest road stage in the Tour's history.

Running from Laval to Blois, the stage covered 194.5 km. With a strong prevailing breeze blowing in from the west, the riders covered an astonishing 52.1 km in the first hour of racing. Equally impressive was the fact that, despite this speed, two riders managed to get clear of the bunch.

France's Anthony Morin and Italy's Gianpaolo Mondini performed heroically to hold the speeding bunch off until the

From Laval

Meslay-du-Maine

2. Cipollini was at his devastating best in 1999, racking up four stage wins in succession starting with this one in Blois, which remains the fastest road stage in the race's history.

1. Never one to shy away from publicity, Cipollini produced all kinds of stunts featuring unauthorized team kit. In 1997, he was fined for coordinating yellow shorts with his Tour leader's yellow jersey. Subsequently, this change to official team kit has become widespread and is now tolerated by the authorities.

Crosmières

La Flèche

Le Lude

Château-la-Vallière

THE TOUR'S FASTEST STAGES

50.355 km/h: Mario Cipollini, Laval–Blois (194.5 km) in 1999

49.938 km/h: Pablo Lastras, Bordeaux–Saint-Maixent-l'École (203.5 km) in 2003

49.417 km/h: Johan Bruyneel, Évreux–Amiens (158 km) in 1993

48.927 km/h: Adri van der Poel, Tarbes–Pau (38 km) in 1988

48.764 km/h: Tom Steels, Tarascon-sur-Ariège–Le Cap d'Agde (222 km) in 1998

48.677 km/h: Patrick Sercu, Freiburg–Freiburg (46 km) in 1977

48.584 km/h: Robbie McEwen, Chambord–Montargis (183 km) in 2005

48.532 km/h: Eddy Merckx, Vouvray–Orléans (112.5 km) in 1974

48.118 km/h: Nico Verhoeven, Berlin–Berlin (105.5 km) in 1987

47.804 km/h: Erik Zabel, Sauternes–Pau (161.5 km) in 1997

47.801 km/h: Guido Bontempi, Nogent-sur-Oise–Wasquehal (196 km) in 1992

47,471 km/h: Jens Heppner, Roscoff–Lorient (169 km) in 1998

47.229 km/h: Charly Mottet, Quimper–Saint-Herblain (246 km) in 1991

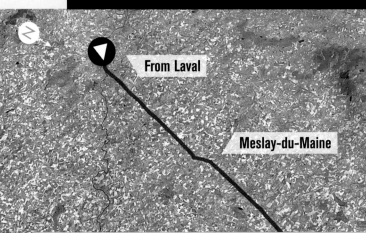

final 10 km. Once they had been caught, Cipollini's red 'train' of Saeco team-mates pushed the pace up to a speed that prevented any other riders breaking clear. Coordinating their efforts perfectly, they kept Cipollini in prime position until 250 m out, when 'SuperMario' let rip. He never looked in any danger of being overhauled.

The stage was completed in less than 4 hours at an average speed of 50.355 km/hour, almost a full kilometre an hour faster than the previous best mark, set by Johan Bruyneel in 1993. Cipollini won on the following three days as well, giving him 12 Tour stage wins in all.

STAGE FACTS

Date: 7 July 1999

Number: 4

Length: 194.5 km

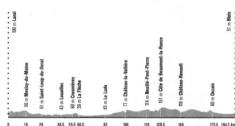

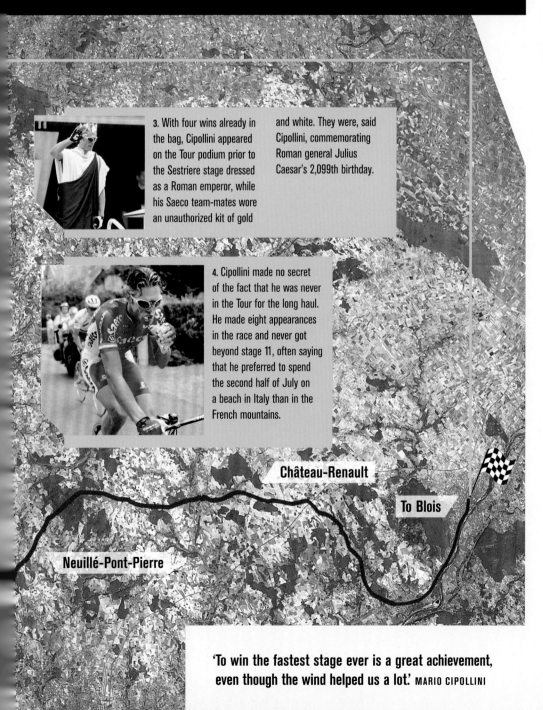

3. With four wins already in the bag, Cipollini appeared on the Tour podium prior to the Sestriere stage dressed as a Roman emperor, while his Saeco team-mates wore an unauthorized kit of gold and white. They were, said Cipollini, commemorating Roman general Julius Caesar's 2,099th birthday.

4. Cipollini made no secret of the fact that he was never in the Tour for the long haul. He made eight appearances in the race and never got beyond stage 11, often saying that he preferred to spend the second half of July on a beach in Italy than in the French mountains.

Château-Renault

To Blois

Neuillé-Pont-Pierre

BEFORE STAGE 4	AFTER STAGE 4
1 Jaan Kirsipuu (Est)	1 Jaan Kirsipuu (Est)
2 Tom Steels (Bel) at 0'17"	2 Stuart O'Grady (Aus) at 0'16"
3 Stuart O'Grady (Aus) at 0'20"	3 Tom Steels (Bel) at 0'21"
Jaan Kirsipuu (Est)	Jaan Kirsipuu (Est)
Mariano Piccoli (Ita)	Mariano Piccoli (Ita)
	Christian Vande Velde (USA)
Christian Vande Velde (USA)	

'To win the fastest stage ever is a great achievement, even though the wind helped us a lot.' MARIO CIPOLLINI

1999

Armstrong's fairytale return

LE GRAND-BORNAND > SESTRIERE

Back at the Tour for the first time in three years following treatment for testicular cancer, Lance Armstrong made a sensational start in winning the prologue time trial, then regained the yellow jersey in the long Metz time trial that preceded the first stage in the mountains. It was clear that Armstrong was a very different rider to the one who had quit the 1996 Tour. Previously solidly muscular, he was now slimmer and clearly faster. But winning time trials was one thing; the big question was whether he could reproduce that speed in the mountains.

The stage that followed the Metz time trial and a rest day took the race over four big climbs before the final run up to the Italian resort of Sestriere. On a wet, very cold day in the Alps, Richard

1. Armstrong abandoning the 1996 Tour initially made few headlines. That changed when, just weeks later, he held a press conference to announce that he had been diagnosed with advanced testicular cancer and was to undergo immediate treatment.

2. Although Armstrong had returned to racing in 1998 and finished fourth in the Tour of Spain and World Championship, he was seen as no more than an outsider for the Tour title. That changed when he crushed the main contenders in the long time trial at Metz that preceded the stages in the Alps.

From Le Grand-Bornand

Col de Montgenèvre

Briançon

3. Armstrong's high-cadence pedalling style in the mountains went against the norm as most riders tended to push as big a gear as possible. However, there was no doubting the effectiveness of the American's technique as no-one was able to cope with his accelerations.

'On the Galibier, I did not feel super. Then I looked at the others and, by the look on their faces, I saw that they were suffering too. Today was brutal. It was cold, very cold.' LANCE ARMSTRONG

Virenque was among the early attackers, picking up useful points in the mountains competition, as race leader Armstrong stayed in the wheels of his US Postal team-mates.

On the final ascent, Armstrong emerged from the pack and went in pursuit of lone leader Alex Zülle. Turning a smallish gear at high cadence in what became his familiar 'egg-beater' style, Armstrong was quickly up and past the Swiss. Fizzing onwards in the gloom, he decimated his most immediate rivals, winning the stage with a flourish and increasing his overall lead to more than 6 minutes. However, a US Anti-Doping Agency investigation over a decade later would strip him of this and his other titles.

STAGE FACTS

Date: 13 July 1999

Number: 9

Length: 213.5 km

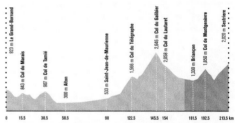

THE TOURS AT SESTRIERE

Although the Giro d'Italia first tackled the climb in 1911, the Tour didn't visit the Italian resort until 1952, when Fausto Coppi took the stage the day after becoming the first rider to win on the Alpe d'Huez.

The Tour crossed the pass again in 1956 and in 1966. Two of the Tour's post-war climbing greats led on those occasions, Charly Gaul and Julio Jiménez, respectively.

More than a quarter of a century passed before the next visit, which produced another sensational solo performance by an Italian rider. Emulating his hero Coppi's achievement, Claudio Chiappucci spent most of the day on the attack, winning the stage and almost wresting the yellow jersey from Miguel Induráin.

In 1996, Bjarne Riis won a weather-shortened stage up to Sestriere, taking the yellow jersey in the process. Then came Armstrong's victory in 1999. The Tour did not return to Sestriere until 2011, when Euskaltel's Rubén Pérez led over the pass and put his name alongside some of the sport's greats.

To Sestriere

BEFORE STAGE 9	AFTER STAGE 9
1 Lance Armstrong (USA)	1 Lance Armstrong (USA)
2 Christophe Moreau (Fra) at 2'20"	2 Abraham Olano (Spa) at 6'03"
3 Abraham Olano (Spa) at 2'33"	3 Christophe Moreau (Fra) at 7'44"
Jaan Kirsipuu (Est)	Stuart O'Grady (Aus)
Mariano Piccoli (Ita)	Richard Virenque (Fra)
Magnus Backstedt (Swe)	Benoît Salmon (Fra)

4. Although many felt that Armstrong could contend for the Tour title, his team was viewed as his Achilles' heel. However, his US Postal team rose to the occasion, particularly on the Sestriere stage, where Kevin Livingston was among those who kept the race under control until Armstrong made his winning move.

Pantani riled by Armstrong's gift

CARPENTRAS > MONT VENTOUX

The race little more than half completed, Lance Armstrong already had his rivals on the run thanks to an impressive performance at the Hautacam summit finish. Although lone breakaway Javier Otxoa managed to hold off the American's full-throttle assault on the Pyrenean peak, all Armstrong's main rivals suffered significant losses.

The next mountain-top finish came just two stages later on the infamous summit of Mont Ventoux. Once again, Armstrong was in command. After his team-mates had set a fearsome pace on the lower slopes, their leader had just six riders for company. Among them was 1998 Tour champion Marco Pantani. Expelled from the 1999 Giro d'Italia just two days from victory, when tests showed irregular blood levels, the Italian was back, but not at his best.

1. Pantani struggled to remain in contact with the lead group heading up through the wooded section of the Ventoux but, once out into the bare moonscape approaching the summit, he came alive with a series of attacks that split the group apart.

3. As the two riders headed up the final ramp to the line, Armstrong surprised everyone when he appeared to ease off and allow Pantani to take the stage win. He confirmed afterwards that he felt it was his way of paying tribute to Pantani. But the Italian didn't appreciate the gesture.

To Mont Ventoux

2. Pantani's attack was good enough to distance everyone except Armstrong. The two men then rode together towards the summit where most expected the American to impose himself, given the historical significance of the mountain.

From Carpentras

Heading up on the steepest part of the Ventoux, Pantani yo-yoed on and off the back of the lead group. Coming out of them, he attacked and kept attacking. With 3 km to go, he went again and only Armstrong was able to respond. At the summit Armstrong appeared to ease off to allow the Italian the stage win. Pantani was withering in his response, saying he felt insulted by the gesture. The spat escalated, Pantani doing all he could to put Armstrong and his team on the back foot in the Alps, taking another stage win in the process before abandoning the race.

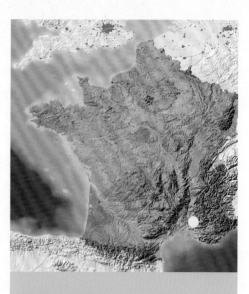

> 'I felt like it was a gift on the Ventoux, and I also feel like it was a mistake to give the gift. He's a great rider, he's a great champion and he's a great climber, but he wasn't the best man on Ventoux and anybody that watched the race will know it.' LANCE ARMSTRONG

STAGE FACTS

Date: 13 July 2000

Number: 12

Length: 149 km

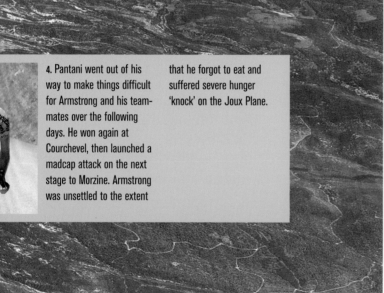

4. Pantani went out of his way to make things difficult for Armstrong and his team-mates over the following days. He won again at Courchevel, then launched a madcap attack on the next stage to Morzine. Armstrong was unsettled to the extent that he forgot to eat and suffered severe hunger 'knock' on the Joux Plane.

BEFORE STAGE 12

1 Lance Armstrong (USA)
2 Jan Ullrich (Ger)
at 4'14"
3 Christophe Moreau (Fra)
at 5'10"

Erik Zabel (Ger)

Javier Otxoa (Spa)

Francisco Mancebo (Spa)

AFTER STAGE 12

1 Lance Armstrong (USA)
2 Jan Ullrich (Ger)
at 4'55"
3 Joseba Beloki (Spa)
at 5'52"

Erik Zabel (Ger)

Javier Otxoa (Spa)

Francisco Mancebo (Spa)

MARCO PANTANI'S TOUR RECORD

1994: Third on general classification, second in King of the Mountains competition and best young rider

1995: Thirteenth on general classification, stage wins at the Alpe d'Huez and Guzet Neige

1997: Third on general classification, stage wins at the Alpe d'Huez and Morzine

1998: First on general classification, stage wins at Plateau de Beille and Les Deux Alpes

2000: Abandoned on stage 17 to Lausanne, stage wins at Mont Ventoux and Courchevel

Pantani's victory at Courchevel turned out to be his final win as a professional. Although he did compete in the Giro d'Italia in 2001–2003, he never appeared at the Tour again. In 2003 his Mercatone Uno team controversially missed out on a wild card invitation. He died as a result of a cerebral oedema and heart failure on 14 February 2004, aged just 34. An inquest revealed acute cocaine poisoning.

2003

Off-roading Armstrong invincible

BOURG-D'OISANS > GAP

During Lance Armstrong's run of seven consecutive Tour wins – which would be stripped from him following a US Anti-Doping Agency investigation in 2012 – the American rarely appeared to be in anything less than total control. An exception occurred in 2003, when he came into the race feeling the effects of a heavy crash at the Dauphiné Libéré and never managed to impose his authority. However, one extraordinary feat highlighted his supreme ability suggesting that, although he was not at his best, he would still not be beaten.

The setting was a series of small climbs into Gap. The last of them was the Côte de la Rochette, from the top of which the riders dropped straight into the finish. Armstrong had struggled

'I couldn't go right because the corner was too sharp, I couldn't go straight because I would hit Beloki, so I had to go left into the field.' LANCE ARMSTRONG

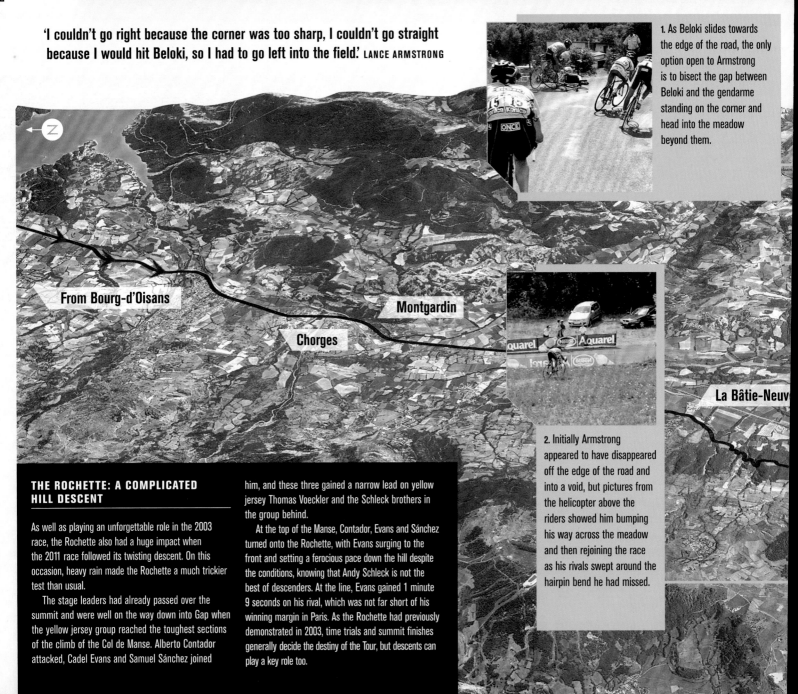

From Bourg-d'Oisans

Chorges

Montgardin

La Bâtie-Neuv

1. As Beloki slides towards the edge of the road, the only option open to Armstrong is to bisect the gap between Beloki and the gendarme standing on the corner and head into the meadow beyond them.

2. Initially Armstrong appeared to have disappeared off the edge of the road and into a void, but pictures from the helicopter above the riders showed him bumping his way across the meadow and then rejoining the race as his rivals swept around the hairpin bend he had missed.

THE ROCHETTE: A COMPLICATED HILL DESCENT

As well as playing an unforgettable role in the 2003 race, the Rochette also had a huge impact when the 2011 race followed its twisting descent. On this occasion, heavy rain made the Rochette a much trickier test than usual.

The stage leaders had already passed over the summit and were well on the way down into Gap when the yellow jersey group reached the toughest sections of the climb of the Col de Manse. Alberto Contador attacked, Cadel Evans and Samuel Sánchez joined

him, and these three gained a narrow lead on yellow jersey Thomas Voeckler and the Schleck brothers in the group behind.

At the top of the Manse, Contador, Evans and Sánchez turned onto the Rochette, with Evans surging to the front and setting a ferocious pace down the hill despite the conditions, knowing that Andy Schleck is not the best of descenders. At the line, Evans gained 1 minute 9 seconds on his rival, which was not far short of his winning margin in Paris. As the Rochette had previously demonstrated in 2003, time trials and summit finishes generally decide the destiny of the Tour, but descents can play a key role too.

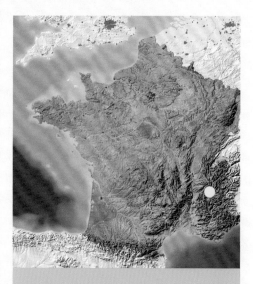

the previous day on the Alpe d'Huez and his rivals were looking to take advantage again in heat that was melting the surface of the roads.

With Alexander Vinokourov already clear heading down the Rochette, Joseba Beloki was setting a fierce pace behind with Armstrong on his wheel. Going into a right-hand bend, Beloki's rear wheel slalomed in the melting tar and the Spaniard hit the road hard. Armstrong's only option in avoiding the prone Spaniard was to continue straight on through the bend. He bounced across an Alpine meadow to the hairpin bend below, hopped off his bike, leapt the ditch, remounted and was off again, having lost just a couple of places in the line.

STAGE FACTS

Date: 14 July 2003

Number: 9

Length: 184.5 km

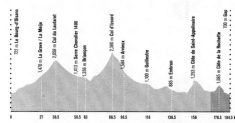

4. Alexander Vinokourov won the stage into Gap to put himself right in contention for the yellow jersey as he moved into second place, just 21 seconds down on Armstrong. He said he had been riding with the power of two men, saying he had been inspired by thoughts of his friend Andrei Kivilev, who had died from head injuries sustained at Paris–Nice four months earlier.

To Gap

3. There was no way back for Beloki, who sustained several fractures, including a bad break in his pelvis, when he crashed. Very much in contention in 2003 and arguably Armstrong's strongest rival, he did return to racing but never reached the same level again.

e de la Rochette

BEFORE STAGE 9	AFTER STAGE 9
1 Lance Armstrong (USA)	1 Lance Armstrong (USA)
2 Joseba Beloki (Spa) at 0'40"	2 Alexander Vinokourov (Kaz) 0'21"
3 Ibán Mayo (Spa) at 1'10"	3 Ibán Mayo (Spa) at 1'02"
Baden Cooke (Aus)	Baden Cooke (Aus)
Richard Virenque (Fra)	Richard Virenque (Fra)
Denis Menchov (Rus)	Denis Menchov (Rus)

Enraged Armstrong is reborn

BAGNÈRES-DE-BIGORRE > LUZ ARDIDEN

Apparently on the ropes when crushed by Jan Ullrich in the Cap Découverte time trial and still vulnerable at the Pyrenean summit finish on Plateau de Bonascre, Lance Armstrong was a rider reborn on the slopes of Luz Ardiden.

The day started hot but conditions had cooled by late afternoon when the yellow jersey group started their ascent of this crucial climb. Armstrong's team-mates beat out a rapid tempo before their leader attacked with just 9 km remaining. However, with Ibán Mayo and Jan Ullrich on his back wheel and refusing to be shaken off, Armstrong looked vulnerable until another twist occurred on this most unpredictable of Tours.

Riding close to the edge of the road, Armstrong's handlebars became entangled with a spectator's bag, bringing him and then

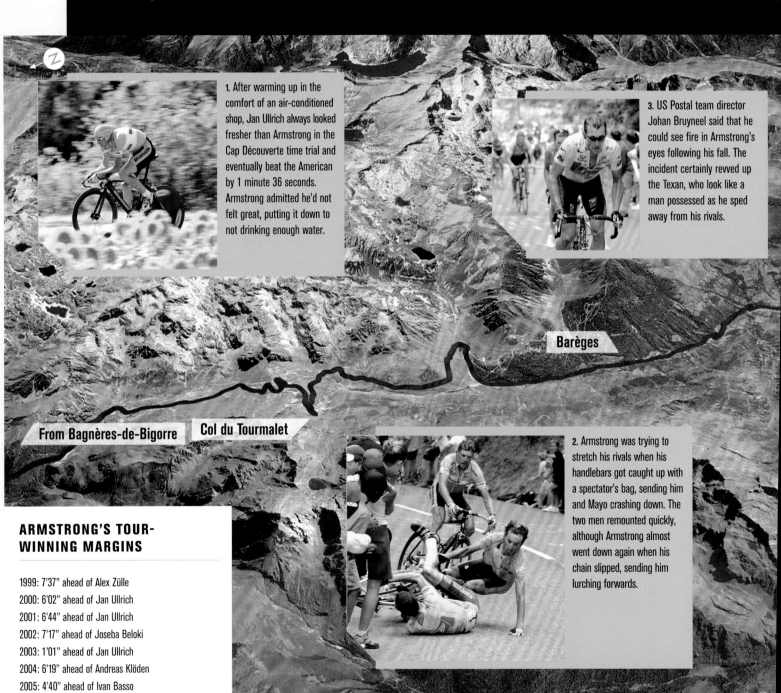

1. After warming up in the comfort of an air-conditioned shop, Jan Ullrich always looked fresher than Armstrong in the Cap Découverte time trial and eventually beat the American by 1 minute 36 seconds. Armstrong admitted he'd not felt great, putting it down to not drinking enough water.

3. US Postal team director Johan Bruyneel said that he could see fire in Armstrong's eyes following his fall. The incident certainly revved up the Texan, who look like a man possessed as he sped away from his rivals.

Barèges

From Bagnères-de-Bigorre   Col du Tourmalet

2. Armstrong was trying to stretch his rivals when his handlebars got caught up with a spectator's bag, sending him and Mayo crashing down. The two men remounted quickly, although Armstrong almost went down again when his chain slipped, sending him lurching forwards.

ARMSTRONG'S TOUR-WINNING MARGINS

1999: 7'37" ahead of Alex Zülle
2000: 6'02" ahead of Jan Ullrich
2001: 6'44" ahead of Jan Ullrich
2002: 7'17" ahead of Joseba Beloki
2003: 1'01" ahead of Jan Ullrich
2004: 6'19" ahead of Andreas Klöden
2005: 4'40" ahead of Ivan Basso

Note Armstrong was stripped of these titles in 2012.

Mayo down. Ullrich swerved but slowed, indicating that other riders should follow suit.

Both stricken men were quickly up, but Armstrong faltered again when his chain slipped. His rage was unmistakeable. Fired up, he swept up to and past his rivals, riding at a fierce rhythm that no-one could follow.

The 40 seconds he gained at the finish gave him the buffer needed to keep Ullrich at arm's length in the final time trial. In Paris, his winning advantage was little more than a minute, enabling him to retain the crown, although a US Anti-Doping Agency investigation nine years later resulted in him being stripped of this and his other titles.

STAGE FACTS

Date: 21 July 2003

Number: 15

Length: 159.5 km

'This has been a Tour of too many problems, too many close calls, too many near misses. I just wish it would stop and I could have some uneventful days.' LANCE ARMSTRONG

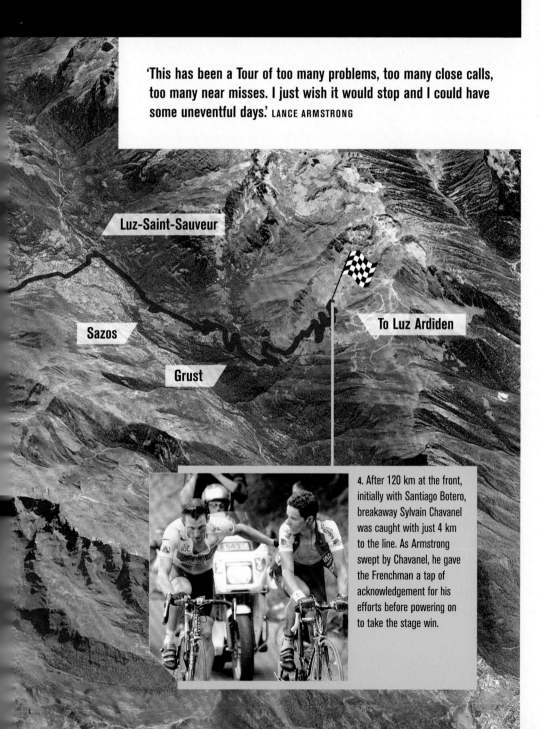

Luz-Saint-Sauveur

Sazos

Grust

To Luz Ardiden

4. After 120 km at the front, initially with Santiago Botero, breakaway Sylvain Chavanel was caught with just 4 km to the line. As Armstrong swept by Chavanel, he gave the Frenchman a tap of acknowledgement for his efforts before powering on to take the stage win.

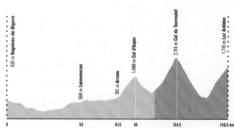

BEFORE STAGE 15	AFTER STAGE 15

1 Lance Armstrong (USA)
2 Jan Ullrich (Ger)
at 0'15"
3 Alexander Vinokourov (Kaz)
at 0'18"

1 Lance Armstrong (USA)
2 Jan Ullrich (Ger)
at 1'07"
3 Alexander Vinokourov (Kaz)
at 2'45"

Baden Cooke (Aus)

Baden Cooke (Aus)

Richard Virenque (Fra)

Richard Virenque (Fra)

Denis Menchov (Rus)

Denis Menchov (Rus)

2004

King of the climbers

LIMOGES > SAINT-FLOUR

Following his involvement in the Festina doping affair that devastated the 1998 Tour, Richard Virenque reinvented himself as a hero in the eyes of French fans with a series of scintillating stage wins following his return from a drug-related ban. After the Ventoux in 2002 and Morzine in 2003, the flamboyant Frenchman completed a hat-trick with a typically courageous ride on a stage including nine categorized climbs into Saint-Flour.

Given the profile of the hilly nature of the stage and the fact it was Bastille Day, Virenque was always likely to be a contender. Consequently, it was no surprise when he got into the early break. More surprising, though, was his decision to go clear with just Axel Merckx for company on the first of

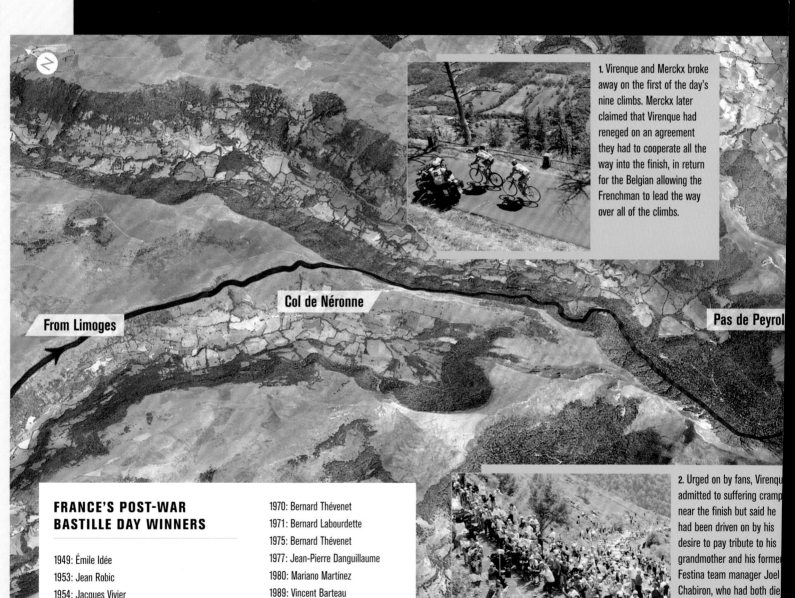

Col de Néronne

From Limoges

Pas de Peyrol

1. Virenque and Merckx broke away on the first of the day's nine climbs. Merckx later claimed that Virenque had reneged on an agreement they had to cooperate all the way into the finish, in return for the Belgian allowing the Frenchman to lead the way over all of the climbs.

2. Urged on by fans, Virenqu admitted to suffering cramp near the finish but said he had been driven on by his desire to pay tribute to his grandmother and his former Festina team manager Joel Chabiron, who had both die in the preceding weeks.

FRANCE'S POST-WAR BASTILLE DAY WINNERS

1949: Émile Idée
1953: Jean Robic
1954: Jacques Vivier
1957: Jean Bourlès
1961: Jacques Anquetil
1964: Jacques Anquetil
1968: Roger Pingeon
1969: Raymond Delisle

1970: Bernard Thévenet
1971: Bernard Labourdette
1975: Bernard Thévenet
1977: Jean-Pierre Danguillaume
1980: Mariano Martínez
1989: Vincent Barteau
1995: Laurent Jalabert
1997: Laurent Brochard
2001: Laurent Jalabert
2004: Richard Virenque
2005: David Moncoutié

those nine ascents. The pair coordinated their efforts over the first six climbs. On the seventh, the Pas de Peyrol, Virenque accelerated away.

More than 60 km remained, but Virenque, urged on by French fans, never looked like being caught. At the finish he took the stage win and a firm grip on the King of the Mountains jersey. This proved to be his first step towards a record-breaking seventh victory in the mountains competition, surpassing the previous mark of six King of the Mountains successes he had held jointly with Federico Bahamontes and Lucien van Impe.

4. A great day for the French was completed when Thomas Voeckler managed to keep the yellow jersey for the fifth day.

To Saint-Flour

3. Virenque bagged a huge 68 points in the mountains competition on the day, taking over leadership of the competition from his Quick Step team-mate Paolo Bettini.

Puy Mary

'We had agreed that he was going to take all the points for the mountains jersey then afterwards we would fight for the finish here and not before. But I guess he has a hard time keeping his word.' AXEL MERCKX

211

2004

STAGE FACTS

Date: 14 July 2004

Number: 10

Length: 237 km

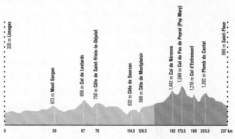

BEFORE STAGE 10		**AFTER STAGE 10**

1 Thomas Voeckler (Fra)
2 Stuart O'Grady (Aus)
  at 2'53"
3 Sandy Casar (Fra)
  at 4'06"

1 Thomas Voeckler (Fra)
2 Stuart O'Grady (Aus)
  at 3'00"
3 Sandy Casar (Fra)
  at 4'13"

Robbie McEwen (Aus)

Robbie McEwen (Aus)

Paolo Bettini (Ita)

Richard Virenque (Fra)

Thomas Voeckler (Fra)

Thomas Voeckler (Fra)

2005

Lance lays down his law

GRENOBLE > COURCHEVEL

The first major mountain stage of the 2005 Tour followed a very familiar pattern to those in the previous six editions. Although Alejandro Valverde narrowly won the battle for the day's spoils in the ski resort of Courchevel, Lance Armstrong was right on the Spaniard's wheel and looked well in control of the longer term war for the yellow jersey.

Set up by some typically brutish pace-making by his Discovery Channel team-mates, Armstrong went to the front with 10 km remaining and just five riders on his wheel. From that point, Armstrong's strength and tactical mastery were absolute. His speed on the climb forced him to brake on one corner to keep to the ideal line, while he combined well with Valverde, Michael Rasmussen and Paco Mancebo to distance much more dangerous rivals.

From Grenoble

1. After some wobbles earlier in the race, Armstrong's team-mates were relentless in crushing almost all opposition on the approach to Courchevel. Their team leader later gave them an 'A' for their efforts.

Moûtiers

2. After Yaroslav Popovych had ramped up the pace going into the final 10 km of the climb, the Ukrainian pulled aside to unleash his team leader Armstrong. Only three riders were able to stay with him.

Brides-les-Bains

3. Valverde won the day and received immediate acknowledgement from the defending champion for his victory on his Tour debut. Wearing the white jersey of best young rider, the Spaniard was forced to quit the race as it left the Alps because of knee trouble.

'We are in a good position with regard to some of the main rivals, so we'll have to protect that and that might mean protecting the jersey and hopefully retiring in it.' LANCE ARMSTRONG

At the finish he didn't look disappointed to lose out to Valverde, giving the Spaniard a pat of congratulation after they had crossed the line. In truth, there was little reason for him to be downcast. He had taken the yellow jersey and had put minutes between himself and the riders hyped as his most likely challengers. A seventh Tour victory was now his for the taking. Once again, the disappointment was felt by his rivals and by many of the watching millions, whose hopes for a drawn-out and unpredictable contest had been smashed by 'Big Tex'. Little did they know that a US Anti-Doping Agency investigation seven years later would result in Armstrong being stripped of this and his other Tour de France titles by the UCI.

Saint-Bon-Tarentaise

To Courchevel

ARMSTRONG'S PERFORMANCES ON THE TOUR'S FIRST SUMMIT FINISHES

1999: Winner at Sestriere, his lead increases to 6'03"

2000: Second at Lourdes-Hautacam, takes yellow jersey and leads by 4'14"

2001: Winner at the Alpe d'Huez, moves up from 23rd to fourth overall, ahead of all of his key rivals

2002: Winner at La Mongie, takes yellow jersey and leads by 1'12"

2003: Third at the Alpe d'Huez, takes yellow jersey and leads by 0'40"

2004: Second at La Mongie, moves up sixth to second, ahead of all of his key rivals

2005: Second at Courchevel, takes yellow jersey and leads by 0'38"

STAGE FACTS

Date: 12 July 2005

Number: 10

Length: 192.5 km

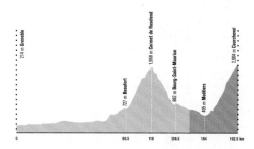

BEFORE STAGE 10	AFTER STAGE 10

1 Jens Voigt (Ger)
2 Christophe Moreau (Fra) at 1'50"
3 Lance Armstrong (USA) at 2'18"

1 Lance Armstrong (USA)
2 Michael Rasmussen (Den) at 0'38"
3 Ivan Basso (Ita) at 2'40"

Tom Boonen (Bel)

Tom Boonen (Bel)

Michael Rasmussen (Den)

Michael Rasmussen (Den)

Vladimir Karpets (Rus)

Alejandro Valverde (Spa)

4. Jan Ullrich (right) was one of the big losers on the climb up to Courchevel, losing more than 2 minutes after an obviously painful effort. Although he finished third in Paris, the Court of Arbitration for Sport later stripped him of all of the results he achieved from May 2005 because of a doping offence.

Lance's last victory

SAINT-ÉTIENNE (TIME TRIAL)

Although Lance Armstrong had never looked like losing the 2005 Tour, there appeared to be a good chance that his final outing in the race would end without him winning a stage. Second at Île de Noirmoutier, Courchevel and Ax 3 Domaines, the American had one final chance in the 55 km time trial in the rolling countryside around Saint-Étienne.

Ivan Basso bested him at the first check point, but the Italian had gone off too fast and faded to fifth. Fittingly, Armstrong's main challenger was perennial rival Jan Ullrich. Finishing the race very strongly, the German came close to denying the Texan a victorious swansong but, as so often in the past, he came up short.

The next day Armstrong duly wrapped up his seventh consecutive success and became the only multiple Tour winner

'I wanted to go out on top. That was the only incentive and that was the only pressure.' LANCE ARMSTRONG

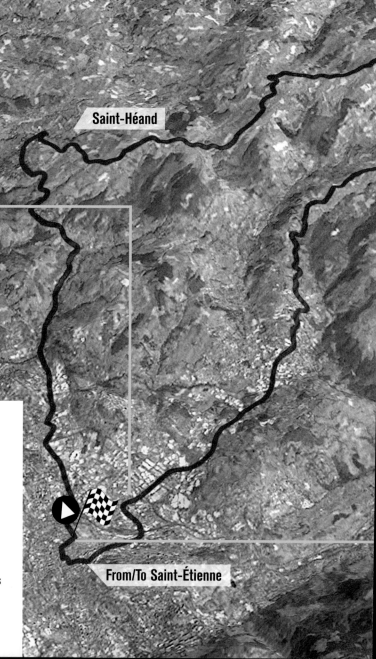

Saint-Héand

From/To Saint-Étienne

1. On a very testing course around Saint-Étienne, Armstrong refused to panic when it was apparent he was behind Ivan Basso at the first check point. Pacing himself perfectly, he averaged a shade over 46 km/hour to beat Jan Ullrich into second on the day.

ARMSTRONG'S TIME TRIAL PERFORMANCES

1999: First, Le Puy du Fou prologue (6.8 km); first, Metz (56.5 km); first, Futuroscope (57 km)

2000: Second, Futuroscope (16.5 km); second, Saint-Nazaire (Team TT, 70 km); first, Mulhouse (58.5 km)

2001: Third, Dunkerque prologue (8.2 km); fourth, Bar-le-Duc (TTT, 67 km); first, Chamrousse (32 km); first, Saint-Amand-Montrond (61 km)

2002: First, Luxembourg prologue (7 km); second, Château-Thierry (TTT, 67.5 km); second, Lorient (52 km); first, Mâcon (50 km)

2003: Seventh, Paris prologue (6.5 km); first, Saint-Dizier (TTT, 69 km); second, Cap Découverte (47 km); third, Nantes (49 km)

2004: Second, Liège prologue (6.1 km); first, Arras (TTT, 64.5 km); first, Alpe d'Huez (15.5 km); first, Besançon (55 km)

2005: Second, Île de Noirmoutier (19 km); first, Blois (TTT, 67.5 km); first, Saint-Étienne (55.5 km)

to retire from the sport on a winning note at the world's biggest race. In his victory address on the podium, he said: 'I'll say to the people who don't believe in cycling, the cynics and the sceptics, I'm sorry for you. I'm sorry that you can't dream big. I'm sorry you don't believe in miracles. But this is one hell of a race.'

A month later, those cynics would have more fuel when French sports daily *L'Équipe* alleged that traces of EPO had been found in Armstrong's samples from the 1999 Tour. In 2012 they were vindicated when a US Anti-Doping Agency investigation revealed evidence of wide-ranging use of doping products by Armstrong and other members of his team. He denied the allegations.

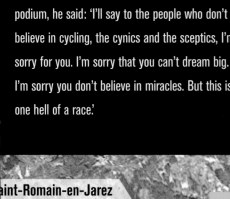

aint-Romain-en-Jarez

Col de la Gachet

2. Lying third going into a time trial that offered some hope to a rider of his supreme climbing ability, Michael Rasmussen cracked, crashing twice and changing his bike no less than three times to fall to seventh overall.

3. A good day for the Armstrong family as dad takes his first stage win of the 2005 Tour. His children, Luke, Grace and Isabella, are on hand to help him celebrate his success.

4. Count them – that's seven consecutive Tour wins. Armstrong poses for the photographers after winning what he had said would be the final race of his career. Victory was short-lived, however, and a USADA investigation resulted in Armstrong being stripped of this and his other titles in 2012.

STAGE FACTS

Date: 23 July 2005

Number: 20

Length: 55.5 km

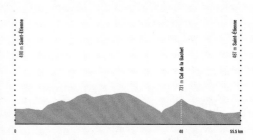

BEFORE STAGE 20	AFTER STAGE 20
1 Lance Armstrong (USA)	1 Lance Armstrong (USA)
2 Ivan Basso (Ita) at 2'46"	2 Ivan Basso (Ita) at 4'40"
3 Michael Rasmussen (Den) at 3'46"	3 Jan Ullrich (Ger) at 6'21"

Thor Hushovd (Nor)	Thor Hushovd (Nor)

Michael Rasmussen (Den)	Michael Rasmussen (Den)

Yaroslav Popovych (Ukr)	Yaroslav Popovych (Ukr)

Escape to victory

BÉZIERS > MONTÉLIMAR

When he'd come into the 2006 Tour de France, Óscar Pereiro had been confident of a finish high up in the top ten. However, the Spaniard struggled in the Pyrenees, plummeting to 46th place overall, almost half an hour down on race leader Floyd Landis, as the riders began the longest stage of the race.

It was a typical 'transition' day and there was little for the overall contenders to worry about when five lowly placed riders went clear with 200 km to the finish. Landis' Phonak team set the pace in the bunch behind the five escapees, but showed no interest in undertaking a serious pursuit.

Alongside Pereiro in the leading quintet were Jens Voigt, Sylvain Chavanel, Manuel Quinziato and Andriy Grivko, all strong

ÓSCAR PEREIRO AT THE TOUR

2004: Tenth overall on debut with Phonak.

2005: Tenth again and also a stage winner in Pau after finishing second on the previous stage.

2006: First following the disqualification of Floyd Landis after a positive dope test. His victory was not confirmed until 20 September 2007.

2007: Tenth.

2008: Abandons as the result of serious injuries sustained in crash on the descent of the Agnel pass. He has a tattoo bearing the place and date of the crash, saying it was the moment of his rebirth.

2009: Abandons the Tour in a feed zone in the Pyrenees, saying his passion for the sport has disappeared.

1. There were no weak links in the five-man breakaway. Although well off the leaders' pace, Pereiro, Voigt, Chavanel, Quinziato and Grivko were strong riders so it was no surprise that the break went the distance.

Anduze

Col de la Cardonille

Puéchabon

2. Pereiro's former Phonak team-mates and managers didn't appear to consider the Spaniard a threat. The pace they set was steady rather than insistent, a huge strategic error as it allowed a strong rider back into contention and suggested that Phonak were struggling with the burden of leading the race.

From Béziers

'I will enjoy every day I wear this yellow jersey and I will try to defend it as long as possible, but I think that the day Floyd decides to get it, he will.' ÓSCAR PEREIRO

riders with their focus firmly set on the stage win. Their lead grew, then ballooned. At the finish, Voigt beat Pereiro to the stage win, but the Spaniard had the huge compensation of the yellow jersey when Landis and the bunch rolled in half an hour later.

Phonak expected Pereiro to fold in the Alps as he had in the Pyrenees, but the yellow jersey gave Pereiro wings. Landis finally clinched it in the deciding time trial, but days after his victory, it was announced the American had tested positive for testosterone. Pereiro regained the yellow jersey, making him arguably the most unexpected victor in Tour history.

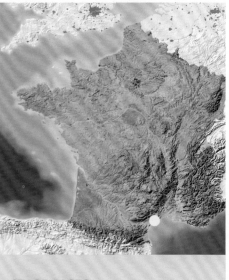

STAGE FACTS

Date: 15 July 2006

Number: 13

Length: 230 km

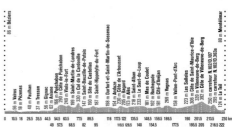

Villeneuve-de-Berg

To Montélimar

Vallon-Pont-d'Arc

3. Although Pereiro suggested that Landis would quickly regain control of the yellow jersey, it didn't turn out to be a straightforward task for the American. After retaking the lead and losing it again, Landis asserted his status as favourite with a long solo break into Morzine on stage 17.

4. Having finally been confirmed as the 2006 Tour winner in September 2007, Pereiro was presented with the yellow jersey at a ceremony in Madrid on 15 October 2007.

BEFORE STAGE 13	AFTER STAGE 13
1 Floyd Landis (USA)	**1** Óscar Pereiro (Spa)
2 Cyril Dessel (Fra) at 0'08"	**2** Floyd Landis (USA) at 1'29"
3 Denis Menchov (Rus) at 1'01"	**3** Cyril Dessel (Fra) at 1'37"
Robbie McEwen (Aus)	Robbie McEwen (Aus)
David De La Fuente (Spa)	David De La Fuente (Spa)

Markus Fothen (Ger)	Markus Fothen (Ger)

London's majestic send-off

PROLOGUE: LONDON

The Tour's two previous visits to Britain had yielded very different results. In 1974, a newly built section of bypass near Plymouth provided a rather functional setting for a stage that drew few spectators and, perhaps fittingly, provided unknown Dutchman Henk Poppe with the only major victory of his career. Two decades on, the Tour finally returned for two stages, finishing in Brighton and Portsmouth. Tens of thousands turned out.

It was more than a decade before the Tour crossed the Channel again and, on this occasion, the setting could not have been any more splendid. Starting in Whitehall and passing the Houses of Parliament and through Hyde Park before finishing on the Mall in front of St James's Palace, it was indisputably one of

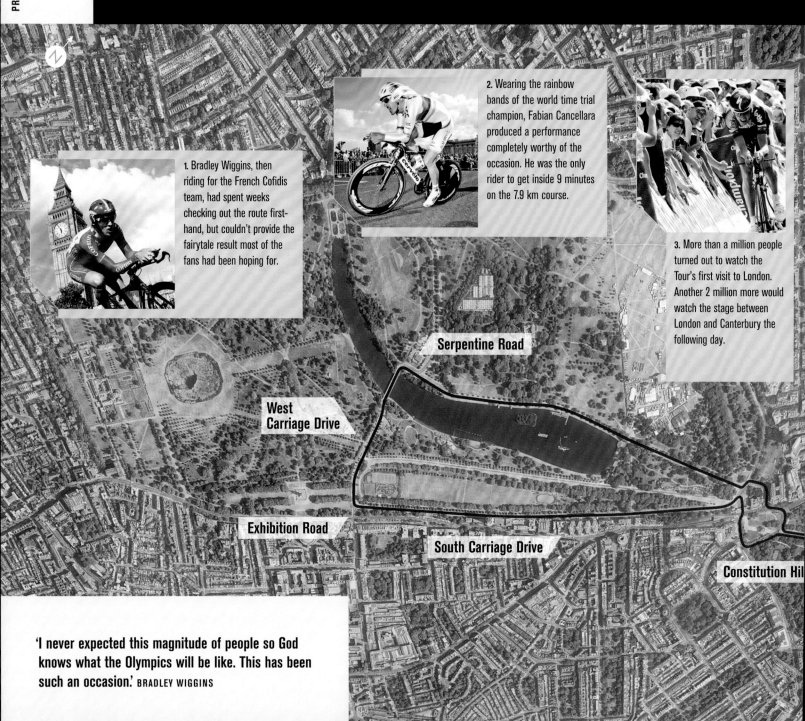

1. Bradley Wiggins, then riding for the French Cofidis team, had spent weeks checking out the route first-hand, but couldn't provide the fairytale result most of the fans had been hoping for.

2. Wearing the rainbow bands of the world time trial champion, Fabian Cancellara produced a performance completely worthy of the occasion. He was the only rider to get inside 9 minutes on the 7.9 km course.

3. More than a million people turned out to watch the Tour's first visit to London. Another 2 million more would watch the stage between London and Canterbury the following day.

Serpentine Road

West Carriage Drive

Exhibition Road

South Carriage Drive

Constitution Hil

'I never expected this magnitude of people so God knows what the Olympics will be like. This has been such an occasion.' BRADLEY WIGGINS

the most spectacular in the race's history. The weather played its part too, the sun emerging and encouraging more than a million fans to line the course.

Home hopes rested on Bradley Wiggins. Huge roars marked the Londoner's rapid progress around the 7.9 km course, but it was not to be his day. He finished fourth. Indeed, the day belonged to just one man: Swiss world time trial champion, Fabian Cancellara. He blasted around the circuit in incomparable fashion. Seven seconds faster than leader Andreas Klöden at halfway, Cancellara finished a staggering 13 seconds clear – almost 2 seconds a kilometre faster than Klöden.

STAGE FACTS

Date: 7 July 2007

Number: Prologue

Length: 7.9 km

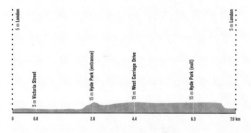

STAGE WINS BY COUNTRY (2012)

1 France (690)	9 United Kingdom (51)	15 Russia (10)	25 Czech Republic (2)
2 Belgium (467)	10 Australia (23)	18 Uzbekistan (9)	25 Latvia (2)
3 Italy (257)	11 United States (20)	19 Kazakhstan (5)	25 Mexico (2)
4 Netherlands (167)	12 Denmark (18)	20 Austria (4)	28 Brazil (1)
5 Spain (123)	13 Norway (14)	20 Estonia (4)	28 Canada (1)
6 Luxembourg (70)	14 Colombia (13)	20 Slovenia (4)	28 Poland (1)
7 Germany (61)	15 Ireland (10)	20 Ukraine (4)	28 South Africa (1)
8 Switzerland (60)	15 Portugal (10)	24 Slovakia (3)	28 Sweden (1)

AFTER PROLOGUE

1 Fabian Cancellara (Swi)
2 Andreas Klöden (Ger)
at 0'13"
3 George Hincapie (USA)
at 0'23"

Fabian Cancellara (Swi)

Not contested

Vladimir Gusev (Rus)

4. Andreas Klöden looked on course for his debut Tour stage win. Riding for Astana, the German was 10 seconds faster than George Hincapie and Wiggins, but ended up being no match for Cancellara.

To The Mall

From Whitehall

Buckingham Palace

Parliament Street

Buckingham Hall

Victoria Street

2007

The yellow jersey's black day

ORTHEZ > GOURETTE, COL D'AUBISQUE

Under fire from the media during the rest day in Pau, race leader Michael Rasmussen attempted to answer his critics with a bravura performance on the Tour de France's final mountain stage. Having found it difficult to cope with Alberto Contador's frequent rapid accelerations at the Plateau de Beille summit finish, Rasmussen set a fierce tempo over the final kilometres of the Aubisque, cracking his young Spanish rival. The stage win made Rasmussen's overall victory of the Tour a virtual certainty.

However, many of those watching were not impressed. The discontented fans who wanted to see the back of Rasmussen were soon to get their wish. Questioned by the management of his Rabobank team about his whereabouts

From Orthez

Béost

Laruns

Eaux-Bonnes

1. As questions began to surface about his whereabouts prior to the Tour, Michael Rasmussen appeared before the press on the rest day in Pau to defend himself against allegations of an anti-doping violation.

3. Hours after Rasmussen's victory on the Aubisque, the media pack in around Rabobank press officer Jacob Bergsma to hear about the team's decision to pull the Dane from the race.

4. Patrice Clerc (right), president of ASO, organizers of the Tour, and Tour director Christian Prudhomme (left) held an impromptu press conference in the start village and backed Rabobank's decision to withdraw Rasmussen from the race.

FAVOURITE FINISHING PLACES

Although it will be no surprise to read that Paris has hosted more stage finishes than any other location, Pau's place at third place is startling given its relatively small size and the fact that it didn't host one until 1930. Pau's popularity with the Tour organization can be explained not only by its position in the foothills of the Pyrenees, but also by the number of hotels in and around the town, which has been a fashionable tourist destination since the 19th century. The Tour often pauses there for a rest day, as was the case when Michael Rasmussen's yellow jersey dreams disappeared with him into the night. Pau was also the setting for Alberto Contador's positive drug test in 2010 that led to him being stripped of that title.

Tour's most popular finish towns:

Paris (135 times)	Briançon (34 times)
Bordeaux (80 times)	Marseille (34 times)
Pau (62 times)	Bayonne (32 times)
Luchon (50 times)	Nantes (30 times)
Metz (40 times)	Belfort (29 times)
Grenoble (38 times)	Montpellier (29 times)
Perpignan (36 times)	Brest (28 times)
Caen (35 times)	Alpe d'Huez (26 times)
Nice (35 times)	

in the weeks prior to the Tour, Rasmussen admitted that he had not been in Mexico, as he had indicated to the anti-doping authorities, but had been training incognito in Italy. Having established that the Dane had clearly violated anti-doping rules, Rabobank pulled him out of the race and sacked him from the team.

Alberto Contador, already in the white jersey as best young rider, inherited the yellow. The Spaniard did just enough to hold off Cadel Evans in the final time trial, taking the title by 23 seconds, with Levi Leipheimer another 8 seconds back in third to provide the Tour's closest podium finish in history.

2. Rasmussen admitted he had found it difficult to cope with Alberto Contador's rapid changes of pace on previous mountain stages, but the Dane stuck with the Spaniard on the Aubisque, before dropping him in the final kilometre.

To Gourette, Col d'Aubisque

STAGE FACTS

Date: 25 July 2007

Number: 16

Length: 218.5 km

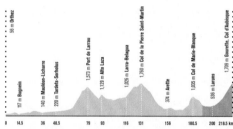

	BEFORE STAGE 16	AFTER STAGE 16
	1 Michael Rasmussen (Den)	1 Michael Rasmussen (Den)
	2 Alberto Contador (Spa) at 2'23"	2 Alberto Contador (Spa) at 3'10"
	3 Cadel Evans (Aus) at 4'00"	3 Cadel Evans (Aus) at 5'03"
	Tom Boonen (Bel)	Tom Boonen (Bel)
	Michael Rasmussen (Den)	Mauricio Soler (Col)
	Alberto Contador (Spa)	Alberto Contador (Spa)

'I accept it and take full responsibility for that [administrative mistake]. I'm sorry that it is now during the Tour de France and that it harms cycling, the sport I love.' MICHAEL RASMUSSEN DURING HIS PAU PRESS CONFERENCE

Sastre's Alp

EMBRUN > ALPE D'HUEZ

The Alpe d'Huez is the Tour's most famous mountain, with 21 hairpin bends leading up to a small ski station. In 2008, it hosted the finish of Stage 17, which covered 210 km from Embrun and included two other 'hors categorie' climbs, the Col du Galibier and the Col de la Croix de Fer (both over 2,000 m). As has often been the case over the 100 Tours, the so-called Dutch Mountain proved decisive. Carlos Sastre started the stage in fourth place, 49 seconds behind leader, his teammate, Fränk Schleck. However, it wasn't Schleck that was in prime position despite being in yellow. Both he and Sastre knew that Australian Cadel Evans and Russian Denis Menchov were strong time trialists and were likely to beat both the CSC riders in the Tour's penultimate time trial stage three days later.

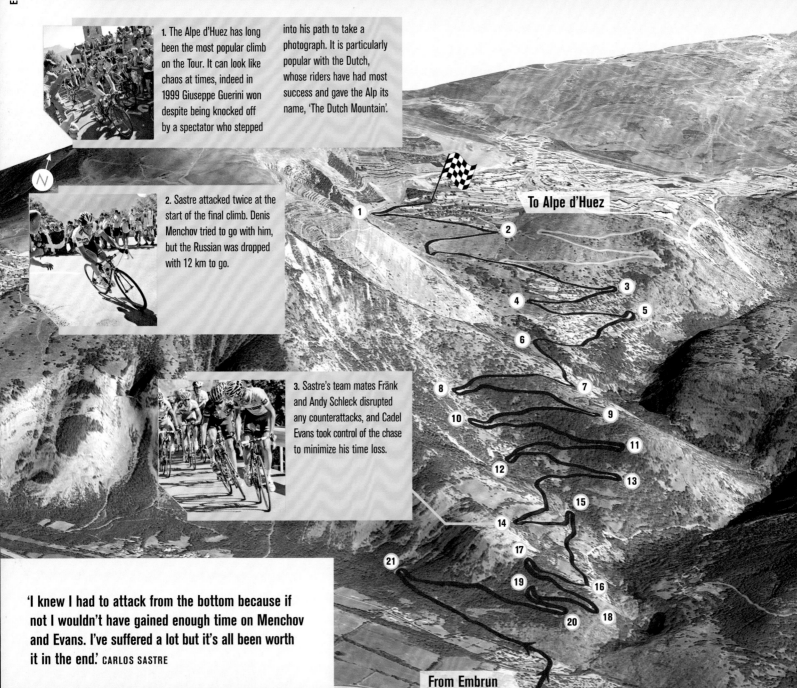

1. The Alpe d'Huez has long been the most popular climb on the Tour. It can look like chaos at times, indeed in 1999 Giuseppe Guerini won despite being knocked off by a spectator who stepped into his path to take a photograph. It is particularly popular with the Dutch, whose riders have had most success and gave the Alp its name, 'The Dutch Mountain'.

2. Sastre attacked twice at the start of the final climb. Denis Menchov tried to go with him, but the Russian was dropped with 12 km to go.

3. Sastre's team mates Fränk and Andy Schleck disrupted any counterattacks, and Cadel Evans took control of the chase to minimize his time loss.

To Alpe d'Huez

From Embrun

'I knew I had to attack from the bottom because if not I wouldn't have gained enough time on Menchov and Evans. I've suffered a lot but it's all been worth it in the end.' CARLOS SASTRE

By the time the Tour arrived at the 17th stage all the riders were tired following two gruelling stages in the Alps. The racing suffered in the early parts, mainly due to the cautiousness of the front runners in the overall standings. Having dragged in an early breakaway the peloton arrived at the bottom of the Alp and Sastre made his move. Menchov tried to go with him, but the CSC team's early pace and the Alpe's brutal gradient destroyed his legs.

Sastre's win on the Alpe d'Huez gave him an overall lead of 1 minute 24 seconds and, despite losing time to Cadel Evans in the final individual time trial, he kept the yellow jersey to win in Paris by 58 seconds. Sastre had ridden the Alp to perfection and glory.

4. After the stage, Sastre explained to journalists, 'We knew we had to attack but going from a long way out was too risky, so we pushed up the rhythm as much as possible during the stage so everybody would get to the final climb after suffering a lot.' The tactic has been described as the most successful piece of outmanoevring in team-sport history. It worked perfectly and Evans and Menchov were left in the wake, desperate to minimize the damage. Sastre finished 2 minutes 3 seconds ahead of Samuel Sánchez and Andy Schleck for his third stage victory in the Tour, following wins in 2003 and 2006. The attack not only set up the yellow jersey, but also helped the Spaniard claim second place in the King of the Mountains classification after Bernhard Kohl. (Kohl was subsequently disqualified for doping.)

STAGE FACTS

Date: 23 July 2008

Number: 17

Length: 210.5 km

SWITCHBACKS

The Alpe d'Huez has been climbed 27 times in the Tour (including twice in 1979). The hairpin bends are named after the winners of stages there, starting at the bottom with bend 21. The naming restarted with the 22nd climb in 2001. The 21 bends in 2011 were named:

21	Fausto Coppi, Lance Armstrong	13	Peter Winnen
		12	Luis Herrera
20	Joop Zoetemelk, Ibán Mayo	11	Bernard Hinault
		10	Federico Echave
19	Hennie Kuiper, Lance Armstrong	9	Steven Rooks
		8	Gert-Jan Theunisse
18	Hennie Kuiper, Fränk Schleck	7	Gianni Bugno
		6	Gianni Bugno
17	Joachim Agostinho, Carlos Sastre	5	Andy Hampsten
		4	Roberto Conti
16	Joop Zoetemelk, Pierre Rolland	3	Marco Pantani
		2	Marco Pantani
15	Peter Winnen	1	Giuseppe Guerini
14	Beat Breu		

BEFORE STAGE 17

1 Fränk Schleck (Lux)
2 Bernhard Kohl (Aut)
 at 0'07"
3 Cadel Evans (Aus)
 at 0'08"

Óscar Freire (Spa)

Bernhard Kohl (Aut)

Andy Schleck (Lux)

AFTER STAGE 17

1 Carlos Sastre (Spa)
2 Fränk Schleck (Lux)
 at 1'24"
3 Bernhard Kohl (Aut)
 at 1'33"

Óscar Freire (Spa)

Bernhard Kohl (Aut)

Andy Schleck (Lux)

2009

Verdict on the Ventoux

MONTÉLIMAR > MONT VENTOUX

The distance separating Paris from France's mountain ranges resulted in a long-standing dilemma for organizers of the Tour de France. The race's mountain stages have almost always decided the destiny of the yellow jersey, but all too often the final verdict was delivered with several days remaining to the finish in Paris, leading to a distinct lack of drama over the closing days. But how could the organizers change this?

Finishing the race anywhere other than Paris has never been considered. However, much improved transport links provided Tour director Christian Prudhomme with a solution: schedule a summit finish on the final Saturday, followed by a TGV transfer to Paris the next morning to complete the final stage.

'I dreamt of this moment last night and to have it come true today is amazing.' JUAN MANUEL GÁRATE

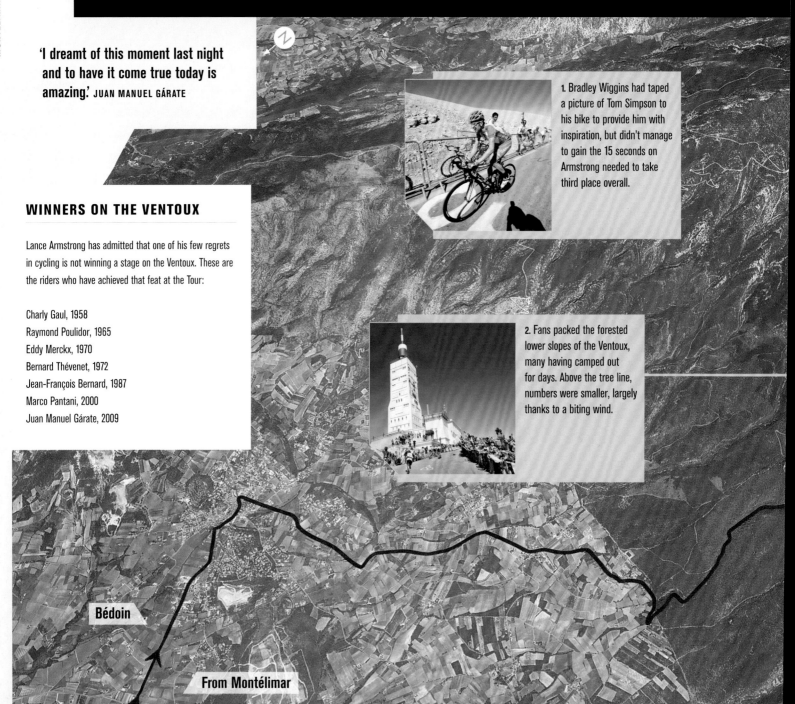

1. Bradley Wiggins had taped a picture of Tom Simpson to his bike to provide him with inspiration, but didn't manage to gain the 15 seconds on Armstrong needed to take third place overall.

WINNERS ON THE VENTOUX

Lance Armstrong has admitted that one of his few regrets in cycling is not winning a stage on the Ventoux. These are the riders who have achieved that feat at the Tour:

Charly Gaul, 1958
Raymond Poulidor, 1965
Eddy Merckx, 1970
Bernard Thévenet, 1972
Jean-François Bernard, 1987
Marco Pantani, 2000
Juan Manuel Gárate, 2009

2. Fans packed the forested lower slopes of the Ventoux, many having camped out for days. Above the tree line, numbers were smaller, largely thanks to a biting wind.

Bédoin

From Montélimar

Mont Ventoux was a fitting choice for the first-ever summit finish on the penultimate day of the Tour. Infamous and unmistakeable, 'The Bald Mountain' stands apart. Better still, as the riders rode towards its sun-bleached slopes, the result was still in the balance. Alberto Contador held the lead, but was being pressed by Andy Schleck and, more controversially, by his own Astana team-mate, Lance Armstrong, back after a four-year absence.

The drama didn't live up to the setting. The favourites tracked each other closely, enabling Spaniard Juan Manuel Gárate to ride off with the greatest win of his career. But half a million were on the Ventoux to see it, justifying Prudhomme's audacious decision.

STAGE FACTS

Date: 25 July 2009

Number: 20

Length: 167 km

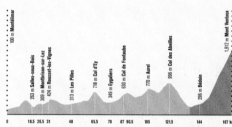

Mont Ventoux

4. Spain's Juan Manuel Gárate and Germany's Tony Martin were the final two survivors of a 16-man group that broke away just 3 km into the stage. Gárate's final attack before the final hairpin eventually saw off his rival.

3. The strong headwind over the treeless 7 km up to the summit made it extremely difficult for riders to attack from the yellow jersey group. Andy Schleck tried to get away but Astana team-mates Alberto Contador and Lance Armstrong always had the legs to counter him.

BEFORE STAGE 20	AFTER STAGE 20

1 Alberto Contador (Spa)
2 Andy Schleck (Lux)
at 4'11"
3 Lance Armstrong (USA)
at 5'24"

1 Alberto Contador (Spa)
2 Andy Schleck (Lux)
at 4'11"
3 Cadel Evans (Aus)
at 5'24"

Thor Hushovd (Nor)

Thor Hushovd (Nor)

Franco Pellizotti (Ita)

Franco Pellizotti (Ita)

Andy Schleck (Lux)

Andy Schleck (Lux)

2009

Cavendish's sprinting masterclass

MONTEREAU-FAULT-YONNE > PARIS CHAMPS-ÉLYSÉES

Having introduced himself to the wider cycling world with four Tour de France stage wins in 2008, 'Manx Missile' Mark Cavendish stepped up another level in 2009, bagging six stage victories in imperious fashion.

The distance between Cavendish and his Tour rivals was sometimes so great that he had time to make cheeky reference to his team's sponsors by waving his sunglasses or pretending to make a call in tribute to his team's backer, HTC.

His best moment, though, came at the very end of the race. The Briton hadn't gone the full distance in his first two Tour outings, but now had the chance to win on the Champs-Élysées, the stage prized above all others by the sprint fraternity.

From Montereau-Fault-Yonne

Place de la Concorde

2. Cavendish's lead-out man, Mark Renshaw, is already starting to celebrate as the Briton, in his typically tucked-down style, powers towards the line for his sixth win of the race.

1. Just as they had all the way through the race, Mark Cavendish's lead-out train kept him safely out of harm's way while also ensuring that any breakaway riders had little chance of capitalizing on their advantage.

STAGE WIN RECORDS

Mark Cavendish's victory on the Champs-Élysées gave him the record for the highest number of bunch sprint wins during one Tour in the post-war period. However, he was still two behind the all-time record for stage wins, which is jointly held by three riders.

Frenchman Charles Pélissier won eight stages during the 1930 race and finished second seven other times that year. In 1970, Eddy Merckx won eight stages including the prologue and two trials and repeated the feat in 1974 when he also won the prologue and a time trial. Two years on, Merckx's Belgian compatriot Freddy Maertens won eight stages on his Tour debut, including the prologue and two time trials.

'It is a dream for every sprinter in the world to cross the finish line in view of the Arc de Triomphe with your arms in the air.' MARK CAVENDISH

Set up perfectly by his team-mates, Cavendish was second in line as the peloton swept through the Place de la Concorde and into the final straight. Glued to the back wheel of his lead-out man, Mark Renshaw, Cavendish made his move with 200 m to go.

His acceleration was startling and, in a flash, he was 10 m clear of the pack behind. They barely closed as he zipped across the line, punching his fists in the air with delight. His six wins hadn't won him the green points jersey, however. He would have to wait another two years for that, by which time he had doubled his stage-winning tally to 20.

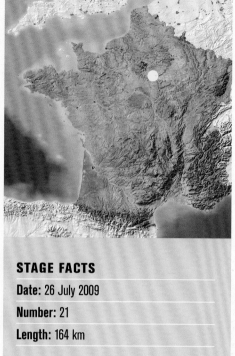

STAGE FACTS

Date: 26 July 2009

Number: 21

Length: 164 km

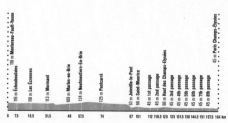

3. Mission accomplished. Having worked seamlessly together coming towards the finish, Cavendish and Renshaw celebrate Cavendish's victory with the same salute. The pair finished first and second on the stage.

To Paris Champs-Élysées

Place Charles de Gaulle

4. Cavendish's fifth victory of the race made him Britain's most successful rider at the Tour de France in terms of stage wins. The record had been held by Barry Hoban since the mid 1970s.

BEFORE STAGE 21

1 Alberto Contador (Spa)
2 Andy Schleck (Lux)
   at 4'11"
3 Lance Armstrong (USA)
   at 5'24"

Thor Hushovd (Nor)

Franco Pellizotti (Ita)

Andy Schleck (Lux)

AFTER STAGE 21

1 Alberto Contador (Spa)
2 Andy Schleck (Lux)
   at 4'11"
3 Lance Armstrong (USA)
   at 5'24"

Thor Hushovd (Nor)

Franco Pellizotti (Ita)

Andy Schleck (Lux)

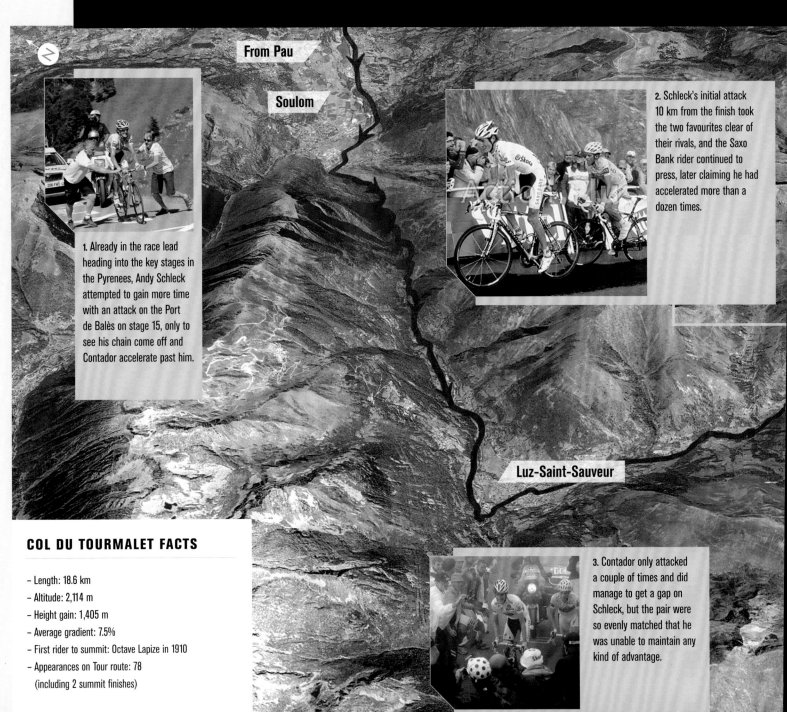

Duel on the Tourmalet

PAU > COL DU TOURMALET

This stage to the summit of the Tourmalet came after three others in the Pyrenean range and provided the culmination of celebrations of a centenary of racing in the high mountains. Fittingly, it pitched the race's two outstanding performers against each other. Relations between Alberto Contador and Andy Schleck had soured after the Spaniard had taken advantage of a mechanical problem encountered by the Luxembourger on a previous Pyrenean stage to take a narrow overall lead.

With 10 km left to the summit, Schleck attacked from the group of main contenders. Contador was the only rider able to respond. The pair were soon on, and then past, lone leader Alexandr Kolobnev. The final kilometres showed how well matched

From Pau

Soulom

Luz-Saint-Sauveur

1. Already in the race lead heading into the key stages in the Pyrenees, Andy Schleck attempted to gain more time with an attack on the Port de Balès on stage 15, only to see his chain come off and Contador accelerate past him.

2. Schleck's initial attack 10 km from the finish took the two favourites clear of their rivals, and the Saxo Bank rider continued to press, later claiming he had accelerated more than a dozen times.

3. Contador only attacked a couple of times and did manage to get a gap on Schleck, but the pair were so evenly matched that he was unable to maintain any kind of advantage.

COL DU TOURMALET FACTS

– Length: 18.6 km
– Altitude: 2,114 m
– Height gain: 1,405 m
– Average gradient: 7.5%
– First rider to summit: Octave Lapize in 1910
– Appearances on Tour route: 78
   (including 2 summit finishes)

the two men were. Schleck set the pace, accelerating frequently in an attempt to disrupt his rival's rhythm. Contador was content to neutralize Schleck's efforts, knowing he was likely to dominate the Luxembourger in the key time trial to come.

At the finish, Contador was happy to let Schleck surge through for the win. When the pair congratulated each other, it appeared they were friends again. However, 18 months later, there was a further twist when the Court for Arbitration of Sport banned Contador after a positive drug test, stripped him of the Tour title and handed what was by now a hollow victory to Schleck.

4. Schleck punches the air as he takes his second mountain stage win of the race, but Contador has the considerable consolation of keeping the yellow jersey – at least until the intervention of the Court for Arbitration of Sport.

To Col du Tourmalet

Barèges

STAGE FACTS

Date: 22 July 2010

Number: 17

Length: 174 km

BEFORE STAGE 17	AFTER STAGE 17
1 Alberto Contador (Spa)	1 Alberto Contador (Spa)
2 Andy Schleck (Lux) at 0'08"	2 Andy Schleck (Lux) at 0'08"
3 Samuel Sánchez (Spa) at 2'00"	3 Samuel Sánchez (Spa) at 3'32"
Thor Hushovd (Nor)	Thor Hushovd (Nor)
Anthony Charteau (Fra)	Anthony Charteau (Fra)

Andy Schleck (Lux)	Andy Schleck (Lux)

'He matched me every time I increased the pace. I tried to break him but I couldn't. But I am still very pleased to win the stage. I am now his equal in the mountains and that is the first time I have been able to say that.' ANDY SCHLECK

2011

Schleck's astounding raid

PINEROLO > GALIBIER SERRE CHEVALIER

The centenary of the Tour's first encounter with the high Alps was marked by an extraordinary stage, both in terms of its aspect and the performances of the leading contenders. It took the riders over the Agnel, the Izoard and, for the first time in Tour history, to a finish on the summit of the mighty Galibier.

It started with the favourites sitting tight in the peloton, apparently waiting for the inevitable showdown on the Galibier. However, often overly cautious in the past, Andy Schleck decided to risk an all-out attack on the Izoard. No-one responded, perhaps wisely, given there were still 62 km to the finish.

Schleck's stunning acceleration quickly carried him across to the breakaway, where he joined Leopard-Trek team-mate Maxime

From Pinerolo

Col d'Izoard

1. Leopard-Trek got their tactics spot on. After Joost Posthuma had paced Andy Schleck on the Izoard, Maxime Monfort took over, guiding his team leader down the descent and then setting a furious pace for him up the Lautaret.

2. Schleck had said beforehand he would attack on this stage. The surprise was not that he did, but that his attack came from so far out. Astonishingly, he maintained his pace all the way into the finish.

Saint-Chaffrey

Cervières

THE TOUR'S HIGHEST STAGE FINISHES

2,646 m Galibier Serre Chevalier in 2011 (stage winner Andy Schleck)

2,413 m Col du Granon in 1986 (Eduardo Chozas)

2,275 m Val Thorens in 1994 (Nelson Rodríguez)

2,240 m Andorra-Arcalís in 1997 (Jan Ullrich) and 2009 (Brice Feillu)

2,114 m Col du Tourmalet in 1974 (Jean-Pierre Danguillaume) and 2010 (Andy Schleck)

2,068 m Montée de Tignes in 2007 (Michael Rasmussen)

2,033 m Sestriere in 1952 (Fausto Coppi), 1992 (Claudio Chiappucci), 1996 (Bjarne Riis) and 1999 (Lance Armstrong)

2,004 m Courchevel in 1997 (Richard Virenque) and 2005 (Alejandro Valverde)

3. Evans showed just as much class as Schleck in his pursuit of the Luxembourger. With no-one else willing, or perhaps able, to assist him the Australian took matters into his own hands, steadily grinding down Schleck's advantage.

Monfort, who sacrificed his own reserves setting a fierce pace for his leader. With 16 km remaining, the Belgian pulled aside and Schleck powered relentlessly on and had, it seemed, ridden himself into the yellow jersey. But there was more drama to come.

Cadel Evans had taken up a dogged one-man pursuit. The battle between Schleck and Evans was the ultimate *mano a mano* as, over the final 10 km, Evans halved Schleck's 4-minute advantage, keeping himself in the hunt for the title. Unwittingly, Evans' effort also enabled Thomas Voeckler to keep the yellow jersey after the Frenchman stuck to his wheel all the way.

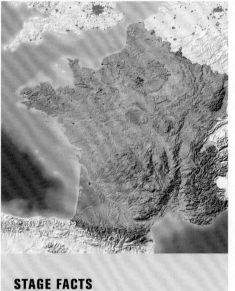

'I said this morning: "No guts, no glory." I took the race by the horns and went all in.' ANDY SCHLECK

STAGE FACTS

Date: 21 July 2011
Number: 18
Length: 200.5 km

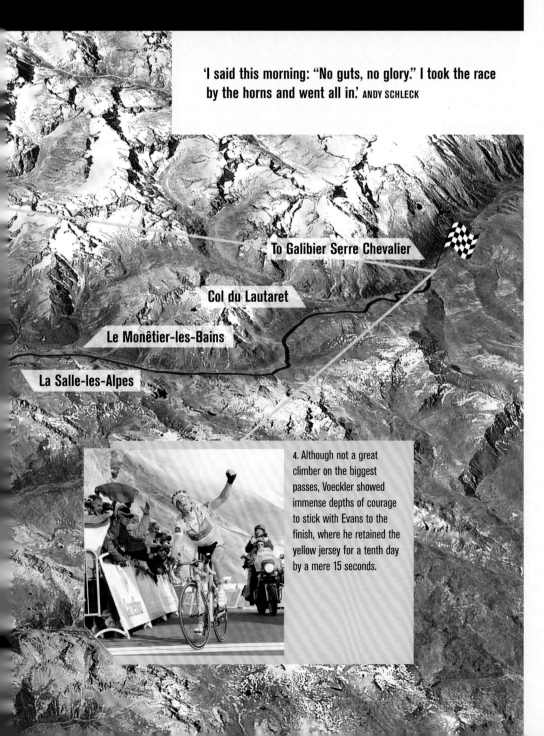

To Galibier Serre Chevalier

Col du Lautaret

Le Monêtier-les-Bains

La Salle-les-Alpes

4. Although not a great climber on the biggest passes, Voeckler showed immense depths of courage to stick with Evans to the finish, where he retained the yellow jersey for a tenth day by a mere 15 seconds.

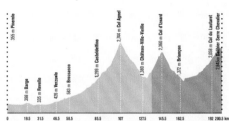

BEFORE STAGE 18

1 Thomas Voeckler (Fra)
2 Cadel Evans (Aus)
at 1'18"
3 Fränk Schleck (Lux)
at 1'22"

Mark Cavendish (UK)

Jelle Vanendert (Bel)

Rigoberto Urán (Col)

AFTER STAGE 18

1 Thomas Voeckler (Fra)
2 Andy Schleck (Lux)
at 0'15"
3 Fränk Schleck (Lux)
at 1'08"

Mark Cavendish (UK)

Jelle Vanendert (Bel)

Rein Taaramäe (Est)

Wiggins climbs towards victory

LUCHON > PEYRAGUDES

Thanks primarily to the large amount of time trialling on the route, Bradley Wiggins went into the race as a favourite. He lived up to that billing in the first of two long time trials, but then faced a series of tough tests in the Alps and Pyrenees. Well shielded by his strong Sky team, Wiggins came through these tests until just one remained: a finish at a summit new to the Tour, the Peyragudes ski station above the Peyresourde pass. Liquigas leader Vincenzo Nibali was best placed to threaten Wiggins and the Italian had his team-mates set the pace for much of the stage, which featured four passes. Nibali went clear of the yellow jersey group on the first of these, the Menté, but then seemed content to wait until the final ascent to make his bid for glory.

'The moment we went over the Peyresourde, I allowed myself to drift and it was the first time I thought maybe I've won the Tour.' BRADLEY WIGGINS

From Luchon

Port de Balès

Col de Peyresourde

1. Mist shrouded long sections of the penultimate climb, the Port de Balès, nullifying Vincenzo Nibali's hopes of an attack on the descent.

2. With Nibali unable to deliver on his team-mate's efforts, Lotto's Jelle Vanendert and Jurgen van den Broeck were the first to attack Wiggins, who briefly appeared to be struggling at this point.

Liquigas's pace whittled down the yellow jersey group to just 14 riders on the Peyresourde. After a brief descent, this group started up the final climb. A flurry of attacks seemed briefly to put Wiggins and right-hand man Chris Froome in difficulty, but both men responded quickly. Riding up to, and then past, their rivals, the two Britons began to close on lone breakaway Alejandro Valverde. They would probably have reached him if Wiggins hadn't asked the surging Froome to ease off. The stage didn't matter. The Tour was won.

BRITAIN'S TOUR FIRSTS

1937: Charles Holland and Bill Burl start the Tour. Burl crashes out on stage 2, Holland is forced out by mechanical failure on stage 14c to Luchon.

1955: Brian Robinson and Tony Hoar finish the Tour.

1958: Robinson wins a stage. He bags another the following year.

1962: Tom Simpson wears the yellow jersey, holding it for one stage.

1969: Barry Hoban wins successive stages.

1974: The Tour visits Britain for a stage in Plymouth.

1984: King of the Mountains Robert Millar wins one of the Tour's main jerseys.

1988: Sean Yates wins a time trial.

1994: Chris Boardman wins the prologue.

2009: Mark Cavendish wins six stages, the final one on the Champs-Élysées.

2011: Cavendish wins the green jersey.

2012: Bradley Wiggins wins the yellow jersey.

STAGE FACTS

Date: 19 July 2012

Number: 17

Length: 143.5 km

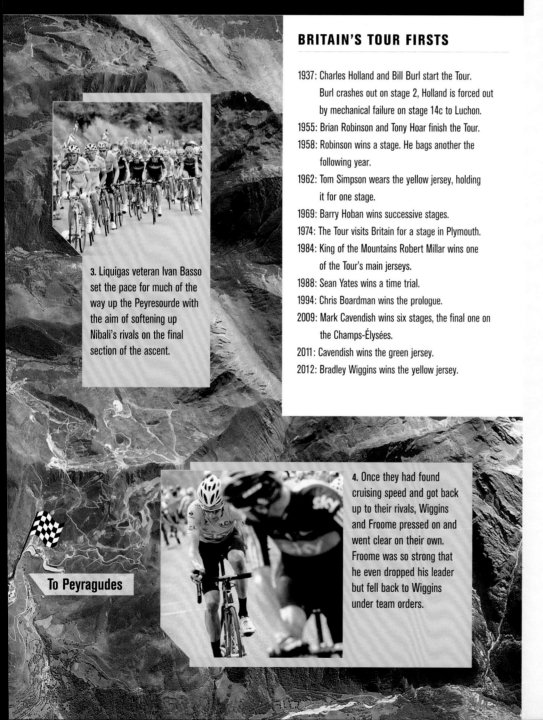

3. Liquigas veteran Ivan Basso set the pace for much of the way up the Peyresourde with the aim of softening up Nibali's rivals on the final section of the ascent.

To Peyragudes

4. Once they had found cruising speed and got back up to their rivals, Wiggins and Froome pressed on and went clear on their own. Froome was so strong that he even dropped his leader but fell back to Wiggins under team orders.

BEFORE STAGE 17	AFTER STAGE 17

1 Bradley Wiggins (UK)
2 Christopher Froome (UK)
  at 2'05"
3 Vincenzo Nibali (Ita)
  at 2'23"

1 Bradley Wiggins (UK)
2 Christopher Froome (UK)
  at 2'05"
3 Vincenzo Nibali (Ita)
  at 2'41"

Peter Sagan (Svk)

Peter Sagan (Svk)

Thomas Voeckler (Fra)

Thomas Voeckler (Fra)

Tejay van Garderen (USA)

Tejay van Garderen (USA)

The atlas
of 100 Tours

1903

1904

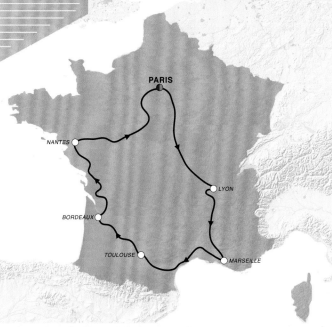

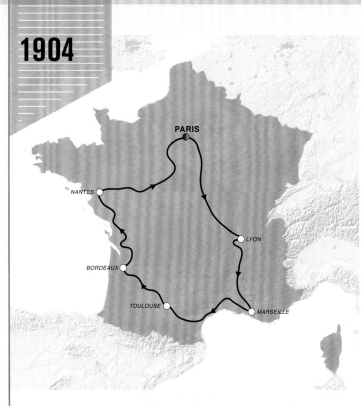

The first Tour de France was a promotional idea by Henri Desgrange, editor of *L'Auto* (forerunner of today's sports daily *L'Équipe*). The stages were very long, but they were not on consecutive days. Competitors could drop out of any stage and start again the next day, although they had to complete all six stages to qualify for the general classification. Of 60 starters, 21 finished the race. Maurice Garin, the pre-race favourite, led throughout the race and won three stages.

The second Tour followed an almost identical route to the first, but the riders this time had to complete all six stages. Initially the winner was also the same as in 1903. However, 12 of the 27 cyclists who finished the race (including the first four in the general classification and all the stage winners) were eventually disqualified for offences such as taking trains during the race. Four months after the race 19-year-old Henri Cornet was declared the winner.

Wednesday 1 July–Sunday 19 July

1	467 km, Paris > Lyon	
2	374 km, Lyon > Marseille	**Overall**
3	423 km, Marseille > Toulouse	1 Maurice Garin (Fra)
4	268 km, Toulouse > Bordeaux	in 93h 33'00"
5	425 km, Bordeaux > Nantes	2 Lucien Pothier (Fra)
6	471 km, Nantes > Paris	at 2h 49'45"
		3 Fernand Augereau (Fra)
		at 4h 29'24"

Saturday 2 July–Sunday 24 July

1	467 km, Paris > Lyon	
2	374 km, Lyon > Marseille	**Overall**
3	423 km, Marseille > Toulouse	1 Henri Cornet (Fra)
4	268 km, Toulouse > Bordeaux	in 96h 05'55"
5	425 km, Bordeaux > Nantes	2 Jean-Baptiste Dortignacq
6	471 km, Nantes > Paris	(Fra)
		at 2h 16'14"
		3 Aloïs Catteau (Bel)
		at 9h 01'25"

1905

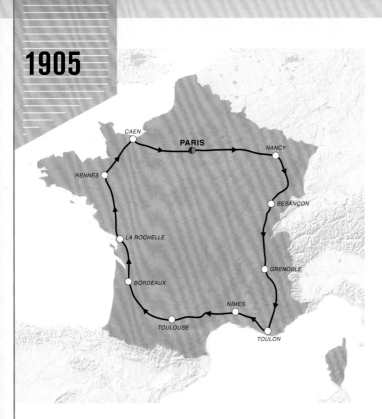

After the scandals of 1904, the third Tour was run under different rules. The stages were more numerous but shorter, and the general classification was decided by points rather than time. The first rider to finish each stage received one point, and each successive rider got an extra point plus one point for every 5 minutes behind the previous rider. A more extensive route included mountains, with the Ballon d'Alsace being the first climb, and an unofficial best climber was named.

Sunday 9 July–Sunday 30 July

1   340 km, Paris > Nancy
2   299 km, Nancy > Besançon
3   327 km, Besançon > Grenoble
4   348 km, Grenoble > Toulon
5   192 km, Toulon > Nîmes
6   307 km, Nîmes > Toulouse
7   268 km, Toulouse > Bordeaux
8   257 km, Bordeaux > La Rochelle
9   263 km, La Rochelle > Rennes
10 167 km, Rennes > Caen
11 253 km, Caen > Paris

Overall
1 Louis Trousselier (Fra)
35 points
2 Hippolyte Aucouturier (Fra)
61 points
3 Jean-Baptiste Dortignacq
(Fra) 64 points

Best Climber
René Pottier (Fra)

1906

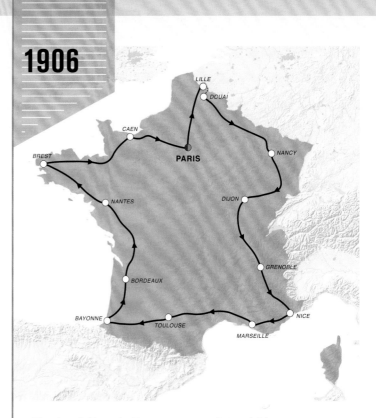

The fourth Tour de France saw a substantial increase in the total distance covered, from 3,021 km in 1905 to 4,637 km in 1906. The average speed of the winner, René Pottier, was 24.5 km/hour which was 3 km/hour slower than the previous year. Of the 76 cyclists who started the race, 49 completed the first stage and a mere 14 finished in the velodrome in Paris at the end of the 13th stage. Only four riders were disqualified.

Wednesday 4 July–Sunday 29 July

1   275 km, Paris > Lille
2   400 km, Douai > Nancy
3   416 km, Nancy > Dijon
4   311 km, Dijon > Grenoble
5   345 km, Grenoble > Nice
6   292 km, Nice > Marseille
7   480 km, Marseille > Toulouse
8   300 km, Toulouse > Bayonne
9   338 km, Bayonne > Bordeaux
10 391 km, Bordeaux > Nantes
11 321 km, Nantes > Brest
12 415 km, Brest > Caen
13 259 km, Caen > Paris

Overall
1 René Pottier (Fra)
31 points
2 Georges Passerieu (Fra)
39 points
3 Louis Trousselier (Fra)
59 points

Best Climber
René Pottier (Fra)

1907

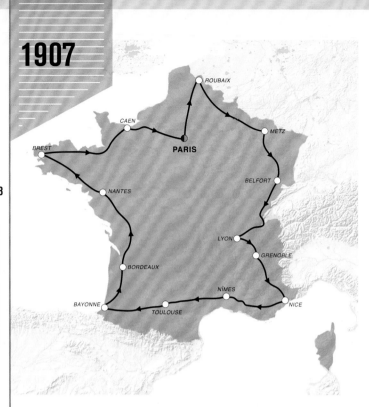

The 1907 Tour followed a now familiar clockwise route around the perimeter of present-day France. In fact, as in the previous year, the riders crossed the border into Germany on stage 2, and this year the race also briefly visited Switzerland, including the western Alps for the first time. Émile Georget won five of the first eight stages, but lost his lead to Lucien Petit-Breton when he was penalized for borrowing a team-mate's bike when his own was broken.

Monday 8 July–Sunday 4 August

1	272 km, Paris > Roubaix	
2	398 km, Roubaix > Metz	
3	259 km, Metz > Belfort	
4	309 km, Belfort > Lyon	
5	311 km, Lyon > Grenoble	
6	345 km, Grenoble > Nice	
7	345 km, Nice > Nîmes	
8	303 km, Nîmes > Toulouse	
9	299 km, Toulouse > Bayonne	
10	269 km, Bayonne > Bordeaux	
11	391 km, Bordeaux > Nantes	
12	321 km, Nantes > Brest	
13	415 km, Brest > Caen	
14	251 km, Caen > Paris	

Overall
1 Lucien Petit-Breton (Fra)
47 points
2 Gustave Garrigou (Fra)
66 points
3 Émile Georget (Fra)
74 points

Best Climber
Émile Georget (Fra)

1908

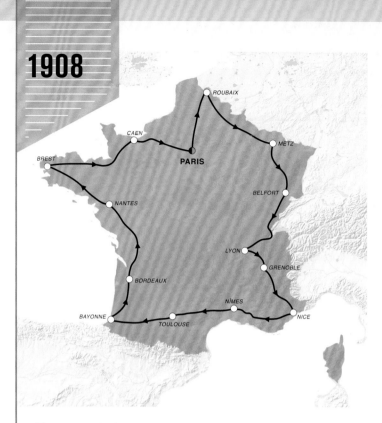

The route of this year's race was virtually identical to the previous year and the winner was also the same. Petit-Breton was helped by the fact that he was a skilled bicycle mechanic, as riders could not change bikes and had to repair their own machines unaided. Of 114 riders who started the race, 36 finished it. French athlete, mountaineer and aviator Marie Marvingt was refused permission to participate. She rode the route after the race, successfully completing it.

Monday 13 July–Sunday 9 August

1	272 km, Paris > Roubaix	
2	398 km, Roubaix > Metz	
3	259 km, Metz > Belfort	
4	309 km, Belfort > Lyon	
5	311 km, Lyon > Grenoble	
6	345 km, Grenoble > Nice	
7	354 km, Nice > Nîmes	
8	303 km, Nîmes > Toulouse	
9	299 km, Toulouse > Bayonne	
10	269 km, Bayonne > Bordeaux	
11	391 km, Bordeaux > Nantes	
12	321 km, Nantes > Brest	
13	415 km, Brest > Caen	
14	251 km, Caen > Paris	

Overall
1 Lucien Petit-Breton (Fra)
36 points
2 François Faber (Lux)
68 points
3 Georges Passerieu (Fra)
75 points

Best Climber
Gustave Garrigou (Fra)

1909

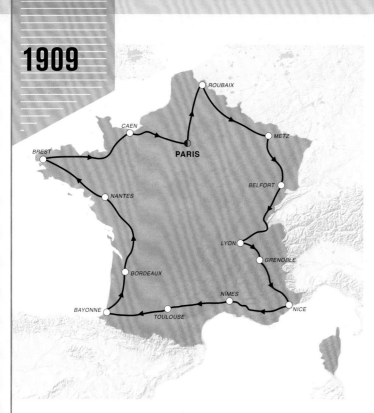

1910

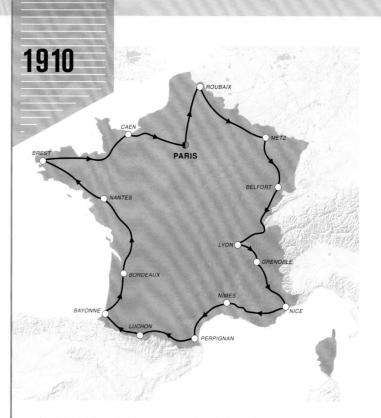

In the absence of Lucien Petit-Breton, François Faber was a clear winner, also taking six stages. More riders than ever before – 150 – started the race, including 19 Italians, 5 Belgians, 4 Swiss, 1 German and 1 Luxembourger; 55 of them finished. Low temperatures, rain and snow made this a difficult edition. The wind was so strong on the Col de Porte that Faber was twice blown off his bike, in addition to having it kicked from under him by a horse.

Monday 5 July–Sunday 1 August

1	272 km, Paris > Roubaix
2	398 km, Roubaix > Metz
3	259 km, Metz > Belfort
4	309 km, Belfort > Lyon
5	311 km, Lyon > Grenoble
6	345 km, Grenoble > Nice
7	345 km, Nice > Nîmes
8	303 km, Nîmes > Toulouse
9	299 km, Toulouse > Bayonne
10	269 km, Bayonne > Bordeaux
11	391 km, Bordeaux > Nantes
12	321 km, Nantes > Brest
13	415 km, Brest > Caen
14	251 km, Caen > Paris

Overall
1 François Faber (Lux)
37 points
2 Gustave Garrigou (Fra)
57 points
3 Jean Alavoine (Fra)
66 points

Best Climber
François Faber (Lux)

The 1910 Tour de France saw the debut of the high mountains, as the race entered the Pyrenees and included the climbs of the Peyresourde, Aspin, Tourmalet and Aubisque on stage 10. After that stage (which had started at 3.30am and finished over 14 hours later) the eventual winner, Octave Lapize, famously described the organizers as assassins. The Tour also saw its first fatality – French cyclist Adolphe Hélière died while swimming during a rest day in Nice.

Sunday 3 July–Sunday 31 July

1	272 km, Paris > Roubaix
2	398 km, Roubaix > Metz
3	259 km, Metz > Belfort
4	309 km, Belfort > Lyon
5	311 km, Lyon > Grenoble
6	345 km, Grenoble > Nice
7	345 km, Nice > Nîmes
8	216 km, Nîmes > Perpignan
9	289 km, Perpignan > Luchon
10	326 km, Luchon > Bayonne
11	269 km, Bayonne > Bordeaux
12	391 km, Bordeaux > Nantes
13	321 km, Nantes > Brest
14	424 km, Brest > Caen
15	262 km, Caen > Paris

Overall
1 Octave Lapize (Fra)
63 points
2 François Faber (Lux)
67 points
3 Gustave Garrigou (Fra)
86 points

Best Climber
Octave Lapize (Fra)

1911

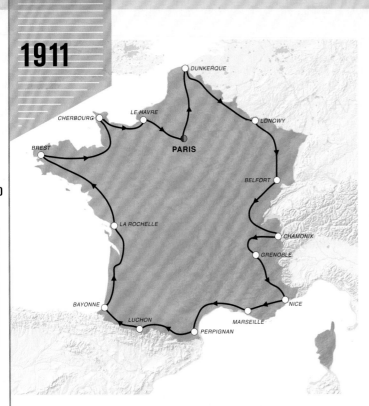

The 1911 race was longer than previous editions, at 5,344 km. The longest stage took almost 18 hours and only 28 of the 84 riders who started made it to Paris. The race again included two stages in the Pyrenees, and this time also visited the high Alps to climb the Col du Galibier; as a result it was considered the first modern Tour. Maurice Brocco was ejected from the race for acting as a *domestique* (a team member whose role is to assist the team leader), a term first used as an insult.

Sunday 2 July–Sunday 30 July

1	351 km, Paris > Dunkerque	
2	388 km, Dunkerque > Longwy	
3	331 km, Longwy > Belfort	
4	344 km, Belfort > Chamonix	
5	366 km, Chamonix > Grenoble	
6	348 km, Grenoble > Nice	
7	334 km, Nice > Marseille	
8	335 km, Marseille > Perpignan	
9	289 km, Perpignan > Luchon	
10	326 km, Luchon > Bayonne	
11	379 km, Bayonne > La Rochelle	
12	470 km, La Rochelle > Brest	
13	405 km, Brest > Cherbourg	
14	361 km, Cherbourg > Le Havre	
15	317 km, Le Havre > Paris	

Overall

1 Gustave Garrigou (Fra)
43 points
2 Paul Duboc (Fra)
61 points
3 Émile Georget (Fra)
84 points

Best Climber
Paul Duboc (Fra)

1912

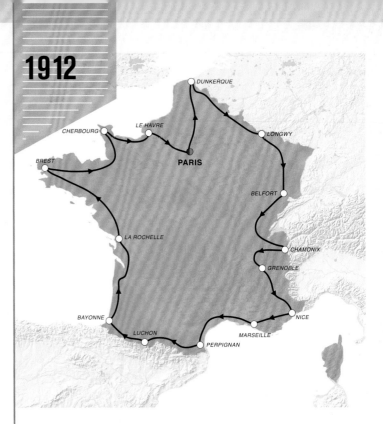

In the last Tour de France to use the points system for the general classification, Belgium had its first winner in 20-year-old Odile Defraye. Some controversy was caused by Belgians who were riding for other teams helping Defraye, and Octave Lapize and his team withdrew from the race in protest. The route was very similar to 1911, including the Alps and the Pyrenees in a clockwise trip around the hexagon. This order is still considered the most classic Tour itinerary.

Sunday 30 June–Sunday 28 July

1	351 km, Paris > Dunkerque	
2	388 km, Dunkerque > Longwy	
3	331 km, Longwy > Belfort	
4	344 km, Belfort > Chamonix	
5	366 km, Chamonix > Grenoble	
6	323 km, Grenoble > Nice	
7	334 km, Nice > Marseille	
8	335 km, Marseille > Perpignan	
9	289 km, Perpignan > Luchon	
10	326 km, Luchon > Bayonne	
11	379 km, Bayonne > La Rochelle	
12	470 km, La Rochelle > Brest	
13	405 km, Brest > Cherbourg	
14	361 km, Cherbourg > Le Havre	
15	317 km, Le Havre > Paris	

Overall

1 Odile Defraye (Bel)
49 points
2 Eugène Christophe (Fra)
108 points
3 Gustave Garrigou (Fra)
140 points

Best Climber
Odile Defraye (Bel)

1913

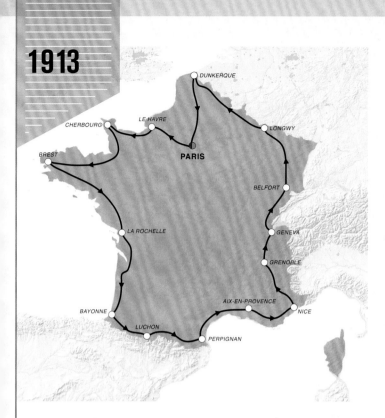

The 1913 Tour reverted to basing the general classification on time, the first since 1904 to do so. It also marked a departure in following an anticlockwise route around France, visiting the Pyrenees before the Alps. Only 25 of the 140 starters finished the race. Eugène Christophe was docked 10 minutes for asking a boy to work the bellows while he spent 4 hours repairing his bicycle following a collision with a car on the descent from the Col du Tourmalet.

Sunday 29 June–Sunday 27 July

1	388 km, Paris > Le Havre	
2	364 km, Le Havre > Cherbourg	
3	405 km, Cherbourg > Brest	
4	470 km, Brest > La Rochelle	
5	379 km, La Rochelle > Bayonne	
6	326 km, Bayonne > Luchon	
7	324 km, Luchon > Perpignan	
8	325 km, Perpignan > Aix-en-Provence	
9	356 km, Aix-en-Provence > Nice	
10	333 km, Nice > Grenoble	
11	325 km, Grenoble > Geneva	
12	335 km, Geneva > Belfort	
13	325 km, Belfort > Longwy	
14	393 km, Longwy > Dunkerque	
15	340 km, Dunkerque > Paris	

Overall
1 Philippe Thys (Bel)
in 197h 54'00"
2 Gustave Garrigou (Fra)
at 8'37"
3 Marcel Buysse (Bel)
at 3h 30'55"

Best Climber
Philippe Thys (Bel)

1914

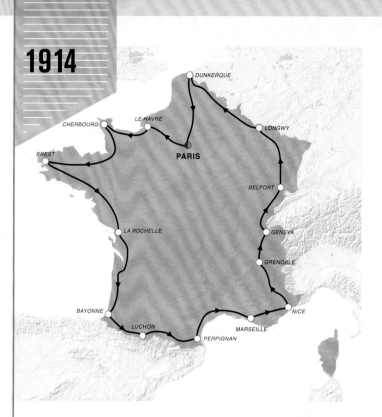

The 1914 Tour de France was the last race before a four-year break for World War I. It began on the same day that Archduke Ferdinand was assassinated in Sarajevo. Belgian Philippe Thys gained the second of his three Tour victories. The presence of seven previous winners and four future winners in the race remains a record. Two competitors from Australia, Don Kirkham and Ivan Munro, competed for the first time; they finished in 17th and 20th places.

Sunday 28 June–Sunday 26 July

1	388 km, Paris > Le Havre	
2	364 km, Le Havre > Cherbourg	
3	405 km, Cherbourg > Brest	
4	470 km, Brest > La Rochelle	
5	379 km, La Rochelle > Bayonne	
6	326 km, Bayonne > Luchon	
7	323 km, Luchon > Perpignan	
8	370 km, Perpignan > Marseille	
9	338 km, Marseille > Nice	
10	323 km, Nice > Grenoble	
11	325 km, Grenoble > Geneva	
12	325 km, Geneva > Belfort	
13	325 km, Belfort > Longwy	
14	390 km, Longwy > Dunkerque	
15	340 km, Dunkerque > Paris	

Overall
1 Philippe Thys (Bel)
in 200h 28'48"
2 Henri Pélissier (Fra)
at 1'50"
3 Jean Alavoine (Fra)
at 36'53"

Best Climber
Firmin Lambot (Bel)

1919

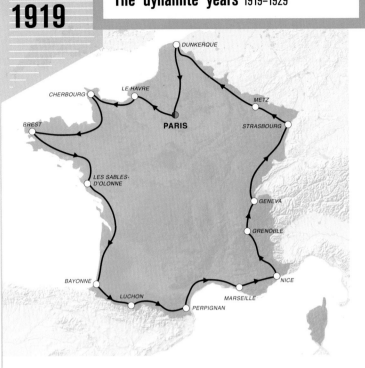

1920

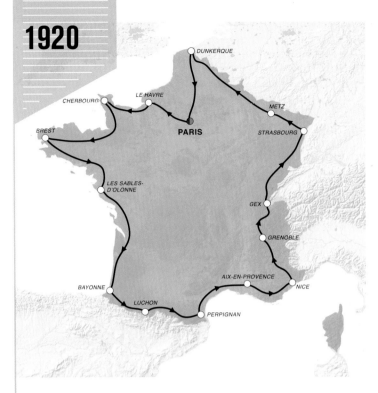

The 13th Tour de France, and the first after World War I, followed a similar course to the 1914 event. Broken forks once again cost Eugène Christophe the race, but he did have the distinction of being the first to wear the yellow jersey, which was introduced after the tenth stage to identify the race leader. He was not happy with the colour as the other riders called him a canary. Firmin Lambot, at 33, was the oldest Tour winner up to that time.

Sunday 29 June–Sunday 27 July

1	388 km, Paris > Le Havre	
2	364 km, Le Havre > Cherbourg	
3	405 km, Cherbourg > Brest	
4	412 km, Brest > Les Sables-d'Olonne	
5	482 km, Les Sables-d'Olonne > Bayonne	
6	326 km, Bayonne > Luchon	
7	323 km, Luchon > Perpignan	
8	370 km, Perpignan > Marseille	
9	338 km, Marseille > Nice	
10	333 km, Nice > Grenoble	
11	325 km, Grenoble > Geneva	
12	371 km, Geneva > Strasbourg	
13	315 km, Strasbourg > Metz	
14	468 km, Metz > Dunkerque	
15	340 km, Dunkerque > Paris	

1 Firmin Lambot (Bel)
in 231h 07'15"
2 Jean Alavoine (Fra)
at 1h 42'54"
3 Eugène Christophe (Fra)
at 2h 26'31"

Best Climber
Honoré Barthélémy (Fra)

The 14th Tour was a triumph for the Belgians, who occupied the first seven places in the general classification and won 15 stages. Philippe Thys became the first man to win three Tours, a feat that would not be repeated until 1955. This was generally considered an unexciting race, with the group finishing together in the first five stages and many of the French favourites dropping out early. Honoré Barthélémy was the top French rider, finishing eighth with a broken shoulder.

Sunday 27 June–Sunday 25 July

1	388 km, Paris > Le Havre	
2	364 km, Le Havre > Cherbourg	
3	405 km, Cherbourg > Brest	
4	412 km, Brest > Les Sables-d'Olonne	
5	482 km, Les Sables-d'Olonne > Bayonne	
6	326 km, Bayonne > Luchon	
7	323 km, Luchon > Perpignan	
8	325 km, Perpignan > Aix-en-Provence	
9	356 km, Aix-en-Provence > Nice	
10	333 km, Nice > Grenoble	
11	362 km, Grenoble > Gex	
12	354 km, Gex > Strasbourg	
13	300 km, Strasbourg > Metz	
14	433 km, Metz > Dunkerque	
15	340 km, Dunkerque > Paris	

1 Philippe Thys (Bel)
in 228h 36'13"
2 Hector Heusghem (Bel)
at 57'21"
3 Firmin Lambot (Bel)
at 1h 39'35"

Best Climber
Firmin Lambot (Bel)

1921

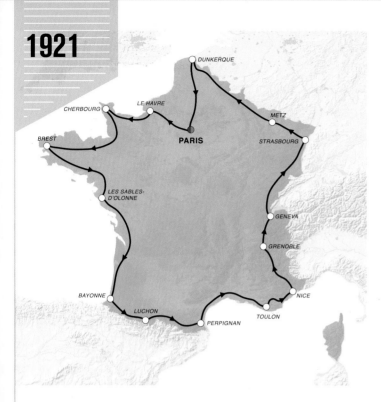

Belgians again dominated the Tour in 1921, while the French Pélissier brothers did not take part due to a disagreement with the organizers. Léon Scieur took the yellow jersey after the second stage and retained it to Paris. Several riders were penalized for not racing competitively on stage 12, and Scieur criticized Hector Heusghem for attacking when he had a puncture. Foreign press covered the Tour de France for the first time, following the race in their own cars.

Sunday 26 June–Sunday 24 July

1	388 km, Paris > Le Havre
2	364 km, Le Havre > Cherbourg
3	405 km, Cherbourg > Brest
4	412 km, Brest > Les Sables-d'Olonne
5	482 km, Les Sables-d'Olonne > Bayonne
6	326 km, Bayonne > Luchon
7	323 km, Luchon > Perpignan
8	411 km, Perpignan > Toulon
9	272 km, Toulon > Nice
10	333 km, Nice > Grenoble
11	325 km, Grenoble > Geneva
12	371 km, Geneva > Strasbourg
13	300 km, Strasbourg > Metz
14	433 km, Metz > Dunkerque
15	340 km, Dunkerque > Paris

1 1 Léon Scieur (Bel)
in 221h 50'26"
2 Hector Heusghem (Bel)
at 18'36"
3 Honoré Barthélémy (Fra)
at 2h 01'00"

Best Climber
Hector Heusghem (Bel)

1922

In 1922 Firmin Lambot won his second Tour de France, making it seven in a row for Belgium. At 36, Lambot is still the oldest Tour winner. Hector Heusghem would almost certainly have won if he hadn't been docked an hour for using a team-mate's bike (with permission from a race judge) when his own broke. The Col d'Izoard was used for the first time, and has since become a regular feature and the scene of many epic battles.

Sunday 25 June–Sunday 23 July

1	388 km, Paris > Le Havre
2	364 km, Le Havre > Cherbourg
3	405 km, Cherbourg > Brest
4	412 km, Brest > Les Sables-d'Olonne
5	482 km, Les Sables-d'Olonne > Bayonne
6	326 km, Bayonne > Luchon
7	323 km, Luchon > Perpignan
8	411 km, Perpignan > Toulon
9	284 km, Toulon > Nice
10	274 km, Nice > Briançon
11	260 km, Briançon > Geneva
12	371 km, Geneva > Strasbourg
13	300 km, Strasbourg > Metz
14	432 km, Metz > Dunkerque
15	340 km, Dunkerque > Paris

1 Firmin Lambot (Bel)
in 222h 08'06"
2 Jean Alavoine (Fra)
at 41'15"
3 Félix Sellier (Bel)
at 42'02"

Best Climber
Jean Alavoine (Fra)

1923

With the return of the Pélissier brothers in 1923, the French public finally saw another home win. Meanwhile Ottavio Bottecchia, whose only French was 'No bananas, lots of coffee, thank you', became the first Italian to wear the yellow jersey. Innovations in the 17th Tour included time bonuses of 2 minutes for stage winners and permission to mend bicycles with spare parts. Riders still had to carry everything they needed for the stage and had to finish with everything they started with.

Sunday 24 June–Sunday 22 July

1   381 km, Paris > Le Havre
2   371 km, Le Havre > Cherbourg
3   405 km, Cherbourg > Brest
4   412 km, Brest > Les Sables-d'Olonne
5   482 km, Les Sables-d'Olonne > Bayonne
6   326 km, Bayonne > Luchon
7   323 km, Luchon > Perpignan
8   427 km, Perpignan > Toulon
9   281 km, Toulon > Nice
10 275 km, Nice > Briançon
11 260 km, Briançon > Geneva
12 377 km, Geneva > Strasbourg
13 300 km, Strasbourg > Metz
14 433 km, Metz > Dunkerque
15 343 km, Dunkerque > Paris

1 Henri Pélissier (Fra)
in 222h 15'30"
2 Ottavio Bottecchia (Ita)
at 30'41"
3 Romain Bellenger (Fra)
at 1h 04'43"

Best Climber
Henri Pélissier (Fra)

1924

Ottavio Bottecchia became the first Italian to win the Tour de France, as well as the first man to wear the yellow jersey from start to finish. He won the first stage, the last stage and both the Pyrenees stages. Reigning champion Henri Pélissier withdrew in protest at officials counting his jerseys as they suspected he was discarding them as he warmed up, breaking the rule that riders had to finish with all they started with. Pélissier later gave an interview listing the drugs taken to survive the long stages.

Sunday 22 June–Sunday 20 July

1   381 km, Paris > Le Havre
2   371 km, Le Havre > Cherbourg
3   405 km, Cherbourg > Brest
4   412 km, Brest > Les Sables-d'Olonne
5   482 km, Les Sables-d'Olonne > Bayonne
6   326 km, Bayonne > Luchon
7   323 km, Luchon > Perpignan
8   427 km, Perpignan > Toulon
9   280 km, Toulon > Nice
10 275 km, Nice > Briançon
11 307 km, Briançon > Gex
12 360 km, Gex > Strasbourg
13 300 km, Strasbourg > Metz
14 433 km, Metz > Dunkerque
15 343 km, Dunkerque > Paris

1 Ottavio Bottecchia (Ita)
in 226h 18'21"
2 Nicolas Frantz (Lux)
at 35'36"
3 Lucien Buysse (Bel)
at 1h 32'13"

Best Climber
Ottavio Bottecchia (Ita)

1925

Following Henri Pélissier's complaints about the difficulty of riding very long stages, the organizers acted by increasing the number of stages in 1925, covering roughly the same distance in 18, rather than 15, stages. Ottavio Bottecchia retained his title, greatly assisted by his team-mate Lucien Buysse who nevertheless managed to finish second. There were six Belgians, three Italians and a Luxembourger in the top ten, but no Frenchmen. Pélissier abandoned his final Tour with a knee problem.

Sunday 21 June–Sunday 19 July

1 340 km, Paris > Le Havre
2 371 km, Le Havre > Cherbourg
3 405 km, Cherbourg > Brest
4 208 km, Brest > Vannes
5 204 km, Vannes > Les Sables-d'Olonne
6 293 km, Les Sables-d'Olonne > Bordeaux
7 189 km, Bordeaux > Bayonne
8 326 km, Bayonne > Luchon
9 323 km, Luchon > Perpignan
10 215 km, Perpignan > Nîmes
11 215 km, Nîmes > Toulon
12 280 km, Toulon > Nice
13 275 km, Nice > Briançon
14 303 km, Briançon > Évian
15 373 km, Évian > Mulhouse
16 334 km, Mulhouse > Metz
17 433 km, Metz > Dunkerque
18 343 km, Dunkerque > Paris

1 Ottavio Bottecchia (Ita)
in 219h 10'18"
2 Lucien Buysse (Bel)
at 54'20"
3 Bartolomeo Aimo (Ita)
at 56'37"

Best Climber
Ottavio Bottecchia (Ita)

1926

The 20th Tour de France was the longest ever, at 5,745 km, and the slowest at 24.06 km/hour. It was the first time it started outside Paris. After his efforts for his team-mate in 1925, Lucien Buysse won the race with an imposing performance on stage 10 in the freezing rain of the Pyrenees in what many consider the toughest ever Tour stage. Rescue parties had to be sent out to find riders, many of whom did not finish until midnight.

Sunday 20 June–Sunday 18 July

1 373 km, Évian > Mulhouse
2 334 km, Mulhouse > Metz
3 433 km, Metz > Dunkerque
4 361 km, Dunkerque > Le Havre
5 357 km, Le Havre > Cherbourg
6 405 km, Cherbourg > Brest
7 412 km, Brest > Les Sables-d'Olonne
8 285 km, Les Sables-d'Olonne > Bordeaux
9 189 km, Bordeaux > Bayonne
10 326 km, Bayonne > Luchon
11 323 km, Luchon > Perpignan
12 427 km, Perpignan > Toulon
13 280 km, Toulon > Nice
14 275 km, Nice > Briançon
15 303 km, Briançon > Évian
16 321 km, Évian > Dijon
17 341 km, Dijon > Paris

1 Lucien Buysse (Bel)
in 238h 44'25"
2 Nicolas Frantz (Lux)
at 1h 22'25"
3 Bartolomeo Aimo (Ita)
at 1h 22'51"

Best Climber
Lucien Buysse (Bel)

1927

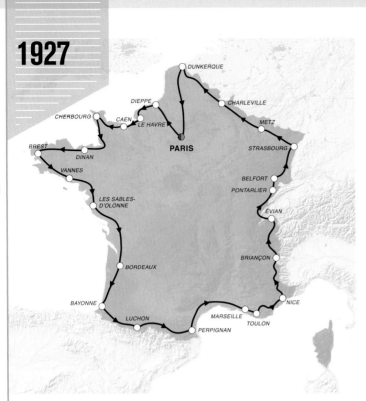

Tour director Henri Desgrange did not like the fact that 10 of the 17 stages in 1926 had finished in bunch sprints, so a different format was used in 1927. The number of stages was increased to 24, and 16 of the flat stages were run as team time trials, with teams setting off at 15-minute intervals. In the absence of Lucien Buysse, Nicolas Frantz was in a class of his own, winning by almost 2 hours.

Sunday 19 June–Sunday 17 July

1	180 km, Paris > Dieppe (TTT)
2	103 km, Dieppe > Le Havre (TTT)
3	225 km, Le Havre > Caen (TTT)
4	140 km, Caen > Cherbourg (TTT)
5	199 km, Cherbourg > Dinan (TTT)
6	206 km, Dinan > Brest (TTT)
7	207 km, Brest > Vannes (TTT)
8	204 km, Vannes > Les Sables-d'Olonne (TTT)
9	285 km, Les Sables-d'Olonne > Bordeaux (TTT)
10	189 km, Bordeaux > Bayonne
11	326 km, Bayonne > Luchon
12	323 km, Luchon > Perpignan
13	360 km, Perpignan > Marseille
14	120 km, Marseille > Toulon (TTT)
15	280 km, Toulon > Nice
16	275 km, Nice > Briançon
17	283 km, Briançon > Évian
18	213 km, Évian > Pontarlier (TTT)
19	119 km, Pontarlier > Belfort (TTT)
20	145 km, Belfort > Strasbourg (TTT)
21	165 km, Strasbourg > Metz (TTT)
22	159 km, Metz > Charleville (TTT)
23	270 km, Charleville > Dunkerque (TTT)
24	344 km, Dunkerque > Paris

1 Nicolas Frantz (Lux)
in 198h 16'42"

2 Maurice Dewaele (Bel)
at 1h 48'21"

3 Julien Vervaecke (Bel)
at 2h 25'06"

Best Climber
Michele Gordini (Ita)

1928

Despite its unpopularity with the public, the team time trial format was used for a second year in 1928. This favoured riders on strong teams, such as the Alcyon-Dunlop team which took all three places on the final podium. Nicolas Frantz retained his title, despite losing 28 minutes on stage 19 when a mechanical problem forced him to ride 100 km on a bike borrowed from a female spectator. The 162 riders starting the race was a record number.

Sunday 17 June–Sunday 15 July

1	207 km, Paris > Caen (TTT)
2	140 km, Caen > Cherbourg (TTT)
3	199 km, Cherbourg > Dinan (TTT)
4	206 km, Dinan > Brest (TTT)
5	208 km, Brest > Vannes (TTT)
6	204 km, Vannes > Les Sables-d'Olonne (TTT)
7	285 km, Les Sables-d'Olonne > Bordeaux (TTT)
8	225 km, Bordeaux > Hendaye (TTT)
9	387 km, Hendaye > Luchon
10	323 km, Luchon > Perpignan
11	363 km, Perpignan > Marseille
12	330 km, Marseille > Nice
13	333 km, Nice > Grenoble
14	329 km, Grenoble > Évian
15	213 km, Évian > Pontarlier (TTT)
16	119 km, Pontarlier > Belfort (TTT)
17	145 km, Belfort > Strasbourg (TTT)
18	165 km, Strasbourg > Metz (TTT)
19	159 km, Metz > Charleville (TTT)
20	271 km, Charleville > Malo-les-Bains (TTT)
21	234 km, Malo-les-Bains > Dieppe (TTT)
22	331 km, Dieppe > Paris

1 Nicolas Frantz (Lux)
in 192h 48'58"

2 André Leducq (Fra)
at 50'07"

3 Maurice Dewaele (Bel)
at 56'16"

Best Climber
Victor Fontan (Fra)

1929

This year the team time trial format was retained only for three stages that were expected to be the slowest. Frenchman Victor Fontan crashed out on stage 10 while wearing the yellow jersey. Maurice Dewaele was helped to victory by his Alcyon team despite illness, leading Henri Desgrange to complain that his race had been won by a corpse. Josef (Jef) Demuysère was relegated from second to third after receiving a 25-minute penalty for taking a drink illegally.

Sunday 30 June–Sunday 28 July

1	206 km, Paris > Caen
2	140 km, Caen > Cherbourg
3	199 km, Cherbourg > Dinan
4	206 km, Dinan > Brest
5	208 km, Brest > Vannes
6	204 km, Vannes > Les Sables-d'Olonne
7	285 km, Les Sables-d'Olonne > Bordeaux
8	182 km, Bordeaux > Bayonne
9	363 km, Bayonne > Luchon
10	323 km, Luchon > Perpignan
11	366 km, Perpignan > Marseille
12	191 km, Marseille > Cannes (TTT)
13	133 km, Cannes > Nice
14	333 km, Nice > Grenoble
15	329 km, Grenoble > Évian
16	283 km, Évian > Belfort
17	145 km, Belfort > Strasbourg
18	165 km, Strasbourg > Metz
19	159 km, Metz > Charleville (TTT)
20	270 km, Charleville > Malo-les-Bains (TTT)
21	234 km, Malo-les-Bains > Dieppe
22	332 km, Dieppe > Paris

1 Maurice Dewaele (Bel)
in 186h 39'16"
2 Giuseppe Pancera (Ita)
at 44'23"
3 Jef Demuysère (Bel)
at 57'10"

Best Climber
Victor Fontan (Fra)

1930

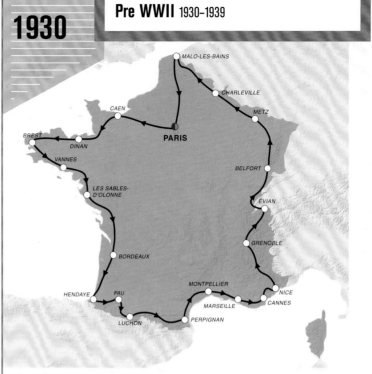

Rather than trade teams, in 1930 the riders rode for national teams. The French won the new team classification as well as having the overall winner and five other men in the top ten. In addition Charles Pélissier won eight stages. The organization paid for competitors' food and accommodation and gave them all yellow bikes to ride. This was funded by a publicity caravan, with the Menier chocolate company vehicle preceding the race and handing out chocolate to the crowds.

Wednesday 2 July–Sunday 27 July

1	206 km, Paris > Caen
2	203 km, Caen > Dinan
3	206 km, Dinan > Brest
4	210 km, Brest > Vannes
5	202 km, Vannes > Les Sables-d'Olonne
6	285 km, Les Sables-d'Olonne > Bordeaux
7	222 km, Bordeaux > Hendaye
8	146 km, Hendaye > Pau
9	231 km, Pau > Luchon
10	322 km, Luchon > Perpignan
11	164 km, Perpignan > Montpellier
12	209 km, Montpellier > Marseille
13	181 km, Marseille > Cannes
14	132 km, Cannes > Nice
15	333 km, Nice > Grenoble
16	331 km, Grenoble > Évian
17	282 km, Évian > Belfort
18	223 km, Belfort > Metz
19	159 km, Metz > Charleville
20	271 km, Charleville > Malo-les-Bains
21	300 km, Malo-les-Bains > Paris

1 André Leducq (Fra)
in 172h 12'16"
2 Learco Guerra (Ita)
at 14'13"
3 Antonin Magne (Fra)
at 16'03"

Best Climber
Benoît Fauré (Fra)

1931

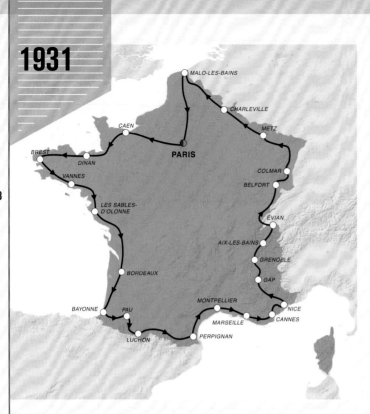

1932

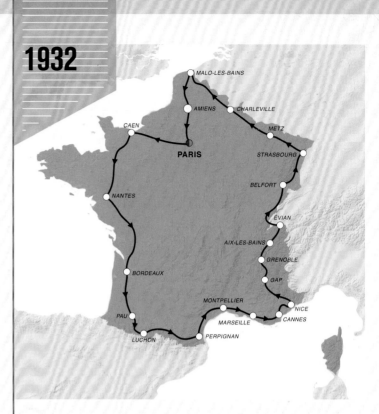

The 25th Tour de France consisted of 24 stages, with only three rest days, and covered 5,091 km at an average speed of 28.74 km/hour. Although the winner was again French, Belgium took the team prize. After an absence of a few years, time bonuses for stage winners were reintroduced. Austrian Max Bulla became the only *touriste-routier* (non-professional cyclist) ever to wear the yellow jersey after winning stage 2 despite starting 10 minutes after the elite riders.

Despite a strong effort by the Italians, who took the team classification, France managed another overall victory in 1932. André Leducq took the yellow jersey after stage 3 and kept it all the way to Paris, winning six stages, including stage 13 over a snowy Col du Galibier. This year there were time bonuses of 4, 2 and 1 minutes for the first three finishers of each stage, aimed at giving sprinters more of a chance in the general classification.

Tuesday 30 June–Sunday 26 July

1	208 km, Paris > Caen
2	212 km, Caen > Dinan
3	206 km, Dinan > Brest
4	211 km, Brest > Vannes
5	202 km, Vannes > Les Sables-d'Olonne
6	338 km, Les Sables-d'Olonne > Bordeaux
7	180 km, Bordeaux > Bayonne
8	106 km, Bayonne > Pau
9	231 km, Pau > Luchon
10	322 km, Luchon > Perpignan
11	164 km, Perpignan > Montpellier
12	207 km, Montpellier > Marseille
13	181 km, Marseille > Cannes
14	132 km, Cannes > Nice
15	233 km, Nice > Gap
16	102 km, Gap > Grenoble
17	230 km, Grenoble > Aix-les-Bains
18	204 km, Aix-les-Bains > Évian
19	282 km, Évian > Belfort
20	209 km, Belfort > Colmar
21	192 km, Colmar > Metz
22	159 km, Metz > Charleville
23	271 km, Charleville > Malo-les-Bains
24	313 km, Malo-les-Bains > Paris

1 **Antonin Magne** (Fra)
in 177h 10'03"
2 **Jef Demuysère** (Bel)
at 12'56"
3 **Antonio Pesenti** (Ita)
at 22'51"

Best Climber
Jef Demuysère (Bel)

Wednesday 6 July–Sunday 31 July

1	208 km, Paris > Caen
2	300 km, Caen > Nantes
3	387 km, Nantes > Bordeaux
4	206 km, Bordeaux > Pau
5	229 km, Pau > Luchon
6	322 km, Luchon > Perpignan
7	168 km, Perpignan > Montpellier
8	206 km, Montpellier > Marseille
9	191 km, Marseille > Cannes
10	132 km, Cannes > Nice
11	233 km, Nice > Gap
12	102 km, Gap > Grenoble
13	230 km, Grenoble > Aix-les-Bains
14	204 km, Aix-les-Bains > Évian
15	291 km, Évian > Belfort
16	145 km, Belfort > Strasbourg
17	165 km, Strasbourg > Metz
18	159 km, Metz > Charleville
19	271 km, Charleville > Malo-les-Bains
20	212 km, Malo-les-Bains > Amiens
21	159 km, Amiens > Paris

1 **André Leducq** (Fra)
in 154h 11'49"
2 **Kurt Stöpel** (Ger)
at 24'03"
3 **Francesco Camusso** (Ita)
at 26'21"

Best Climber
Vicente Trueba (Spa)

1933

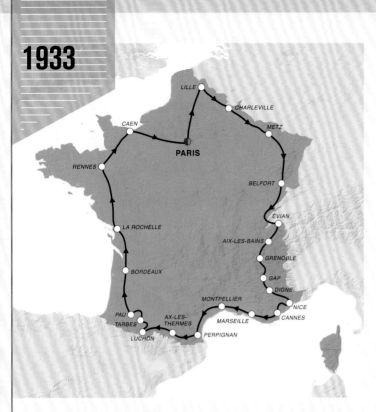

This was the first Tour since 1912 to follow a clockwise route around France. It also saw the introduction of an official mountains classification, calculated by points, which was won by Spaniard Vicente Trueba, who reached 9 of the 16 peaks first. Georges Speicher, in his second year as a professional, gave the French their fourth consecutive win. France also won the team classification. Without the time bonus of 2 minutes for a stage win, Giuseppe Martano would have won the race.

Tuesday 27 June–Sunday 23 July

1 262 km, Paris > Lillle
2 192 km, Lille > Charleville
3 166 km, Charleville > Metz
4 220 km, Metz > Belfort
5 293 km, Belfort > Évian
6 207 km, Évian > Aix-les-Bains
7 229 km, Aix-les-Bains > Grenoble
8 102 km, Grenoble > Gap
9 227 km, Gap > Digne
10 156 km, Digne > Nice
11 128 km, Nice > Cannes
12 208 km, Cannes > Marseille
13 168 km, Marseille > Montpellier
14 166 km, Montpellier > Perpignan
15 158 km, Perpignan > Ax-les-Thermes
16 165 km, Ax-les-Thermes > Luchon
17 91 km, Luchon > Tarbes
18 185 km, Tarbes > Pau
19 233 km, Pau > Bordeaux
20 183 km, Bordeaux > La Rochelle
21 266 km, La Rochelle > Rennes
22 169 km, Rennes > Caen
23 222 km, Caen > Paris

1 Georges Speicher (Fra)
in 147h 51'37"
2 Learco Guerra (Ita)
at 4'01"
3 Giuseppe Martano (Ita)
at 5'08"

King of the Mountains
Vicente Trueba (Spa)

1934

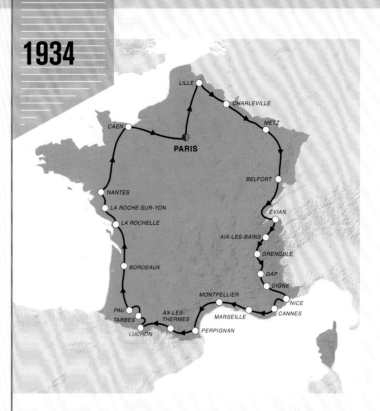

An innovation in the 28th Tour de France was the inclusion of the first individual time trial, with the 21st stage split into a morning road stage and an afternoon test against the clock. The French were dominant, wining 19 stages and holding the yellow jersey all the way through. René Vietto sacrificed his chances for his team-mate Antonin Magne by twice giving him a wheel in the Pyrenees. The 4,363-km course was ridden at an average speed of 30.36 km/hour.

Tuesday 3 July–Sunday 29 July

1 262 km, Paris > Lille
2 192 km, Lille > Charleville
3 161 km, Charleville > Metz
4 220 km, Metz > Belfort
5 293 km, Belfort > Évian
6 207 km, Évian > Aix-les-Bains
7 229 km, Aix-les-Bains > Grenoble
8 102 km, Grenoble > Gap
9 227 km, Gap > Digne
10 156 km, Digne > Nice
11 126 km, Nice > Cannes
12 195 km, Cannes > Marseille
13 172 km, Marseille > Montpellier
14 177 km, Montpellier > Perpignan
15 158 km, Perpignan > Ax-les-Thermes
16 165 km, Ax-les-Thermes > Luchon
17 91 km, Luchon > Tarbes
18 172 km, Tarbes > Pau
19 215 km, Pau > Bordeaux
20 183 km, Bordeaux > La Rochelle
21a 81 km, La Rochelle > La Roche-sur-Yon
21b 90 km, La Roche-sur-Yon > Nantes (ITT)
22 275 km, Nantes > Caen
23 221 km, Caen > Paris

1 Antonin Magne (Fra)
in 147h 13'58"
2 Giuseppe Martano (Ita)
at 27'31"
3 Roger Lapébie (Fra)
at 52'15"

King of the Mountains
René Vietto (Fra)

1935

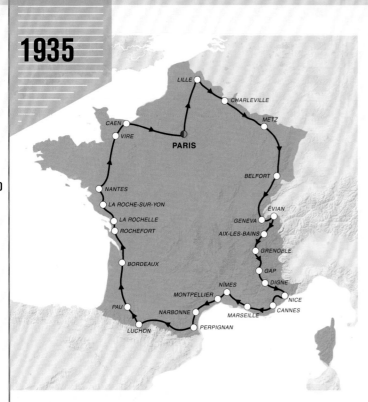

Outsider Romain Maes took the first stage after passing a level crossing ahead of the peloton just before it closed; he led for the rest of the race. Favourite Antonin Magne withdrew after being hit by a car on stage 7. On the same stage Spaniard Francisco Cepeda became the Tour's first racing fatality after he fell on the descent of the Galibier. The split-stage format with individual time trials was used six times this year.

Thursday 4 July–Sunday 28 July

1	262 km, Paris > Lille	
2	192 km, Lille > Charleville	
3	161 km, Charleville > Metz	
4	220 km, Metz > Belfort	
5a	262 km, Belfort > Geneva (Swi)	
5b	58 km, Geneva > Évian (ITT)	
6	207 km, Évian > Aix-les-Bains	
7	229 km, Aix-les-Bains > Grenoble	
8	102 km, Grenoble > Gap	
9	227 km, Gap > Digne	
10	156 km, Digne > Nice	
11	126 km, Nice > Cannes	
12	195 km, Cannes > Marseille	
13a	112 km, Marseille > Nîmes	
13b	56 km, Nîmes > Montpellier (ITT)	
14a	103 km, Montpellier > Narbonne	
14b	63 km, Narbonne > Perpignan (ITT)	
15	325 km, Perpignan > Luchon	
16	194 km, Luchon > Pau	
17	224 km, Pau > Bordeaux	
18a	159 km, Bordeaux > Rochefort	
18b	33 km, Rochefort > La Rochelle (ITT)	
19a	81 km, La Rochelle > La Roche-sur-Yon	
19b	95 km, La Roche-sur-Yon > Nantes (ITT)	
20a	220 km, Nantes > Vire	
20b	55 km, Vire > Caen (ITT)	
21	221 km, Caen > Paris	

1 **Romain Maes** (Bel)
in 141h 32'00"

2 Ambrogio Morelli (Ita)
at 17'52"

3 Félicien Vervaecke (Bel)
at 24'06"

King of the Mountains
Félicien Vervaecke (Bel)

1936

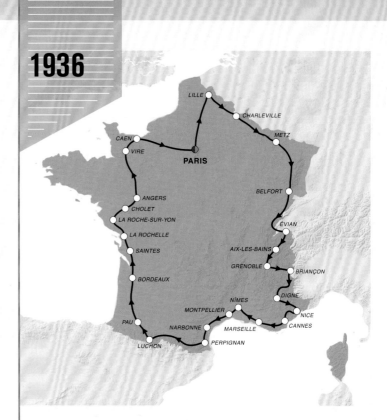

The 30th Tour was Henri Desgrange's last as Director. He was ill and was replaced by Jacques Goddet after stage 2. The Tour was won by Sylvère Maes. Although sharing a surname, he was not related to fellow Belgian Romain Maes, who dropped out with bronchitis during stage 7. That Alpine stage was won by Theo Middelkamp, the first Dutch stage winner, who had never seen a mountain before. No Italian competitors were present this year, following Mussolini's invasion of Ethiopia.

Tuesday 7 July–Sunday 2 August

1	258 km, Paris > Lille	
2	192 km, Lille > Charleville	
3	161 km, Charleville > Metz	
4	220 km, Metz > Belfort	
5	298 km, Belfort > Évian	
6	212 km, Évian > Aix-les-Bains	
7	230 km, Aix-les-Bains > Grenoble	
8	194 km, Grenoble > Briançon	
9	220 km, Briançon > Digne	
10	156 km, Digne > Nice	
11	126 km, Nice > Cannes	
12	195 km, Cannes > Marseille	
13a	112 km, Marseille > Nîmes	
13b	52 km, Nîmes > Montpellier (ITT)	
14a	103 km, Montpellier > Narbonne	
14b	63 km, Narbonne > Perpignan (ITT)	
15	325 km, Perpignan > Luchon	
16	194 km, Luchon > Pau	
17	229 km, Pau > Bordeaux	
18a	117 km, Bordeaux > Saintes	
18b	75 km, Saintes > La Rochelle (ITT)	
19a	81 km, La Rochelle > La Roche-sur-Yon	
19b	65 km, La Roche-sur-Yon > Cholet (ITT)	
19c	67 km, Cholet > Angers	
20a	204 km, Angers > Vire	
20b	55 km, Vire > Caen (ITT)	
21	234 km, Caen > Paris	

1 **Sylvère Maes** (Bel)
in 142h 47'32"

2 Antonin Magne (Fra)
at 26'55"

3 Félicien Vervaecke (Bel)
at 27'53"

King of the Mountains
Julián Berrendero (Spa)

1937

A multitude of split stages resulted in 31 'stages' in 1937, including both team time trials and an individual time trial. This was the first Tour in which bicycles with gears were allowed. It also saw the first two British competitors – Charles Holland and Bill Burl – and the first participation by Italian Gino Bartali, winner of the 1936 and 1937 Giro d'Italia. The Belgian team withdrew during the race because of what they saw as French chauvinism and bias.

Wednesday 30 June–Sunday 25 July

1	263 km, Paris > Lille
2	192 km, Lille > Charleville
3	161 km, Charleville > Metz
4	220 km, Metz > Belfort
5a	175 km, Belfort > Lons-le-Saunier
5b	34 km, Lons-le-Saunier > Champagnole (TTT)
5c	93 km, Champagnole > Geneva (Swi)
6	180 km, Geneva > Aix-les-Bains
7	228 km, Aix-les-Bains > Grenoble
8	194 km, Grenoble > Briançon
9	220 km, Briançon > Digne
10	251 km, Digne > Nice
11a	169 km, Nice > Toulon
11b	65 km, Toulon > Marseille (TTT)
12a	112 km, Marseille > Nîmes
12b	51 km, Nîmes > Montpellier
13a	103 km, Montpellier > Narbonne
13b	63 km, Narbonne > Perpignan
14a	99 km, Perpignan > Bourg-Madame
14b	59 km, Bourg-Madame > Ax-les-Thermes
14c	167 km, Ax-les-Thermes > Luchon
15	194 km, Luchon > Pau
16	235 km, Pau > Bordeaux
17a	123 km, Bordeaux > Royan
17b	37 km, Royan > Saintes
17c	67 km, Saintes > La Rochelle
18a	81 km, La Rochelle > La Roche-sur-Yon
18b	172 km, La Roche-sur-Yon > Rennes
19a	114 km, Rennes > Vire
19b	59 km, Vire > Caen (ITT)
20	234 km, Caen > Paris

1 Roger Lapébie (Fra) in 138h 58'31"
2 Mario Vicini (Ita) at 7'17"
3 Leo Amberg (Swi) at 26'13"

King of the Mountains
Félicien Vervaecke (Bel)

1938

After falling in a river and being forced to withdraw while wearing the yellow jersey in 1937, Gino Bartali returned to win the Tour de France in 1938, having skipped the Giro d'Italia. He won an epic stage 14 in the Alps, leading over every climb. Time bonuses were reduced to 1 minute for stage winners and 1 minute for the first rider over a classified climb. This was the final appearance of double Tour winners André Leducq and Antonin Magne.

Tuesday 5 July–Sunday 31 July

1	215 km, Paris > Caen
2	237 km, Caen > Saint-Brieuc
3	238 km, Saint-Brieuc > Nantes
4a	62 km, Nantes > La Roche-sur-Yon
4b	83 km, La Roche-sur-Yon > La Rochelle
4c	83 km, La Rochelle > Royan
5	198 km, Royan > Bordeaux
6a	53 km, Bordeaux > Arcachon
6b	171 km, Arcachon > Bayonne
7	115 km, Bayonne > Pau
8	193 km, Pau > Luchon
9	260 km, Luchon > Perpignan
10a	63 km, Perpignan > Narbonne
10b	27 km, Narbonne > Béziers (ITT)
10c	73 km, Béziers > Montpellier
11	223 km, Montpellier > Marseille
12	199 km, Marseille > Cannes
13	284 km, Cannes > Digne
14	219 km, Digne > Briançon
15	311 km, Briançon > Aix-les-Bains
16	284 km, Aix-les-Bains > Besançon
17a	89 km, Besançon > Belfort
17b	143 km, Belfort > Strasbourg
18	186 km, Strasbourg > Metz
19	196 km, Metz > Reims
20a	48 km, Reims > Laon
20b	42 km, Laon > Saint-Quentin (ITT)
20c	107 km, Saint-Quentin > Lille
21	279 km, Lille > Paris

1 Gino Bartali (Ita) in 148h 29'12"
2 Félicien Vervaecke (Bel) at 18'27"
3 Victor Cosson (Fra) at 29'26"

King of the Mountains
Gino Bartali (Ita)

1939

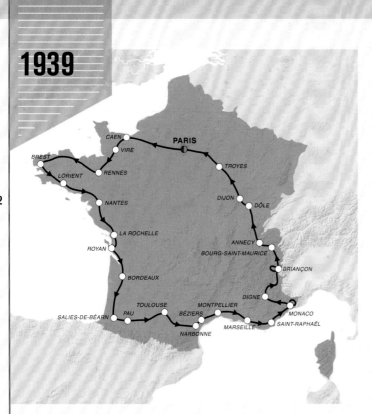

Like the 1938 edition, the 1939 Tour de France followed an anticlockwise route. It included the first mountain time trial, up the 2,770-m high Col de l'Iseran, won by overall winner Sylvère Maes. This last Tour before a seven-year break for World War II did not include riders from Germany, Italy or Spain. In the absence of several French champions, the way was clear for Belgian domination. However, this was to be the last Belgian victory for 30 years.

Monday 10 July–Sunday 30 July

1	215 km, Paris > Caen
2a	64 km, Caen > Vire (ITT)
2b	119 km, Vire > Rennes
3	244 km, Rennes > Brest
4	174 km, Brest > Lorient
5	207 km, Lorient > Nantes
6a	144 km, Nantes > La Rochelle
6b	107 km, La Rochelle > Royan
7	198 km, Royan > Bordeaux
8a	210 km, Bordeaux > Salies-de-Béarn
8b	69 km, Salies-de-Béarn > Pau (ITT)
9	311 km, Pau > Toulouse
10a	149 km, Toulouse > Narbonne
10b	27 km, Narbonne > Béziers (ITT)
10c	70 km, Béziers > Montpellier
11	212 km, Montpellier > Marseille
12a	157 km, Marseille > Saint-Raphaël
12b	122 km, Saint-Raphaël > Monaco (Mon)
13	101 km, Monaco > Monaco
14	175 km, Monaco > Digne
15	219 km, Digne > Briançon
16a	126 km, Briançon > Briançon
16b	64 km, Bonneval-sur-Arc > Bourg-Saint-Maurice (ITT)
16c	104 km, Bourg-Saint-Maurice > Annecy
17a	226 km, Annecy > Dôle
17b	59 km, Dôle > Dijon (ITT)
18a	151 km, Dijon > Troyes
18b	201 km, Troyes > Paris

1 Sylvère Maes (Bel)
in 132h 03'17"
2 René Vietto (Fra)
at 30'38"
3 Lucien Vlaemynck (Bel)
at 32'08"

King of the Mountains
Sylvère Maes (Bel)

1947

The Louison Bobet, Maître Jacques and Eddy Merckx years 1947–1975

The first Tour de France after World War II started at the Palais Royale in Paris, with one hundred riders in national and regional teams. It included no split stages. There was no German team and the Italian team comprised Franco–Italians living in France. Jean Robic is one of only two men to have won the Tour de France without wearing the yellow jersey, as he took the lead for the first time in the final stage. Italy took the team prize.

Wednesday 25 June–Sunday 20 July

1	236 km, Paris > Lille
2	182 km, Lille > Brussels (Bel)
3	314 km, Brussels > Luxembourg (Lux)
4	223 km, Luxembourg > Strasbourg
5	248 km, Strasbourg > Besançon
6	249 km, Besançon > Lyon
7	172 km, Lyon > Grenoble
8	185 km, Grenoble > Briançon
9	217 km, Briançon > Digne
10	255 km, Digne > Nice
11	230 km, Nice > Marseille
12	165 km, Marseille > Montpellier
13	172 km, Montpellier > Carcassonne
14	253 km, Carcassonne > Luchon
15	195 km, Luchon > Pau
16	195 km, Pau > Bordeaux
17	272 km, Bordeaux > Les Sables-d'Olonne
18	236 km, Les Sables-d'Olonne > Vannes
19	139 km, Vannes > Saint-Brieuc (ITT)
20	235 km, Saint-Brieuc > Caen
21	257 km, Caen > Paris

1 Jean Robic (Fra)
in 148h 11'25"
2 Édouard Fachleitner (Fra)
at 3'58"
3 Pierre Brambilla (Ita)
at 10'07"

King of the Mountains
Pierre Brambilla (Ita)

1948

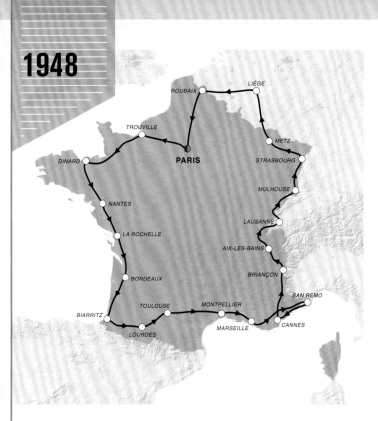

1948 saw the triumphant return of Gino Bartali ten years after his first Tour win and the emergence of a new French talent in Louison Bobet, who led for much of the race and finished fourth. The 35th Tour was truly international, visiting Italy, Belgium and Switzerland. In stages 3–18 the rider in last place in the general classification was eliminated. The arrival at the Paris velodrome in 1948 was the first live television broadcast from the Tour de France.

Wednesday 30 June–Sunday 25 July

1	237 km, Paris > Trouville
2	259 km, Trouville > Dinard
3	251 km, Dinard > Nantes
4	166 km, Nantes > La Rochelle
5	262 km, La Rochelle > Bordeaux
6	244 km, Bordeaux > Biarritz
7	219 km, Biarritz > Lourdes
8	261 km, Lourdes > Toulouse
9	246 km, Toulouse > Montpellier
10	248 km, Montpellier > Marseille
11	245 km, Marseille > San Remo (Ita)
12	170 km, San Remo > Cannes
13	274 km, Cannes > Briançon
14	263 km, Briançon > Aix-les-Bains
15	256 km, Aix-les-Bains > Lausanne (Swi)
16	243 km, Lausanne > Mulhouse
17	120 km, Mulhouse > Strasbourg (ITT)
18	195 km, Strasbourg > Metz
19	249 km, Metz > Liège (Bel)
20	228 km, Liège > Roubaix
21	286 km, Roubaix > Paris

1 Gino Bartali (Ita)
in 147h 10'36"
2 Briek Schotte (Bel)
at 26'16"
3 Guy Lapébie (Fra)
at 28'48"

King of the Mountains
Gino Bartali (Ita)

1949

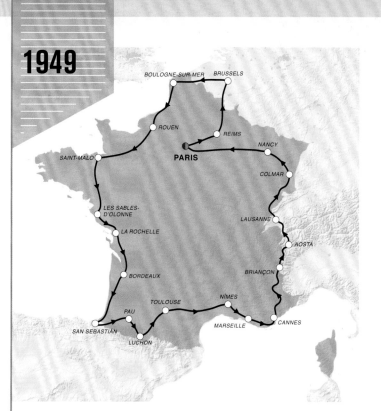

Two Italians – Fausto Coppi and Gino Bartali – dominated the 1949 event; Coppi became the first rider to win the Giro d'Italia and the Tour in the same year, a feat he would repeat in 1952. The two managed to work together despite strained relations within the team. In addition to Belgium, Switzerland and Italy, the route entered Spain for the first time. Stages finished and started in San Sebastián. The 4,808 km were covered at an average speed of 32.12 km/hour.

Thursday 30 June–Sunday 24 July

1	182 km, Paris > Reims
2	273 km, Reims > Brussels (Bel)
3	211 km, Brussels > Boulogne-sur-Mer
4	185 km, Boulogne-sur-Mer > Rouen
5	293 km, Rouen > Saint-Malo
6	305 km, Saint-Malo > Les Sables-d'Olonne
7	92 km, Les Sables-d'Olonne > La Rochelle (ITT)
8	262 km, La Rochelle > Bordeaux
9	228 km, Bordeaux > San Sebastián (Spa)
10	192 km, San Sebastián > Pau
11	193 km, Pau > Luchon
12	134 km, Luchon > Toulouse
13	289 km, Toulouse > Nîmes
14	199 km, Nîmes > Marseille
15	215 km, Marseille > Cannes
16	275 km, Cannes > Briançon
17	257 km, Briançon > Aosta (Ita)
18	265 km, Aosta > Lausanne (Swi)
19	283 km, Lausanne > Colmar
20	137 km, Colmar > Nancy (ITT)
21	340 km, Nancy > Paris

1 Fausto Coppi (Ita)
in 149h 40'49"
2 Gino Bartali (Ita)
at 10'55"
3 Jacques Marinelli (Fra)
at 25'13"

King of the Mountains
Fausto Coppi (Ita)

1950

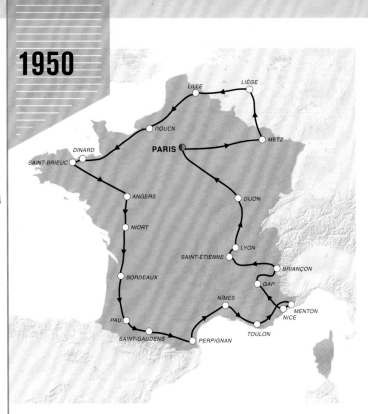

In the absence of an injured Fausto Coppi, Gino Bartali led the Italian team but withdrew – along with all his compatriots (including race leader Fiorenzo Magni) – when he was assaulted by French spectators who accused him of causing Louison Bobet to fall on the Col d'Aspin. Ferdy Kübler of Switzerland took over the lead and kept it until the end of the Tour. This year every stage was covered live on television and the winner received one million French francs.

Thursday 13 July–Monday 7 August

1	307 km, Paris > Metz
2	241 km, Metz > Liège (Bel)
3	233 km, Liège > Lille
4	231 km, Lille > Rouen
5	316 km, Rouen > Dinard
6	78 km, Dinard > Saint-Brieuc (ITT)
7	248 km, Saint-Brieuc > Angers
8	181 km, Angers > Niort
9	206 km, Niort > Bordeaux
10	202 km, Bordeaux > Pau
11	230 km, Pau > Saint-Gaudens
12	233 km, Saint-Gaudens > Perpignan
13	215 km, Perpignan > Nîmes
14	222 km, Nîmes > Toulon
15	206 km, Toulon > Menton
16	96 km, Menton > Nice
17	229 km, Nice > Gap
18	165 km, Gap > Briançon
19	291 km, Briançon > Saint-Étienne
20	98 km, Saint-Étienne > Lyon (ITT)
21	233 km, Lyon > Dijon
22	314 km, Dijon > Paris

1 Ferdy Kübler (Swi)
in 145h 36'56"
2 Stan Ockers (Bel)
at 9'30"
3 Louison Bobet (Fra)
at 22'19"

King of the Mountains
Louison Bobet (Fra)

1951

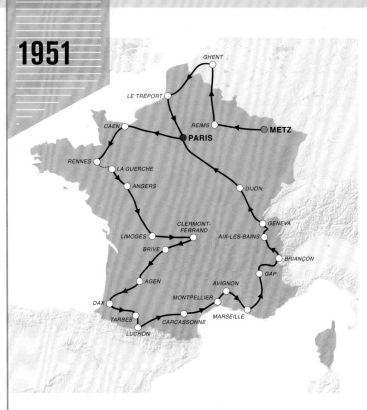

In 1951 the Tour started outside Paris for only the second time, left the perimeter of France to visit the Massif Central for the first time, and made its first ascent of Mont Ventoux, the 'giant of Provence'. Hugo Koblet brought Switzerland a second consecutive victory with five stage wins including two time trials and a solo breakaway of over 100 km. Wim van Est became the first Dutchman to hold the yellow jersey, but fell down a ravine while wearing it.

Wednesday 4 July–Sunday 29 July

1	185 km, Metz > Reims
2	228 km, Reims > Ghent (Bel)
3	219 km, Ghent > Le Tréport
4	188 km, Le Tréport > Paris
5	215 km, Paris > Caen
6	182 km, Caen > Rennes
7	85 km, La Guerche > Angers (ITT)
8	241 km, Angers > Limoges
9	236 km, Limoges > Clermont-Ferrand
10	216 km, Clermont-Ferrand > Brive
11	177 km, Brive > Agen
12	185 km, Agen > Dax
13	201 km, Dax > Tarbes
14	142 km, Tarbes > Luchon
15	213 km, Luchon > Carcassonne
16	192 km, Carcassonne > Montpellier
17	224 km, Montpellier > Avignon
18	173 km, Avignon > Marseille
19	208 km, Marseille > Gap
20	165 km, Gap > Briançon
21	201 km, Briançon > Aix-les-Bains
22	97 km, Aix-les-Bains > Geneva (Swi) (ITT)
23	197 km, Geneva > Dijon
24	322 km, Dijon > Paris

1 Hugo Koblet (Swi)
in 142h 20'14"
2 Raphaël Géminiani (Fra)
at 22'00"
3 Lucien Lazaridès (Fra)
at 24'16"

King of the Mountains
Raphaël Géminiani (Fra)

1952

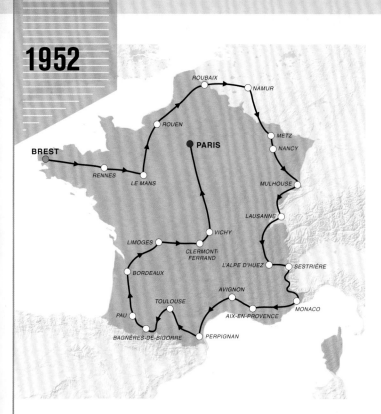

Two innovations in 1952 were mountain top finishes and an award to the most combative rider each day. Fausto Coppi was the first stage winner on the Alpe d'Huez and went on to win his second Tour de France. He was also first to the top of the other new climbs of Sestriere and Puy-de-Dôme. The time trials were shorter this year, as they were felt to have had too great an influence on the final result in previous years.

Wednesday 25 June–Saturday 19 July

1	246 km, Brest > Rennes	
2	181 km, Rennes > Le Mans	
3	189 km, Le Mans > Rouen	
4	232 km, Rouen > Roubaix	
5	197km, Roubaix > Namur (Bel)	
6	228 km, Namur > Metz	
7	60 km, Metz > Nancy (ITT)	
8	252 km, Nancy > Mulhouse	
9	238 km, Mulhouse > Lausanne	
10	266 km, Lausanne > Alpe d'Huez	
11	182 km, Bourg-d'Oisans > Sestriere (Ita)	
12	251 km, Sestriere > Monaco (Mon)	
13	214 km, Monaco > Aix-en-Provence	
14	178 km, Aix-en-Provence > Avignon	
15	275 km, Avignon > Perpignan	
16	200 km, Perpignan > Toulouse	
17	204 km, Toulouse > Bagnères-de-Bigorre	
18	149 km, Bagnères-de-Bigorre > Pau	
19	195 km, Pau > Bordeaux	
20	228 km, Bordeaux > Limoges	
21	245 km, Limoges > Clermont-Ferrand/ Puy-de-Dôme	
22	63 km, Clermont-Ferrand > Vichy (ITT)	
23	354 km, Vichy > Paris	

1 Fausto Coppi (Ita)
in 151h 57'20"
2 Stan Ockers (Bel)
at 28'17"
3 Bernardo Ruiz (Spa)
at 34'38"

King of the Mountains
Fausto Coppi (Ita)

1953

To commemorate the 50th anniversary of the first Tour de France the organizers introduced the points competition, with a green jersey for its leader. Louison Bobet finally won the Tour on his sixth attempt, with a commanding performance on the Col d'Izoard. Fausto Coppi did not ride, for reasons that are not clear, but this was the first Tour for future stars Charly Gaul and André Darrigade. Wout Wagtmans of the Netherlands won the first-ever overall combativity award.

Friday 3 July–Sunday 26 July

1	195 km, Strasbourg > Metz	
2	227 km, Metz > Liège (Bel)	
3	221 km, Liège > Lille	
4	188 km, Lille > Dieppe	
5	200 km, Dieppe > Caen	
6	206 km, Caen > Le Mans	
7	181 km, Le Mans > Nantes	
8	345 km, Nantes > Bordeaux	
9	197 km, Bordeaux > Pau	
10	103 km, Pau > Cauterets	
11	115 km, Cauterets > Luchon	
12	228 km, Luchon > Albi	
13	189 km, Albi > Béziers	
14	214 km, Béziers > Nîmes	
15	173 km, Nîmes > Marseille	
16	236 km, Marseille > Monaco (Mon)	
17	261 km, Monaco > Gap	
18	165 km, Gap > Briançon	
19	227 km, Briançon > Lyon	
20	70 km, Lyon > Saint-Étienne (ITT)	
21	210 km, Saint-Étienne > Montluçon	
22	328 km, Montluçon > Paris	

1 Louison Bobet (Fra)
in 129h 23'25"
2 Jean Malléjac (Fra)
at 14'18"
3 Giancarlo Astrua (Ita)
at 15'02"

Fritz Schär (Swi)

King of the Mountains
Jesús Loroño (Spa)

1954

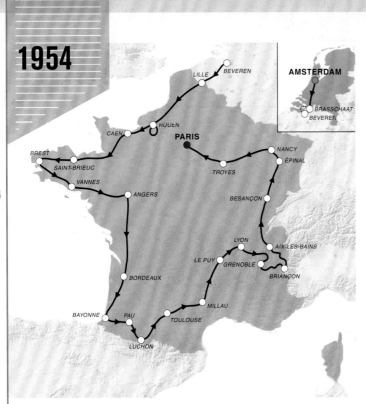

AMSTERDAM

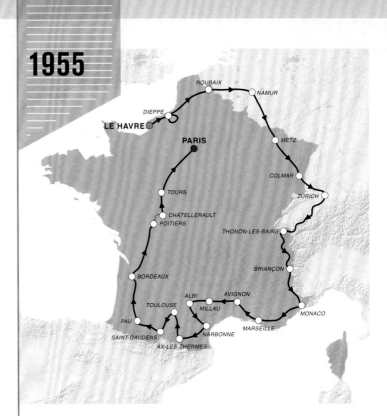

The 1954 Tour de France covered 4,669 km at an average speed of 34.74 km/hour. It saw the reintroduction of split stages and the inclusion of both individual and team time trials. For the first time the Tour started outside France, with a stage in Holland. The Italian federation did not send a team following a strike during the Giro d'Italia. The Swiss had a successful Tour, finishing second and third overall; France's Louison Bobet won his second consecutive Tour.

Thursday 8 July–Sunday 1 August

1	216 km, Amsterdam > Brasschaat (Ned)
2	225 km, Beveren (Ned) > Lille
3	219 km, Lille > Rouen
4a	10.4 km, Rouen/Circuit des Essarts (TTT)
4b	131 km, Rouen > Caen
5	224 km, Caen > Saint-Brieuc
6	179 km, Saint-Brieuc > Brest
7	211 km, Brest > Vannes
8	190 km, Vannes > Angers
9	343 km, Angers > Bordeaux
10	202 km, Bordeaux > Bayonne
11	241 km, Bayonne > Pau
12	161 km, Pau > Luchon
13	203 km, Luchon > Toulouse
14	225 km, Toulouse > Millau
15	197 km, Millau > Le Puy
16	194 km, Le Puy > Lyon
17	182 km, Lyon > Grenoble
18	216 km, Grenoble > Briançon
19	221 km, Briançon > Aix-les-Bains
20	243 km, Aix-les-Bains > Besançon
21a	134 km, Besançon > Épinal
21b	72 km, Épinal > Nancy (ITT)
22	216 km, Nancy > Troyes
23	180 km, Troyes > Paris

1 Louison Bobet (Fra)
in 140h 06'05"
2 Ferdy Kübler (Swi)
at 15'49"
3 Fritz Schär (Swi)
at 21'46"

Ferdy Kübler (Swi)

King of the Mountains
Federico Bahamontes (Spa)

1955

In the 42nd Tour de France Louison Bobet became the first man to win the race in three consecutive years. He managed it despite very painful saddle sores that later required surgery. This was the first time since World War II that any German riders competed, as well as the first time that a British team entered. Luxembourger Charly Gaul emerged as a major climbing talent, while Miguel Poblet became the first Spaniard to wear the yellow jersey.

Thursday 7 July–Saturday 30 July

1a	102 km, Le Havre > Dieppe
1b	12.5 km, Dieppe (TTT)
2	204 km, Dieppe > Roubaix
3	210 km, Roubaix > Namur (Bel)
4	225 km, Namur > Metz
5	229 km, Metz > Colmar
6	195 km, Colmar > Zurich (Swi)
7	267 km, Zurich > Thonon-les-Bains
8	253 km, Thonon-les-Bains > Briançon
9	275 km, Briançon > Monaco (Mon)
10	240 km, Monaco > Marseille
11	198 km, Marseille > Avignon
12	240 km, Avignon > Millau
13	205 km, Millau > Albi
14	156 km, Albi > Narbonne
15	151 km, Narbonne > Ax-les-Thermes
16	123 km, Ax-les-Thermes > Toulouse
17	249 km, Toulouse > Saint-Gaudens
18	206 km, Saint-Gaudens > Pau
19	195 km, Pau > Bordeaux
20	243 km, Bordeaux > Poitiers
21	68.6 km, Châtellerault > Tours (ITT)
22	229 km, Tours > Paris

1 Louison Bobet (Fra)
in 130h 29'26"
2 Jean Brankart (Bel)
at 4'53"
3 Charly Gaul (Lux)
at 11'30"

Stan Ockers (Bel)

King of the Mountains
Charly Gaul (Lux)

1956

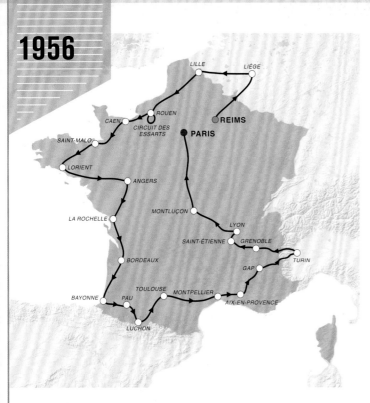

The line-up this year included no previous winners. An unknown French rider called Roger Walkowiak was part of a 31-man group that gained over 18 minutes on the peloton on stage 7. As he had also been in a breakaway group on stage 4, he took the yellow jersey and managed to stay with the specialist climbers in the mountains to win the race. Another Frenchman, Roger Hassenforder, won four stages, including a solo breakaway of 187 km on stage 21.

Thursday 5 July–Saturday 28 July

1	223 km, Reims > Liège (Bel)
2	217 km, Liège > Lille
3	225 km, Lille > Rouen
4a	15.1 km, Rouen/Circuit des Essarts (ITT)
4b	125 km, Rouen > Caen
5	189 km, Caen > Saint-Malo
6	192 km, Saint-Malo > Lorient
7	244 km, Lorient > Angers
8	180 km, Angers > La Rochelle
9	219 km, La Rochelle > Bordeaux
10	201 km, Bordeaux > Bayonne
11	255 km, Bayonne > Pau
12	130 km, Pau > Luchon
13	176 km, Luchon > Toulouse
14	231 km, Toulouse > Montpellier
15	204 km, Montpellier > Aix-en-Provence
16	203 km, Aix-en-Provence > Gap
17	234 km, Gap > Turin (Ita)
18	250 km, Turin > Grenoble
19	173 km, Grenoble > Saint-Étienne
20	73 km, Saint-Étienne > Lyon (ITT)
21	237 km, Lyon > Montluçon
22	331 km, Montluçon > Paris

1 Roger Walkowiak (Fra)
in 124h 01'16"
2 Gilbert Bauvin (Fra)
at 1'25"
3 Jan Adriaenssens (Bel)
at 3'44"

Stan Ockers (Bel)

King of the Mountains
Charly Gaul (Lux)

1957

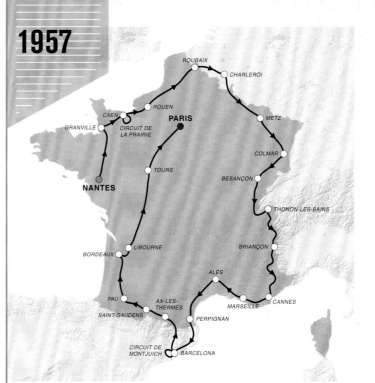

The 1957 event was a good one for the French and saw the remarkably successful debut of a true Tour de France superstar in 23-year-old Jacques Anquetil. He built this and subsequent wins on powerful time trial performances and was renowned for his elegant style. For the first time since 1930 riders were allowed to have advertising on their jerseys. Reporter Alex Virot and his motorcycle driver René Wagner died following a crash in bad weather in the Pyrenees.

Thursday 27 June–Saturday 20 July

1	204 km, Nantes > Granville
2	226 km, Granville > Caen
3a	15 km, Caen/Circuit de la Prairie (TTT)
3b	134 km, Caen > Rouen
4	232 km, Rouen > Roubaix
5	170 km, Roubaix > Charleroi (Bel)
6	248 km, Charleroi > Metz
7	223 km, Metz > Colmar
8	192 km, Colmar > Besançon
9	188 km, Besançon > Thonon-les-Bains
10	247 km, Thonon-les-Bains > Briançon
11	286 km, Briançon > Cannes
12	239 km, Cannes > Marseille
13	160 km, Marseille > Alès
14	246 km, Alès > Perpignan
15a	197 km, Perpignan > Barcelona (Spa)
15b	9.8 km, Barcelona/Circuit de Montjuich (ITT)
16	220 km, Barcelona > Ax-les-Thermes
17	236 km, Ax-les-Thermes > Saint-Gaudens
18	207 km, Saint-Gaudens > Pau
19	194 km, Pau > Bordeaux
20	66 km, Bordeaux > Libourne (ITT)
21	317 km, Libourne > Tours
22	227 km, Tours > Paris

1 Jacques Anquetil (Fra)
in 135h 44'42"
2 Marcel Janssens (Bel)
at 14'56"
3 Adolf Christian (Aut)
at 17'20"

Jean Forestier (Fra)

King of the Mountains
Gastone Nencini (Ita)

1958

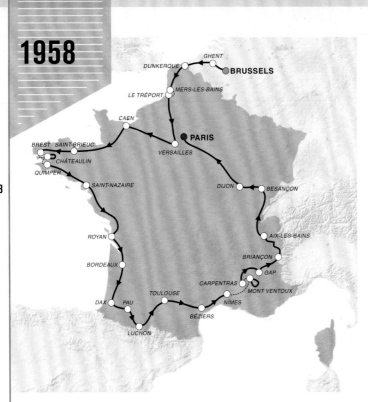

The 45th Tour started in Brussels in honour of the World Fair. There were no rest days this year. Charly Gaul won all three time trials, including one up Mont Ventoux. The yellow jersey changed hands a record 11 times, with Gaul taking it in the final time trial. Jacques Anquetil, who was several minutes behind and feeling ill, withdrew before stage 23. In the final sprint in Paris André Darrigade collided with a race official, Constant Wouters, who died 11 days later.

Thursday 26 June–Saturday 19 July

1	184 km, Brussels (Bel) > Ghent (Bel)
2	198 km, Ghent > Dunkerque
3	177 km, Dunkerque > Mers-les-Bains
4	205 km, Le Tréport > Versailles
5	232 km, Versailles > Caen
6	223 km, Caen > Saint-Brieuc
7	170 km, Saint-Brieuc > Brest
8	46 km, Châteaulin (ITT)
9	206 km, Quimper > Saint-Nazaire
10	255 km, Saint-Nazaire > Royan
11	137 km, Royan > Bordeaux
12	161 km, Bordeaux > Dax
13	230 km, Dax > Pau
14	129 km, Pau > Luchon
15	176 km, Luchon > Toulouse
16	187 km, Toulouse > Béziers
17	189 km, Béziers > Nîmes
18	21.5 km, Mont Ventoux (ITT)
19	178 km, Carpentras > Gap
20	165 km, Gap > Briançon
21	219 km, Briançon > Aix-les-Bains
22	237 km, Aix-les-Bains > Besançon
23	74 km, Besançon > Dijon (ITT)
24	320 km, Dijon > Paris

1 Charly Gaul (Lux)
in 116h 59'05"
2 Vito Favero (Ita)
at 3'10"
3 Raphaël Géminiani (Fra)
at 3'41"

Jean Graczyk (Fra)

King of the Mountains
Federico Bahamontes (Spa)

1959

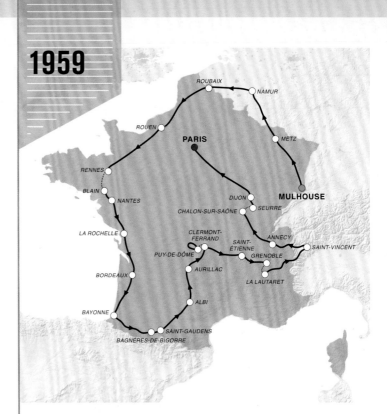

In 1959 specialist climber Federico Bahamontes, known as the 'Eagle of Toledo', profited from rivalry among the French national and regional teams to become the first Spanish winner of the Tour. This was the last Tour for previous winners Jean Robic and Louison Bobet. The course distance of 4,391 km was covered at an average speed of 35.47 km/hour and 65 of the 120 starters finished the race. Helicopters were used for television coverage for the first time this year.

Thursday 25 June–Saturday 18 July

1	238 km, Mulhouse > Metz
2	240 km, Metz > Namur (Bel)
3	217 km, Namur > Roubaix
4	230 km, Roubaix > Rouen
5	286 km, Rouen > Rennes
6	45.3 km, Blain > Nantes (ITT)
7	190 km, Nantes > La Rochelle
8	201 km, La Rochelle > Bordeaux
9	207 km, Bordeaux > Bayonne
10	235 km, Bayonne > Bagnères-de-Bigorre
11	119 km, Bagnères-de-Bigorre > Saint-Gaudens
12	184 km, Saint-Gaudens > Albi
13	219 km, Albi > Aurillac
14	231 km, Aurillac > Clermont-Ferrand
15	12.5 km, Puy-de-Dôme (ITT)
16	210 km, Clermont-Ferrand > Saint-Étienne
17	197 km, Saint-Étienne > Grenoble
18	243 km, Le Lautaret > Saint-Vincent (Ita)
19	251 km, Saint-Vincent > Annecy
20	202 km, Annecy > Chalon-sur-Saône
21	69.2 km, Seurre > Dijon (ITT)
22	331 km, Dijon > Paris

1 Federico Bahamontes (Spa)
in 123h 46'45"
2 Henry Anglade (Fra)
at 4'01"
3 Jacques Anquetil (Fra)
at 5'05"

André Darrigade (Fra)

King of the Mountains
Federico Bahamontes (Spa)

1960

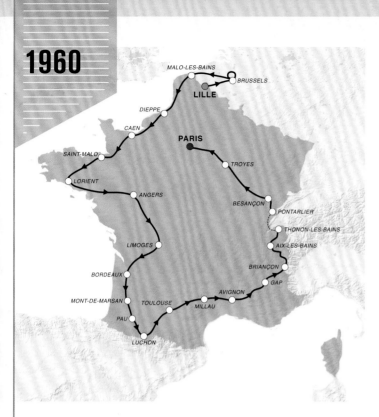

In the absence of Jacques Anquetil, tired after winning the Giro d'Italia, Roger Rivière was the French favourite. Trying to keep up with eventual winner Gastone Nencini on the descent of the Col de Perjuret, Rivière fell into a ravine and broke his back, ending his career. It is thought that the opiates he had taken numbed his hands and impaired his braking. This was the first Tour de France for British rider Tom Simpson, who finished 29th.

Sunday 26 June–Sunday 17 July

1a	108 km, Lille > Brussels (Bel)
1b	27.8 km, Brussels (ITT)
2	206 km, Brussels > Malo-les-Bains
3	209 km, Malo-les-Bains > Dieppe
4	211 km, Dieppe > Caen
5	189 km, Caen > Saint-Malo
6	191 km, Saint-Malo > Lorient
7	244 km, Lorient > Angers
8	240 km, Angers > Limoges
9	225 km, Limoges > Bordeaux
10	228 km, Mont-de Marsan > Pau
11	161 km, Pau > Luchon
12	176 km, Luchon > Toulouse
13	224 km, Toulouse > Millau
14	217 km, Millau > Avignon
15	187 km, Avignon > Gap
16	172 km, Gap > Briançon
17	229 km, Briançon > Aix-les-Bains
18	215 km, Aix-les-Bains > Thonon-les-Bains
19	83 km, Pontarlier > Besançon (ITT)
20	229 km, Besançon > Troyes
21	200 km, Troyes > Paris

1 Gastone Nencini (Ita)
in 112h 08'42"
2 Graziano Battistini (Ita)
at 5'02"
3 Jan Adriaenssens (Bel)
at 10'24"

Jean Graczyk (Fri)

King of the Mountains
Imerio Massignan (Ita)

1961

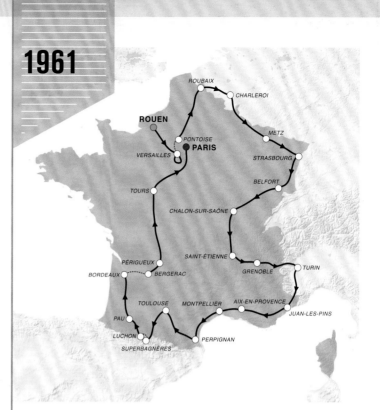

The first clockwise Tour since 1957 saw the same winner as in that year. The French team was united behind Jacques Anquetil and he held the yellow jersey from the time trial on the opening day to the end in Paris. Second and third places were closely contested, with Guido Carlesi taking the runner-up spot by 2 seconds from Charly Gaul on the final day. Imerio Massignan won the mountain top finish at Superbagnères and retained his King of the Mountains title.

Sunday 25 June–Sunday 16 July

1a	136.5 km, Rouen > Versailles
1b	28.5 km, Versailles (ITT)
2	230.5 km, Pontoise > Roubaix
3	197.5 km, Roubaix > Charleroi (Bel)
4	237.5 km, Charleroi > Metz
5	221 km, Metz > Strasbourg
6	180.5 km, Strasbourg > Belfort
7	214.5 km, Belfort > Chalon-sur-Saône
8	240.5 km, Chalon-sur-Saône > Saint-Étienne
9	230 km, Saint-Étienne > Grenoble
10	250.5 km, Grenoble > Turin (Ita)
11	225 km, Turin > Juan-les-Pins
12	199 km, Juan-les-Pins > Aix-en-Provence
13	177.5 km, Aix-en-Provence > Montpellier
14	174 km, Montpellier > Perpignan
15	206 km, Perpignan > Toulouse
16	208 km, Toulouse > Superbagnères
17	197 km, Luchon > Pau
18	207 km, Pau > Bordeaux
19	74.5 km, Bergerac > Périgueux (ITT)
20	309.5 km, Périgueux > Tours
21	252.5 km, Tours > Paris

1 Jacques Anquetil (Fra)
in 122h 01'33"
2 Guido Carlesi (Ita)
at 12'14"
3 Charly Gaul (Lux)
at 12'16"

André Darrigade (Fra)

King of the Mountains
Imerio Massignan (Ita)

1962

1963

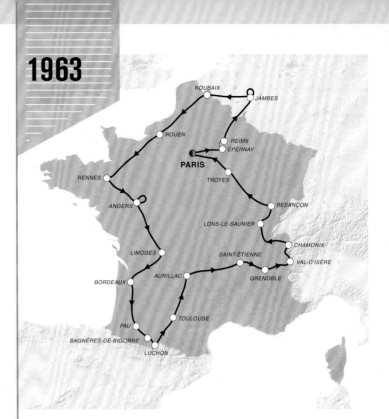

The 1962 Tour was the first since 1929 to be contested by trade teams rather than national and regional teams. For the first time there were more Italian riders (52) than French (50). Jacques Anquetil became the third man to win three Tours, taking the yellow jersey in the final time trial. Tom Simpson was the first British rider to wear the yellow jersey and finished the Tour in sixth place. Raymond Poulidor rode the first of his 14 Tours.

In the 50th Tour de France the organizers reduced the amount of time trialling to 79 km from 130 km the previous year, in an attempt to reduce the dominance of Jacques Anquetil. He responded by winning not only both the individual time trials but also two mountain stages to gain his fourth overall victory. Rik van Looy, a specialist sprinter, also won four stages and took the green points jersey. Seamus Elliott became the first Irishman to wear the yellow jersey.

Sunday 24 June–Sunday 15 July

1	253 km, Nancy > Spa (Bel)
2a	147 km, Spa > Herentals (Bel)
2b	23 km, Herentals (TTT)
3	210 km, Brussels (Bel) > Amiens
4	196.5 km, Amiens > Le Havre
5	215 km, Pont l'Évêque >Saint-Malo
6	235.5 km, Dinard > Brest
7	201 km, Quimper > Saint-Nazaire
8a	155 km, Saint-Nazaire > Luçon
8b	43 km, Luçon > La Rochelle (ITT)
9	214 km, La Rochelle > Bordeaux
10	184.5 km, Bordeaux > Bayonne
11	155.5 km, Bayonne > Pau
12	207.5 km, Pau > Saint-Gaudens
13	18.5 km, Luchon > Superbagnères (ITT)
14	215 km, Luchon > Carcassonne
15	196.5 km, Carcassonne > Montpellier
16	185 km, Montpellier > Aix-en-Provence
17	201 km, Aix-en-Provence > Juan-les-Pins
18	241.5 km, Juan-les-Pins > Briançon
19	204.5 km, Briançon > Aix-les-Bains
20	68 km, Bourgoin > Lyon (ITT)
21	232 km, Lyon > Pougues-les-Eaux
22	271 km, Pougues-les-Eaux > Paris

1 Jacques Anquetil (Fra)
in 114h 31'54"
2 Jef Planckaert (Bel)
at 4'59"
3 Raymond Poulidor (Fra)
at 10'24"

Rudi Altig (Ger)

King of the Mountains
Federico Bahamontes (Spa)

Sunday 23 June–Sunday 14 July

1	152.5 km, Paris > Épernay
2a	185.5 km, Reims > Jambes (Bel)
2b	21.6 km, Jambes (TTT)
3	223.5 km, Jambes > Roubaix
4	235.5 km, Roubaix > Rouen
5	285 km, Rouen > Rennes
6a	118.5 km, Rennes > Angers
6b	24.5 km, Angers (ITT)
7	236 km, Angers > Limoges
8	231.5 km, Limoges > Bordeaux
9	202 km, Bordeaux > Pau
10	148.5 km, Pau > Bagnères-de-Bigorre
11	131 km, Bagnères-de-Bigorre > Luchon
12	172.5 km, Luchon > Toulouse
13	234 km, Toulouse > Aurillac
14	236.5 km, Aurillac > Saint-Étienne
15	174 km, Saint-Étienne > Grenoble
16	202 km, Grenoble > Val-d'Isère
17	227.5 km, Val-d'Isère > Chamonix
18	225 km, Chamonix > Lons-le-Saunier
19	54.5 km, Lons-le-Saunier > Besançon (ITT)
20	233.5 km, Besançon > Troyes
21	185.5 km, Troyes > Paris

1 Jacques Anquetil (Fra)
in 113h 30'05"
2 Federico Bahamontes (Spa)
at 3'35"
3 José Pérez-Francés (Spa)
at 10'14"

Rik van Looy (Bel)

King of the Mountains
Federico Bahamontes (Spa)

1964

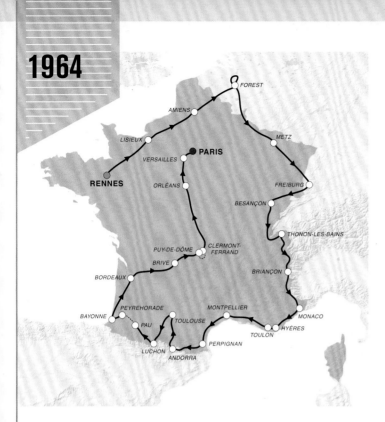

In 1964 Jacques Anquetil became the first man to win five Tours and the first since Fausto Coppi to win the Giro d'Italia and the Tour in the same year. In one of the most memorable races ever, Anquetil's winning margin over Raymond Poulidor was less than a minute. Federico Bahamontes was King of the Mountains for the sixth and last time. This year was the first time the Tour visited Andorra and the first time it finished with a time trial.

Monday 22 June–Tuesday 14 July

1	215 km, Rennes > Lisieux
2	208 km, Lisieux > Amiens
3a	196.5 km, Amiens > Forest (Bel)
3b	21.3 km, Forest (TTT)
4	291.5 km, Forest > Metz
5	161.5 km, Metz > Freiburg (Ger)
6	200 km, Freiburg > Besançon
7	195 km, Besançon > Thonon-les-Bains
8	248.5 km, Thonon-les-Bains > Briançon
9	239 km, Briançon > Monaco (Mon)
10a	187.5 km, Monaco > Hyères
10b	20.8 km, Hyères > Toulon (ITT)
11	250 km, Toulon > Montpellier
12	174 km, Montpellier > Perpignan
13	170 km, Perpignan > Andorra (And)
14	186 km, Andorra > Toulouse
15	203 km, Toulouse > Luchon
16	197 km, Luchon > Pau
17	42.6 km, Peyrehorade > Bayonne (ITT)
18	187 km, Bayonne > Bordeaux
19	215.5 km, Bordeaux > Brive
20	237.5 km, Brive > Puy-du-Dôme
21	311 km, Clermont-Ferrand > Orléans
22a	118.5 km, Orléans > Versailles
22b	27.5 km, Versailles > Paris (ITT)

1 Jacques Anquetil (Fra)
in 127h 09'44"
2 Raymond Poulidor (Fra)
at 0'55"
3 Federico Bahamontes (Spa)
at 4'44"

Jan Janssen (Ned)

King of the Mountains
Federico Bahamontes (Spa)

1965

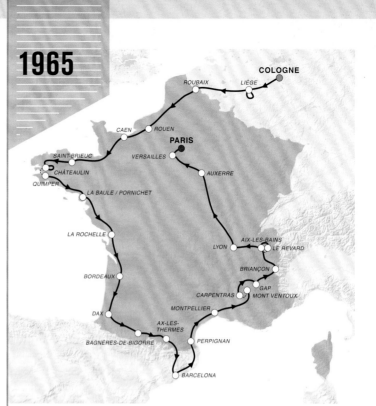

The 52nd Tour de France started in Germany for the first time, continuing into Belgium and also visiting Spain. It included a finish at the top of Mont Ventoux and a mountain time trial, finishing with a time trial into Paris for the second year running. Raymond Poulidor was a strong favourite in the absence of Jacques Anquetil, but he only managed second place again. He was beaten by 23-year-old Tour debutant Felice Gimondi, a last-minute replacement in the Salvarani team.

Tuesday 22 June–Wednesday 14 July

1a	149 km, Cologne (Ger) > Liège (Bel)
1b	22.5 km, Liège (TTT)
2	200.5 km, Liège > Roubaix
3	240 km, Roubaix > Rouen
4	227 km, Caen > Saint-Brieuc
5a	147 km, Saint-Brieuc > Châteaulin
5b	26.7 km, Châteaulin (ITT)
6	210.5 km, Quimper > La Baule/Pornichet
7	219 km, La Baule/Pornichet > La Rochelle
8	197.5 km, La Rochelle > Bordeaux
9	226.5 km, Dax > Bagnères-de-Bigorre
10	222.5 km, Bagnères-de-Bigorre > Ax-les-Thermes
11	240.5 km, Ax-les-Thermes > Barcelona (Spa)
12	219 km, Barcelona > Perpignan
13	164 km, Perpignan > Montpellier
14	173 km, Montpellier > Mont Ventoux
15	167.5 km, Carpentras > Gap
16	177 km, Gap > Briançon
17	193.5 km, Briançon > Aix-les-Bains
18	26.9 km, Aix-les-Bains > Le Revard (ITT)
19	165 km, Aix-les-Bains > Lyon
20	298.5 km, Lyon > Auxerre
21	225.5 km, Auxerre > Versailles
22	37.8 km, Versailles > Paris (ITT)

1 Felice Gimondi (Ita)
in 116h 42'06"
2 Raymond Poulidor (Fra)
at 2'40"
3 Gianni Motta (Ita)
at 9'18"

Jan Janssen (Ned)

King of the Mountains
Julio Jiménez (Spa)

1966

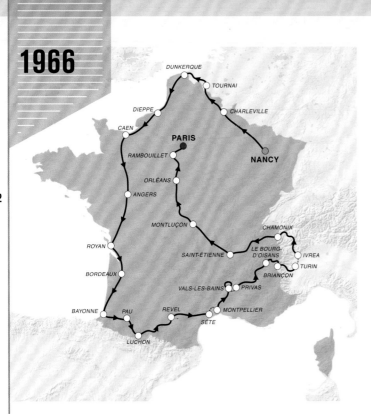

In 1966 Jan Janssen became the first Dutchman to stand on the final Tour de France podium. The Tour's first dope test led to a short strike by the riders during stage 9. Raymond Poulidor once again failed to win a race for which he was the favourite, concentrating on a sick Jacques Anquetil in his farewell Tour instead of the latter's team-mate Lucien Aimar, who got into a breakaway on stage 10 and took the yellow jersey after stage 16.

Tuesday 21 June–Thursday 14 July

1	208.5 km, Nancy > Charleville
2	198 km, Charleville > Tournai (Bel)
3a	20.8 km, Tournai (TTT)
3b	131.5 km, Tournai > Dunkerque
4	205 km, Dunkerque > Dieppe
5	178.5 km, Dieppe > Caen
6	216.5 km, Caen > Angers
7	252.5 km, Angers > Royan
8	137.5 km, Royan > Bordeaux
9	201 km, Bordeaux > Bayonne
10	234.5 km, Bayonne > Pau
11	188 km, Pau > Luchon
12	218.5 km, Luchon > Revel
13	191.5 km, Revel > Sète
14a	144 km, Montpellier > Vals-les-Bains
14b	20 km, Vals-les-Bains (ITT)
15	203.5 km, Privas > Bourg-d'Oisans
16	148.5 km, Bourg-d'Oisans > Briançon
17	160 km, Briançon > Turin (Ita)
18	188 km, Ivrea (Ita) > Chamonix
19	264.5 km, Chamonix > Saint-Étienne
20	223.5 km, Saint-Étienne > Montluçon
21	232.5 km, Montluçon > Orléans
22a	111 km, Orléans > Rambouillet
22b	51.3 km, Rambouillet > Paris (ITT)

1 Lucien Aimar (Fra)
in 117h 34'21"

2 Jan Janssen (Ned)
at 1'07"

3 Raymond Poulidor (Fra)
at 2'02"

Willy Planckaert (Bel)

King of the Mountains
Julio Jiménez (Spa)

1967

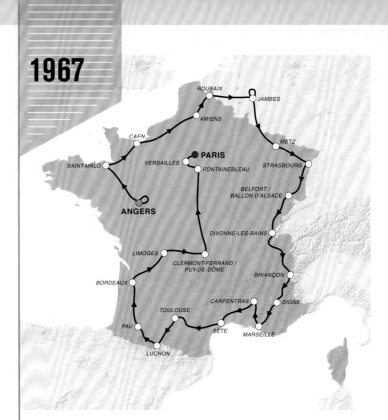

The 1967 Tour was contested by national teams. It was topped and tailed by individual time trials, with stage 1a being the first of what is now known as a prologue. The finish of the race was the last one in the Parc des Princes velodrome, which was demolished soon after. Stage 13, on 13 July, saw the death of British rider Tom Simpson on the slopes of Mont Ventoux as a result of alcohol, amphetamines, the climb and the heat.

Thursday 29 June–Sunday 23 July

1a	5.775 km, Angers (ITT)
1b	185.5 km, Angers > Saint-Malo
2	180 km, Saint-Malo > Caen
3	248 km, Caen > Amiens
4	191 km, Amiens > Roubaix
5a	172 km, Roubaix > Jambes (Bel)
5b	17 km, Jambes (TTT)
6	238 km, Jambes > Metz
7	205.5 km, Metz > Strasbourg
8	215 km, Strasbourg > Belfort/Ballon d'Alsace
9	238.5 km, Belfort > Divonne-les-Bains
10	243 km, Divonne-les-Bains > Briançon
11	197 km, Briançon > Digne
12	207.5 km, Digne > Marseille
13	211.5 km, Marseille > Carpentras
14	201.5 km, Carpentras > Sète
15	230.5 km, Sète > Toulouse
16	188 km, Toulouse > Luchon
17	250 km, Luchon > Pau
18	206.5 km, Pau > Bordeaux
19	217 km, Bordeaux > Limoges
20	222 km, Limoges > Clermont-Ferrand/ Puy-de-Dôme
21	359 km, Clermont-Ferrand > Fontainebleau
22a	104 km, Fontainebleau > Versailles
22b	46.6 km, Versailles > Paris (ITT)

1 Roger Pingeon (Fra)
in 136h 53'50"

2 Julio Jiménez (Spa)
at 3'40"

3 Franco Balmamion (Ita)
at 7'23"

Jan Janssen (Ned)

King of the Mountains
Julio Jiménez (Spa)

1968

The 55th Tour was the last one to be contested by national teams. The first Dutch Tour winner, Jan Janssen, covered the 4,684.8 km at an average speed of 34.894 km/hour, taking the yellow jersey only in the final time trial into the Vélodrome de Vincennes. The unlucky Raymond Poulidor withdrew following a collision with a motorbike. Team cars were allowed to give the riders water for the first time and compulsory drug tests took place after each stage.

Thursday 27 June–Sunday 21 July

1a	6.1 km, Vittel (ITT)
1b	189 km, Vittel > Esch-sur-Alzette (Lux)
2	210.5 km, Arlon (Bel) > Forest (Bel)
3a	22 km, Forest (TTT)
3b	112 km, Forest > Roubaix
4	238 km, Roubaix > Rouen
5a	165 km, Rouen > Bagnoles-de-l'Orne
5b	154.5 km, Bagnoles-de-l'Orne > Dinard
6	188 km, Dinard > Lorient
7	190 km, Lorient > Nantes
8	223 km, Nantes > Royan
9	137.5 km, Royan > Bordeaux
10	202.5 km, Bordeaux > Bayonne
11	183.5 km, Bayonne > Pau
12	226.5 km, Pau > Saint-Gaudens
13	208.5 km, Saint-Gaudens > La Seu d'Urgell (Spa)
14	231.5 km, La Seu d'Urgell > Perpignan
15	250.5 km, Font-Romeu > Albi
16	199 km, Albi > Aurillac
17	236.5 km, Aurillac > Saint-Étienne
18	235 km, Saint-Étienne > Grenoble
19	200 km, Grenoble > Sallanches
20	242.5 km, Sallanches > Besançon
21	242 km, Besançon > Auxerre
22a	136 km, Auxerre > Melun
22b	55.2 km, Melun > Paris (ITT)

1 Jan Janssen (Ned)
in 133h 49'42"

2 Herman van Springel (Bel)
at 0'38"

3 Ferdinand Bracke (Bel)
at 3'03"

Franco Bitossi (Ita)
[NB. the points jersey was actually red this year]

King of the Mountains
Aurelio González (Spa)

1969

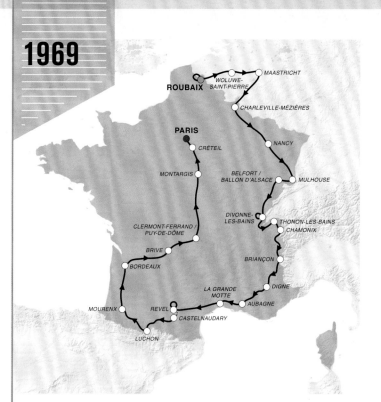

In 1969 Belgian prodigy Eddy Merckx, angry after being removed from the Giro d'Italia for a positive drug test (he denied any wrongdoing), dominated his first Tour de France. In addition to the yellow jersey, which he took after stage 6 and reinforced with a 140-km solo breakaway in the Pyrenees on stage 17, he won the points, mountains and combined classifications, as well as the overall combativity award. His team, Faema, also claimed the team prize on the return to trade teams.

Saturday 28 June–Sunday 20 July

Prologue	10.4 km, Roubaix (ITT)
1a	147 km, Roubaix > Woluwe-Saint-Pierre (Bel)
1b	15.6 km, Woluwe-Saint-Pierre (TTT)
2	181.5 km, Woluwe-Saint-Pierre > Maastricht (Ned)
3	213.5 km, Maastricht > Charleville
4	214 km, Charleville > Nancy
5	193.5 km, Nancy > Mulhouse
6	133.5 km, Mulhouse > Belfort/Ballon d'Alsace
7	241 km, Belfort > Divonne-les-Bains
8a	8.8 km, Divonne-les-Bains (ITT)
8b	136.5 km, Divonne-les-Bains > Thonon-les-Bains
9	111 km, Thonon-les-Bains > Chamonix
10	220.5 km, Chamonix > Briançon
11	198 km, Briançon > Digne
12	161.5 km, Digne > Aubagne
13	195.5 km, Aubagne > La Grande-Motte
14	234.5 km, La Grande-Motte > Revel
15	18.5 km, Revel (ITT)
16	199 km, Castelnaudary > Luchon
17	214.5 km, Luchon > Mourenx/Ville Nouvelle
18	201 km, Mourenx > Bordeaux
19	192.5 km, Bordeaux > Brive
20	198 km, Brive > Clermont-Ferrand/Puy-de-Dôme
21	329.5 km, Clermont-Ferrand > Montargis
22a	111.5 km, Montargis > Créteil
22b	36.8 km, Créteil > Paris (ITT)

1 Eddy Merckx (Bel)
in 116h 16'02"

2 Roger Pingeon (Fra)
at 17'54"

3 Raymond Poulidor (Fra)
at 22'13"

Eddy Merckx (Bel)

King of the Mountains
Eddy Merckx (Bel)

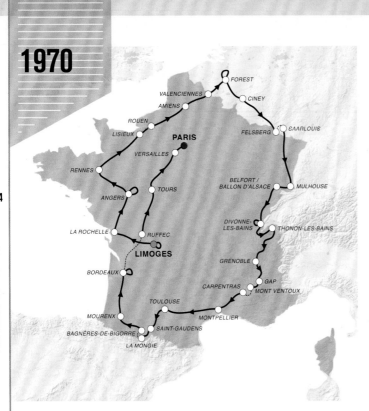

1971

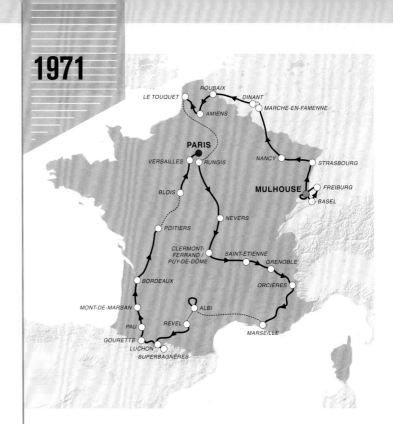

As in the previous edition, the 1970 Tour de France included no rest days and there were even more of the financially successful split stages this year. Eddy Merckx dominated again, winning eight stages, wearing the yellow jersey for 18 days, winning the mountains classification and the combativity award and coming second in the points competition. The 22-year-old Bernard Thévenet showed his potential by winning the stage to La Mongie, the first time this climb had been used in the Tour.

1971 saw the first transfer by plane (from Marseille to Albi), a prologue team time trial and the introduction of bonus seconds for intermediate sprints. Despite fewer time trials this year, Eddy Merckx won a third consecutive Tour. He was trailing Luis Ocaña by almost 10 minutes after the latter's impressive win on stage 11 in the Alps, but the Spaniard crashed while descending the Col de Menté in a storm on stage 14 and had to abandon the race.

Saturday 27 June–Sunday 19 July

Prologue	7.4 km, Limoges (ITT)
1	224.5 km, Limoges > La Rochelle
2	200 km, La Rochelle > Angers
3a	10.7 km, Angers (TTT)
3b	140 km, Angers > Rennes
4	229 km, Rennes > Lisieux
5a	94.5 km, Lisieux > Rouen
5b	113 km, Rouen > Amiens
6	135.5 km, Amiens > Valenciennes
7a	120 km, Valenciennes > Forest (Bel)
7b	7.2 km, Forest (ITT)
8	232.5 km, Ciney (Bel) > Felsberg (Ger)
9	269.5 km, Saarlouis (Ger) > Mulhouse
10	241 km, Belfort > Divonne-les-Bains
11a	8.8 km, Divonne-les-Bains (ITT)
11b	139.5 km, Divonne-les-Bains > Thonon-les-Bains
12	194 km, Thonon-les-Bains > Grenoble
13	194.5 km, Grenoble > Gap
14	170 km, Gap > Mont Ventoux
15	144.5 km, Carpentras > Montpellier
16	259.5 km, Montpellier > Toulouse
17	190 km, Toulouse > Saint-Gaudens
18	135.5 km, Saint-Gaudens > La Mongie
19	185.5 km, Bagnères-de-Bigorre > Mourenx
20a	231 km, Mourenx > Bordeaux
20b	8.2 km, Bordeaux (ITT)
21	191.5 km, Ruffec > Tours
22	238.5 km, Tours > Versailles
23	54 km, Versailles > Paris (ITT)

1 Eddy Merckx (Bel)
in 119h 31'49"

2 Joop Zoetemelk (Ned)
at 12'41"

3 Gösta Pettersson (Swe)
at 15'54"

Walter Godefroot (Bel)

King of the Mountains
Eddy Merckx (Bel)

Saturday 26 June–Sunday 18 July

Prologue	11 km, Mulhouse (TTT)
1a	59.5 km, Mulhouse > Basle (Swi)
1b	90 km, Basle > Freiburg (Ger)
1c	74 km, Freiburg > Mulhouse
2	144 km, Mulhouse > Strasbourg
3	165.5 km, Strasbourg > Nancy
4	242 km, Nancy > Marche-en-Famenne (Bel)
5	208.5 km, Dinant (Bel) > Roubaix
6a	127.5 km, Roubaix > Amiens
6b	133.5 km, Amiens > Le Touquet
7	257.5 km, Rungis > Nevers
8	221 km, Nevers > Clermont Ferrand/Puy-de-Dôme
9	153 km, Clermont-Ferrand > Saint-Étienne
10	188.5 km, Saint-Étienne > Grenoble
11	134 km, Grenoble > Orcières-Merlette
12	251 km, Orcières > Marseille
13	16.3 km, Albi (ITT)
14	214.5 km, Revel > Luchon
15	19.6 km, Luchon > Superbagnères
16a	145 km, Luchon > Gourette
16b	57.5 km, Gourette > Pau
17	188 km, Mont-de-Marsan > Bordeaux
18	244 km, Bordeaux > Poitiers
19	185 km, Blois > Versailles
20	53.8 km, Versailles > Paris (ITT)

1 Eddy Merckx (Bel)
in 96h 45'14"

2 Joop Zoetemelk (Ned)
at 9'51"

3 Lucien van Impe (Bel)
at 11'06"

Eddy Merckx (Bel)

King of the Mountains
Lucien van Impe (Bel)

1972

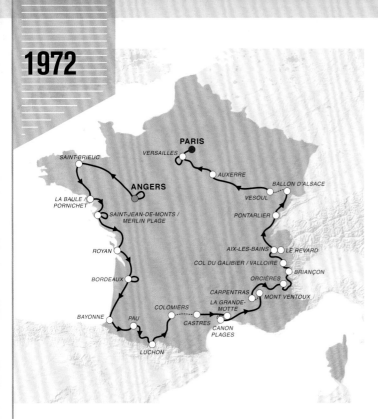

The 1972 Tour de France was the first one since 1947 to take place entirely within the borders of France. Luis Ocaña was forced to abandon again, this time with a lung infection, and the main challenge to Eddy Merckx came from Cyrille Guimard. However, the Frenchman also had to quit the race with knee pain, leaving the way clear for 'the Cannibal' to win a fourth successive Tour. The 36-year-old Raymond Poulidor collected yet another podium place.

Saturday 1 July–Sunday 23 July

Prologue	7.2 km, Angers (ITT)
1	235.5 km, Angers > Saint-Brieuc
2	206.5 km, Saint-Brieuc > La Baule
3a	161 km, Pornichet > Saint-Jean-de-Monts
3b	16.2 km, Merlin-Plage (TTT)
4	236 km, Merlin-Plage > Royan
5a	133.5 km, Royan > Bordeaux
5b	12.7 km, Bordeaux (ITT)
6	205 km, Bordeaux > Bayonne
7	220.5 km, Bayonne > Pau
8	163.5 km, Pau > Luchon
9	179 km, Luchon > Colomiers
10	210 km, Castres > La Grande-Motte
11	207 km, Carnon Plage > Mont Ventoux
12	192 km, Carpentras > Orcières
13	201 km, Orcières > Briançon
14a	51 km, Briançon > Col du Galibier
14b	151 km, Valloire > Aix-les-Bains
15	28 km, Aix-les-Bains > Le Revard
16	198.5 km, Aix-les-Bains > Pontarlier
17	213 km, Pontarlier > Ballon d'Alsace
18	257.5 km, Vesoul > Auxerre
19	230 km, Auxerre > Versailles
20a	42 km, Versailles (ITT)
20b	89 km, Versailles > Paris

1 Eddy Merckx (Bel)
in 108h 17'18"
2 Felice Gimondi (Ita)
at 10'41"
3 Raymond Poulidor (Fra)
at 11'34"

Eddy Merckx (Bel)

King of the Mountains
Lucien van Impe (Bel)

1973

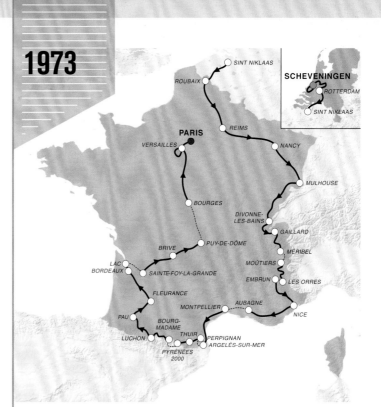

The 60th Tour de France covered 4,140.4 km at an average speed of 33.918 km/hour, the slowest since 1954. Eddy Merckx, having already won both the Vuelta a España and the Giro d'Italia in 1973, did not participate. No Italian teams took part in protest over the lack of French riders at the Giro. The riders complained about the long days and the numbers of transfers necessitated by the multitude of split stages. Luis Ocaña took six stages and the overall win.

Saturday 30 June–Sunday 22 July

Prologue	7.1 km, Scheveningen (Ned) (ITT)
1a	84 km, Scheveningen > Rotterdam (Ned)
1b	137.5 km, Rotterdam > Sint-Niklaas (Bel)
2a	12.4 km, Sint-Niklaas (TTT)
2b	138 km, Sint Niklaas > Roubaix
3	226 km, Roubaix > Reims
4	214 km, Reims > Nancy
5	188 km, Nancy > Mulhouse
6	244.5 km, Mulhouse > Divonne-les-Bains
7a	86.5 km, Divonne-les-Bains > Gaillard
7b	150.5 km, Gaillard > Méribel
8	237.5 km, Moûtiers > Les Orres
9	234.5 km, Embrun > Nice
10	222.5 km, Nice > Aubagne
11	238 km, Montpellier > Argelès-sur-Mer
12a	28.3 km, Perpignan > Thuir (ITT)
12b	76 km, Thuir > Pyrénées 2000
13	235 km, Bourg-Madame > Luchon
14	227.5 km, Luchon > Pau
15	137 km, Pau > Fleurance
16a	210 km, Fleurance > Bordeaux
16b	12.4 km, Bordeaux > Lac (ITT)
17	248 km, Sainte-Foy-la-Grande > Brive
18	216.5 km, Brive > Puy-de-Dôme
19	233.5 km, Bourges > Versailles
20a	16 km, Versailles (ITT)
20b	89 km, Versailles > Paris

1 Luis Ocaña (Spa)
in 122h 25'34"
2 Bernard Thévenet (Fra)
at 15'51"
3 José Manuel Fuente (Spa)
at 17'15"

Herman van Springel (Bel)

King of the Mountains
Pedro Torres (Spa)

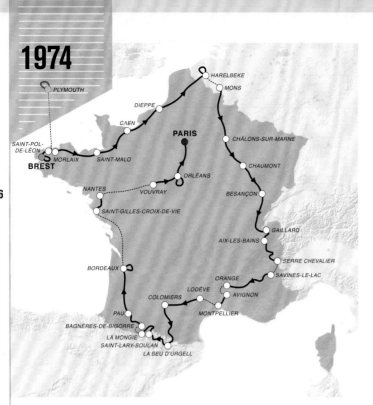

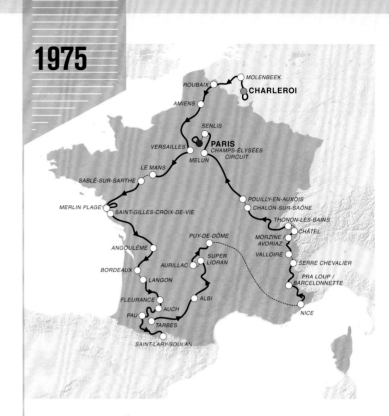

THE ATLAS OF 100 TOURS

The Tour de France entered the UK for the first time in 1974, crossing the Channel by boat for a single stage in the south-west of England which was not popular with the riders. Eddy Merckx returned to be the second man to win five Tours, and the first to win the first five he participated in. He won eight stages this year. Raymond Poulidor also returned at the age of 38 to claim another second place in Paris.

This year saw the introduction of the polkadot mountains jersey and the white jersey for the best young rider, which was taken by Francesco Moser in the only Tour de France he ever rode. It was the only Tour between 1962 and 1995 not to include a team time trial and the first one to finish with a circuit on the Champs-Élysées. Eddy Merckx was leading until he was punched in the stomach by a spectator on stage 14.

Thursday 27 June–Sunday 21 July

Prologue	7.1 km, Brest (ITT)	
1	144 km, Brest > Saint-Pol-de-Léon	
2	163.7 km, Plymouth > Plymouth (UK)	
3	190 km, Morlaix > Saint Malo	
4	184.5 km, Saint Malo > Caen	
5	165 km, Caen > Dieppe	
6a	239 km, Dieppe > Harelbeke (Bel)	
6b	9 km, Harelbeke (TTT)	
7	221.5 km, Mons (Bel) > Châlons-sur-Marne	
8a	136 km, Châlons-sur-Marne > Chaumont	
8b	152 km, Chaumont > Besançon	
9	241 km, Besançon > Gaillard	
10	131.5 km, Gaillard > Aix-les-Bains	
11	199 km, Aix-les-Bains > Serre Chevalier	
12	231 km, Savins-le-Lac > Orange	
13	126 km, Avignon > Montpellier	
14	248.5 km, Lodève > Colomiers	
15	225 km, Colomiers > La Seu d'Urgell (Spa)	
16	209 km, La Seu d'Urgell > Saint-Lary-Soulan	
17	119 km, Saint-Lary-Soulan > La Mongie	
18	141.5 km, Bagnères-de-Bigorre > Pau	
19a	195.5 km, Pau > Bordeaux	
19b	12.4 km, Bordeaux (ITT)	21a	112.5 km, Vouvray > Orléans
20	117 km, Saint-Gilles-Croix-de-Vie > Nantes	21b	37.5 km, Orléans (ITT)
		22	146 km, Orléans > Paris

1 Eddy Merckx (Bel)
in 116h 16'58"
2 Raymond Poulidor (Fra)
at 8'04"
3 Vicente López-Carril (Spa)
at 8'09"

Patrick Sercu (Bel)

King of the Mountains
Domingo Perurena (Spa)

Thursday 26 June–Sunday 20 July

Prologue	6.25 km, Charleroi (Bel) (ITT)	
1a	94 km, Charleroi > Molenbeek (Bel)	
1b	108.5 km, Molenbeek > Roubaix	
2	121.5 km, Roubaix > Amiens	
3	169.5 km, Amiens > Versailles	
4	223 km, Versailles > Le Mans	
5	222.5 km, Sablé-sur-Sarthe > Merlin-Plage	
6	16 km, Merlin-Plage (ITT)	
7	235.5 km, Saint-Gilles-Croix-de-Vie > Angoulême	
8	134 km, Angoulême > Bordeaux	
9a	131 km, Langon > Fleurance	
9b	37.4 km, Fleurance > Auch (ITT)	
10	206 km, Auch > Pau	
11	160 km, Pau > Saint-Lary-Soulan	
12	242 km, Tarbes > Albi	
13	260 km, Albi > Super Lioran	
14	173.5 km, Aurillac > Puy-de-Dôme	
15	217.5 km, Nice > Pra Loup	
16	107 km, Barcelonnette > Serre Chevalier	
17	225 km, Valloire > Morzine Avoriaz	
18	40 km, Morzine > Châtel (ITT)	
19	229 km, Thonon-les-Bains > Chalon-sur-Saône	
20	256 km, Pouilly-en-Auxois > Melun	
21	220.5 km, Melun > Senlis	
22	163.5 km, Paris/ Champs-Élysées Circuit	

1 Bernard Thévenet (Fra)
in 114h 35'31"
2 Eddy Merckx (Bel)
at 2'47"
3 Lucien van Impe (Bel)
at 5'01"

Rik van Linden (Bel)

Lucien van Impe (Bel)

Francesco Moser (Ita)

1976

The Bernard Hinault years – the last champion of the old school 1976–1988

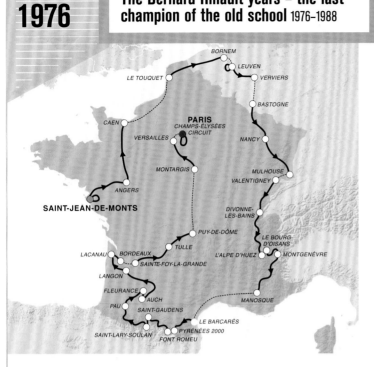

The 1976 Tour de France was a good one for Belgium despite the absence of Eddy Merckx. Specialist climber Lucien van Impe profited from a hilly course to win the overall classification, and Freddy Maertens won eight stages (including three time trials) in his first Tour. In his 14th and final Tour, at the age of 40, Raymond Poulidor finished third for the fifth time. He had also managed three second places, but he never wore the yellow jersey.

Thursday 24 June–Sunday 18 July

Prologue	8 km, Saint-Jean-de-Monts (ITT)
1	173 km, Saint-Jean-de-Monts > Angers
2	236.5 km, Angers > Caen
3	37 km, Le Touquet (ITT)
4	258 km, Le Touquet > Bornem (Bel)
5a	4.3 km, Leuven (Bel) (TTT)
5b	144 km, Leuven > Verviers (Bel)
6	209 km, Bastogne (Bel) > Nancy
7	205.5 km, Nancy > Mulhouse
8	220.5 km, Valentigney > Divonne-les-Bains
9	258 km, Divonne-les-Bains > Alpe d'Huez
10	166 km, Bourg-d'Oisans > Montgenèvre
11	224 km, Montgenèvre > Manosque
12	205.5 km, Le Barcarès > Pyrénées 2000
13	188 km, Font-Romeu > Saint-Gaudens
14	139 km, Saint-Gaudens > Saint-Lary-Soulan
15	195 km, Saint-Lary-Soulan > Pau
16	152 km, Pau > Fleurance
17	38.75 km, Fleurance > Auch (ITT)
18a	86 km, Auch > Langon
18b	123 km, Langon > Lacanau
18c	70.5 km, Lacanau > Bordeaux
19	219.5 km, Sainte-Foy-la-Grande > Tulle
20	220 km, Tulle > Puy-de-Dôme
21	145.5 km, Montargis > Versailles
22a	6 km, Paris/Champs-Élysées Circuit (ITT)
22b	90.7 km, Paris/Champs-Élysées Circuit

1 Lucien van Impe (Bel)
in 116h 22'23"
2 Joop Zoetemelk (Ned)
at 4'14"
3 Raymond Poulidor (Fra)
at 12'08"

Freddy Maertens (Bel)

Giancarlo Bellini (Ita)

Enrique Martínez Heredia (Spa)

1977

1977 was Eddy Merckx's last Tour de France; he finished sixth, more than 12 minutes down on Bernard Thévenet, who won his second Tour. There were fewer mountain top finishes this year and five individual time trials. Dutchman Hennie Kuiper won stage 17 at the top of the Alpe d'Huez in an epic battle with Thévenet after Lucien van Impe was hit by a television car while leading on the final climb. Thévenet's winning margin over Kuiper was the smallest since 1968.

Thursday 30 June–Sunday 24 July

Prologue	5 km, Fleurance (ITT)
1	237 km, Fleurance > Auch
2	253 km, Auch > Pau
3	248.2 km, Oloron-Sainte-Marie > Vitoria (Spa)
4	256 km, Vitoria > Seignosse le Penon
5a	138.5 km, Morcenx > Bordeaux
5b	30.2 km, Bordeaux/Circuit du Lac (ITT)
6	225.5 km, Bordeaux > Limoges
7a	139.5 km, Jaunay-Clan > Angers
7b	4 km, Angers (TTT)
8	246.5 km, Angers > Lorient
9	187 km, Lorient > Rennes
10	174 km, Bagnoles-de-l'Orne > Rouen
11	242.5 km, Rouen > Roubaix
12	192.5 km, Roubaix > Charleroi
13a	46 km, Freiburg > Freiburg (Ger)
13b	159.5 km, Altkirch > Besançon
14	230 km, Besançon > Thonon-les-Bains
15a	105 km, Thonon-les-Bains > Morzine
15b	14 km, Morzine > Avoriaz (ITT)
16	121 km, Morzine > Chamonix
17	184.5 km, Chamonix > Alpe d'Huez
18	199.5 km, Rossignol Voirin > Saint-Étienne
19	171.5 km, Saint-Trivier > Dijon
20	50 km, Dijon (ITT)
21	141.5 km, Montereau > Versailles
22a	6 km, Paris/Champs-Élysées (ITT)
22b	90.7 km, Paris/Champs-Élysées Circuit

1 Bernard Thévenet (Fra)
in 115h 38'30"
2 Hennie Kuiper (Ned)
at 0'48"
3 Lucien van Impe (Bel)
at 3'32"

Jacques Esclassan (Fra)

Lucien van Impe (Bel)

Dietrich Thurau (Ger)

1978

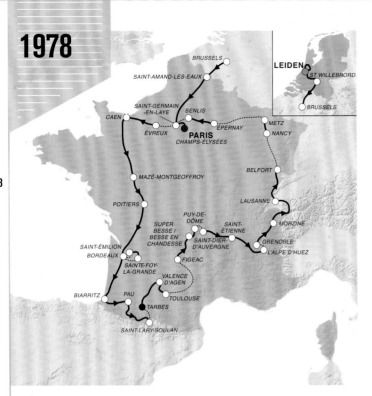

1979

The 1978 Tour de France, which covered 3,908 km at an average speed of 36.084 km/hour, was won by Bernard Hinault who was competing in his first Tour. Stage 12a was annulled after the riders crossed the finishing line on foot in protest about difficult racing conditions and split stages. Belgian Michel Pollentier won the stage to the Alpe d'Huez to take the overall lead, but he was disqualified for trying to cheat a dope test by using a fake urine sample.

Following the riders' protest in 1978, the 1979 Tour contained no split stages. It is the only edition to have two stage finishes on the Alpe d'Huez. Of 150 starters, 89 riders finished the race. Bernard Hinault took his second victory, also winning seven stages. Joop Zoetemelk finished second again, despite a 10-minute doping penalty, and Joachim Agostinho of Portugal was placed third again at the age of 37. The Tour was broadcast in the USA for the first time.

Thursday 29 June–Sunday 23 July

Prologue	5.2 km, Leiden (Ned) (ITT)
1a	135 km, Leiden > St Willebrord (Ned)
1b	100 km, St Willebrord > Brussels (Bel)
2	199 km, Brussels > Saint-Amand-les-Eaux
3	243.5 km, Saint-Amand-les-Eaux > Saint-Germain-en-Laye
4	153 km, Évreux > Caen (TTT)
5	244 km, Caen > Mazé Montgeoffroy
6	166.2 km, Mazé Montgeoffroy > Poitiers
7	242 km, Poitiers > Bordeaux
8	59.3 km, Saint-Émilion > Sainte-Foy-la-Grande (ITT)
9	233 km, Bordeaux > Biarritz
10	191.5 km, Biarritz > Pau
11	161 km, Pau > Saint-Lary-Soulan
12a	Tarbes > Valence d'Agen (cancelled)
12b	96 km, Valence d'Agen > Toulouse
13	221 km, Figeac > Super Besse
14	52.5 km, Besse-en-Chandesse > Puy-de-Dôme (ITT)
15	196 km, Sainte-Dier-d'Auvergne > Saint-Étienne
16	240.5 km, Saint-Étienne > Alpe d'Huez
17	225 km, Grenoble > Morzine
18	137.5 km, Morzine > Lausanne (Swi)
19	181.5 km, Lausanne > Belfort
20	72 km, Metz > Nancy (ITT)
21	207.5 km, Épernay > Senlis
22	161.5 km, Saint-Germain-en-Laye > Paris/Champs-Élysées

1 Bernard Hinault (Fra)
in 108h 18'02"
2 Joop Zoetemelk (Ned)
at 3'56"
3 Joaquim Agostinho (Por)
at 6'54"

Freddy Maertens (Bel)

Mariano Martínez (Fra)

Henk Lubberding (Ned)

Wednesday 27 June–Sunday 22 July

Prologue	5 km, Fleurance (ITT)
1	225 km, Fleurance > Luchon
2	23.9 km, Luchon > Superbagnères (ITT)
3	180.5 km, Luchon > Pau
4	86.6 km, Captieux > Bordeaux (TTT)
5	145.5 km, Neuville-de-Poitou > Angers
6	238.5 km, Angers > Saint-Brieuc
7	158.2 km, Saint-Hilaire-du-Harcouët > Deauville
8	90.2 km, Deauville > Le Havre (TTT)
9	201.2 km, Amiens > Roubaix
10	124 km, Roubaix > Brussels (Bel)
11	33.4 km, Brussels (ITT)
12	193 km, Rochefort (Bel) > Metz
13	202 km, Metz > Ballon d'Alsace
14	248.2 km, Belfort > Évian
15	54.2 km, Évian > Morzine Avoriaz (ITT)
16	201.3 km, Morzine > Les Menuires
17	166.5 km, Les Menuires > Alpe d'Huez
18	118.5 km, Alpe d'Huez > Alpe d'Huez
19	162 km, Alpe d'Huez > Saint-Priest
20	239.6 km, Saint-Priest > Dijon
21	48.8 km, Dijon (ITT)
22	189 km, Dijon > Auxerre
23	205 km, Auxerre > Nogent-sur-Marne
24	180.3 km, Le-Perreux-sur-Marne > Paris/Champs-Élysées

1 Bernard Hinault (Fra)
in 103h 06'50"
2 Joop Zoetemelk (Ned)
at 13'07"
3 Joaquim Agostinho (Por)
at 26'53"

Bernard Hinault (Fra)

Giovanni Battaglin (Ita)

Jean-René Bernaudeau (Fra)

1980

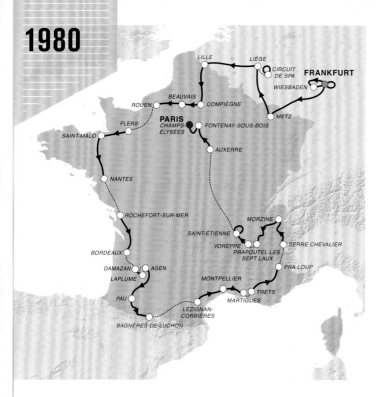

Bernard Hinault was again the favourite in the 1980 Tour, but he had to pull out after stage 12 with an injured knee while leading the race. Joop Zoetemelk finally managed to win at his tenth attempt, after five second places, with Dutchmen also taking the runner-up spot and the white jersey for best young rider. To prevent too much competition for the Lanterne Rouge, the last man on the general classification was eliminated from stages 14–20.

Thursday 26 June–Sunday 20 July

Prologue	7.6 km, Frankfurt (Ger) (ITT)
1a	133 km, Frankfurt > Wiesbaden (Ger)
1b	45.8 km, Wiesbaden > Frankfurt (TTT)
2	276 km, Frankfurt > Metz
3	282 km, Metz > Liège (Bel)
4	34.6 km, Circuit de Spa (Bel) (ITT)
5	249.6 km, Liège > Lille
6	215.8 km, Lille > Compiègne
7a	65 km, Compiègne > Beauvais (TTT)
7b	92 km, Beauvais > Rouen
8	164.2 km, Flers > Saint-Malo
9	205.3 km, Saint-Malo > Nantes
10	203 km, Rochefort-sur-Mer > Bordeaux
11	51.5 km, Damazan > Laplume (ITT)
12	194.1 km, Agen > Pau
13	200.4 km, Pau > Luchon
14	189.5 km, Lézignan-Corbières > Montpellier
15	160 km, Montpellier > Martigues
16	208.6 km, Trets > Pra Loup
17	242 km, Serre Chevalier > Morzine
18	198.8 km, Morzine > Prapoutel les Sept Laux
19	139.7 km, Voreppe > Saint-Étienne
20	34.5 km, Saint-Étienne (ITT)
21	208 km, Auxerre > Fontenay-sous-Bois
22	186.1 km, Fontenay-sous-Bois > Paris/Champs-Élysées

1 Joop Zoetemelk (Ned)
in 109h 19'14"
2 Hennie Kuiper (Ned)
at 6'55"
3 Raymond Martin (Fra)
at 7'56"

Rudy Pévenage (Bel)

Raymond Martin (Fra)

Johan van der Velde (Ned)

1981

Bernard Hinault returned to form for the 68th Tour, swapping his world championship jersey for the yellow one after stage 6 and increasing his lead from then on. Phil Anderson was the only real challenger to 'the Badger'. He was the first Australian to wear the yellow jersey (on stage 6), and kept second place until he lost 17 minutes on the stage to the Alpe d'Huez. This year saw the return of time bonuses at the end of flat stages.

Thursday 25 June–Sunday 19 July

Prologue	5.8 km, Nice (ITT)
1a	97 km, Nice > Nice
1b	40 km, Nice (TTT)
2	254 km, Nice > Martigues
3	232 km, Martigues > Narbonne
4	77.2 km, Narbonne > Carcassonne (TTT)
5	117.5 km, Saint-Gaudens > Saint-Lary-Soulan
6	26.7 km, Nay > Pau (ITT)
7	227 km, Pau > Bordeaux
8	182 km, Rochefort-sur-Mer > Nantes
9	196.5 km, Nantes > Le Mans
10	264 km, Le Mans > Aulnay-sous-Bois
11	246 km, Compiègne > Roubaix
12a	107.3 km, Roubaix > Brussels (Bel)
12b	137.8 km, Brussels > Zolder (Bel)
13	157 km, Beringen (Bel) > Hasselt (Bel)
14	38.5 km, Mulhouse (ITT)
15	231 km, Besançon > Thonon-les-Bains
16	199.5 km, Thonon-les-Bains > Morzine
17	230.5 km, Morzine > Alpe d'Huez
18	131 km, Bourg-d'Oisans > Le Pleynet
19	117.5 km, Veurey > Saint-Priest
20	46.5 km, Saint-Priest (ITT)
21	207 km, Auxerre > Fontenay-sous-Bois
22	186.8 km, Fontenay-sous-Bois > Paris/Champs-Élysées

1 Bernard Hinault (Fra)
in 96h 19'38"
2 Lucien van Impe (Bel)
at 14'34"
3 Robert Alban (Fra)
at 17'04"

Freddy Maertens (Bel)

Lucien van Impe (Bel)

Peter Winnen (Ned)

1982

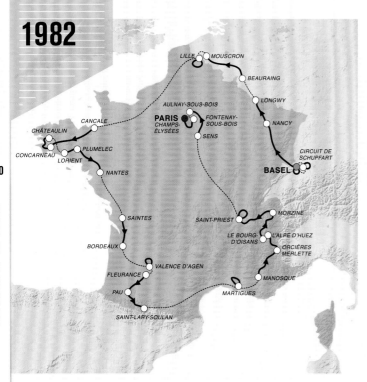

In 1982 Bernard Hinault won his fourth Tour de France, as well as the Giro d'Italia. Phil Anderson led until stage 11 and was the best young rider. Dutch riders took second, third and fourth places overall, while Irishman Sean Kelly dominated the green jersey competition. Lucien van Impe was absent for the first time since 1969. The stage 5 team time trial had to be cancelled when striking steelworkers blocked the road; it was replaced by stage 9a.

Friday 2 July–Sunday 25 July

Prologue 7.4 km, Basle (Swi) (ITT)
1   207 km, Möhlin/Circuit de Schupfart (Swi)
2   250 km, Basle > Nancy
3   134 km, Nancy > Longwy
4   219 km, Beauraing (Bel) > Mouscron (Bel)
5   Orchies > Fontaine au Pire (TTT) (cancelled)
6   233 km, Lille > Lille
7   234.5 km, Cancale > Concarneau
8   200.8 km, Concarneau > Châteaulin
9a   69 km, Lorient > Plumelec (TTT)
9b   138.5 km, Plumelec > Nantes
10   147.2 km, Saintes > Bordeaux
11   57.3 km, Valence d'Agen (ITT)
12   249 km, Fleurance > Pau
13   122 km, Pau > Saint-Lary-Soulan/Plat d'Adet
14   32.5 km, Martigues (ITT)
15   208 km, Manosque > Orcières Merlette
16   123 km, Orcières Merlette > Alpe d'Huez
17   251 km, Bourg-d'Oisans > Morzine
18   233 km, Morzine > Saint-Priest
19   48 km, Saint-Priest (ITT)
20   161 km, Sens > Aulnay-sous-Bois
21   186.8 km, Fontenay-sous-Bois > Paris/Champs-Élysées

1 Bernard Hinault (Fra)
in 92h 08'46"
2 Joop Zoetemelk (Ned)
at 6'21"
3 Johan van der Velde (Ned)
at 8'59"

Sean Kelly (Ire)

Bernard Vallet (Fra)

Phil Anderson (Aus)

1983

The 70th Tour de France was an open one in the absence of Bernard Hinault, who had tendinitis. Pascal Simon took the yellow jersey on stage 10, but fell and broke his shoulder-blade the next day. He held on until stage 17, when 23-year-old Tour debutant Laurent Fignon took over the lead and held it to the end. Lucien van Impe returned to win the polka dot jersey again, while Sean Kelly retained the green jersey and led for one day.

Friday 1 July–Sunday 24 July

Prologue 5.5 km, Fontenay-sous-Bois (ITT)
1   163 km, Nogent-sur-Marne > Créteil
2   100 km, Soissons > Fontaine-au-Pire (TTT)
3   152 km, Valenciennes > Roubaix
4   300 km, Roubaix > Le Havre
5   257 km, Le Havre > Le Mans
6   58.5 km, Châteaubriant > Nantes (ITT)
7   216 km, Nantes > Île d'Oléron
8   222 km, La Rochelle > Bordeaux
9   207 km, Bordeaux > Pau
10   201 km, Pau > Luchon
11   177 km, Luchon > Fleurance
12   261 km, Fleurance > Roquefort-sur-Soulzon
13   210 km, Roquefort-sur-Soulzon > Aurillac
14   149 km, Aurillac > Issoire
15   15.6 km, Clermont-Ferrand > Puy-de-Dôme (ITT)
16   144.5 km, Issoire > Saint-Étienne
17   223 km, La Tour-du-Pin > Alpe d'Huez
18   247 km, Bourg-d'Oisans > Morzine
19   15 km, Morzine > Avoriaz (ITT)
20   291 km, Morzine > Dijon
21   50 km, Dijon (ITT)
22   195 km, Alfortville > Paris/Champs-Élysées

1 Laurent Fignon (Fra)
in 105h 07'52"
2 Ángel Arroyo (Spa)
at 4'04"
3 Peter Winnen (Ned)
at 4'09"

Sean Kelly (Ire)

Lucien van Impe (Bel)

Laurent Fignon (Fra)

1984

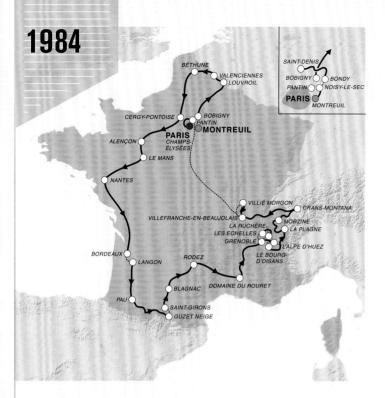

Laurent Fignon retained his title in style, wining all three long individual time trials as well as two Alpine stages. Vincent Barteau held the yellow jersey from stages 6–17. Colombian Luis Herrera's victory on the Alpe d'Huez was the first stage win by a South American, while Greg LeMond was the first US rider to finish on the podium. Robert Millar was the first British rider to claim a jersey – the polka dot one – in Paris.

Friday 29 June–Sunday 22 July

Prologue	5.4 km, Montreuil-sous-Bois > Noisy-le-Sec (ITT)
1	148.5 km, Bondy > Saint-Denis
2	249.5 km, Bobigny > Louvroil
3	51 km, Louvroil > Valenciennes (TTT)
4	83 km, Valenciennes > Béthune
5	207 km, Béthune > Cergy-Pontoise
6	202 km, Cergy-Pontoise > Alençon
7	67 km, Alençon > Le Mans (ITT)
8	192 km, Le Mans > Nantes
9	338 km, Nantes > Bordeaux
10	198 km, Langon > Pau
11	226.5 km, Pau > Guzet Neige
12	111 km, Saint-Girons > Blagnac
13	220.5 km, Blagnac > Rodez
14	227.5 km, Rodez > Domaine de Rouret
15	241.5 km, Domaine de Rouret > Grenoble
16	22 km, Les Échelles > La Ruchère (ITT)
17	151 km, Grenoble > Alpe d'Huez
18	185 km, Bourg-d'Oisans > La Plagne
19	186 km, La Plagne > Morzine
20	140.5 km, Morzine > Crans-Montana (Swi)
21	320.5 km, Crans-Montana > Villefranche-en-Beaujolais
22	51 km, Villié-Morgon > Villefranche-en-Beaujolais (ITT)
23	196.5 km, Pantin > Paris/Champs-Élysées

1 Laurent Fignon (Fra)
in 112h 03'40"
2 Bernard Hinault (Fra)
at 10'32"
3 Greg LeMond (USA)
at 11'46"

Frank Hoste (Bel)

Robert Millar (UK)

Greg LeMond (USA)

1985

In the absence of an injured Laurent Fignon, Bernard Hinault became the third rider to win five Tours despite breaking his nose in a crash on stage 14. Stephen Roche was the first Irishman on the podium. This was the first Tour for future Spanish star Miguel Indurain, who pulled out on stage 4. Among several mountain top finishes was the new climb of Luz Ardiden where Greg LeMond was instructed to wait for his team-mate Hinault and lost several minutes.

Friday 28 June–Sunday 21 July

Prologue	6.8 km, Plumelec (ITT)
1	256 km, Vannes > Lanester
2	242 km, Lorient > Vitré
3	73 km, Vitré > Fougères (TTT)
4	239 km, Fougères > Pont-Audemer
5	224 km, Neufchâtel-en-Bray > Roubaix
6	221.5 km, Roubaix > Reims
7	217.5 km, Reims > Nancy
8	75 km, Sarrebourg > Strasbourg (ITT)
9	173.5 km, Strasbourg > Épinal
10	204.5 km, Épinal > Pontarlier
11	195 km, Pontarlier > Morzine Avoriaz
12	269 km, Morzine > Lans-en-Vercors
13	31.8 km, Villard-de-Lans (ITT)
14	179 km, Autrans > Saint-Étienne
15	237.5 km, Saint-Étienne > Aurillac
16	247 km, Aurillac > Toulouse
17	209.5 km, Toulouse > Luz Ardiden
18a	52.5 km, Luz-Saint-Sauveur > Col d'Aubisque
18b	83.5 km, Laruns > Pau
19	203 km, Pau > Bordeaux
20	225 km, Montpon-Ménestérol > Limoges
21	45.7 km, Circuit du Lac de Vassivière (ITT)
22	196 km, Orléans > Paris/Champs-Élysées

1 Bernard Hinault (Fra)
in 113h 24'23"
2 Greg LeMond (USA)
at 1'42"
3 Stephen Roche (Ire)
at 4'29"

Sean Kelly (Ire)

Luis Herrera (Col)

Fabio Parra (Col)

1986

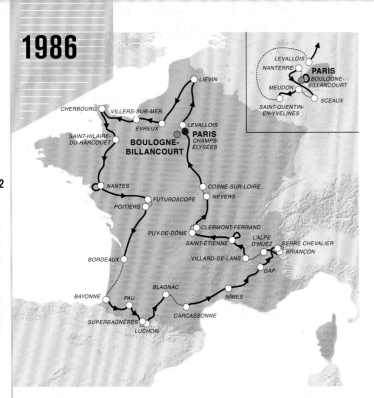

272

THE ATLAS OF 100 TOURS

1987

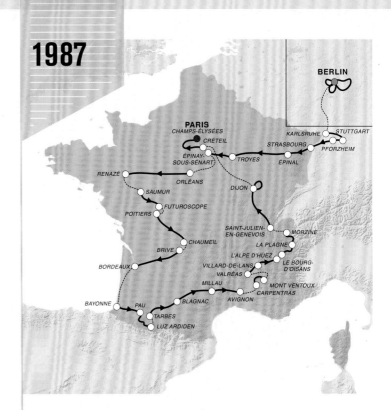

The 1986 Tour covered 4,083 km at an average speed of 37.02 km/hour and 132 of the 210 riders who started completed the course. Bernard Hinault had promised to help Greg LeMond this year but constantly attacked, including on the Alpe d'Huez where LeMond caught him; the two crossed the line hand-in-hand. Another American, Andy Hampsten, won the white jersey while Alex Stieda was the first Canadian to wear the yellow jersey. Hinault retired shortly after the race.

The first few stages of this tough and mountainous Tour de France were held in Germany. The large field (209 riders started) led to numerous crashes, which the European riders blamed on the Colombians. Greg LeMond did not take part, following a serious shooting accident. Jean-François Bernard won the time trial up Mont Ventoux, but was unable to consolidate his lead. An epic battle between Stephen Roche and Pedro Delgado was resolved only in the final time trial.

Friday 4 July–Sunday 27 July

Prologue 4.6 km, Boulogne-Billancourt (ITT)
1   85 km, Nanterre > Sceaux
2   56 km, Meudon > Saint-Quentin-en-Yvelines (TTT)
3   214 km, Levallois > Liévin
4   243 km, Liévin > Évreux
5   124.5 km, Évreux > Villers-sur-Mer
6   200 km, Villers-sur-Mer > Cherbourg
7   201 km, Cherbourg > Saint-Hilaire-du-Harcouët
8   204 km, Saint-Hilaire-du-Harcouët > Nantes
9   61.5 km, Nantes (ITT)
10 183 km, Nantes > Futuroscope
11 258.3 km, Poitiers > Bordeaux
12 217.5 km, Bayonne > Pau
13 186 km, Pau > Superbagnères
14 154 km, Luchon > Blagnac
15 225.5 km, Carcassonne > Nîmes
16 246.5 km, Nîmes > Gap
17 190 km, Gap > Serre Chevalier
18 162.5 km, Briançon > Alpe d'Huez
19 179.5 km, Villard-de-Lans > Saint-Étienne
20 58 km, Saint-Étienne (ITT)
21 190 km, Saint-Étienne > Puy-de-Dôme
22 194 km, Clermont-Ferrand > Nevers
23 255 km, Cosne-sur-Loire > Paris/ Champs-Élysées

1 Greg LeMond (USA)
in 110h 35'19"
2 Bernard Hinault (Fra)
at 3'10"
3 Urs Zimmermann (Swi)
at 10'54"

Eric Vanderaerden (Bel)

Bernard Hinault (Fra)

Andy Hampsten (USA)

Wednesday 1 July–Sunday 26 July

Prologue 6.1 km, Berlin (Ger) (ITT)
1   105.5 km, Berlin > Berlin
2   40.5 km, Berlin (TTT)
3   219 km, Karlsruhe (Ger) > Stuttgart (Ger)
4   79 km, Stuttgart > Pforzheim (Ger)
5   112.5 km, Pforzheim > Strasbourg
6   169 km, Strasbourg > Épinal
7   211 km, Épinal > Troyes
8   205.5 km, Troyes > Épinay-sous-Sénart
9   260 km, Orléans > Renazé
10 87.5 km, Saumur > Futuroscope (ITT)
11 255 km, Poitiers > Chaumeil
12 228 km, Brive > Bordeaux
13 219 km, Bayonne > Pau
14 166 km, Pau > Luz Ardiden
15 164 km, Tarbes > Blagnac
16 216.5 km, Blagnac > Millau
17 239 km, Millau > Avignon
18 36.5 km, Carpentras > Mont Ventoux (ITT)
19 185 km, Valréas > Villard-de-Lans
20 201 km, Villard-de-Lans > Alpe d'Huez
21 185.5 km, Bourg-d'Oisans > La Plagne
22 186 km, La Plagne > Morzine
23 224.5 km, Saint-Julien-en-Genevois > Dijon
24 38 km, Dijon (ITT)
25 192 km, Créteil > Paris/ Champs-Élysées

1 Stephen Roche (Ire)
in 115h 27'42"
2 Pedro Delgado (Spa)
at 0'40"
3 Jean-François Bernard (Fra)
at 2'13"

Jean-Paul van Poppel (Ned)

Luis Herrera (Col)

Raúl Alcalá (Mex)

1988

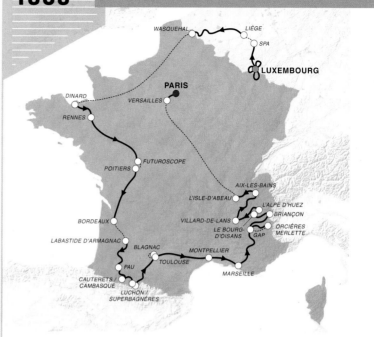

The 75th Tour started with a prelude in which lead riders were launched by their teams for a flying 1 km that did not count towards the overall time. Stephen Roche was injured and Pedro Delgado won the race in controversial circumstances. He led from stage 12 onwards but tested positive for probenecid, a steroid-masking agent that was not added to the list of prohibited drugs until after the Tour. He could not be disqualified, and declined to leave voluntarily.

Monday 4 July–Sunday 24 July
Prologue 1 km, Pornichet > La Baule (T/ITT)
1   91.5 km, Pontchateau > Machecoul
2   48 km, La Haye Fouassière > Ancenis (TTT)
3   213.5 km, Nantes > Le Mans
4   158 km, Le Mans > Évreux
5   147.5 km, Neufchâtel-en-Bray > Liévin
6   52 km, Liévin > Wasquehal (ITT)
7   225.5 km, Wasquehal > Reims
8   219 km, Reims > Nancy
9   160.5 km, Nancy > Strasbourg
10   149.5 km, Belfort > Besançon
11   232 km, Besançon > Morzine
12   227 km, Morzine > Alpe d'Huez
13   38 km, Grenoble > Villard-de-Lans (ITT)
14   163 km, Blagnac > Guzet Neige
15   187.5 km, Saint-Girons > Luz Ardiden
16   38 km, Tarbes > Pau
17   210 km, Pau > Bordeaux
18   93.5 km, Ruelle-sur-Touvre > Limoges
19   188 km, Limoges > Puy-de-Dôme
20   223.5 km, Clermont-Ferrand > Chalon-sur-Saône
21   46 km, Santenay (ITT)
22   172.5 km, Nemours > Paris/Champs-Élysées

1 Pedro Delgado (Spa)
in 84h 27'53"
2 Steven Rooks (Ned)
at 7'13"
3 Fabio Parra (Col)
at 9'58"

Eddy Planckaert (Bel)

Steven Rooks (Ned)

Erik Breukink (Ned)

1989

This memorable Tour began with Pedro Delgado starting the prologue 2 minutes 54 seconds late, a deficit that he never made up. Throughout the race no more than 53 seconds separated Greg LeMond, returning following his shooting accident, and Laurent Fignon. The Frenchman led by 50 seconds going into the final time trial into Paris, but the American overturned this advantage to win by the smallest ever margin. Sean Kelly won the green jersey for the fourth and final time.

Saturday 1 July–Sunday 23 July
Prologue 7.8 km, Luxembourg (Lux) (ITT)
1   135.5 km, Luxembourg > Luxembourg
2   46 km, Luxembourg (TTT)
3   241 km, Luxembourg > Spa (Bel)
4   255 km, Liège (Bel) > Wasquehal
5   73 km, Dinard > Rennes (ITT)
6   259 km, Rennes > Futuroscope
7   258.5 km, Poitiers > Bordeaux
8   157 km, Labastide-d'Armagnac > Pau
9   147 km, Pau > Cauterets/Cambasque
10   136 km, Cauterets > Superbagnères
11   158 km, Luchon > Blagnac
12   242 km, Toulouse > Montpellier
13   179 km, Montpellier > Marseilles
14   240 km, Marseilles > Gap
15   39 km, Gap > Orcières Merlette (ITT)
16   175 km, Gap > Briançon
17   165 km, Briançon > Alpe d'Huez
18   91.5 km, Bourg-d'Oisans > Villard-de-Lans
19   125 km, Villard-de-Lans > Aix-les-Bains
20   130 km, Aix-les-Bains > L'Isle-d'Abeau
21   24.5 km, Versailles > Paris/Champs-Élysées (ITT)

1 Greg LeMond (USA)
in 87h 38'35"
2 Laurent Fignon (Fra)
at 0'08"
3 Pedro Delgado (Spa)
at 3'34"

Sean Kelly (Ire)

Gert-Jan Theunisse (Ned)

Best Young Rider
Fabrice Philipot (Fra)

1990

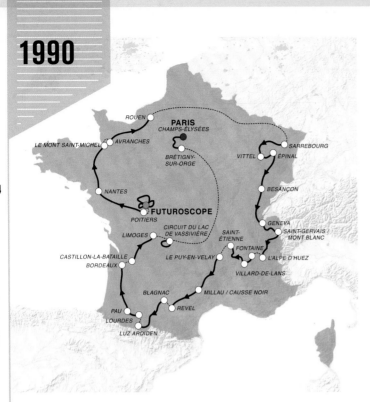

1991

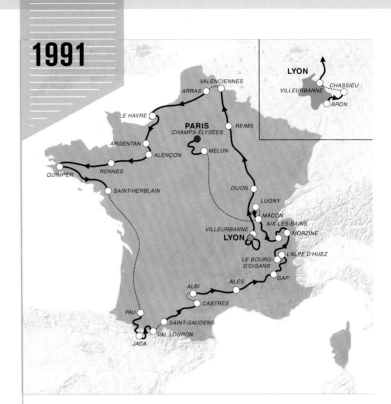

After the dramatic final day time trial in 1989, the 1990 Tour reverted to the familiar final stage on the Champs-Élysées. A break including Italian climber Claudio Chiappucci finished 9 minutes ahead of the peloton on stage 1. Chiappucci took the yellow jersey on stage 12 and held it until Greg LeMond claimed it on stage 20. He was the first Italian for 15 years to wear the jersey. Dmitri Konyshev was the first Soviet rider to win a stage.

1991 saw Thierry Marie escape on stage 6 for one of the longest ever lone breaks (234 km). Miguel Indurain, in his seventh Tour, took over the lead on stage 13 when Greg LeMond was distanced on the Col du Tourmalet, and held it to achieve the first of his five overall victories. Gianni Bugno won at the top of the Alpe d'Huez to claim second place on the podium. Green jersey winner Djamolidine Abdoujaparov crashed spectacularly on the Champs-Élysées.

Saturday 30 June–Sunday 22 July

Prologue	6.3 km, Futuroscope (ITT)
1	138.5 km, Futuroscope > Futuroscope
2	44.5 km, Futuroscope (TTT)
3	233 km, Poitiers > Nantes
4	203 km, Nantes > Mont Saint-Michel
5	301 km, Avranches > Rouen
6	202.5 km, Sarrebourg > Vittel
7	61.5 km, Vittel > Épinal (ITT)
8	181.5 km, Épinal > Besançon
9	196 km, Besançon > Geneva (Swi)
10	118.5 km, Geneva > Saint-Gervais/ Mont Blanc
11	182.5 km, Saint-Gervais > Alpe d'Huez
12	33.5 km, Fontaine > Villard-de-Lans (ITT)
13	149 km, Villard-de-Lans > Saint-Étienne
14	205 km, Le Puy-en-Velay > Millau/ Causse Noir
15	170 km, Millau > Revel
16	215 km, Blagnac > Luz Ardiden
17	150 km, Lourdes > Pau
18	202 km, Pau > Bordeaux
19	182.5 km, Castillon-la-Bataille > Limoges
20	45.5 km, Circuit du Lac de Vassivière (ITT)
21	182.5 km, Brétigny-sur-Orge > Paris/ Champs-Élysées

1 Greg LeMond (USA)
in 90h 43'20"

2 Claudio Chiappucci (Ita)
at 2'16"

3 Erik Breukink (Ned)
at 2'29"

Olaf Ludwig (Ger)

Thierry Claveyrolat (Fra)

Best Young Rider
Gilles Delion (Fra)

Saturday 6 July–Sunday 28 July

Prologue	5.4 km, Lyon (ITT)
1	114.5 km, Lyon > Lyon
2	36.5 km, Bron > Chassieu (TTT)
3	210.5 km, Villeurbanne > Dijon
4	286 km, Dijon > Reims
5	149.5 km, Reims > Valenciennes
6	259 km, Arras > Le Havre
7	167 km, Le Havre > Argentan
8	73 km, Argentan > Alençon (ITT)
9	161 km, Alençon > Rennes
10	207.5 km, Rennes > Quimper
11	246 km, Quimper > Saint-Herblain
12	192 km, Pau > Jaca (Spa)
13	232 km, Jaca > Val Louron
14	172.5 km, Saint-Gaudens > Castres
15	235 km, Albi > Alès
16	215 km, Alès > Gap
17	125 km, Gap > Alpe d'Huez
18	255 km, Bourg-d'Oisans > Morzine
19	177 km, Morzine > Aix-les-Bains
20	160 km, Aix-les-Bains > Mâcon
21	57 km, Lugny > Mâcon (ITT)
22	178 km, Melun > Paris/ Champs-Élysées

1 Miguel Indurain (Spa)
in 101h 01'20"

2 Gianni Bugno (Ita)
at 3'36"

3 Claudio Chiappucci (Ita)
at 5'56"

Djamolidine Abdoujaparov
(USSR)

Claudio Chiappucci (Ita)

Best Young Rider
Álvaro Mejía (Col)

1992

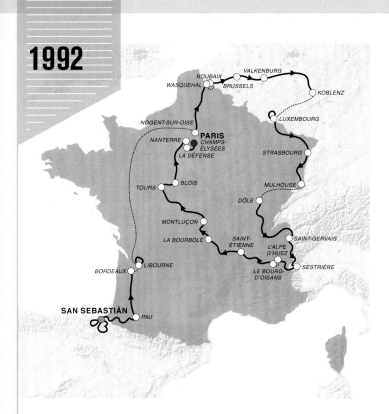

The 1992 Tour visited six countries in addition to France to celebrate the Maastricht Treaty. The same three men stood on the final podium as in the previous year. Miguel Indurain added his second Tour to his victory in the Giro d'Italia. Claudio Chiappucci climbed into second place after a 125-km lone break into Sestriere and retained the polka dot jersey. Andy Hampsten won on the Alpe d'Huez. Emerging French talents included Laurent Jalabert, Luc Leblanc, Richard Virenque and Pascal Lino.

Saturday 4 July–Sunday 26 July

Prologue	8 km, San Sebastián (Spa) (ITT)
1	194.5 km, San Sebastián > San Sebastián
2	255 km, San Sebastián > Pau
3	210 km, Pau > Bordeaux
4	63.5 km, Libourne (TTT)
5	196 km, Nogent-sur-Oise > Wasquehal
6	167 km, Roubaix > Brussels (Bel)
7	196.5 km, Brussels > Valkenburg (Ned)
8	206.5 km, Valkenburg > Koblenz (Ger)
9	65 km, Luxembourg (Lux) (ITT)
10	217 km, Luxembourg > Strasbourg
11	249.5 km, Strasbourg > Mulhouse
12	267.5 km, Dôle > Saint-Gervais
13	254.5 km, Saint-Gervais > Sestriere (Ita)
14	186.5 km, Sestriere > Alpe d'Huez
15	198 km, Bourg-d'Oisans > Saint-Étienne
16	212 km, Saint-Étienne > La Bourboule
17	189 km, La Bourboule > Montluçon
18	212 km, Montluçon > Tours
19	64 km, Tours > Blois (ITT)
20	222 km, Blois > Nanterre
21	141 km, La Défense > Paris/Champs-Élysées

1 Miguel Indurain (Spa)
in 100h 49'30"

2 Claudio Chiappucci (Ita)
at 4'35"

3 Gianni Bugno (Ita)
at 10'49"

Laurent Jalabert (Fra)

Claudio Chiappucci (Ita)

Best Young Rider
Eddy Bouwmans (Ned)

1993

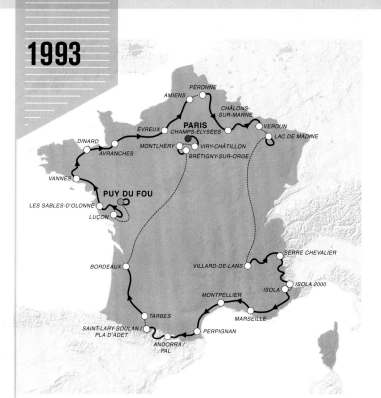

In the 80th Tour de France Miguel Indurain won for the third year running and completed his second Giro-Tour double. Tony Rominger was the main challenger, but lost vital minutes in a poor team time trial. Indurain took the lead after stage 9 and never looked in danger of losing it. Zenon Jaskula was the first Polish rider to mount the final podium. The French had no rider in the top ten and only one stage victory, by Pascal Lino.

Saturday 3 July–Sunday 25 July

Prologue	6.8 km, Le Puy du Fou (ITT)
1	215 km, Luçon > Les Sables-d'Olonne
2	227.5 km, Les Sables-d'Olonne > Vannes
3	189.5 km, Vannes > Dinard
4	81 km, Dinard > Avranches (TTT)
5	225.5 km, Avranches > Évreux
6	158 km, Évreux > Amiens
7	199 km, Péronne > Châlons-sur-Marne
8	184.5 km, Châlons-sur-Marne > Verdun
9	59 km, Lac de Madine (ITT)
10	203 km, Villard-de-Lans > Serre Chevalier
11	179 km, Serre Chevalier > Isola 2000
12	286.5 km, Isola > Marseille
13	181.5 km, Marseille > Montpellier
14	223 km, Montpellier > Perpignan
15	231.5 km, Perpignan > Andorra (And)
16	230 km, Andorra > Saint-Lary-Soulan/ Pla d'Adet
17	190 km, Tarbes > Pau
18	199.5 km, Orthez > Bordeaux
19	48 km, Brétigny-sur-Orge > Montlhéry (ITT)
20	196.5 km, Viry-Châtillon > Paris/ Champs-Élysées

1 Miguel Indurain (Spa)
in 95h 57'09"

2 Tony Rominger (Swi)
at 4'59"

3 Zenon Jaskula (Pol)
at 5'48"

Djamolidine Abdoujaparov
(Uzb)

Tony Rominger (Swi)

Best Young Rider
Antonio Martín (Spa)

1994

British time trial specialist Chris Boardman took the yellow jersey in the prologue but lost it in the team time trial before the race crossed the Channel for two stages in southern England. His fellow countryman Sean Yates also held it for one day before Miguel Indurain took the lead after stage 9. A policeman taking a photo in Armentières caused a spectacular crash and serious injury to Laurent Jalabert, while Richard Virenque beat Marco Pantani in the mountains competition.

Saturday 2 July–Sunday 2 July
Prologue 7.2 km, Lille (ITT)

1	234 km, Lille > Armentières
2	203.5 km, Roubaix > Boulogne-sur-Mer
3	66.5 km, Calais > Eurotunnel (TTT)
4	204.5 km, Dover (UK) > Brighton (UK)
5	187 km, Portsmouth > Portsmouth (UK)
6	270.5 km, Cherbourg > Rennes
7	259.5 km, Rennes > Futuroscope
8	218.5 km, Poitiers > Trélissac
9	64 km, Périgueux > Bergerac (ITT)
10	160.5 km, Bergerac > Cahors
11	263.5 km, Cahors > Lourdes/Hautacam
12	204.5 km, Lourdes > Luz Ardiden
13	223 km, Bagnères-de-Bigorre > Albi
14	202 km, Castres > Montpellier
15	231 km, Montpellier > Carpentras
16	224.5 km, Valréas > Alpe d'Huez
17	149 km, Bourg-d'Oisans > Val Thorens
18	174.5 km, Moûtiers > Cluses
19	47.5 km, Cluses > Morzine/Alvoriaz (ITT)
20	208.5 km, Morzine > Lac Saint-Point
21	175 km, Disneyland Paris > Paris/Champs-Élysées

1 Miguel Indurain (Spa)
in 103h 38'38"
2 Piotr Ugrumov (Lat)
at 5'39"
3 Marco Pantani (Ita)
at 7'19"

Djamolidine Abdoujaparov (Uzb)

Richard Virenque (Fra)

Best Young Rider
Marco Pantani (Ita)

1995

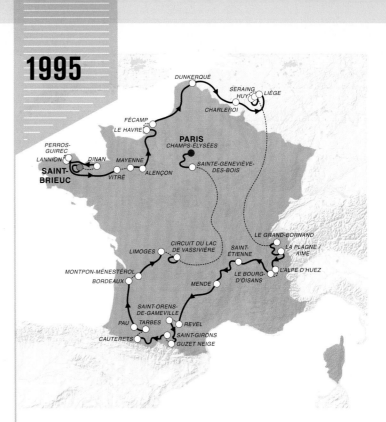

In 1995 Miguel Indurain became the first man to win five consecutive Tours. Marco Pantani won the stage to the Alpe d'Huez and Laurent Jalabert led a long breakaway to win in Mende on Bastille Day. The Tour was marred by the death of Olympic champion Fabio Casartelli on the descent of the Portet d'Aspet on stage 15. The next stage was annulled, with the Motorola team crossing the line together. Casartelli's team-mate Lance Armstrong went on to win stage 18.

Saturday 1 July–Sunday 23 July
Prologue 7.3 km, Saint-Brieuc (ITT)

1	233.5 km, Dinan > Lannion
2	235.5 km, Perros-Guirec > Vitré
3	67 km, Mayenne > Alençon (TTT)
4	162 km, Alençon > Le Havre
5	261 km, Fécamp > Dunkerque
6	202 km, Dunkerque > Charleroi (Bel)
7	203 km, Charleroi > Liège (Bel)
8	54 km, Huy (Bel) > Seraing (Bel) (ITT)
9	160 km, Le Grand-Bornand > La Plagne
10	162.5 km, Aime La Plagne > Alpe d'Huez
11	199 km, Bourg-d'Oisans > Saint-Étienne
12	222.5 km, Saint-Étienne > Mende
13	245 km, Mende > Revel
14	164 km, Saint-Orens-de-Gameville > Guzet Neige
15	206 km, Saint-Girons > Cauterets
16	149 km, Tarbes > Pau (neutralized)
17	246 km, Pau > Bordeaux
18	166.5 km, Montpon-Ménestérol > Limoges
19	46.5 km, Limousin/Lac de Vassivière (ITT)
20	155 km, Sainte-Geneviève-des-Bois > Paris/Champs-Élysées

1 Miguel Indurain (Spa)
in 92h 44'59"
2 Alex Zülle (Swi)
at 4'35"
3 Bjarne Riis (Den)
at 6'47"

Laurent Jalabert (Fra)

Richard Virenque (Fra)

Best Young Rider
Marco Pantani (Ita)

1996

Miguel Indurain was again the favourite in 1996 but struggled with illness in the first week and never recovered. Bjarne Riis took the yellow jersey after winning in Sestriere on a stage shortened by snow, and went on to be the first Danish winner. He later admitted to using performance-enhancing EPO during the race, as did green jersey winner Erik Zabel. This was the first Tour since 1975 not to include a team time trial. Lance Armstrong withdrew, feeling ill, on stage 7.

Saturday 29 June–Sunday 21 July

Prologue 9.4 km, 's-Hertogenbosch (Ned) (ITT)

1	209 km, 's-Hertogenbosch > 's-Hertogenbosch
2	247.5 km, 's-Hertogenbosch > Wasquehal
3	195 km, Wasquehal > Nogent-sur-Oise
4	232 km, Soissons > Lac de Madine
5	242 km, Lac de Madine > Besançon
6	207 km, Arc-et-Senans > Aix-les-Bains
7	200 km, Chambéry > Les Arcs
8	30.5 km, Bourg-Saint-Maurice > Val-d'Isère (ITT)
9	46 km, Le Monêtier-les-Bains > Sestriere (Ita)
10	208.5 km, Turin (Ita) > Gap
11	202 km, Gap > Valence
12	143.5 km, Valence > Le Puy-en-Velay
13	177 km, Le Puy-en-Velay > Super Besse
14	186.5 km, Besse-en-Chandesse > Tulle
15	176 km, Brive > Villeneuve-sur-Lot
16	199 km, Agen > Lourdes/Hautacam
17	262 km, Argelès-Gazost > Pamplona (Spa)
18	154.5 km, Pamplona > Hendaye
19	226.5 km, Hendaye > Bordeaux
20	63.5 km, Bordeaux > Saint-Émilion (ITT)
21	147.5 km, Palaiseau > Paris/Champs-Élysées

1 Bjarne Riis (Den)
in 95h 57'16"

2 Jan Ullrich (Ger)
at 1'41"

3 Richard Virenque (Fra)
at 4'37"

Erik Zabel (Ger)

Richard Virenque (Fra)

Best Young Rider
Jan Ullrich (Ger)

1997

The 1997 Tour covered 3942.3 km at an average speed of 39.22 km/hour and 139 of the 198 starters finished the race. Jan Ullrich, after finishing second in his first Tour at the age of 22, became the first German to win the overall classification. Richard Virenque won the polka dot jersey for the fourth consecutive year and also finished second overall ahead of another specialist climber, Marco Pantani, who won two Alpine stages, including the one to the Alpe d'Huez.

Saturday 5 July–Sunday 27 July

Prologue 7.3 km, Rouen (ITT)

1	192 km, Rouen > Forges-les-Eaux
2	262 km, Saint-Valéry-en-Caux > Vire
3	224 km, Vire > Plumelec
4	223 km, Plumelec > Le Puy du Fou
5	261.5 km, Chantonnay > La Châtre
6	215.5 km, Le Blanc > Marennes
7	194 km, Marennes > Bordeaux
8	161.5 km, Sauternes > Pau
9	182 km, Pau > Loudenvielle/Vallée du Louron
10	252.5 km, Luchon > Andorra Arcalís (And)
11	192 km, Andorra > Perpignan
12	55.5 km, Saint-Étienne (ITT)
13	203.5 km, Saint-Étienne > Alpe d'Huez
14	148 km, Bourg-d'Oisans > Courchevel
15	208.5 km, Courchevel > Morzine
16	181 km, Morzine > Fribourg (Swi)
17	218.5 km, Fribourg > Colmar
18	175.5 km, Colmar > Montbéliard
19	172 km, Montbéliard > Dijon
20	63 km, Disneyland Paris (ITT)
21	149.5 km, Disneyland Paris > Paris/Champs-Élysées

1 Jan Ullrich (Ger)
in 100h 30'35"

2 Richard Virenque (Fra)
at 9'09"

3 Marco Pantani (Ita)
at 14'03"

Erik Zabel (Ger)

Richard Virenque (Fra)

Best Young Rider
Jan Ullrich (Ger)

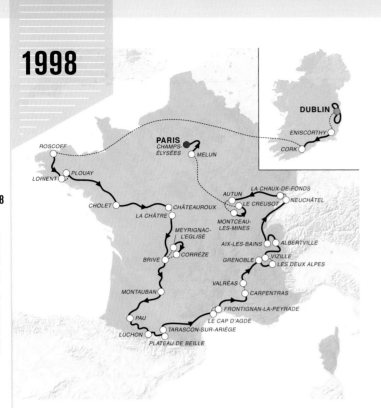

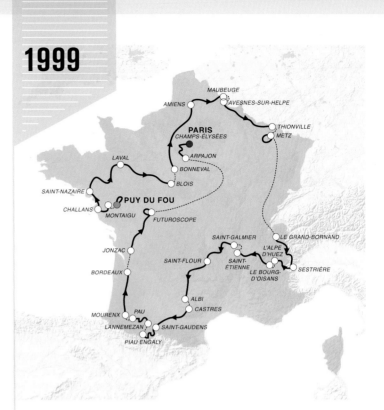

The 85th Tour de France began in Ireland with Chris Boardman winning the prologue with an impressive 54.2 km/hour ride. Thereafter it turned into the 'Tour du Dopage', with the scandal of the Festina affair. The whole Festina team pulled out after the discovery of drugs in a *soigneur*'s car, followed by all the Spanish teams in protest against police raids. Marco Pantani added the Tour to his Giro d'Italia win, while Jan Ullrich took both individual time trials.

In 1999 Lance Armstrong rode the Tour de France for the first time since being diagnosed with testicular cancer in 1996, and gained the first of his seven victories. There were no French stage winners for the first time since 1926, while Mario Cipollini won four consecutive stages to set a post-World War II record. Giuseppe Guerini was brought down by a cameraman who jumped out in front of him near the top of the Alpe d'Huez, but continued to win the stage.

Saturday 11 July–Sunday 2 August

Prologue	5.6 km, Dublin (Ire) (ITT)
1	180.5 km, Dublin > Dublin
2	205.5 km, Enniscorthy (Ire) > Cork (Ire)
3	169 km, Roscoff > Lorient
4	252 km, Plouay > Cholet
5	228.5 km, Cholet > Châteauroux
6	204.5 km, La Châtre > Brive
7	58 km, Meyrignac-l'Église > Corrèze (ITT)
8	190.5 km, Brive > Montauban
9	210 km, Montauban > Pau
10	196.5 km, Pau > Luchon
11	170 km, Luchon > Plateau de Beille
12	222 km, Tarascon-sur-Ariège > Le Cap d'Agde
13	196 km, Frontignan-la-Peyrade > Carpentras
14	186.5 km, Valréas > Grenoble
15	189 km, Grenoble > Les Deux Alpes
16	204 km, Vizille > Albertville
17	149 km, Albertville > Aix-les-Bains
18	218.5 km, Aix-les-Bains > Neuchâtel (Swi)
19	242 km, La Chaux-de-Fonds (Swi) > Autun
20	52 km, Montceau-les-Mines > Le Creusot (ITT)
21	147.5 km, Melun > Paris/Champs-Élysées

1 Marco Pantani (Ita)
in 92h 49'46"
2 Jan Ullrich (Ger)
at 3'21"
3 Bobby Julich (USA)
at 4'08"

Erik Zabel (Ger)

Christophe Rinero (Fra)

Best Young Rider
Jan Ullrich (Ger)

Saturday 3 July–Sunday 25 July

Prologue	6.8 km, Le Puy du Fou (ITT)
1	208 km, Montaigu > Challans
2	176 km, Challans > Saint-Nazaire
3	194.5 km, Saint-Nazaire > Laval
4	194.5 km, Laval > Blois
5	233.5 km, Bonneval > Amiens
6	171.5 km, Amiens > Maubeuge
7	227 km, Avesnes-sur-Helpe > Thionville
8	56.5 km, Metz (ITT)
9	213.5 km, Le Grand-Bornand > Sestriere (Ita)
10	220.5 km, Sestriere > Alpe d'Huez
11	198.5 km, Bourg-d'Oisans > Saint-Étienne
12	201.5 km, Saint-Galmier > Saint-Flour
13	236.5 km, Saint-Flour > Albi
14	199 km, Castres > Saint-Gaudens
15	173 km, Saint-Gaudens > Piau Engaly
16	192 km, Lannemezan > Pau
17	200 km, Mourenx > Bordeaux
18	184.5 km, Jonzac > Futuroscope
19	57 km, Futuroscope (ITT)
20	143.5 km, Arpajon > Paris/Champs-Élysées

1 Lance Armstrong (USA)*
in 91h 32'16"
2 Alex Zülle (Swi)
at 7'37"
3 Fernando Escartín (Spa)
at 10'26"

Erik Zabel (Ger)

Richard Virenque (Fra)

Best Young Rider
Benoît Salmon (Fra)

* Title stripped in 2012.
No replacement winner declared.

2000

The first Tour de France of the new millennium started with a 16.5 km time trial (won by David Millar of Scotland) instead of the usual prologue, and saw the first team time trial for five years. Lance Armstrong took the yellow jersey on stage 10 and kept it for the rest of the race. Armstrong and Marco Pantani arrived together at the top of Mont Ventoux; Armstrong said that he gifted the stage to Pantani, but the latter denied this.

Saturday 1 July–Sunday 23 July
1. 16.5 km, Futuroscope (ITT)
2. 194 km, Futuroscope > Loudun
3. 161.5 km, Loudun > Nantes
4. 70 km, Nantes > Saint-Nazaire (TTT)
5. 202 km, Vannes > Vitré
6. 198.5 km, Vitré > Tours
7. 205.5 km, Tours > Limoges
8. 203.5 km, Limoges > Villeneuve-sur-Lot
9. 181 km, Agen > Dax
10. 205 km, Dax > Lourdes/Hautacam
11. 218.5 km, Bagnères-de-Bigorre > Revel
12. 149 km, Carpentras > Mont Ventoux
13. 185.5 km, Avignon > Draguignan
14. 249.5 km, Draguignan > Briançon
15. 173.5 km, Briançon > Courchevel
16. 196.5 km, Courchevel > Morzine
17. 155 km, Évian-les-Bains > Lausanne (Swi)
18. 246.5 km, Lausanne > Freiburg (Ger)
19. 58.5 km, Freiburg > Mulhouse (ITT)
20. 254.5 km, Belfort > Troyes
21. 138 km, Paris/Eiffel Tower > Paris/Champs-Élysées

1 Lance Armstrong (USA)*
in 92h 33'08"
2 Jan Ullrich (Ger)
at 6'02"
3 Joseba Beloki (Spa)
at 10'04"

Erik Zabel (Ger)

Santiago Botero (Col)

Francisco Mancebo (Spa)

* Title stripped in 2012.
No replacement winner declared.

2001

The 2001 Tour de France was shorter than previous editions, at 3,455 km, but was a difficult one with a long team time trial, two individual time trials and five consecutive mountain top finishes. The final podium was the same as the previous year, with Jan Ullrich achieving his fourth second place, while Erik Zabel won a record sixth consecutive green jersey. Lance Armstrong was more dominant than ever and Laurent Jalabert transformed from a sprinter to a climber.

Saturday 7 July–Sunday 29 July
Prologue 8.2 km, Dunkerque (ITT)
1. 194.5 km, Saint-Omer > Boulogne-sur-Mer
2. 218.5 km, Calais > Antwerp (Bel)
3. 198.5 km, Antwerp > Seraing (Bel)
4. 215 km, Huy (Bel) > Verdun
5. 67 km, Verdun > Bar-le-Duc (TTT)
6. 211.5 km, Commercy > Strasbourg
7. 162.5 km, Strasbourg > Colmar
8. 222.5 km, Colmar > Pontarlier
9. 185 km, Pontarlier > Aix-les-Bains
10. 209 km, Aix-les-Bains > Alpe d'Huez
11. 32 km, Grenoble > Chamrousse (TTT)
12. 166.5 km, Perpignan > Ax-les-Thermes/
Plateau de Bonascre
13. 194 km, Foix > Saint-Lary-Soulan/Pla d'Adet
14. 141.5 km, Tarbes > Luz Ardiden
15. 232.5 km, Pau > Lavaur
16. 229.5 km, Castelsarrasin > Sarran
17. 194 km, Brive > Montluçon
18. 61 km, Montluçon > Saint-Amand-Montrond (ITT)
19. 149.5 km, Orléans > Évry
20. 160.5 km, Corbeil-Essonnes > Paris/Champs-Élysées

1 Lance Armstrong (USA)*
in 86h 17'28"
2 Jan Ullrich (Ger)
at 6'44"
3 Joseba Beloki (Spa)
at 9'05"

Erik Zabel (Ger)

Laurent Jalabert (Fra)

Óscar Sevilla (Spa)

* Title stripped in 2012.
No replacement winner declared.

2002

The total distance was reduced again in 2002, to 3,277.5 km, with slightly shorter stages than previously to discourage doping. In the absence of Jan Ullrich, Lance Armstrong took his fourth victory with ease, at an average speed of 39.93 km/hour. Joseba Beloki took second after two third places. Laurent Jalabert retained the polka dot jersey in his final Tour de France. Colombian Santiago Botero surprised everyone by beating Armstrong in the first time trial.

Saturday 6 July–Sunday 28 July

Prologue	7 km, Luxembourg (Lux) (ITT)
1	192.5 km, Luxembourg > Luxembourg
2	181 km, Luxembourg > Sarrbrücken (Ger)
3	174.5 km, Metz > Reims
4	67.5 km, Épernay > Château-Thierry (TTT)
5	195 km, Soissons > Rouen
6	199.5 km, Forges-les-Eaux > Alençon
7	176 km, Bagnoles-de-l'Orne > Avranches
8	217.5 km, Saint-Martin-de-Landelles > Plouay
9	52 km, Lanester > Lorient (ITT)
10	147 km, Bazas > Pau
11	158 km, Pau > La Mongie
12	199.5 km, Lannemezan > Plateau de Beille
13	171 km, Lavelanet > Béziers
14	221 km, Lodève > Mont Ventoux
15	226.5 km, Vaison-la-Romaine > Les Deux Alpes
16	179.5 km, Les Deux Alpes > La Plagne
17	142 km, Aime > Cluses
18	176.5 km, Cluses > Bourg-en-Bresse
19	50 km, Régnié-Durette > Mâcon (ITT)
20	144 km, Melun > Paris/Champs-Élysées

1 Lance Armstrong (USA)*
in 82h 05'12"
2 Joseba Beloki (Spa)
at 7'17"
3 Raimondas Rumšas (Lit)
at 8'17"

Robbie McEwen (Aus)

Laurent Jalabert (Fra)

Ivan Basso (Ita)

* Title stripped in 2012.
No replacement winner declared.

2003

The Tour marked its centenary with a route entirely within France and visiting the six start/finish towns from the 1903 event. Jan Ullrich returned to push Lance Armstrong closer than ever, but the American gained his fifth consecutive victory. Joseba Beloki was only 40 seconds behind Armstrong when he was seriously injured in a crash while descending into Gap on stage 9, causing the Texan to take a detour through a field. Tyler Hamilton finished fourth with a broken collar-bone.

Saturday 5 July–Sunday 27 July

Prologue	6.5 km, Paris (ITT)
1	168 km, Saint-Denis/Montgeron > Meaux
2	204.5 km, La Ferté-sous-Jouarre > Sedan
3	167.5 km, Charleville > Saint-Dizier
4	69 km, Joinville > Saint-Dizier (TTT)
5	196.5 km, Troyes > Nevers
6	230 km, Nevers > Lyon
7	230.5 km, Lyon > Morzine
8	219 km, Sallanches > Alpe d'Huez
9	184.5 km, Bourg-d'Oisans > Gap
10	219.5 km, Gap > Marseille
11	153.5 km, Narbonne > Toulouse
12	47 km, Gaillac > Cap Découvert (ITT)
13	197.5 km, Toulouse > Plateau de Bonsacre
14	191.5 km, Saint-Girons > Loudenvielle
15	159.5 km, Bagnères-de-Bigorre > Luz Ardiden
16	197.5 km, Pau > Bayonne
17	181 km, Dax > Bordeaux
18	203.5 km, Bordeaux > Saint-Maixent-l'École
19	49 km, Pornic > Nantes (ITT)
20	152 km, Ville-d'Avray > Paris/Champs-Élysées

1 Lance Armstrong (USA)*
in 83h 41'12"
2 Jan Ullrich (Ger)
at 1'01"
3 Alexander Vinokourov (Kaz)
at 4'14"

Baden Cooke (Aus)

Richard Virenque (Fra)

Denis Menchov (Rus)

* Title stripped in 2012.
No replacement winner declared.

2004

WATERLOO
WASQUEHAL
ARRAS NAMUR LIÈGE
AMIENS CAMBRAI CHARLEROI

PARIS
CHAMPS-ÉLYSÉES

SAINT-BRIEUC CHÂTRES MONTEREAU-FAULT-YONNE
LAMBALLE BONNEVAL
QUIMPER CHÂTEAUBRIANT
ANGERS BESANÇON
LONS-LE-SAUNIER
GUÉRET ANNEMASSE
LIMOGES SAINT-LÉONARD-DE-NOBLAT LE GRAND-BORNAND
SAINT-FLOUR VILLARD- L'ALPE D'HUEZ
FIGEAC DE-LANS LE BOURG-
VALRÉAS D'OISANS
CASTELSARRASIN NÎMES
LANNEMEZAN
CARCASSONNE
LA MONGIE PLATEAU DE BEILLE

In 2004 Lance Armstrong dominated once more. The route included a mountain time trial up the Alpe d'Huez, won by Armstrong. This edition was enlivened by the performance of Thomas Voeckler, a young French rider who got into a successful breakaway on stage 5 and held the yellow jersey against all odds through the Pyrenees before conceding it to Armstrong on stage 15. Richard Virenque won his seventh and last polka dot jersey.

Saturday 3 July–Sunday 25 July

Prologue 6.1 km, Liège (Bel) (ITT)
1   202.5 km, Liège > Charleroi (Bel)
2   197 km, Charleroi > Namur (Bel)
3   210 km, Waterloo (Bel) > Wasquehal
4   64.5 km, Cambrai > Arras (TTT)
5   200.5 km, Amiens > Chartres
6   196 km, Bonneval > Angers
7   204.5 km, Châteaubriant > Saint-Brieuc
8   168 km, Lamballe > Quimper
9   160.5 km, Saint-Léonard-de-Noblat > Guéret
10   237 km, Limoges > Saint-Flour
11   164 km, Saint-Flour > Figeac
12   197.5 km, Castelsarrasin > La Mongie
13   205.5 km, Lannemezan > Plateau de Beille
14   192.5 km, Carcassonne > Nîmes
15   180.5 km, Valréas > Villard-de-Lans
16   15.5 km, Bourg-d'Oisans > Alpe d'Huez (ITT)
17   204.5 km, Bourg-d'Oisans > Le Grand-Bornand
18   166.5 km, Annemasse > Lons-le-Saunier
19   55 km, Besançon (ITT)
20   163 km, Montereau-Fault-Yonne > Paris/
     Champs-Élysées

1 Lance Armstrong (USA)*
in 83h 36'02"
2 Andreas Klöden (Ger)
at 6'19"
3 Ivan Basso (Ita)
at 6'40"

Robbie McEwen (Aus)

Richard Virenque (Fra)

Vladimir Karpets (Rus)

* Title stripped in 2012.
No replacement winner declared.

2005

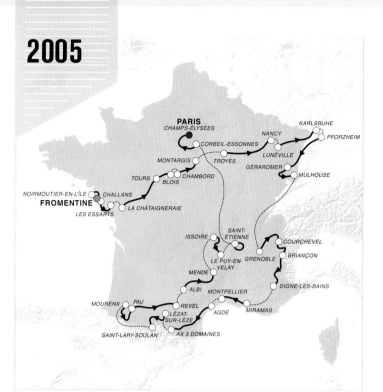

PARIS
CHAMPS-ÉLYSÉES
KARLSRUHE
NANCY PFORZHEIM
CORBEIL-ESSONNES LUNÉVILLE
MONTARGIS TROYES GÉRARDMER
TOURS CHAMBORD MULHOUSE
BLOIS
NOIRMOUTIER-EN-L'ÎLE CHALLANS
FROMENTINE LA CHÂTAIGNERAIE
LES ESSARTS
SAINT-
ISSOIRE ÉTIENNE COURCHEVEL
LE PUY-EN- GRENOBLE BRIANÇON
VELAY
MENDE
ALBI DIGNE-LES-BAINS
MONTPELLIER
MOURENX PAU MIRAMAS
REVEL AGDE
LÉZAT-
SUR-LÈZE
SAINT-LARY-SOULAN AX 3 DOMAINES

The 2005 Tour saw Lance Armstrong's seventh and final victory. It started with a 19 km individual time trial instead of a prologue. The 3,592.5 km route was covered at an average speed of 41.654 km/hour. In the final time trial Michael Rasmussen dropped from third to seventh place after multiple falls and several bike changes. Armstrong wore the yellow jersey for 17 of the 21 days. Jan Ullrich's third place was declared void in 2012 after his doping ban.

Saturday 2 July–Sunday 24 July

1   19 km, Fromentine > Île de Noirmoutier (ITT)
2   181.5 km, Challans > Les Essarts
3   212.5 km, La Châtaigneraie > Tours
4   67.5 km, Tours > Blois (TTT)
5   183 km, Chambord > Montargis
6   199 km, Troyes > Nancy
7   228.5 km, Lunéville > Karlsruhe (Ger)
8   231.5 km, Pforzheim (Ger) > Gérardmer
9   171 km, Gérardmer > Mulhouse
10   192.5 km, Grenoble > Courchevel
11   173 km, Courchevel > Briançon
12   187 km, Briançon > Digne
13   173.5 km, Miramas > Montpellier
14   220.5 km, Agde > Ax 3 Domaines
15   205.5 km, Lézat-sur-Lèze > Saint-Lary-Soulan/Pla d'Alet
16   180.5 km, Mourenx > Pau
17   239.5 km, Pau > Revel
18   189 km, Albi > Mende
19   153.5 km, Issoire > Le Puy-en-Velay
20   55.5 km, Saint-Étienne (ITT)
21   144.5 km, Corbeil-Essonnes > Paris/Champs-Élysées

1 Lance Armstrong (USA)*
in 86h 15'02"
2 Ivan Basso (Ita)
at 4'40"
3 Jan Ullrich (Ger)
at 6'21"

Thor Hushovd (Nor)

Michael Rasmussen (Den)

Yaroslav Popovych (Ukr)

* Title stripped in 2012.
No replacement winner declared.

2006

The Tour today 2006–2013

2007

The 93rd Tour de France visited five other countries – Luxembourg, the Netherlands, Belgium, Spain and Germany. Controversy began before the race with the exclusion of two favourites, Ivan Basso and Jan Ullrich, as a result of a doping scandal. Spaniard Óscar Pereiro took the yellow jersey after gaining 30 minutes on the peloton in a breakaway on stage 13. Although Pereiro was later overtaken by Floyd Landis, he was eventually declared the winner after Landis was disqualified for doping.

The 2007 Tour started with a prologue in London. Alberto Contador emerged as a major force in stage racing this year. He announced his arrival in the Pyrenees with a win at Plateau de Beille and took the yellow jersey when Michael Rasmussen was withdrawn by his team after stage 16 for missed drug tests. Contador subsequently managed to hold off superior time triallists Cadel Evans and Levi Leipheimer, with only 31 seconds between the three riders at the finish.

Saturday 1 July–Sunday 23 July

Prologue	7.1 km, Strasbourg (ITT)
1	184.5 km, Strasbourg > Strasbourg
2	228.5 km, Obernai > Esch-sur-Alzette (Lux)
3	216.5 km, Esch-sur-Alzette (Lux) > Valkenburg (Ned)
4	207 km, Huy (Bel) > Saint-Quentin
5	225 km, Beauvais > Caen
6	189 km, Lisieux > Vitré
7	52 km, Saint-Grégoire > Rennes
8	181 km, Saint-Méen-le-Grand > Lorient
9	169.5 Bordeaux > Dax
10	190.5 km, Cambo-les-Bains > Pau
11	206.5 km, Tarbes > Val d'Aran/ Pla de Beret
12	211.5 km, Luchon > Carcassonne
13	230 km, Béziers > Montélimar
14	180.5 km, Montélimar > Gap
15	187 km, Gap > Alpe d'Huez
16	182 km, Bourg-d'Oisans > La Toussuire
17	200.5 km, Saint-Jean-de-Maurienne > Morzine
18	197 km, Morzine > Mâcon
19	57 km, Le Creusot > Monceau-les-Mines (ITT)
20	154.5 km, Antony/ Parc de Sceaux > Paris/ Champs-Élysées

1 Óscar Pereiro (Spa)
in 89h 40'27"
2 Andreas Klöden (Ger)
at 0'32"
3 Carlos Sastre (Spa)
at 2'16"

Robbie McEwen (Aus)

Michael Rasmussen (Den)

Damiano Cunego (Ita)

Saturday 7 July–Sunday 29 July

Prologue	7.9 km, London (UK) (ITT)
1	203 km, London > Canterbury (UK)
2	168.5 km, Dunkerque > Ghent (Bel)
3	236.5 km, Waregem (Bel) > Compiègne
4	193 km, Villers-Cotterêts > Joigny
5	182.5 km, Chablis > Autun
6	199.5 km, Semur-en-Auxois > Bourg-en-Bresse
7	197.5 km, Bourg-en-Bresse > Le Grand-Bornand
8	165 km, Le Grand-Bornand > Tignes
9	159.5 km, Val-d'Isère > Briançon
10	229.5 km, Tallard > Marseille
11	182.5 km, Marseille > Montpellier
12	178.5 km, Montpellier > Castres
13	54 km, Albi (ITT)
14	197 km, Mazamet > Plateau de Beille
15	196 km, Foix > Loudenvielle/ Le Louron
16	218.5 km, Orthez > Gourette/ Col d'Aubisque
17	188.5 km, Pau > Castelsarrasin
18	211 km, Cahors > Angoulême
19	55.5 km, Cognac > Angoulême (ITT)
20	146 km, Marcoussis > Paris/ Champs-Élysées

1 Alberto Contador (Spa)
in 91h 00'26"
2 Cadel Evans (Aus)
at 0'23"
3 Levi Leipheimer (USA)
at 0'31"

Tom Boonen (Bel)

Mauricio Soler (Col)

Alberto Contador (Spa)

2008

BREST
SAINT-BRIEUC
SAINT-MALO
AURAY
PLUMELEC
NANTES
CHOLET
CHÂTEAUROUX
SAINT-AMAND-MONTROND
CÉRILLY
MONTLUÇON
AIGURANDE
ROANNE
SAINT-ÉTIENNE
SUPER BESSE
BRIOUDE
L'ALPE D'HUEZ
AURILLAC
LE BOURG-D'OISANS
FIGEAC
EMBRUN
CUNEO
PRATO NEVOSO
LANNEMEZAN
JAUSIERS
DIGNE-LES-BAINS
PAU
TOULOUSE
NÎMES
FOIX
NARBONNE
LOURDES
HAUTACAM
BAGNÈRES-DE-BIGORRE
LAVELANET
PARIS
CHAMPS-ÉLYSÉES
ÉTAMPES

The 95th Tour de France had no prologue, starting instead with a road stage in Brittany and there were no time bonuses this year. Alberto Contador was unable to defend his title, as his team (Astana) was not invited to participate because of doping problems. His fellow countryman Carlos Sastre won the race after a solo break to the Alpe d'Huez. After the Tour Bernhard Kohl was stripped of third place overall and of the mountains classification when he tested positive for CERA.

Saturday 5 July–Sunday 27 July

1. 197.5 km, Brest > Plumelec
2. 164.5 km, Auray > Saint-Brieuc
3. 208 km, Saint-Malo > Nantes
4. 29.5 km, Cholet (ITT)
5. 232 km, Cholet > Châteauroux
6. 195.5 km, Aigurande > Super Besse
7. 159 km, Brioude > Aurillac
8. 172.5 km, Figeac > Toulouse
9. 224 km, Toulouse > Bagnères-de-Bigorre
10. 156 km, Pau > Lourdes/Hautacam
11. 167.5 km, Lannemezan > Foix
12. 168.5 km, Lavelanet > Narbonne
13. 182 km, Narbonne > Nîmes
14. 194.5 km, Nîmes > Digne
15. 183 km, Embrun > Prato Nevoso (Ita)
16. 157 km, Cuneo (Ita) > Jausiers
17. 210.5 km, Embrun > Alpe d'Huez
18. 196.5 km, Bourg-d'Oisans > Saint-Étienne
19. 165.5 km, Roanne > Montluçon
20. 53 km, Cérilly > Saint-Amand-Montrond (ITT)
21. 143 km, Étampes > Paris/Champs-Élysées

1 Carlos Sastre (Spa)
in 87h 52'52"
2 Cadel Evans (Aus)
at 0'58"
3 None

Óscar Freire (Spa)

None

Andy Schleck (Lux)

2009

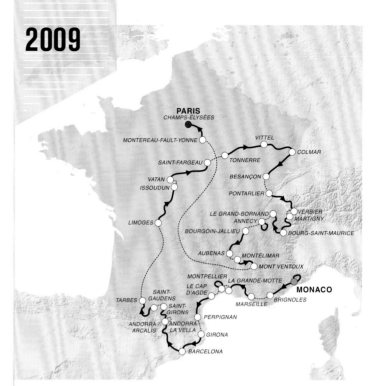

PARIS
CHAMPS-ÉLYSÉES
MONTEREAU-FAULT-YONNE
VITTEL
SAINT-FARGEAU
TONNERRE
COLMAR
VATAN
BESANÇON
ISSOUDUN
PONTARLIER
VERBIER
MARTIGNY
LE GRAND-BORNAND
ANNECY
LIMOGES
BOURG-SAINT-MAURICE
BOURGOIN-JALLIEU
AUBENAS
MONTÉLIMAR
MONT VENTOUX
MONTPELLIER
LA GRANDE-MOTTE
LE CAP
D'AGDE
MONACO
TARBES
SAINT-
GAUDENS
MARSEILLE
BRIGNOLES
SAINT-
GIRONS
PERPIGNAN
ANDORRA
ARCALIS
ANDORRA
LA VELLA
GIRONA
BARCELONA

The 2009 Tour started with a time trial in the principality of Monaco and also visited Spain, Andorra and Switzerland. Lance Armstrong came out of retirement to finish third behind his team-mate Alberto Contador, but this result was voided in 2012, with third being awarded to Britain's Bradley Wiggins. Fellow Briton Mark Cavendish won six stages, including the final one on the Champs-Élysées. Franco Pellizotti was stripped of the mountains classification in 2011 because of irregular values in a blood sample taken for his biological passport.

Saturday 4 July–Sunday 26 July

1. 15.5 km, Monaco (Mon) (ITT)
2. 187 km, Monaco > Brignoles
3. 196.5 km, Marseille > La Grande-Motte
4. 39 km, Montpellier (TTT)
5. 196.5 km, Le Cap d'Agde > Perpignan
6. 181.5 km, Girona (Spa) > Barcelona (Spa)
7. 224 km, Barcelona > Andorra Arcalís (And)
8. 176.5 km, Andorra la Vella (And) > Saint-Girons
9. 160.5 km, Saint-Gaudens > Tarbes
10. 194.5 km, Limoges > Issoudun
11. 192 km, Vatan > Saint-Fargeau
12. 211.5 km, Tonnerre > Vittel
13. 200 km, Vittel > Colmar
14. 199 km, Colmar > Besançon
15. 207.5 km, Pontarlier > Verbier (Swi)
16. 159 km, Martigny (Swi) > Bourg-Saint-Maurice
17. 169.5 km, Bourg-Saint-Maurice > Le Grand-Bornand
18. 40.5 km, Annecy (ITT)
19. 178 km, Bourgoin-Jallieu > Aubenas
20. 167 km, Montélimar > Mont Ventoux
21. 164 km, Montereau-Fault-Yonne > Paris/Champs-Élysées

1 Alberto Contador (Spa)
in 85h 48'35"
2 Andy Schleck (Lux)
at 4'11"
3 Bradley Wiggins (UK)
at 6'01"

Thor Hushovd (Nor)

None

Andy Schleck (Lux)

2010

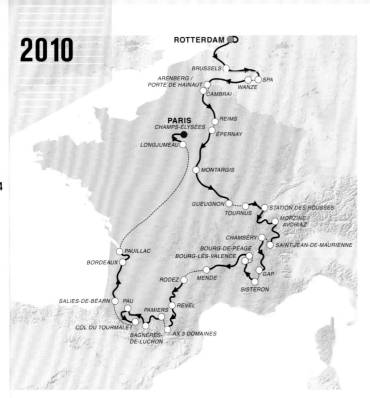

This year's Tour was unusual in only having one time trial in addition to the prologue. The Col du Tourmalet was climbed twice to celebrate the centenary of the inclusion of the Pyrenees. In the race Andy Schleck finished 39 seconds behind Alberto Contador. However, the latter was stripped of the result in 2012 because of a positive test for clenbuterol, with Schleck being promoted to first place. Mark Cavendish won five stages, including a repeat victory in Paris.

Saturday 3 July–Sunday 25 July

Prologue 8.9 km, Rotterdam (Ned) (ITT)
1   223.5 km, Rotterdam > Brussels (Bel)
2   201 km, Brussels > Spa (Bel)
3   213 km, Wanze (Bel) > Arenberg/Porte de Hainaut
4   153.5 km, Cambrai > Reims
5   187.5 km, Épernay > Montargis
6   227.5 km, Montargis > Gueugnon
7   165.5 km, Tournus > Station des Rousses
8   189 km, Station des Rousses > Morzine Avoriaz
9   204.5 km, Morzine Avoriaz > Saint-Jean-de-Maurienne
10 179 km, Chambéry > Gap
11 184.5 km, Sisteron > Bourg-lès-Valence
12 210.5 km, Bourg-de-Péage > Mende
13 196 km, Rodez > Revel
14 184.5 km, Revel > Ax 3 Domaines
15 187.5 km, Pamiers > Luchon
16 199.5 km, Luchon > Pau
17 174 km, Pau > Col du Tourmalet
18 198 km, Salies-de-Béarn > Bordeaux
19 52 km, Bordeaux > Pauillac (ITT)
20 102.5 km, Longjumeau > Paris/Champs-Élysées

1 Andy Schleck (Lux)
in 91h 59'27"
2 Denis Menchov (Rus)
at 1'22"
3 Samuel Sánchez (Spa)
at 3'40"

Alessandro Petacchi (Ita)

Anthony Charteau (Fra)

Andy Schleck (Lux)

2011

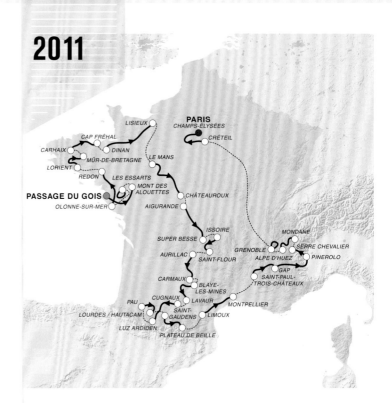

In 2011 Cadel Evans became the first Australian winner of the Tour de France and, at 34, the oldest post-war winner. Fränk Schleck joined his younger brother on the final podium. Thomas Voeckler emulated his achievement from 2004, this time holding the yellow jersey for ten days and finishing the race in fourth overall. Mark Cavendish again won five stages, also taking the green jersey, while two Norwegians – Thor Hushovd and Edvald Boasson Hagen – won two stages each.

Saturday 2 July–Sunday 24 July

1   191.5 km, Passage du Gois > Mont des Alouettes
2   23 km, Les Essarts (TTT)
3   198 km, Olonne-sur-Mer > Redon
4   172.5 km, Lorient > Mûr-de-Bretagne
5   164.5 km, Carhaix > Cap Fréhel
6   226.5 km, Dinan > Lisieux
7   218 km, Le Mans > Châteauroux
8   189 km, Aigurande > Super Besse/Sancy
9   208 km, Issoire > Saint-Flour
10 158 km, Aurillac > Carmaux
11 167.5 km, Blaye-les-Mines > Lavaur
12 211 km, Cugnaux > Luz Ardiden
13 152.5 km, Pau > Lourdes/Hautacam
14 168.5 km, Saint-Gaudens > Plateau de Beille
15 192.5 km, Limoux > Montpellier
16 162.5 km, Saint-Paul-Trois-Châteaux > Gap
17 179 km, Gap > Pinerolo (Ita)
18 200.5 km, Pinerolo > Galibier/Serre Chevalier
19 109.5 km, Mondane > Alpe d'Huez
20 42.5 km, Grenoble (ITT)
21 95 km, Créteil > Paris/Champs-Élysées

1 Cadel Evans (Aus)
in 86h 12'22"
2 Andy Schleck (Lux)
at 1'34"
3 Fränk Schleck (Lux)
at 2'30"

Mark Cavendish (UK)

Samuel Sánchez (Spa)

Pierre Rolland (Fra)

2012

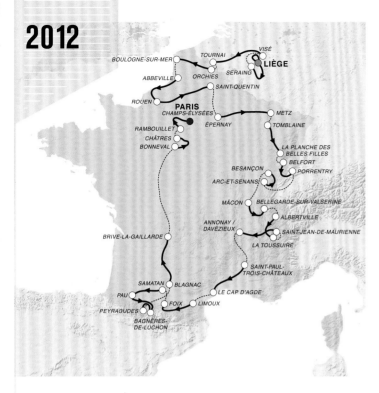

2013

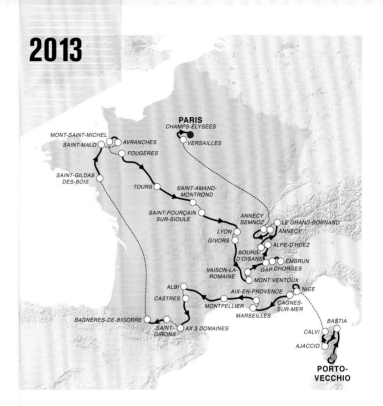

The 99th Tour included more individual time trialling than the previous few editions but no team time trial. Bradley Wiggins became the first British rider to win the race, wearing the yellow jersey from stage 7, with his team-mate Chris Froome in second place. The 22-year-old Slovakian Peter Sagan won three stages in his debut Tour, as did Mark Cavendish, who also won the final stage for the fourth successive year. Frenchman Thomas Voeckler won two stages as well as the mountains jersey.

The 100th Tour de France will be the first in 10 years to stay entirely inside France. It starts with three stages in Corsica, the only French region never to have hosted the Tour. After a brief visit to the Pyrenees the race will transfer to Brittany and then head south-east. The final few days in the Alps include a mountain time trial and two ascents of the Alpe d'Huez in a single day before an evening finish on the Champs-Élysées.

Saturday 30 June–Sunday 22 July

Prologue	6.4 km, Liège (Bel) (ITT)
1	198 km, Liège > Seraing (Bel)
2	207.5 km, Visé (Bel) > Tournai (Bel)
3	197 km, Orchies > Boulogne-sur-Mer
4	214.5 km, Abbeville > Rouen
5	196.5 km, Rouen > Saint-Quentin
6	207.5 km, Épernay > Metz
7	199 km, Tomblaine > La Planche des Belles Filles
8	157.5 km, Belfort > Porrentruy (Swi)
9	41.5 km, Arc-et-Senans > Besançon (ITT)
10	194.5 km, Mâcon > Bellegarde-sur-Valserine
11	148 km, Albertville > La Toussuire/Les Sybelles
12	226 km, Saint-Jean-de-Maurienne > Annonay/Davézieux
13	217 km, Saint-Paul-Trois-Châteaux > Cap d'Agde
14	191 km, Limoux > Foix
15	158.5 km, Samatan > Pau
16	197 km, Pau > Luchon
17	143.5 km, Luchon > Peyragudes
18	222.5 km, Blagnac > Brive
19	53.5 km, Bonneval > Chartres (ITT)
20	120 km, Rambouillet > Paris/Champs-Élysées

1 Bradley Wiggins (UK)
in 87h 34'47"
2 Chris Froome (UK)
at 3'21"
3 Vincenzo Nibali (Ita)
at 6'19"

Peter Sagan (Svk)

Thomas Voeckler (Fra)

Tejay van Garderen (USA)

Saturday 29 June–Sunday 21 July

1	212 km, Porto-Vecchio > Bastia (Cor)
2	154 km, Bastia > Ajaccio (Cor)
3	145 km, Ajaccio > Calvi (Cor)
4	25 km, Nice (TTT)
5	219 km, Cagnes-sur-Mer > Marseille
6	176 km, Aix-en-Provence > Montpellier
7	205 km, Montpellier > Albi
8	194 km, Castres > Ax 3 Domaines
9	165 km, Saint-Girons > Bagnères-de-Bigorre
10	193 km, Saint-Gildas-des-Bois > Saint-Malo
11	33 km, Avranches > Mont-Saint-Michel (ITT)
12	218 km, Fougères > Tours
13	173 km, Tours > Saint-Amand-Montrond
14	191 km, Saint-Pourçain-sur-Sioule > Lyon
15	242 km, Givors > Mont Ventoux
16	168 km, Vaison-la-Romaine > Gap
17	32 km, Embrun > Chorges (ITT)
18	168 km, Gap > Alpe-d'Huez
19	204 km, Bourg-d'Oisans > Le Grand-Bornand
20	125 km, Annecy > Annecy–Semnoz
21	118 km, Versailles > Paris Champs-Élysées

Index

Picture credits and acknowledgements

MAIN CREDIT:

Offside/*L'Équipe* have provided the majority of the images appearing in this book.

Octopus Publishing would like to acknowledge and thank David Wilkinson and Mark Leech from Offside (www.welloffside.com) in London and their colleagues at *L'Équipe* in Paris for their help with this publication.

OTHER CREDITS:

Action Plus Stefano Sirotti 226 above, 228 above right

Bibliothèque Nationale de France Agence Meurisse 58 above left; Agence Rol 53, 57 above

Corbis Gilbert Iundt/Jean-Yves Ruszniewski/TempSport 25 above, 26, 198 below left; Hulton-Deutsch Collection 25 below; Leo Mason 23; Selwyn Tait/Sygma 144; Stephane Ruet/Sygma 196 below; Tim de Waele/TDWsport.com/Corbis 5; Universal/TempSport 24, 136 below, 137

Getty Images 22, AFP 83, 114 above, 171, 184 below, 188 below, 193 above, 218 left; AFP/Image Forum 27 right, 72 below, 73 below, 74 above, 75 above, 82 above, 85 above, 98 below, 100 above, 102 below left; Chris Cole 190 left; Doug Pensinger 29 above, 30; Gamma-Keystone 21 above, 126 above; Gamma-Rapho 153; Mike Powell 189 below, 193 below; Roger Viollet 11 main, 21 below, 45 below, 47, 54 below right, 61, 91 below; Universal Images Group 11 above

Mary Evans Picture Library Epic 40 above

Offside MarcaMedia 27 left

Photoshot AP/Bas Czerwinski 222 centre; Nicolas Bouvy 223

Press Association Images AP 174 below; AP/Bas Czerwinski 222 above, 226 below; AP/Bernard Papon 222 below

Rex Features Sipa Press 215 above

Spaarnestad Photo Nationaal Archief/Het Leven/Fotograaf onbekend 75 below

TopFoto Alinari 117 above; RogerViollet 38 above

IN-HOUSE ACKNOWLEDGEMENTS:

Editorial Director Trevor Davies
Deputy Art Director Yasia Williams-Leedham
Senior Editor Leanne Bryan
Picture Research Manager Giulia Hetherington
Production Manager Peter Hunt
Foreign Rights Executive Marta Pascual Argente
Editorial Assistant Irina Polianina

EXTERNAL ACKNOWLEDGEMENTS:

Book Design and Layout Grade Design www.gradedesign.com
Cartography Cosmographics Ltd
Aerial photographs © IGN / PlanetObserver – 2012
Satellite images © PlanetObserver
Digital Elevation Models © PlanetObserver
Aerial photography of London and Plymouth
  Supplied by Bluesky © GeoPerspectives
Gazetteer Cartography Geoff Borin
Jacket Illustration David Juniper
Additional Editorial Research Halldora Magnusdottir
Copy Editor Jane Birch
Picture Researchers Roland and Sarah Smithies
Proofreaders Miranda Harrison and Jo Murray
Indexer Isobel McLean